CARICATURE AND REALISM IN THE ROMANTIC NOVEL

What was caricature to novelists in the Romantic period? Why does Jane Austen call Mr Dashwood's wife 'a strong caricature of *him*self'? Why does Mary Shelley describe the body of Frankenstein's creature as 'in proportion', but then 'distorted in its proportions' – and does caricature have anything to do with it? This book answers those questions, shifting our understanding of 'caricature' as a literary-critical term in the decades when 'the English novel' was first defined and canonised as a distinct literary entity. Novels incorporated caricature talk and anti-caricature rhetoric to tell readers what different realisms purported to show them. Recovering the period's concept of caricature, *Caricature and Realism in the Romantic Novel* sheds light on formal realism's self-reflexivity about the 'caricature' of artifice, exaggeration and imagination. This title is part of the Flip it Open Programme and may also be available on Open Access. Check our website Cambridge Core for details.

OLIVIA FERGUSON is a library worker, editorial consultant and writer based in North East Scotland. She has degrees in literature and linguistics from McGill University, the University of Victoria and the University of Edinburgh. She has published research articles in *Studies in Romanticism*, *Persuasions On-Line*, *Notes and Queries* and *Gothic Studies*, and has a chapter in the forthcoming *Edinburgh Companion to Jane Austen and the Arts*. Ferguson was a research fellow at the Institute of Advanced Studies in the Humanities, University of Edinburgh, from 2018 to 2019, and was Lecturer in Romanticism at Birkbeck College, University of London, from 2019 to 2020.

CAMBRIDGE STUDIES IN ROMANTICISM

Founding Editor
Marilyn Butler, University of Oxford

General Editor
James Chandler, University of Chicago

Editorial Board
Claire Connolly, University College Cork
Paul Hamilton, University of London
Claudia Johnson, Princeton University
Essaka Joshua, University of Notre Dame
Nigel Leask, University of Glasgow
Alan Liu, University of California, Santa Barbara
Deidre Lynch, Harvard University
Jerome McGann, University of Virginia
David Simpson, University of California, Davis

This series aims to foster the best new work in one of the most challenging fields within English literary studies. From the early 1780s to the early 1830s, a formidable array of talented men and women took to literary composition, not just in poetry, which some of them famously transformed, but in many modes of writing. The expansion of publishing created new opportunities for writers, and the political stakes of what they wrote were raised again by what Wordsworth called those 'great national events' that were 'almost daily taking place': the French Revolution, the Napoleonic and American wars, urbanization, industrialization, religious revival, an expanded empire abroad, and the reform movement at home. This was an enormous ambition, even when it pretended otherwise. The relations between science, philosophy, religion, and literature were reworked in texts such as *Frankenstein* and *Biographia Literaria*; gender relations in *A Vindication of the Rights of Woman* and *Don Juan*; journalism by Cobbett and Hazlitt; and poetic form, content, and style by the Lake School and the Cockney School. Outside Shakespeare studies, probably no body of writing has produced such a wealth of commentary or done so much to shape the responses of modern criticism. This indeed is the period that saw the emergence of those notions of literature and of literary history, especially national literary history, on which modern scholarship in English has been founded.

The categories produced by Romanticism have also been challenged by recent historicist arguments. The task of the series is to engage both with a challenging corpus of Romantic writings and with the changing field of criticism they have helped to shape. As with other literary series published by Cambridge University Press, this one will represent the work of both younger and more established scholars on either side of the Atlantic and elsewhere.

See the end of the book for a complete list of published titles.

CARICATURE AND REALISM IN THE ROMANTIC NOVEL

OLIVIA FERGUSON

Shaftesbury Road, Cambridge CB2 8EA, United Kingdom

One Liberty Plaza, 20th Floor, New York, NY 10006, USA

477 Williamstown Road, Port Melbourne, VIC 3207, Australia

314–321, 3rd Floor, Plot 3, Splendor Forum, Jasola District Centre, New Delhi – 110025, India

103 Penang Road, #05–06/07, Visioncrest Commercial, Singapore 238467

Cambridge University Press is part of Cambridge University Press & Assessment, a department of the University of Cambridge.

We share the University's mission to contribute to society through the pursuit of education, learning and research at the highest international levels of excellence.

www.cambridge.org
Information on this title: www.cambridge.org/9781009274241
DOI: 10.1017/9781009274227

© Olivia Ferguson 2023

This work is in copyright. It is subject to statutory exceptions and to the provisions of relevant licensing agreements; with the exception of the Creative Commons version the link for which is provided below, no reproduction of any part of this work may take place without the written permission of Cambridge University Press.

An online version of this work is published at http://dx.doi.org/10.1017/9781009274227 under a Creative Commons Open Access license CC-BY-NC 4.0 which permits re-use, distribution and reproduction in any medium for non-commercial purposes providing appropriate credit to the original work is given and any changes made are indicated. To view this license, visit https://creativecommons.org/licenses/by-nc/4.0

All versions of this work may contain content reproduced under license from third parties. Permission to reproduce this third-party content must be obtained from these third-parties directly.

When citing this work, please include a reference to the DOI: 10.1017/9781009274227

First published 2023
First paperback edition 2025

A catalogue record for this publication is available from the British Library

ISBN 978-1-009-27426-5 Hardback
ISBN 978-1-009-27424-1 Paperback

Cambridge University Press & Assessment has no responsibility for the persistence or accuracy of URLs for external or third-party internet websites referred to in this publication and does not guarantee that any content on such websites is, or will remain, accurate or appropriate.

Contents

Preface	*page* vii
Acknowledgements	ix

PART I CARICATURE TALK

1	Defining Caricature	3
2	Denying Caricature	28
3	Caricature Talk and the *Spectator*	50

PART II NOVEL CARICATURES

Caricature Talk and Characterisation Technique	91

4	Jane Austen and Anti-caricature	93
5	Walter Scott and Historical Caricatures	126
6	Mary Shelley, Flesh-Caricature and Horrid Realism	169

Afterword	204
Notes	207
Bibliography	233
Index	255

Preface

What was caricature to novelists in the Romantic period? Why is Mr Dashwood's wife 'a strong caricature of *him*self' in *Sense and Sensibility*? Why does *The Heart of Mid-Lothian* imagine that its detailed account of eighteenth-century Edinburgh might 'serve as an illustration of Kay's caricatures'? Why is the body of Frankenstein's creature 'in proportion', but then 'distorted in its proportions' – and does caricature have anything to do with it? This book answers those questions, and shifts our understanding of *caricature* as a critical term for literature in the decades when 'the English novel' was defined and canonised as a distinct literary entity.

Literary scholarship has often taken 'caricature' to be the disreputable doppelgänger of 'character', and caricaturing as the antithesis of good characterisation. 'Caricature', its conceptual difficulty left unexamined, has long been used as a critical tool for debating the relative quality of fictive characters. However, caricature has historically played a more complex role alongside character – both in fiction readers' understandings of fictive character, literary form and literary realism, and in realism's intensified self-consciousness about using 'the real' to amuse, charm and shock readers in new ways. Novelists in the Romantic period incorporate concepts of caricature into their narration: they integrate caricature talk and anti-caricature rhetoric with characterisation technique, in order to 'tell' readers what different realisms are purporting to 'show' them. Meanwhile, in Romantic character criticism, caricature talk involves and generates readers' knowledge and feelings about fictive characters as 'realist' writing.

Part I, 'Caricature Talk', collates source material from periodicals, newspapers, books and dictionaries to establish the full scope of caricature's significance for literature and letters in the Romantic period. In Chapters 1 and 2, by comparing the ways in which the word 'caricature' was used, I recover meanings lying outside notions of caricature as either 'a satirical representation' or 'a humorous portrait', extricate the Romantic period's understanding of textual caricature from the contemporary genres of single-sheet caricature prints and *ritratti carichi*, and explain the relation of prosopographic textual caricature to fictive textual caricature. The primary purpose of Chapters 2 and 3 is to trace a central thread in the criticism and writing of the Romantic novel, a grouping of vocabulary, concepts and rhetoric about textual exaggeration that I call 'caricature talk'. To illustrate caricature talk, Chapter 3 analyses key passages from *The Spectator* (1711–12) and its critical reception between the 1770s and the 1820s. I suggest that the caricature talk that features in the critical recognition and writing of the Romantic novel derived key topics of interest – diversion, originality and realism – from the *Spectator* and other humorous character-driven periodicals of the early eighteenth century; and I show how anti-caricature rhetoric became conventionalised in essays that sought to explain and promote the appeal of Addison and Steele's character Sir Roger de Coverley.

Part II, 'Novel Caricatures', opens with a note on the question of textual caricature having a formal existence in the Romantic novel. If Part I has shown that *concepts* of caricature are important to the novel, might Part II show how *techniques* of caricature were used by novelists? I argue that different novelistic realisms incorporate specific meanings and usages of 'caricature' from among the range discussed in Chapters 1 and 2, in telling readers the significance and effects of characterisation techniques that purport to show real minds and bodies. Each chapter describes how a single writer's oeuvre engages with concepts of caricature in unique ways – but since I focus on three writers now considered so definitive of different strains of realist prose fiction, I hope that my reader will find some generalisable insights: to the comic, moralist and contemporary from Austen, to the 'compendious' and historical for Scott, and to 'body horror' from Shelley. Several themes converge and diverge between chapters, and there is no chronological or conceptual narrative implied by my ordering of the chapters. For example, Chapters 4 and 5 both discuss how novelists use anti-caricature rhetoric in their novels; all chapters discuss realism's habilitation of 'explained caricatures'; and all chapters engage with realism's forced grotesquing of deviant bodies, as enabled by social critique's literalisation of caricature into flesh – fat bodies in Austen's novels, dwarfism in Scott's and Shelley's fiction, and dead and 'straight-laced bodies' in *Frankenstein*.

This is a history of literature's caricature, which cannot be taken in at one glance, or encapsulated in a sentence. Starting with the dictionaries in which the Romantic-period reader might have sought a deeper understanding of *caricatúra*, I build a picture of a literary 'caricature' that branched and varied, yet retained definition.

Acknowledgements

I acknowledge the generous support of the Social Sciences and Humanities Research Council of Canada, the Wolfson Foundation, and the Institute for Advanced Studies in the Humanities (IASH) at the University of Edinburgh, which funded the PhD and postdoctoral research on which this project is based.

I am grateful for permission to include content from work published elsewhere. Passages from my chapter 'Jane Austen and Caricature' in the forthcoming *Edinburgh Companion to Jane Austen and the Arts* (eds. Joe Bray and Hannah Moss) and from my article 'Walter Scott and the Future of Caricature in the Novel' (published in *Studies in Romanticism* in 2021) reappear, in revised form, in Chapters 4 and 5 respectively. Full citations of these works are included in the bibliography.

Thanks to my supervisors and supporters at the University of Edinburgh, particularly Penny Fielding and Bob Irvine. Thanks to the team at IASH, and to the staff at the National Library of Scotland.

Thank you to the Department of English at the University of Victoria for your teaching and mentorship. I gratefully acknowledge the entrance scholarship that allowed me to pursue a Master's degree, and the support of the Hugh Campbell and Marion Alice Small Fund for Scottish Studies.

Thanks to those who have offered insightful and kindly helpful comments on my PhD and journal articles: Freya Johnston, Rebecca Tierney-Hynes, David Stewart and the peer reviewers for *Studies in Romanticism*. Thanks to the two peer reviewers for Cambridge University Press who read the draft of my monograph and inspired me to make it better than it was.

Much of this book was rewritten several times between 2019 and 2022. I give my most personal thanks to those who have imparted moral support above and beyond any professional commitments, at crucial times over the last four years – particularly Mike Bintley, Rebecca Tierney-Hynes, Katie Halsey and Georgina Barker.

PART I

Caricature Talk

CHAPTER I

Defining Caricature

Say that a reader in the Romantic period noticed the word *caricatura* when they were reading the works of Thomas Browne, or when they encountered a reference in the *Scots Magazine* to Alexander Pope being 'hurt by the caricatura of his figure'.[1] Say that they recognised this word as Italian and were curious about its origins. Which reference work could they have turned to?

The best choice, I think, would have been one of the many editions of Giuseppe Baretti's *Dictionary of the English and Italian Languages*. Samuel Johnson's *Dictionary of the English Language* was not an option: Johnson did not define 'caricature', and though a brief entry was added posthumously then expanded by H. J. Rodd in the 1818 edition, it contains no helpful information about the word's Italian origins. Pocket editions of Johnson's dictionary define caricature simply as 'a ludicrous, droll likeness',[2] while Thomas Sheridan's *Complete Dictionary* (1790) defines it as 'exaggerated resemblance in drawings'. If the reader was uncertain how to pronounce the word and looked it up in John Walker's *Critical Pronouncing Dictionary* (1823), they would have been referred to Baretti's dictionary.[3] Alternatively, they might have picked up the latest edition of Giuspano Graglia's *New Pocket Dictionary of the Italian and English Languages*, titled *An Italian and English Pocket Dictionary* when first published in 1787 and in its seventeenth edition by 1837.

What light would Italian have shed, for British readers in the Romantic period, on the meaning of *caricatúra*, assimilated into English as 'caricature'?

From *Caricatúra* to Caricature: A History of the Word in English

Looking it up in Baretti's dictionary, the reader does not immediately find the kind of definition they might expect from an Italian–English dictionary: a definition written in English. Baretti's first 1760 edition explains *caricatúra* in Italian – 'dicesi anche di ritratto ridicolo in cui siensi grandemente accresciati i diffetti' – and notes that '[t]he English have adopted the word. See *caricare in* [sic] *ritratto*'.⁴ Graglia's 1787 pocket dictionary, which reproduces content from Baretti, defines *caricatúra* only as 'a caricature'. Thus, to understand the meaning of *caricatúra*, the reader must look higher on the page, where a series of definitions trace the word's etymology.

First, we have *cárica* ('charge, burden, load') and *cáricare* ('to charge, to load, to burden, to lay a burden upon'), with several examples of figurative usage such as 'to charge one with something, to lay the fault upon him'. Graglia's dictionary has *caricárla ad uno*, 'to play tricks with one', and *caricársi*, 'to take upon one's self'. In one of Baretti's examples, the reader will find a definition of pictorial caricature: to *caricare un ritratto* is 'to paint a portrait so, that the original may appear ridiculous by a kind of exaggeration of the parts of his face, yet without losing the resemblance'. Baretti's definition would have helped the English reader with *caricatúra* as it appears in *Letter to a Friend* (1690), where Browne describes the face of a dying man with a reference to Italian *caricatúra* drawings:

> [A] weak Physiognomist might say at first eye, This was a face of Earth, and that *Morta* had set her Hard-Seal upon his Temples, easily perceiving what *Caricatura* Draughts Death makes upon pined faces.⁵

This is one of the earliest references to *caricatúra* in an English-language text. Two decades later in no. 537 of the *Spectator*, John Hughes saves his reader the trouble of consulting a dictionary by providing his own definition of 'those burlesk pictures, which the Italians call Caricatura's'.⁶ By the late eighteenth century, when English readers were expected to know what 'caricature' meant, Baretti's dictionary was there for any reader interested to know the history of this Italian-sounding word – especially when encountering it in its original Italian form, as in Walter Scott's *Rob Roy* (1818). After asking Frank to describe his father, a businessman, Rashleigh responds:

> 'O rare-painted portrait! [...] Vandyke was a dauber to you, Frank. I see thy sire before me in all his strength and weakness, loving and honouring the King as a sort of lord mayor of the empire, or chief of the board of trade, venerating the Commons, for the acts regulating the export trade, and respecting the Peers, because the Lord Chancellor sits on a wool-sack.'
> 'Mine was a likeness, Rashleigh; yours is a *caricatura*.'⁷

Rob Roy being set in 1715, Scott uses the period-appropriate '*caricatura*' rather than the assimilated 'caricature' in this dialogue. Baretti's explanation of *caricare un ritratto* is clearly relevant to this analogy between the two young men's opposing verbal descriptions of Mr Osbaldistone and

Defining Caricature 5

two different styles of portraiture, the Flemish painting and the exaggerated comic *ritratto*.

So far, so good. But say that this reader in the Romantic period had also come across other uses of the word 'caricature' where the 'caricatures' in question are clearly not literally *ritratti*, pictures or graphic portraits, but rather instances of writing, reviewing, editing and public speaking. Letters to the editor, newspaper advertisements for comic plays, Mary Wollstonecraft's *Vindication of the Rights of Woman*, the *Scots Magazine*'s review of *Frankenstein* – all these refer to textual or verbal caricatures. Would Baretti's dictionary have provided any helpful context for such references to written or spoken *caricatúra*?

> I have been told formerly, that it is the office of a Critic to discover the *beauties* as well as the *defects* of a work. Our modern reviewers present us with nothing but *caricature* (*Morning Post*, 1775).

> The best method, I believe, that can be adopted to correct a fondness for novels is to ridicule them; [...] if a judicious person, with some turn for humour, would read several to a young girl, and point out [...] how foolishly and ridiculously they caricatured human nature, just opinions might be substituted instead of romantic sentiments (Wollstonecraft, 1792).

> The taste of the day leans entirely to caricature: We have lost our relish for the simple beauties of nature. The caricature in acting, in novel-writing, in preaching, in parliamentary eloquence is entirely in rage. We are no longer satisfied with propriety and neatness; we must have something grotesque and disproportioned, cumbrous with ornament and gigantic in its dimensions (*Morning Chronicle*, 1796).

> This present evening Their Majesties Servants will act (never performed) a new Dramatick Caricature, in one act, called THE UGLY CLUB (*Morning Post and Gazetteer*, 1798).

> The Brain-Sucker. Or, the Distress of Authorship. A Serio-Comic Caricature. In a Letter from Farmer Homely, to an absent Friend (*Morning Star*, 1798).

> SIR,—After seeing my letter of the 10th instant, in your Register of Sunday last, chequered, caricatured in Italics, and pared away, as it there appeared, *ad libitum*, for to suit your own purpose, I had almost resolved to desert the correspondence (*Cobbett's Weekly Register*, 1807).

> 'The Lord of the Manor' was performed yesterday, and the House, as on Monday, was crowded to an overflow. JONES played *Young Contrast* with all that pleasantry of caricature which made the character so

important when the Opera was first revived at this Theatre (*Morning Post*, 1814).

Here is one of the productions of the modern school in its highest style of caricature and exaggeration [. . .]. There never was a wilder story imagined, yet like most of the fictions of this age, it has an air of reality attached to it, by being connected with the favourite projects and passions of the times (*Scots Magazine*, 1818).⁸

None of these examples ask the reader to think specifically of drawings or graphic portraits. The *Morning Chronicle* gives several examples of caricature, all of which involve verbal expression and none of which are pictorial. For the *Scots Magazine* writer, caricature is a 'style' of writing.

Readers could have thought of these expressions as metaphors, analogies that apply Baretti's definition of an exaggerated portrait – *caricare un ritratto* – to a 'portrait' in textual or verbal form. Indeed, verbal and textual caricatures are occasionally compared with graphic *ritratti*, whether implicitly (as in the *Gentleman's Magazine*'s profile of the Shakespearean commentator George Steevens) or explicitly (as in John Hughes's letter to *The Spectator* advertising his own 'Ode to the Creator of the World'):

A characteristic bon mot, is a kind of oral caricature, copies of which, are multiplied by every tongue that utters it (*The Gentleman's Magazine*, 1800).⁹

Politicians can resolve the most shining actions among men into artifice and design; others, who are soured by discontent, repulses, or ill usage, are apt to mistake their spleen for philosophy; men of profligate lives, and such as find themselves incapable of rising to any distinction among their fellow-creatures, are for pulling down all appearances of merit, which seem to upbraid them: and satirists describe nothing but deformity. From all these hands we have seen such draughts of mankind as are represented in those burlesk pictures, which the Italians call Caricatura's; where the art consists in preserving, amidst distorted proportions and aggravated features, some distinguishing likeness of the person, but in such a manner as to transform the most agreeable beauty into the most odious monster (John Hughes, no. 537 of *The Spectator*).¹⁰

But despite the analogies, these 'caricatures' were not simply textual versions of caricature *ritratti*, humorous portraits of individuals' distinctive physical features. None of the oral or written caricatures mentioned in these examples involve people's physical features, and only some of them are humorous; others are noted for having satirical or aesthetic impact, or being misinformative. Would a reader who consulted Baretti's explanation of *caricare un ritratto* ('to paint a portrait so, that the original may appear ridiculous') and his definition of *caricatúra* ('ritratto ridicolo') have thought that, in being applied so diversely to verbal 'caricatures', the English borrowing of *caricatúra* was losing its meaning?

Perhaps not, since Baretti does offer the anglophone reader an Italian precedent for 'caricature' as exaggerated speech or writing. The last of the dictionary's examples for the verb *cáricare* is 'Caricare (accrescere in parlando la cosa più che veramente sia)'. Baretti renders his definition into English as 'to enlarge, to be more vehement than it is need [sic], to exaggerate', omitting to translate his phrase 'in parlando' – 'in speaking' or 'in the telling'. The English reader could have found further linguistic justification for the 'caricature' that was not a *ritratto ridicolo* in the alternative definition for *caricare un ritratto* included in some editions of Baretti's dictionary, 'to overshadow a picture', suggesting exaggerated contrasts rather than enlarged features. If they read through all Baretti's entries under *carica–*, they would have found that *caricatúra* also meant 'the charge of a gun' ('certa quantità di munizione'), and that to *caricar l'inimico* was 'to charge or attack the enemy' – a double meaning suggesting that an exaggerated 'caricature' might be more violent and hurtful than humorous and ridiculous. Baretti's dictionary, where *caricatúra* appears alongside definitions of *cárica* and *cáricare* – and next to explanations of phrases like 'caricare un archibuso', 'caricar l'orza', 'caricare (accusare)' and 'caricare (in parlando)' – calls the English reader's attention to the fact that *caricatúra*, when it describes a graphic or verbal likeness, is a figurative usage of *cáricare*. To use the word 'caricature' to describe an overblown sermon, a distorting abridgement of one's letter to the editor about the Poor Laws, or the style of the new novel *Frankenstein*, was not to misapply *caricatúra* but to reinvest it with some of *cáricare*'s many idioms – contrast, force, impact, plenitude, addition, emphasis – that were subordinated in the *ritratto ridicolo* definition. Any reader who jumped from *Cobbett's Weekly Register* or the *Scots Magazine* to Baretti's dictionary would have been reassured that 'caricature' – used so freely of texts and speeches in the English language – was securely in the linguistic tradition of *caricatúra*.

I like to think that this scenario of mine is not hypothetical: that many readers in the Romantic period really did consult Baretti's entry for *caricatúra* – or familiarise themselves with the word's etymology elsewhere. In his *Rules for Drawing Caricaturas* (1788), Francis Grose implicitly recognises that the *ritratto ridicolo* is a 'charged' picture but not necessarily an 'overcharged' one, when he advises the amateur graphic caricaturist 'not to overcharge the peculiarities of their subjects, as they would thereby become hideous instead of ridiculous, and instead of laughter excite horror'.[11] Wollstonecraft insists that her satirical description of the dependent woman is 'not an overcharged picture'.[12] Austen's manuscript of readers' opinions about characters in *Emma* records one reader thinking that Miss Bates might be 'overcharged', and Thomas Babington Macaulay describes Fanny Burney's characters as 'extravagantly overcharged'.[13] English's use of 'overcharged' to mean 'over-exaggerated' indicates that English readers and writers continued to be aware of caricature's linguistic ties with *cárica* and *cáricare*.

When, in the late Georgian period, Britain's political graphic satirists became more adept in the techniques of the *ritratto ridicolo*, writers recognised these distinctive designs as 'caricature prints' – but caricature's semantic range was not eclipsed by the strengthened association with satirical prints. A letter to the *Morning Post*, in 1776, describes Robert D'Arcy, 4th Earl of Holdernesse, as 'foremost in the patronage of operas, opera singers, and every species of foreign taste, and foreign *vertu*'; thus, the writer thinks – referring to a print titled *The Idol* (c. 1756–58) – '[t]he well known satyrical print of his Lordship at the feet of Mingotti was not a *caricature*'.[14] When 'caricature' is used in late eighteenth-century newspapers and periodicals to mean a graphic portrait, it usually alludes to drawings and amateur sketches – except where there is a discussion or advertisement specifically about satirical prints, such as a notice in the *Morning Herald* that '[t]his day is published by W. Holland [. . .] A Caricature Print of Lloyd's Coffee-House, and another of Wright's Oyster-Room, the first 4s, the other 3s'.[15]

The richness of Baretti's entries under *carica–*, and the varied ways 'caricature' was used in the Romantic period as just quoted, suggest that the history of the modern graphic caricature – its development in Renaissance Italy and its export to Britain in the seventeenth and eighteenth centuries – is not quite as relevant as I once assumed, when it comes to the history of literature's caricature in the Romantic period. In the following pages, some context on the Italian *ritratti carichi* and on that genre's appropriation by the British elite, gives a background for British writers' understanding of graphic caricature as an artistic tradition long preceding the satirical prints of the late Georgian period.

Literature and the Caricature Print in the Romantic Period

The inception of Romanticism in British culture and literature coincides with what twentieth-century scholarship dubbed the 'Age of Caricature' (sometimes the 'golden age of caricature'), a period understood to span the

1770s to the 1820s. In this common shorthand, 'caricature' means the genre of single-sheet satirical prints that possessed a distinctive aesthetic and that seems to have attained an artistic high point in the late Georgian period. The very phrase 'Age of Caricature' tempts literary scholars – me among them – into imagining that poets and novelists in the Romantic period might have been struck by the 'caricature' of the satirical prints, might have incorporated the prints' qualities into their own works, or might have been influenced by prints via some larger cultural phenomenon that graphic satirists helped create, with satirical prints representative of caricature as a 'spirit of the age'. Such claims often lean on phrases denoting contemporaneity ('the age of ', 'of the day', 'in the period when'): for example, Michael O'Neill remarks that '[g]reat Romantic short lyrics have something in common with the caricaturist's eye for the telling detail (this is the age of Gillray, after all)'.[16] What was the relationship between the satirical prints and the new literature being published in the Romantic period? On the way to answering that question, several points should be made about the relation of the word 'caricature' to the satirical print genre, the social status of the satirical print, and how the satirical prints and Romantic literature represented each other.

The satirical prints of the late Georgian era, laden with text and intertextual allusions, are a literary genre in their own right. Literary critics' recent forays into the study of the genre are made possible by decades of work by print and art historians – most significantly the eleven-volume *Catalogue of Political and Personal Satires Preserved in the Department of Prints and Drawings in the British Museum*, which not only systematised the British Museum's collection of thousands of single-sheet prints and caricature drawings but also annotated them with relevant historical information and identified the individuals depicted. Between 1868 and 1883 Frederic George Stephens, founder member of the Pre-Raphaelite Brotherhood, compiled the first four volumes, comprising BM Sat 1 to 4838. Historian Mary Dorothy George took up the project in 1930, completing seven further volumes between 1935 and 1954. At the end of the twentieth century a new generation of print historians aimed to understand the genre in its broader cultural and socio-economic contexts, with Eirwen E.C Nicholson's 1994 PhD thesis, a review and critical analysis of scholarship on political prints c. 1640–c. 1832, in the vanguard. Critics have had the benefit of print historian Diana Donald's persuasively titled *The Age of Caricature: Satirical Prints in the Reign of George III* (1996); and for any literary critic with a serious interest in the topic, James Baker's account of the genre's socio-economic history in *The Business of Satirical Prints in Late-Georgian England* (2017) is indispensable.

Now a new generation of scholars subject the eighteenth-century satirical print to cultural historicism, critical theory and close-reading techniques – notably Amelia Rauser's ground-breaking study *Caricature Unmasked: Irony, Authenticity and Individualism in Eighteenth-Century English Prints* (2008), *The Efflorescence of Caricature, 1759–1838*, a collection of essays edited by Todd Porterfield (2011), Ian Haywood's *Romanticism and Caricature* (2014), Temi Odumosu's *Africans in English Caricature, 1769–1819* (2017) and David Taylor's *The Politics of Parody: A Literary History of Caricature, 1760–1830* (2018).[17] While Odumosu uses a more capacious definition where 'caricature' can refer to satirical characterisations in plays, novels and periodicals as well as in satirical prints, generally these book titles reflect the pattern that has emerged in the study of satirical prints as a literary genre, of the word 'caricature' habitually standing in for the genre of the single-sheet satirical print. It is true that, as scholars acknowledge, the Georgian satirical print drew heavily on the techniques of Italian caricature portraiture, and some artists often used more extravagant, fantastic imagery than previous 'emblematic' political prints had done. However, caricature was not synonymous with the single-sheet satirical print at any point during 'the Age of Caricature' itself. Nor is it clear that we can expect to find significant lines of influence running directly between satirical prints and the new literature published in the Romantic period.

Due to the satirical prints' borrowing from an established literary canon – Shakespeare, *Paradise Lost, Don Quixote, Gulliver's Travels*[18] – as well as from Gothic imagery and from the idioms of the press, it is inevitable that there are coincidences in imagery and wording between Cruikshank and Scott, between Gillray and Shelley. For example, as Haywood points out, *Frankenstein* shares its subtitle with George Cruikshank's satire on Napoleon exiled to Elba, *The Modern Prometheus, or Downfall of Tyranny* (1814).[19] Cruikshank certainly did not invent the phrase: it appears in a wide range of contemporary publications, for example referring to the electro-magnetic therapist James Graham in 1781, and to the anti-vaccination Benjamin Moseley in 1805, before being applied to Napoleon in 1815.[20] Shaftesbury may have coined the phrase to cast aspersion on con artists, writing in *The Moralists* (1709) of 'our modern PROMETHEUS'S, *the Mountebanks*, who perform'd such Wonders [...]. Shou'd we dare to make such *Empiricks* of the Gods, and such a *Patient* of poor Nature?'[21] Perhaps most pertinently, given the link between Galvanism and Frankenstein's electrified oak tree, the epithet was applied to Benjamin Franklin. A poem published in the *London Evening*

Post in 1777 portrays Franklin ascending to heaven 'in chains of wire, / To perish by his stolen fire', describing him in a footnote as 'this arch patriot, philosopher, modern Prometheus, and rebel'.[22] Contemporary references to Napoleon as Prometheus – including Cruikshank's print – dwell on Prometheus chained rather than on Promethean fire. Shelley's tagging of Frankenstein as a Prometheus draws on any number of negative associations the 'modern Prometheus' had gathered since Shaftesbury's ironic statement in the early 1700s.

Looking beyond such coincidences of imagery and allusion between literature and satirical prints, it can be argued that the late-Georgian satirical print 'evokes a parallel with Romantic aesthetics' more generally, as Haywood does: 'to the extent that it showcases a distorting application of the inspirational imagination, we can regard caricature as renegade Romanticism'.[23] E. H. Gombrich supposes that around the time of the late-Georgian print, Romanticism was inculcating a taste for 'the weirdest combinations of symbols, the most grotesque conglomerations of images, [...] phantoms, nightmares, and apparitions'.[24] Robert Patten sees the late-Georgian caricature print as 'another manifestation of the Romantic movement' in the sense of 'the exploration of individuality and difference which confuted Augustan assumptions about universal norms'.[25]

I would suggest, however, that the extravagant imagery of some late-Georgian satirical prints – most prominently Gillray's – should not be allowed to dominate any discussion of 'caricature' as a cultural phenomenon with close connections to literature in the Romantic period. Parallels between Romanticism and late-Georgian satirical prints cannot be grounded in an argument that novelists and poets of the Romantic period generally saw satirical prints as the model for a 'caricature' applicable beyond the most topical political events and matters of high society. Moreover, the comic and grotesque artistic techniques that became associated with *caricatúra* preceded the satirical print genre by hundreds of years – marginal drawings in medieval manuscripts, stone gargoyles, the 'fancy head' genre – and British connoisseurs were well aware of the modern caricature portrait's origins in the Italian Renaissance, with *Bell's Court and Fashionable Magazine* in 1815 observing that '[i]t is to no less persons than to those eminent restorers of the art of painting, Michel Angelo, and Leonardi di Vinci, that we are indebted for some of the first caricatures which have ever appeared in modern times'.[26]

British interest in modern graphic *caricatúra* was sparked by the comic *ritratti carichi* of sixteenth-century Italy that are credited to Annibale Carracci, a Bolognese painter of altarpieces and frescoes paid for by elite families. These early modern graphic caricatures followed a literary fad for short satirical 'portraits' in verse, and Donald Posner suggests that the first *ritratti carichi* were pictorial illustrations for these verses.[27] Only a few examples survive of the caricatures by Carracci and his fellows: Malvasia's *Life of the Carracci* mentions drawings of people depicted variously as dwarfed and hunchbacked, with animalistic physiognomies, or made to resemble inanimate objects. E. H. Gombrich identifies these techniques with 'the theoretical discovery of the difference between likeness and equivalence'.[28] Carracci named the *perfetta deformità* ('perfect deformity'), a distinctive physical aberration supposed to contain the essence of a person's real physical likeness, and which could be exaggerated or made the basis of a fantastic portrait that still, thanks to the perfect deformity, resembled the subject.[29] Anne Summerscale notes that Carracci conceived of his *caricatúra* as something greater and more intellectual than mere 'comic distortion'; rather, it was a realism born of perverse creativity, which sat alongside the Carracci family's artistic reform movement.[30] In 1582, when the Carracci founded a school for artists in Bologna, the Academia degli Incamminati ('Academy of Those Who Are Making Progress'), fine art was dominated by the strand of Renaissance art that came to be seen as exaggeratedly elegant, 'Mannerism'. The Carracci advocated a return to nature, flouting church doctrine by allowing artists to draw nudes from live models.[31] *Ritratti carichi*, visual jokes that captured individuals' physical likenesses in unflattering ways, became fashionable in the elite society that patronised the Academia's painting. Noble men and women tried their hands at caricaturing each other, as well as commissioning professional portraits of themselves, their family and friends. The trend was imported to Britain by connoisseurs who returned from their Grand Tour with group portraits of themselves and their travelling companions: desirable souvenirs, especially if drawn by an acclaimed artist such as Pier Leone Ghezzi or the Italian-trained English painter Thomas Patch.[32] When the British elites took up caricaturing as a hobby, enterprising publishers offered engraving and printing services so that amateur caricaturists could distribute copies of their drawings around the social circle that would recognise the likeness.

The most prominent of the publishers were Mary and Matthew Darly, who engraved portraits by George Marquess Townshend. Mary Darly created a drawing manual, *A Book of Carricaturas* (1762), to appeal to her clientele. In a run-on sentence introducing the book, she calls attention to caricaturing's fashionably aristocratic and Continental origins, while patriotically endorsing the British upper ranks' talent for this new pastime:

> Carricatura is the burlesque of Character, or an exaggeration of nature, when not very pleasing it's a manner of drawing that has & still is held in great esteem both by the Italiens [sic] & French, some of our Nobility & Gentility at this time do equal, if not excel any thing of the kind that has ever been done in any other country, tis the most diverting species of designing & will certainly keep those that practise it out of the hippo [hypochondria], or Vapours & that it may have such an effect on her friends is the wish of M^y Darly.[33]

Darly's emphasis on amateur caricaturing as a way of dispelling the kinds of 'nervous' disorders now understood as 'depression' and 'anxiety' accords with eighteenth-century *caricatúra* as a hobby carried out behind closed doors and among peers: social, entertaining, even therapeutic. Manuals like Darly's play into the social pressure or encouragement to become a caricaturist, promising to teach caricaturing even to readers not talented at drawing with artistic formulae and diagrams. *A Book of Carricaturas* recommends that the would-be caricaturist begin by examining their subject's linear profile and sorting it into one of four categories – straight, convex, concave, or with the S-shaped curve of the ogive arch or 'ogee'. Later in the century, antiquarian Francis Grose attempts a more granular categorisation of faces into types of noses and mouths. His *Rules for Drawing Caricaturas* (1788) also gives tips for using these categories to caricature faces briefly glimpsed: 'When a caricaturist wishes to delineate any face he may see in a place where it would be improper or impossible to draw it, he may commit it to his memory, by parsing it in his mind (as school-boys term it) by naming the contour and the different species of features of which it is constructed, as school-boys point out the different parts of the speech in a Latin sentence.'[34] This grammar of the face helped artists to draw from life, and quickly, with a sketchy quality being part of the desired aesthetic. In some surviving examples of amateur caricaturing, multiple *ritratti carichi* float in empty space on a single page (in the manner of Leonardo Da Vinci's sheets of grotesque and 'fancy heads'), usually untitled and sometimes using reusing paper, such as with George Clerk's drawing on a printed legal document catalogued as 'Heads of Two Men'.[35] Looking back on the inscrutable fashions of the past, a writer for *The Athenaeum* in 1888 remarks with wonder that Grose's manual was 'one of several books professing to give instructions in an art which nowadays no one would think of taking lessons in, though a century ago it seems to have been regarded as a "genteel accomplishment"'.[36]

The appeal of caricaturing as a pursuit for gentlemen and gentlewoman amateurs continued into the nineteenth century, when it was less exclusive to the highest ranks of British society. In Walter Scott's circles, John Gibson Lockhart and Charles Kirkpatrick Sharpe were known for *ritratti carichi* of private acquaintances. Writing to Lord Montagu in 1824, Scott asks, 'Did you get Lockhart set to drawing Caricatures—he has a pretty talent that way'.[37] Jonathan Henry Christie reports how, in their Balliol days, Lockhart 'was an incessant caricaturist [. . .] his papers, his books, and the walls of his rooms [. . .] crowded with portraits of his friends and himself'.[38] *Redgauntlet* draws inspiration from Lockhart's penchant for caricaturing as a law student, describing Darsie Latimer's notebook 'filled with caricatures of the professors and my fellow students'.[39] Whereas Lockhart gave up the practice in later life, Sharpe used his talent to illustrate Bannatyne Club publications, and had a volume of his drawings printed as *Portraits of an Amateur* (1833). Thackeray – known for his essay on the professional graphic satirist George Cruikshank – shows awareness of *caricatúra*'s status as a private entertainment for elite amateurs in *Vanity Fair*, where Becky Sharp endears herself to Lord Steyne by verbally 'caricaturing Lady Jane and her ways', and by sketching 'a caricature of Sir Pitt Crawley'.[40] Caricaturing continued to be practised for the enjoyment of the artists and their circles, from the watercolour comic tableaux of Jemima Blackburn, to Edward Lear's self-portraits, to Virginia Woolf and Vanessa Bell's private magazine *Hyde Park Gate News*. Blackburn routinely associated with earls and countesses her contemporary amateur caricaturist Ella Taylor also moved in high society, indicating that in the second half of the nineteenth century *ritratti carichi* continued to be a creative outlet for upper-class British men and women.[41]

The late Georgian period saw the emergence of single-sheet satirical prints enhanced by the techniques of *ritratti carichi*. These prints were the work of professional artists and were printed and distributed more widely than the Darlys' customers' designs. However, commercial 'caricature prints' still effectively *belonged* to those elites. In the 1780s, artists including James Sayers, Richard Newton, Thomas Rowlandson, David Allan, John Kay and Isaac Cruikshank capitalised on the fashion for amateur caricaturing with new kinds of *ritratti carichi* that would interest well-connected consumers. The intended consumer of single-sheet satirical prints had intimate knowledge through social acquaintance of the people depicted in them – their personal histories and rivalries, their faces and physiques, their mannerisms and speech tics. In many cases, these graphic satirists offered an enhanced version of the Darlys' services: they would gratify their clients with professionally executed designs based on the clients' sketches and ideas. Most of James Gillray's prints were based on submissions from gentlemen amateurs: drawings, verbal descriptions of scenes and brief textual prompts. David Taylor gives an account of an extensive collaboration between Gillray and Captain Thomas Bradyll, son of an MP and heir to estates in Cumbria, for the 1803 print *The King of Brobdingnag, and Gulliver*.[42] Gillray's correspondence shows that he corresponded about designs with politicians including George Canning, John Hookham Frere, Sir John Dalrymple, Nathaniel Sneyd and Lord Bateman – and many more letters to Gillray are unsigned.[43] One note from Canning suggests that Gillray could be kept on a tight leash, though instructions were delivered politely: 'It is particularly wished that the Print of Mr. Sheridan No. 5 of the French Habits, which Mr. Gillray was so good as to send for inspection to-day, may not be published. If Mr. G. can call to-morrow, the reason will be explained to him.'[44] Nineteenth-century commentators on Georgian satirical prints, unaware of the extent to which Gillray and Cruikshank were satirists for hire who served individuals in government, misrepresent them as independent agents with their own political agendas. An essay in *The Athenaeum* describes Gillray as 'a sort of public and private spy', 'a caterpillar on the green-leaf of reputation' who 'loved to crawl over those whom Fame had marked as her own' and who felt personal hatred for 'his political adversaries'.[45] In general, however, the prints toed the line by expressing socially conservative, politically reactionary and royalist attitudes – especially when the focus moved from parliamentary conflicts to wider social or diplomatic concerns. A satire on Pitt in a Gillray print was not a call to revolution. Nicholson's work systematically presents research to dispel the myth that the single-sheet satirical print addressed a large public and could appeal 'even [or] especially to the illiterate', as some scholars had suggested.[46]

Indeed, most satirical prints were neither priced nor designed to be accessed and understood by the lower classes. Prolific collectors were Sarah Sophia Banks, George III, George IV and Sir William Augustus Fraser, who bequeathed his eleven morocco-bound folios of caricature prints to the House of Lords Library. The prints' consumers were often, like the satirists' clients, members of the political classes. Nicholson presents a compelling account of the satirical prints as peer-to-peer satire.[47] Baker gives an account of the late-Georgian print shop and the 'polite classes' who were its core market.[48] H. T. Dickinson highlights that most political satirical prints assumed a high level of political literacy, and Taylor demonstrates the high level of cultural literacy that readers would need to appreciate the prints' dense parodies of classical texts.[49] Many prints include phrases and quotations in French and Latin. There are comic imitations of fashionably controversial fine art, such as the burlesques of Fuseli's 1781 painting *The Nightmare*, and Gillray's 1798 print *The Apotheosis of Hoche*, suggested to him by the MP and *Anti-Jacobin* contributor John Hookham Frere.[50] Graphic satirists also assumed, of course, that their patrons were connoisseurs of comic *caricatúra*. By using portraiture techniques distinctive to the *ritratti carichi* brought back from Italy and emulated by amateur caricaturists in British high society, late-Georgian satirical prints created an aesthetic that was familiarly high-end.

Where novelists in the Romantic period use the word 'caricature' in referring to satirical prints, they thematise the prints as material objects associated with the frivolous leisure pursuits of aristocrats and with the machinations of political elites – a fair representation of the social world discussed in the last section. Mary Brunton's novel *Self-control* (1811), for example, gives an authentic view of the market for caricature prints, with print shop owners on the lookout for a wealthy lady wanting 'to make some addition to her cabinet', and protagonist Laura encountering 'the elegant, the accomplished, Colonel Hargrave' – 'one of the best bred men in the kingdom', an individual of 'the highest polish' – in a print shop. Hargrave does not notice Laura at first because he is 'busied in examining a book of caricatures', and she 'hoped that the caricatures would not long continue so very interesting'.[51] Hargrave's caricatures resonate with Robert Ferrars's jewelled pin in *Sense and Sensibility*: costly, fascinating and (in the novel's view) trivial objects from which the man's interest must be detached if the heroine is to advance *her* interest. Brunton evokes the 'book of caricatures' as something perhaps beyond the genteel reader's income, yet certainly beneath her attention. For Brunton, caricature portraits – whether professional or amateur – are neither artistically valuable nor satirically purposeful but merely a material trapping of petty vices. The protagonist in *Discipline* (1814) teases her guardian by 'hid[ing] her prayer-book' and 'past[ing] caricatures on the inside of her pew in church';[52] later, when she draws caricature portraits of people at an auction of expensive objects, she becomes a participant in the scene she is attempting to satirise:

> As the sale proceeded, a hundred useless toys were exposed, and called forth a hundred vain and unlovely emotions [...]. I took out my pencil to caricature a group, in which a spare dame, whose face combined no common contrast of projection and concavity, was darting from her sea-green eyes sidelong flames upon a china jar, which was surveyed with complacent smiles by its round and rosy purchaser. But my labours were

interrupted, and from an amused spectator of the scene, I was converted into a keen actor, when the auctioneer exposed a tortoise-shell dressing-box, magnificently inlaid with gold.[53]

Edgeworth, the only writer who refers to specific prints in her novels, shares Brunton's association of caricature drawing and satirical prints with a dissolute elite society: in an episode involving caricature drawings in *Belinda* (1801), she alludes to the prints that satirised Duchess of Devonshire's alleged methods of political canvassing in 1784;[54] in *Ennui* (1809), one character compares another to an Irish satirical print, exclaiming that he is '"the caricature of *the English fire-side* outdone!"';[55] and in *Helen* (1834), party guests are presented with 'a heap of coarse caricatures [...] party caricatures' as after-dinner entertainment. The novel's protagonist hides them under the table '"[f]or the honour of England"', and substitutes 'a portfolio of caricatures in a different style'.[56] When Edgeworth meditates that 'humour only can ensure [these prints'] permanence; the personality dies with the person', she gives the example of 'the famous old print of the minister rat-catcher, in the Westminster election' – a timely reference since readers in the 1830s could have recalled the newest spate of prints on the theme of 'placemen ratters', which mocked Wellington's soliciting of votes for the passage of the Roman Catholic Relief Act. Robert Southey and Samuel Taylor Coleridge capitalised on that trend in the prints by reissuing an updated anti-Catholic version of their satirical ballad 'The Devil's Thoughts' as *The Devil's Walk*, with plates by Robert Cruikshank including an image of Wellington associating with the Devil calculated to please ultra-tory readers.[57]

The ways that living writers themselves feature in late-Georgian satirical prints makes plain the genre's association with celebrity and social exclusivity. Southey and Charles Lamb are represented as political radicals in the inaugural number of the *Anti-Jacobin* (1797–99), founded by George Canning while Secretary of State for Foreign Affairs, endorsed by Pitt and supported by the Treasury. At the time, Southey and Lamb did not have significant public profiles; being unfamiliar with the writers' actual physical appearances, Gillray represents them as an ass and a frog, without caricaturing their real faces. For Southey, the experience was gratifying rather than humiliating, and in multiple letters he encourages his friends and family to seek out a copy of the magazine: 'Did you know that I have been caricatured in the Anti-Jacobine [sic] Magazine together with Lloyd, Lamb, the Duke of Bedford—Fox &c &c &c? the fellow has not however libelled my likeness, because he did not know it—so he has clapt an Asse's head on my shoulders.'[58] Here, the word 'caricature' is used to mean a mocking, ludicrous representation rather than an artistic technique of linear exaggerated resemblance. Southey is apparently delighted at being satirised in the company of more illustrious 'jacobins' such as Fox and the Duke of Bedford. Since the *Anti-Jacobin*'s readership is relatively small and pro-government, he cannot trust that his acquaintances will come across it of their own accord, and at two shillings the illustrated magazine is not cheap: 'If you have not already seen your acquaintance caricatured', he writes to a friend, 'pray send for the first number of the Anti-Jacobine Magazine. the caricature is worth two shillings, & you will not be amused the less for not recognizing the likeness'.[59] Despite the lack of physical likeness, this print was proof positive that Southey was not beneath the notice of people in high places. He could have imagined lords and ladies noticing him as they read the *Anti-Jacobin* over breakfast in bed. Concluding another letter Southey mentions, 'you have I suppose seen my asinine honours in the Jacobine Magazine'.[60] Gillray's portrait of the writer as an ass labelled 'Southey', in a magazine so closely tied to Pitt's government, had little power to damage his reputation before his reading public and could even enhance his standing. Even if his face and physique were unknown, he was someone worth satirising.

Canning himself would have understood Southey's delighted reaction to appearing in one of Gillray's elaborate designs: Canning's personal relationship with Gillray began when, through their mutual acquaintance John Sneyd, he persuaded the artist to include his portrait in a satirical print. As Taylor explains, for Canning's peers this inclusion 'would unequivocally signal his arrival on the political stage'.[61] Similarly, an appearance in a satirical print suggested that a writer had considerable cultural impact. Scott was the most frequently portrayed, appearing in prints by Charles Williams, Thomas Hood, Robert Cruikshank, Henry Thomas Aiken and John Doyle between 1812 and 1827.[62] Due to Byron's status as an aristocrat and a 'fashionable' individual, his physical likeness, manners and deeds were far better known, and the satires correspondingly more personal.[63] Southey's excitement about being raised from obscurity into the colourful pages of the *Anti-Jacobin* – 'Did you know I have been caricatured' – and Lord Byron's celebrity in the prints, both fit with the satirical print genre's reputation as a 'low' genre for high society.

I have hunted for references to the 'caricature' of London-centric satirical print culture among the published works of the writers who most strongly represent the Romantic period in literary scholarship. Besides Edgeworth's thematising of caricature prints in *Belinda*, *Ennui* and

Helen, there is a possible reference to the satirical print genre in Percy Shelley's satirical closet drama *Oedipus Tyrannus; or, Swellfoot the Tyrant* (1820), where government ministers plot to smear Queen Caroline in the press. The litigious 'green bag' supposed to contain evidence of her guilt actually contains a 'fatal liquor' that will make her appear in the public eye like 'a ghastly caricature / Of what was human' and '[b]e called adulterer, drunkard, liar, wretch' regardless of what she has actually done.[64] Shelley may be alluding here to the graphic caricature of satirical prints, given the green bag's power to transform Caroline's physical appearance from 'gentlest looks / To savage, foul, and fierce deformity'. However, Shelley is almost certainly referring to the power of the journalistic press more generally, to apotheosise individuals as well as satirise them – and his emphasis on the press's influence over common people suggests that the green bag contains more newspapers and pamphlets than satirical prints, which were expensive to purchase or hire. In *Oedipus Tyrannus*, the House of Lords tells a crowd of gullible pigs that if Caroline is innocent, the contents of the bag will transform her into an angel raining down 'blessings in the shape of comfits': 'just the sort of thing / Swine will believe'.

In none of these examples does the writer position the satirical prints as the genre of caricature, or as particularly important to ideas about emphasis and exaggeration that could be applied to literary works. Walter Scott's interest in John Kay is the exception that proves the rule. While Kay did produce satirical prints and portraits with distinct political meanings, Scott's reference to 'Kay's caricatures' in *The Heart of Mid-Lothian* is clearly aimed at graphic caricature's potential for social documentary and historical record. Kay's portraits of Edinburgh characters have been thought to be comparatively 'gentle' and 'polite',[65] too different from Gillray's and the Cruikshanks' prints to be comfortably included in overviews of late-Georgian satire. Scott was a collector of political satirical prints and held Gillray to be the best artist in the genre.[66] But his admiring reference to 'Kay's caricatures' in *The Heart of Mid-Lothian* indicates that the pre-Gillray understanding of *caricatúra* was alive and well in the early nineteenth century. I consider Kay's significance to Scott's novel-writing in Chapter 3.

It is unfortunate for literary criticism that Kay has been marginalised in the study of late-Georgian graphic caricature, when his are the only 'caricatures' explicitly claimed as a model for a literary work's textual description of people and places. Neglecting Kay's work in Edinburgh, and the collection of prints Scott kept at Abbotsford,[67] is convenient to scholarship's tendency to overlook Scottishness in the phenomenon of late-Georgian graphic satire. For scholars working on British graphic satire, Kay is an afterthought when he is mentioned at all. Some have used phrases like 'the golden age of *English* caricature', despite the fact that Gillray's and the Cruikshank family's connections with Scotland should be well known from scholarship such as Robert Patten's work on George Cruikshank.[68] Early in his career, Isaac moved his family from Edinburgh (where he may have picked up professional caricaturing from Kay) to London, where the Cruikshanks attended a Scottish church; and dialogue in one of George and Robert's collaborative prints shows familiarity with Scottish English despite living in London their whole adult lives.

These satirists' Scottish origins were common knowledge during their lifetimes, with Gillray and Cruikshank being recognisably Scottish names, and were emphasised in nineteenth-century biographies. Whereas Gillray's Lanarkshire father fought under the Duke of Cumberland in Flanders, the Cruikshanks were historically Jacobites. In 1833, the *Monthly Magazine* highlights the Cruikshanks' Jacobite credentials on both sides of the family line:

> Prior to the famous "forty-five," the name of Cruikshank, or as it used to be spelt by its Scotch proprietors, Crookshank, appears to have been recorded only in the Highland fogs. The mother of George was a Mac Naghten. The Crookshanks and the Mac Naghtens were both Charlie Stewart's men. Many of them were killed and more of them wounded at Preston Pans, and Culloden.[69]

The *Morning Chronicle*'s 1851 retrospective of 'Gillray's Caricatures' identifies him as 'the son of a Scotsman, who lost an arm at Fontenoy'.[70] Gillray, notorious for alcoholism and dementia in the last years of his life,[71] was not then proudly claimed as an English caricaturist, the brightest star of a golden age.

If any graphic satirist could be seen to fill that role, it was William Hogarth. John Barrell notes that the adjective 'Hogarthian' appeared in print during Hogarth's lifetime.[72] Commentators in the Romantic period describe Hogarth's works as 'comic paintings' and 'portraits', or as 'caricatures' so good they were scarcely caricatures at all. The *Monthly Magazine*, reviewing *Melincourt* in 1817, declares that Peacock 'finishes his portraits like Hogarth, while the portraits in [some other comic novels] are mere sign-posts or coarse caricatures'.[73] Hazlitt claims that the faces in Hogarth's works 'go to the very verge of caricature and yet never (we believe in any single instance) go beyond it'.[74] In an essay in *The Athenaeum*, Hogarth and his works are praised, yet denied the immortality of artistic 'genius', sharing Edgeworth's idea of graphic satire in *Helen* as ephemeral, fatally concerned with temporary goings-on:

> The political caricatures of that wonderful man [Hogarth] were felt and understood in their day [...] but to the children of this age they appear only as extravagant riddles, which no one has the patience to solve. They have gone to that oblivion from which there is no redemption: indeed, the most successful of caricatures can be only for a passing moment. They deal only with the personal defects or the fleeting follies of the creatures of the hour [...]. In caricatures, as in candles, there are wicks which will soon consume them; and the memories of the artists themselves may be safely permitted to perish with them.[75]

Hogarth could still be lumped in with the late-Georgian satirists, on the grounds that 'you had to be there' to appreciate his jokes.

The literati's conceptions in the Romantic period of amateur caricaturing and caricature prints – highly exclusive, highly specific and thus short-lived – are at odds with a fundamental ideal of literary realism, the 'originality' of individualised characters that are particularised without being comic or satirically rendered portraits of unique and living individuals. Writers would have hoped to achieve broader appeal, make light reading more respectable and give readers more lasting pleasure, by distancing the idea that leisure reading offered characters as identities to be deciphered and narratives as puzzles to be solved. In Chapter 2, I consider the Romantic literary sphere's wariness of prosopographic caricature as a context for the values of realist character-writing that emerge in the late eighteenth century's critical reception of *The Spectator*.

Distorted People, Distorted Texts: 'Caricature' in Critique

I have pointed out that British literary culture's understanding of 'caricature' as a term applicable to texts precedes the distinctive late-Georgian satirical print with its increased use of Italianate caricature portraiture. The caricature talk that emerged in the late eighteenth-century literary sphere originated in the appropriation of 'caricature' from the *ritratti carichi* brought to Britain by the Grand Tour: literary culture transferred *caricatúra*'s sense of techniques for exaggerated visual resemblance (more differentiated lines, darker shadows) to *caricatúra* in the sense of techniques for exaggerated textual description (too much, too often, too incongruously or contrastingly), with varied usage of 'caricature' recapturing the richness of *caricatúra*'s connotations and etymology in Italian.

But there was an intermediate step, I argue, in this transfer from the critique of pictures to the critique of texts. From the early years of *ritratti carichi* and *caricatúra* becoming known in Britain, anglophone writers used the vocabulary of caricature to describe real human bodies – and later, real human minds. 'Caricature' was a pliable metaphor for evoking the disturbing effect of a physical body that was unnatural and real, uncanny in its distorted resemblance of what it should ideally be. In Chapter 6, I discuss these descriptions of 'flesh-caricatures' in writing by Thomas Browne, John Locke, Jean-Jacques Rousseau and Mary Wollstonecraft as precursors to the 'horrid realism' local to grotesque bodies in Mary Shelley's *Frankenstein* and 'Transformation', as well as in Scott's novels, from *The Black Dwarf* to *The Talisman*. By metaphorising *caricatúra* – effectively saying that 'this person resembles a picture that exaggerates yet resembles a person' – writers literalise *caricatúra*, imagining an artistic representation of a real thing into the thing itself.

When Thomas Holcroft translated Johann Caspar Lavater's *Physiognomische Fragmente* (1775–78) into English, the author's reliance on the literalisation of *caricatúra* to evoke physical deformity frustrated the translator's preference for varying vocabulary. Lavater uses 'Carricatur' and 'Karikatur' often enough that Holcroft runs out of synonyms:

> By *Caricature*, the Author appears to mean nothing more than an imperfect drawing, and by *Ideal*, sometimes perfect beauty, sometimes a fancy piece. These words occur so frequently that they must inevitably be often retained in the translation.[76]

Whether or not Holcroft manages to pick up all the connotations of Lavater's 'Carricatur' with his various synonyms, his translation is an instance of a Romantic-period reader needing to figure out what 'caricature' could mean for writers engaged in social and cultural critique. Clearly, Lavater was not making a straightforward analogy with the *caricatúra* of the *ritratti carichi*, which were deliberately distorted and intended to be comic or otherwise entertaining. The bodies and faces he saw around him were failures, 'imperfect drawings' of the human form, pitiable or horrific:

> Carrikaturen aller Arten treff' ich an.—Die Bemerkung entgeht mir nie, dass der Pobel zusammengenommen ordentlich die grobste Carrikatur des National-Stadt-Dorf-characters ist.[77]

Holcroft translates:

> I constantly find that the vulgar, collectively, whether of nation, town, or village, are the most distorted.

Omitting to translate the first sentence as 'I meet all kinds of caricatures', and substituting the phrase 'most distorted' instead of 'die grobste Carrikatur', Holcroft may have wanted to avoid readers assuming that Lavater finds these beings humorous, or sees them as distinctive individuals. These connotations of 'caricature' would be at odds with Lavater's disgusted tone or would contradict his seeing the common people *zusammengenommen*. Holcroft retains the word 'caricature' in a passage about family (mis)resemblance, where individual human beings are distorted versions of other particular human beings: if men 'abandon themselves to their passions' and sink 'deep in degeneracy', Lavater warns in Holcroft's translation, 'what variety of more or less gross, vulgar, caricatures will rise in succession, from father to son!'[78] I imagine Holcroft, suspicious of Lavater's seemingly figurative uses of 'Carrikaturen', picking up Baretti's dictionary to reassure himself that 'Carrikatur' had an etymological link with *caricare un ritratto* in the sense of failing to copy reality closely enough.

Indeed, this meaning of *caricatúra* – an inadvertently bad drawing, particularly of a human body – was influential in the Romantic literary sphere's appropriation of 'caricature' as a term of criticism, and fundamental to the anti-caricature rhetoric in Romantic character talk that I will discuss later. The distinction between a deliberate *caricatúra* and a *ritratto caricato* is debated in an exchange of letters published in successive numbers of the *Monthly Review* in 1758. The first letter in the exchange (signed 'B') is better known to scholars, for its response to Hogarth's caption for *The Bench* (1758): Lynch mentions it in her analysis of the stance Hogarth takes on 'caricature' in *The Analysis of Beauty* (1743) and his caption for *Characters and Caricaturas* (1743).[79] A second letter, responding to the first, contextualises 'B' and Hogarth's disagreement over the meaning of *caricatúra* in the difference between *caricato* and *caricatúra* as technical terms for visual art.

Seen as part of a conversation about the meaning of caricature, these letters show a desire to categorise *caricatúra* as either a pejorative term or a name for a particular set of techniques and their aesthetic effects. In his caption for *The Bench*, Hogarth – like Holcroft in his translation of Lavater – tries to relegate 'caricature' to a single meaning: 'That which has, of late years, got the name of *Caracatura*, is, or ought to be, totally divested of every stroke that hath a tendency to good Drawing.' He compares it to 'the early scrawlings of a child' that make a reductive and inadvertently 'comical resemblance' of the human form, as opposed to '*Outré*', which 'signifies [. . .] the exaggerated outlines of a figure, all the parts of which may be in other respects, a perfect and true picture of nature'. (To illustrate this, Hogarth gives an example that metaphorises and literalises pictorial exaggeration, suggesting that '[a] Giant or Dwarf may be called a common man *Outré*'.)

B, writing to the *Monthly Review*, requests that Hogarth give up his definition of caricature as an inadvertently bad drawing for the deliberately exaggerated *ritratto ridicolo*, referring to the Carracci's *perfetta deformità*:

> I must beg leave to differ with the Author [Hogarth], as to what he says of the meaning of those words [*Caracatura* and *Outré*] being commonly mistaken. I have conversed a good deal with Painters, with Connoisseurs, and with people entirely ignorant of Painting; and yet never remember to have heard them misapplied *before*: nor, indeed, do I recollect any three terms of art, in the meaning of which mankind are generally agreed. With submission to so great an Artist, I must beg leave to say, that his definition of *Caracatura* is entirely wrong [. . .]. *Caracatura*, means the distinguishing figure of a person or thing ludicrously exaggerated, yet so as to preserve the similitude of the original, regardless of any circumstances that may arise for good or bad Drawing. As to the word *Outré*, it never meant any thing more than simply exaggerated.[80]

A third gentleman writes in from Worcester to agree with B's definition, which he thinks 'follows the surer guidance of the common sense and general acceptation, of the word'. The Worcester connoisseur's main purpose, however, is to point out that the similarity in the words 'character' and 'caricature' is mere coincidence, that they are not etymologically linked, arguing that 'caricature' should be used only as part of the specialised vocabulary of the visual arts. After correcting Hogarth's and B's spelling of the word, he separates the *ritratto caricato* from the *ritratto ridicolo* or *ritratto carichi*:

> CARACATURA has (some people will be suprized at it) no meaning whatever: nor is there any such word in the Italian, the French, or the English Dictionaries. There is, indeed, a word used by Italian painters, which is written *Caricatura*, which in English we should translate [to] a charging, or a loading, and perhaps an over-charging, or an over-loading,— and is derived from *carica*, a charge or load; hence *caricato*, loaded. [. . .]
>
> But to return to *Caricato* and *Caricatura*, as technical terms of painting, we shall observe, that the masters in Italy have frequent occasion for the first of these words, when they point out the faults of their disciples, who, in the copies they make, commonly exaggerate those almost imperceptible flexures and curvatures of the outlines [. . .]. The master then says, *Avete troppo caricato questo muscolo, questo naso, questo Ginocchio, &c*. That is, you have loaded, or charged, or exaggerated, this muscle, this nose, this knee, &c.

Two years later, the Worcester connoisseur might have read with approval Baretti's entries under *carica–*. What Hogarth calls 'Caracatura', he explains, is actually the drawing *troppo caricato*, whereas the exaggerations of *caricatúra* are intentional:

> *Una Caricatura* is the technical term used precisely to express a kind of drawing, which delights in an artificial exaggeration of particular features, by means of which exaggeration the portrait of a very decent person may appear strikingly like, and at the same time be rendered whimsically ridiculous.
>
> Of these *Caricaturas* excellent examples may be seen among the works of Leonardo da Vinci, Annibale Caracci, Carlo Marratti, &c. and even of Mr. Hogarth, *that are not totally divested of every stroke which hath a tendency to good drawing.*[81]

Hogarth and his respondents attempt to disentangle the different ways in which *caricatúra* was being used and mark some usages as erroneous, whereas later in the century – when 'caricature' is increasingly written and pronounced in an anglicised fashion – caricature talk is more accepting of the word's fluidity.

Caricature talk in the Romantic period accepts *caricatúra*'s multivalence and applicability, beyond graphic satire and beyond the visual arts altogether. Hazlitt makes the generalised pronouncement that '[a]rt is at once a miniature and a caricature of nature', and accuses Michelangelo's sculptures of 'tread[ing] on the verge of caricature' with '*extreme* forms, massy, gigantic, supernatural'.[82] Felix Mendelssohn deplores the 'perverted caricatures' in the 'distorted cantus firmus of the "Dies Irae," to which the witches are dancing' in Berlioz's *Symphonie Fantastique*.[83] Francis Jeffrey complains of 'harsh caricature' in Scott's *Guy Mannering*.[84] The *Critical Review* accuses Byron of 'having collected together a greater mass of offensive and disgusting objects than any poet ever did before – of having aspired to heap together caricatures of enormous guilt'.[85] The *Monthly Review* makes a case for deliberately exaggerating physicalised emotion on the stage: 'In the language of the theatre, the expression of every emotion ought to be not merely distinct, but obvious; the object should be magnified, *colossalized*, (if we may coin such an expression,) into conspicuousness. Like the pictured passions of Charles Le Brun, those of the playhouse ought somewhat to caricature nature, in order to be instantly and definitely visible and distinguishable'.[86] Painting, sculpture, music, novels, poetry, stage performance: this freedom of usage, where 'caricature' is limited neither to graphic satire, nor satire nor the visual arts generally, is reflected in several dictionaries published during the Romantic period. In H. J. Rodd's 1818 edition of Johnson's *Dictionary of the English Language*,

Rodd's examples for 'caricature' and 'to caricature' include caricature drawings, but he defines the terms without reference to visual art, as 'the representation of a person or circumstance, so as to render the original ridiculous, without losing the resemblance' and 'to ridicule; to represent unfairly'. Walker's *Critical Pronouncing Dictionary*, first published in 1823, argues that using 'caricature' to describe any kind of representation or imitation simply extends what is already a 'metaphorical signification' in using *caricatúra* to mean an exaggerated drawing:

> This word, though not in Johnson, I have not scrupled to insert, from its frequent and legitimate usage. Baretti tells us that the literal sense of this word is *certa quantita di munizione che si mettee nell' archibuso o altro*, which, in English, signifies the charge of a gun; but its metaphorical signification, and the only one in which the English use it, as he tells us, *dichesi anche di ritratto ridicolo in cui sensei grandemente accresciute [sic]i diffetti*, when applied to paintings, chiefly portraits, the heightening of some features, and lowering others, which we call in English overcharging, and which will make a very ugly picture, not unlike a handsome person: whence any exaggerated character, which is redundant in some of its parts, and defective in others, is called a Caricature.[87]

This definition's easy transition from the deliberate *ritratto ridicolo* to 'any exaggerated character' is one of several instances suggesting Romantic-period English's acceptance that 'caricature' comprised multiple interrelated definitions and could have positive or negative connotations depending on the context.

For example, in Wollstonecraft's *Vindication*, we have not only the deliberate caricature *and* the incompetent caricature, the accurate caricature *and* the misrepresenting caricature, the pictorial caricature *and* the textual caricature, but also the literalised caricature as in Lavater's social critique. Wollstonecraft imagines that 'the discriminating outline of a caricature' could fully capture the details that her text does not include, 'the domestic miseries and petty vices' diffused by warped femininity. When she offers a description of dependent womanhood, she insists that it is 'not an overcharged' representation. She claims to have noticed a woman's eye, having 'glanced coldly over a most exquisite picture, rest, sparkling with pleasure, on a caricature rudely sketched'. She refers to silly novels 'caricatur[ing] human nature', and (in the first edition of the *Vindication*) to artificially sentimental literary style: 'pretty superlatives' that are actually 'nothings— these caricatures of the real beauty of sensibility'.[88] Finally, Wollstonecraft claims that the Protestant Dissenter's body, like the female body, has been physically caricatured alongside the distortion of mental character:

> Were not dissenters [...] a class of people, with strict truth characterized by cunning? And may I not lay some stress on this fact to prove, that when any power but reason curbs the free spirit of man, dissimulation is practised, and the various shifts of art are naturally called forth? Great attention to decorum, which was carried to a degree of scrupulosity, and all that puerile bustle about trifles and consequential solemnity, which Butler's caricature of a dissenter brings before the imagination, shaped their persons as well as their minds in the mould of prim littleness. [...] Oppression thus formed many of the features of their character perfectly to coincide with that of the oppressed half of mankind; for is it not notorious, that dissenters were like women, fond of deliberating together, and asking advice of each other, till by a complication of little contrivances, some little end was brought about?[89]

Here, Wollstonecraft alludes to the titular character of *Hubridas* (1663–78), referring to a comic textual caricature simultaneously with literalising caricature into a horrifically shrunken body. Such 'flesh-caricatures', which I explore further in Chapter 6, use the *troppo caricato* definition of caricature for social critique.

Literary criticism in the Romantic period, on the other hand, uses *troppo caricato* in an anti-caricature rhetoric deploring supposedly exaggerated or disproportioned textual properties of literary works: their style, their structure, their variegation. Critique's literalisation of 'caricature' into flesh-caricature played a role in cementing this rhetorical use of 'caricature' – in association with other terms like 'disproportion', 'distortion' and 'exaggeration' – to deplore works that apparently failed to shape their content into proper forms.

2

Denying Caricature

The Romantic period's caricature talk about novels is dominated by anti-caricature rhetoric that seeks to establish the literary quality and verisimilitude of 'strong' characterisations that might otherwise be accused of being 'caricatured' or 'overcharged'. To describe and judge the quality of artistic and literary works' 'likeness' to reality, anti-caricature rhetoric uses a variety of elements from the Romantic period's capacious concept of caricature, including social critique's literalisation of the *troppo caricato* as flesh-caricature. In Romantic caricature talk, 'caricature' associates with the terms found in its contemporary dictionary definitions, such as 'exaggerated', 'overcharged' and 'overdone'; as well as *troppo caricato* terms denoting grotesque delineation ('disproportioned', 'distorted', 'misshapen', 'monstrous', 'gigantic' etc.), phrases relating to the *caricare un ritratto* meaning of caricature (excessive 'contrast', 'overcoloured') and vocabulary evoking caricature's etymological associations with weight, effort and impact ('forced', 'striking', 'violent', etc.). To convey their perceptions of caricature in the work, critics use spatial metaphors (the work's distance from, or proximity to, caricature), painterly metaphors ('strokes' and 'touches' versus 'daubs' and 'glare') and imagery of gigantic and disproportioned bodies. In anti-caricature rhetoric, high value is placed on the 'delicate', 'modest' and 'natural', whereas 'caricature' and its associated terms are frequently modified by pejorative adjectives such as 'coarse', 'gross', 'unnatural', 'ghastly' and so on. James Beattie, for example, draws on anti-caricature vocabulary to illuminate the novel's transition from romance to realism, a contrast dramatised by Cervantes in *Don Quixote*:

> The extravagance of [the books of chivalry that influence Don Quixote] being placed, as it were, in the same groupe with the appearances of nature and the real business of life, the hideous disproportion of the former becomes so glaring by contrast. [...] *Don Quixote* occasioned the death of the Old Romance, and gave birth to the New. Fiction henceforth divested herself of her gigantick size, tremendous aspect, and frantick demeanour.[1]

While anti-caricature rhetoric sometimes insists on caricature's total absence from a work, generally 'anti-caricature' rhetoric is not absolutely against caricature: as I remark in Chapter 4, critics frequently propose that novelists should offer a 'heightened' and 'striking' reality that approaches caricature without crossing over into it, or which judiciously incorporates caricature while keeping it subordinate to other elements in the narrative. Often the vocabulary of caricature talk is used to critique a work's overall style or structure for lacking restraint, discipline or self-consciousness in its representation of a reality.

As George Levine has argued, nineteenth-century realism 'was not a solidly self-satisfied vision based in a misguided objectivity and faith in representation, but a highly self-conscious attempt to explore or create a new reality. Its massive self-confidence implied a radical doubt, its strategies of truth telling, a profound self-consciousness'.² Part I of this book describes how a 'caricature talk' dominated by anti-caricature rhetoric functions in literary realism's self-consciousness during the Romantic period. Anti-caricature rhetoric, I argue, does not just 'prop up' novelistic realism but actually helps constitute it in the Romantic period – by habilitating for realism the elements of fiction that might seem exaggeratedly humorous, grotesque or 'romantic'; by foregrounding and testing the theoretical distinction between resemblance and equivalence; and by turning novels' fictitious 'reality' into a competition where characters are rated, and novelists ranked against each other. Later, I explore anti-caricature rhetoric in Romantic-period retrospectives on the *Spectator* (Chapter 3), in the long critical tradition on characters in Jane Austen's published and unpublished fiction (Chapter 4), and in the contemporary critical reception of Scott's characters (Chapter 5), as well as analysing how Austen and Scott incorporate anti-caricature rhetoric in the self-conscious realisms of their novels.

Literary criticism of the Romantic period speaks caricature talk most frequently when discussing fictive characters in novels; and non-protagonist characters framed as humorous or satirical are those most likely to attract caricature talk, with anti-caricature rhetoric used to distinguish outright 'caricatures' from the realist solidity of strong characters. In the first part of this chapter, I highlight caricature talk's relationship with literary form in the literary criticism of the Romantic period and put my research in conversation with scholarship on the history of literary character criticism – writing and talking about fictive characters – in order to explain where caricature talk's rhetorical denial of caricature fits in a literary history of the concept of literary character. The second part of this chapter provides an essential context for Chapter 3's discussion of character 'originality' by giving an account of how prosopographic caricature was conceived of as distinct from imaginative literary characterisation in the Romantic period.

Anti-caricature and Literary Form in the Novel

Anti-caricature rhetoric, alert to the potential 'deformity' of lengthy prose fiction, lends itself in the Romantic period to the formalist imagining of literary works as textual assemblages of parts. In caricature talk about novels, for example, individual characters are parsed into qualities and characteristics, and placed into moral categories; casts of characters are subdivided into principal and subordinate characters; descriptions and characters are separated out from story; and story is conceived as a succession of incidents of different sizes, shapes and shades.

In the worst cases, the literary work might strike the reader as an under-structured 'pile' or 'mass' of content, accumulated through an additive process and striving for novelty and impact by making each example more extreme than the last. Josiah Conder writes that Byron's poem 'Darkness' is 'Fuseli *out-Fuselied*; horror accumulated upon horror in naked hideousness, up to the highest point of exaggeration'; and, in a backhanded compliment, concedes that 'it required indeed a very extraordinary power of conception to make such a rabble of misshapen and ghastly ideas pass before the mind'.[3] Often in such critiques, there is a latent distinction between form and content. Recycling the episode in *Frankenstein* where Victor's opium dream shifts into a series of nightmarish images, the *British Critic* argues that while Shelley's novel has no organisation in its ideas – 'these volumes have neither principle, object, nor moral' – though the horrific content might have been formed into some recognisable didactic or scientific purpose: 'the horror which abounds in [*Frankenstein*] is too grotesque and *bizarre* ever to approach neither the sublime [...] and yet we suspect, that the diseased and wandering imagination, which has stepped out of all legitimate bounds, to frame these disjointed combinations and unnatural adventures, might be disciplined into something better'.[4]

Anti-caricature rhetoric could also serve critiques of narrative structure and length, as in Scott's apology for a single-volume *Black Dwarf* in the introduction to the Magnum Opus edition. 'The story was intended to be longer, and the catastrophe more artificially brought out' – but after receiving advice that the character of the Black Dwarf 'was of a kind too revolting, and more likely to disgust than interest the reader', Scott chose to cut the story short: 'I got off my subject by hastening the story to an end, as fast as it was possible; and by huddling into one volume, a tale which was designed to occupy two, have perhaps produced a narrative as much disproportioned and distorted, as the Black Dwarf who is its subject.'[5]

The targets of anti-caricature rhetoric – disproportion, disjointedness, discordance perceived to result from the mishandling of subject matter and content – might be endemic to the novel as a literary form so reliant on the concatenation of parts. Since novelistic narratives were relatively prolonged and tended to contain more numerous and various settings, incidents and characters than other literary works, critics felt responsible for pointing out the good and bad points that readers might miss, as a writer for the *Scots Magazine* suggests in a review of *Rob Roy*:

> A story is not like a picture or a statue, the whole of which we can take in at one glance, and of course immediately perceive whether there is any absurdity or incongruity in the composition. Our attention is rather successively occupied with different parts than with the whole, and if we are much interested, we shall be very ready either not to perceive or to forget the perplexities in which the narrator has involved himself.

Carving Scott's novel into parts, the reviewer identifies strengths and weaknesses. Descriptions of places are excellent, and characterisations are impressive – but the plot is less interesting: '[I]t is to the character and the descriptions, much more than to the story, that our attention is rivetted in this [novel . . .] and we think the peculiar merit of the piece before us consists in the truth, and the little exaggeration of its leading features'. For this reviewer, *Rob Roy*'s leading features are its characters. With each character delineated in a 'style of accurate drawing, without the slightest distortion or exaggeration', it matters less if the novel as a whole is not well formed. Quoting Hamlet's advice to the players at Elsinore, the *Scots Magazine* reviewer criticises Scott's characterisation of Helen Campbell – who 'out-herods Herod' (*Hamlet* 3.2.14) – and commends other characterisations that 'o'erstep not the modesty of nature' (3.2.19):

> They are the characters of unexaggerated nature [. . .] that we prize by far the most highly in this work, and in some of them the author has shown infinite skill, the weaving together of discordant qualities, with so happy a regard to the due limits and proportions of each, that the result of the whole is the production of a perfectly natural character, even in cases where, 'to overstep the modesty of nature,' was almost unavoidable.[6]

Anti-caricature rhetoric brings fictive characters to the fore in its view of the novelist's ability to construct a strong realism made convincing by 'limits' and 'proportions' as well as 'particulars'. While I have quoted some less typical examples here, most of the Romantic-period caricature talk about novels focuses on characters, and on non-protagonists in particular – using the vocabulary of caricature talk to evaluate how entertaining, how interesting and how strongly related to reality fictive characters are.

John Frow proposes that while the concept of character is 'perhaps the most widely-used of all critical tools, at all levels of analysis', it is 'perhaps the most problematic and the most undertheorized of the basic categories of narrative theory', with 'its sheer obviousness disguis[ing] the conceptual difficulties it presents'.[7] Caricature too has seemed obvious, and like character its use as a critical tool has a history worth investigating. I agree with the argument in Lynch's work on 'character's changing conditions of legibility': that character has no 'true identity' to unmask, but rather consists in historically and materially contingent ways of explaining the human world and making it meaningful.[8] In other words, literary characters are used, often very persuasively, to think, say and effect ideas about ourselves and – perhaps more frequently and more confidently – about others. As Lynch puts it, the history of character can be illuminated by '[t]he cultural historian's task [. . .] of investigating reading and writing practices as local accomplishments – as social technologies that depend on certain verbal forms, practical exercises, codes of deportment, and capacities for pleasure and that permit their users to engage in particular sets of activities'.[9] One of these activities might be the cultural phenomenon that Toril Moi calls 'character talk', a language-game where we 'talk [and write] about fictive characters in much the same way we talk about real people, and yet we don't get confused, we don't begin to mistake fiction for reality'.[10]

In the Romantic period's iteration of the language-game of literary characters, caricature talk explicitly plays with this idea of fictive characters being mistaken for real ones. Here I return to my idea that literature's caricature – the doppelgänger of 'character' as a critical tool – has historically brought consciousness of form and formal 'realism' into the discussion of literary characters, through caricature talk and anti-caricature rhetoric. The Victorian critic Anna Murphy Jameson, one of many character critics who might be accused of 'naïvely realist' psychological analysis, conveys the premise that characters can seem more real *because* they are fictive, not in the sense of being false or of belonging only to fiction, but in the sense of being intensively formed: ideas and facts densely interconnected through language and narrative. She contrasts Shakespeare's 'wicked women' characters – 'more terrible, because more credible and intelligible' – with 'those monstrous caricatures we meet with in history [...] where isolated facts and actions are recorded, without any relation to causes or motives, or connecting feelings; and pictures exhibited, from which the considerate mind turns in disgust, and the feeling heart has no relief but in positive and, I may add, reasonable incredulity'.[11] Caricature talk – often rhetorically pretending that the character's existence pre-exists or exceeds the text – periodically orients character criticism to the text, the author, to characterisation, putting the '-ism' in realism.

Lynch identifies 'character appreciations' like Jameson's with 'romantic faith in unsoundable depths' of mind and feeling, and 'pretext for endless moral invigilation and self-revision'.[12] Early examples of this critical genre include Maurice Morgann's *An Essay on the Dramatic Character of Sir John Falstaff* (1777), Henry Mackenzie's essays on Hamlet in *The Mirror* (1780) and on Falstaff in *The Lounger* (1786), William Richardson's essays on Shakespeare's characters in the 1780s, and Thomas Robertson's *Essay on the Character of Hamlet* (1788). In the Victorian era, Lynch observes, Shakespearean heroines take over from Falstaff and Hamlet as paradigmatic of ethical or psychological character criticism, with Jameson's *Shakespeare's Heroines: Characteristics of Women, Moral, Poetical and Historical* (1832) preceding Mary Cowden Clarke's *The Girlhood of Shakespeare's Heroines, in a Series of Tales* (1851). Clarke's projection of the heroines' extra-textual lives has been seen as an extreme example of the kind of criticism L. C. Knights protested in 'How Many Children Had Lady Macbeth?' – though as Lynch's analysis of passages from Morgann's 1777 essay demonstrates, the key elements of genre – its styles, its emphases, its aims – were already firmly in place in *belles lettres* literary scholarship of the second half of the eighteenth century. Romantic character criticism, Lynch argues, '*produces* the depth that needs explicating and with it the textual effects that signal the psychological real'.[13] Frow identifies this 'representational' character criticism as the most culturally dominant mode of literary criticism, the one which – with reference to Fredric Jameson's definition of 'ethical' and 'psychological' analysis – 'deals in notions of personal identity, of the quest for self'.[14]

The professionalised academy had come to think of 'character appreciation' as women's (and children's) reading, associating it with the amateur literary debates of women's book clubs and the secularised moral education of English Literature lessons. As Frow puts it, 'the methodology of ethical analysis is, at its simplest (for example in the "character appreciation" that is at the heart of much of the literature syllabus in secondary schools), the discussion of the moral make-up, the *ethos* of characters, as though they were acquaintances whose virtues and shortcomings one were dissecting'.[15] This idea that people naively discuss fictional characters 'as though they were real people' risks underselling the abilities of secondary school teachers, and the cultural literacy of their pupils, by assuming that readers have not already learned, through their enjoyment and discussion of narrative media, how to talk about real people 'as though they were' more or less sophisticatedly fictive characters. We might also forget how extensively people's personal ethics may actually be derived largely from fictive and historical characters encountered through narrative media, rather than primarily from their direct observation of their acquaintances, or from dedicated religious or ethical instruction.

In the Romantic period's language-games about fictive characters, anti-caricature rhetoric is not used only to judge the verisimilitude of fiction and segregate 'realistic' characters from 'unrealistic' ones. On the one hand, anti-caricature rhetoric describes verisimilitude in literary fiction, saying what is like reality and what is not; on the other hand, anti-caricature rhetoric also articulates why some characters are more pleasurably (or painfully) 'real' than others. Not only denying and distancing 'caricature' but also acknowledging caricature's perverse realism, reading and writing practices engage in a caricature talk that, on the way to establishing the extra-textual 'character' (of the author, their time period, a historical figure, a nation, etc.), problematises fictive 'character' by emphasising authorial technique and talent for characterisation. The vocabulary of caricature talk, whether used pejoratively or not, raises the issue of the novelist's simulated 'reality' as an intervention of style, humour, feeling, personality – and the text as a composition of 'parts', 'marks', 'touches' and 'relations'.

Perhaps talking about characters has been one of the most pleasurable and useful aspects of the novel in large part because we *do* confuse fiction and reality when we engage in it, but not because we are stupid or naive. When readers declare their love for Sir Roger de Coverley or Mr Collins, the vocabulary and rhetoric of caricature talk tends to assume that the 'originality' confusion is a deliberate part of the literary work's form, and that we seem to think, believe and feel things about 'characters' as discrete and credible human entities because writers do more than merely 'record' or 'copy' reality.

While literati in the Romantic period may not have theorised the concept of character in ways acceptable to modern formalist critics, the conceptual richness of their 'caricature' indicates that romantic faith in fictive characters' potential for 'depths' and 'roundness' has always existed alongside caricature talk's interest in what makes and unmakes the strength of characters' realism.

Prosopographic Caricature in the Romantic Literary Sphere

Critics and writers who extol the superiority of created characters over copied ones do so, in the Romantic period, against a background of prosopographic writing – reviews, biographies, romans à clef and the 'silver fork' novels – that promises insider information about the personal lives of public figures. Some of this writing uses detailed characterisation that highlights its subject's least ideal qualities, including the particulars of their body and physical appearance, simulating the intimacy of personal acquaintance with the individual depicted that was crucial to the perverse realism of amateur caricature drawings and late-Georgian caricature prints.

There are, however, several key differences between pictorial *caricatúra* of real people and textual 'caricatures' of real people, which made it important in the Romantic literary sphere to differentiate the 'reality' of texts' most distinctive characters. For one thing, whereas the caricature print's aesthetic tends to present its portraits as playful burlesques, humorous for the ways in which they distort as much as for the distortion of their subjects, the textuality of 'caricatures' in books and periodicals arguably gives them a stronger claim to candour. Second, prosopographic caricatures were not limited to a small elite group, where personal caricaturing was a mutual social activity and actually contributed to an individual's status; instead, they were imagined to bring the subject before a miscellaneous 'reading public'. Third, prosopographic writing appeared in publication contexts where personal caricature was selective, targeted at certain individuals for particular reasons. Fourth, since detailed prosopography requires a certain level of intimacy with the subject, inevitably writers were most likely to caricature other writers, potentially devaluing their most precious intellectual property, the authorial persona – whether compromising either the authority of an anonymous writer's impersonality, or the attraction of a writer's cultivated individualism. Caricature drawings and prints (mis)represented subjects who were supposed to be 'public' to the viewer in other ways, through social acquaintance, political speeches, ownership and development of land and properties, and news reporting about society and politics. By contrast, textual prosopographic 'caricatures' in books and periodicals could have more impact (psychological and financial) on a subject whose public reputation consisted primarily of books and periodicals.

What I am calling prosopographic 'caricature' was understood in the Romantic period as a textual representation of an individual character that relies on the author being able to recall first-hand or find out particulars about their subject's figure in society (including their works and deeds, career and connections, speech and manners and/or physical appearance); and which frames some of those particulars as extreme, singular or unflatteringly material; and by which the reader might be able to recognise the real individual by their verbal expression, social behaviour or physical appearance. While some texts vulnerable to the charge of prosopographic caricature restricted their 'particulars' to material that was already published in textual form, or attempted to synthesise prosopographic referents into imaginary characters, others were ready to justify their personal 'attacks' on individual targets.

Here, I examine the Romantic literary sphere's wariness of textual characterisations that meet the criteria for prosopographic caricature just listed, alongside writers' justifications for this style of prosopography – looking at examples from *Blackwood's Magazine* and Peacock's comic symposia, and making points of comparison with Edgeworth's characterisation of John Langan in *Castle Rackrent* and Scott's of David Ritchie in *The Black Dwarf*. Placing caricature talk and anti-caricature rhetoric's emphasis on artistic 'originality' in its social context, I give an account of the notion that distinctive textual characterisations would ideally be limited by propriety and civility, but I also notice when and why it was acceptable for writers to suspend these self-imposed rules.

The literary periodical press in the early nineteenth century used *personality* to mean 'a statement or remark referring to or aimed at a particular person, and usually disparaging or offensive in nature' (OED n. 6b). For a remark to count as a 'personality' in the literary sphere, the person had to be named or otherwise clearly identified, and the statement had to be published, for example in a review of the person's work. Wilson, in *Blackwood's Magazine*, referred to one such review as 'one of those wicked, and we-know-not-what-to-call-them, things, which afflict the spirits of so many of our contemporaries'.[16] The most offensive 'personalities' had a high degree of particularity, and capitalised on some degree of personal acquaintance with the subject as an individual. Writers for literary periodicals were conscious that even their most harshly critical reviews should avoid describing personal traits such as physical appearance and psychological temperament. They were to review writers' works, not the writers themselves.

Thus William Blackwood, in 1817, knew that he could seize writers' and readers' attention with uncivil caricatures that disturbed the notion of the literary sphere as a sociable little public of idealists. *Blackwood's Edinburgh Magazine* published some exceptionally personal literary criticism in its first number of October 1817, all of which was unsigned by its authors: John Wilson's review of Coleridge's autobiography *Biographia Literaria*, the first of John Gibson Lockhart's essays on the 'Cockney School of Poetry', and a satire on literary Edinburgh written in pseudo-biblical prose and titled 'A Translation from an Ancient Chaldee Manuscript'. A collaboration between Wilson, Lockhart and Hogg, this account of the rivalry between Blackwood and Archibald Constable, publisher of the *Edinburgh Review*, provoked charges of libel and slander – and even blasphemy – against Blackwell. But all publicity was good publicity. The 'Chaldee Manuscript' defined *Blackwood's* as a uniquely vitriolic publication.[17] Once the first print run sold out, Blackwell made a show of contrition: the number was reissued with a statement of apology, the 'Chaldee Manuscript' removed and the first 'Cockney School' essay heavily revised. Blackwood established a fund in preparation for any future lawsuits, seeming to accept legal fees as part of the cost of doing business, and enshrining over-personal literary criticism in the magazine's modus operandi. Macvey Napier went to the trouble of bringing out an anonymous pamphlet titled *Hypocrisy Unveiled and Calumny Detected in a Review of Blackwood's Magazine*, accusing the reviewers of 'hold[ing] up personal defects, peculiarities, and misfortunes, to ridicule and scorn', and threatening retaliation: 'We know them well—all and each of them,—their names, characters, and schemes.'[18] Scholarship on *Blackwood's Edinburgh Magazine* has emphasised the extremity of its writers' personal attacks on other writers and other periodicals.[19] Yet *Blackwood's* writers did not disregard the taboo against personal criticism, nor did they flout it indiscriminately; rather, they tried to justify their attacks as well-deserved caricatures of particular writers.

Blackwood's reissue of the first number retracts the more personal elements of Lockhart's invective against Leigh Hunt. References to the writer's private character and physical mannerisms are scrupulously removed, redirecting the harshest criticisms from the man to his writings.[20] When Lockhart (signing himself as 'Z') makes another anonymous attack on Hunt's character, he does so more cannily. The third 'Cockney School' essay excuses itself as a critique of Hunt's moral character, where the boundary between private life and public reputation cannot be maintained, because Hunt has already degraded his character in published writing:

> There can be no radical distinction allowed between the private and public character of a poet. If a poet sympathizes with and justifies wickedness in his poetry, he is a wicked man. It matters not that his private life may be free from wicked actions. [...] It is therefore of little or no importance, whether Leigh Hunt be or be not a bad private character. [...] The world is not fond of ingenious distinctions between the theory and practice of morals. The public are justified in refusing to hear a man plead in favour of his character, when they hold in their hands a work of his in which all respect to character is forgotten.[21]

This statement could be read as a manifesto for *Blackwood's Magazine*'s rebellious approach to literary criticism, or even as an argument for the legitimacy of personal attacks in literary reviewing generally. By Lockhart's reasoning, reviewing a literary work is always a review of its author, and vice versa: it is impossible to avoid commenting on an author's character, when the work's faults are its author's. The statement primes the reader to notice that the insults Z fires at Hunt's muse – claiming to expose her as a painted whore dressed in fashionably 'transparent drapery' – are personal criticisms of Hunt.[22] Lockhart's erasure of the distinction between private and public character might be read not as a deliberate intervention, sincerely meant, in the long-established consensus that personal satire should not feature in the literary sphere, but as a case for highly personal criticism in exceptional cases. Criticism becomes caricature when Lockhart uses a description of Hunt's personal manners and psychology to justify his essay's antagonism towards the poet. Hunt's character is defined by personal antagonism, Z argues: he has an 'irritable temper which keeps [him...] in a perpetual fret with himself and all the world beside, and that shews itself equally in his deadly enmities and capricious friendships' (453). Such personal comments were extraordinarily offensive, as Keats understands in a letter to Benjamin Bailey: 'There has been a flaming attack upon Hunt in the Endinburgh [sic] Magazine—I never read anything so virulent—accusing him of the greatest Crimes—dep[r]eciating his Wife his Poetry—his Habits—his company, his Conversation.'[23]

But *Blackwood's* could claim that Hunt had started it. As editor of *The Examiner* and *The Reflector*, Hunt had himself written combative reviews and satires that conflated writers with their works, most notably *The Feast of Poets* (1811). Furthermore, he had been imprisoned for the crimes of seditious and blasphemous libel of the Prince Regent, printing Charles Lamb's 'Triumph of the Whale' in 1812 and his own article 'The Prince on St. Patrick's Day' in 1813.[24] 'The Story of Rimini', a poem Hunt produced while he was in prison and supplied with material by Byron, was a sympathetic treatment of the historical figure Francesca da Rimini, who is depicted in Dante's *Inferno* as consigned to the second circle of Hell, murdered by her husband after being discovered in bed with his younger brother. Hunt dedicated his poem to Byron. Other readers were less disposed to admire Francesca and Hunt's poem about her, which they could easily interpret as an atheistic endorsement of adultery, incest and lust.[25] As they saw it, sympathetic writing about Francesca da Rimini was pornography barely concealed beneath the respectability of its literary sources. Lockhart's anti-jacobin imagery, which links the immorality of *The Story of Rimini* with Hunt's radical politics, suggests that Z's purportedly general statement is aimed pointedly at Hunt. Z's phrase 'no radical distinction' is a dog whistle for Hunt's republicanism, and implies that praise of Hunt's literary works would be complicit in those radical opinions. It is not just any poet who loses the privilege of privacy, here, but the exceptionally seditious, blasphemous, bilious Hunt.

Blackwood's could also justify personal criticisms of writers who had overreached themselves in search of personal celebrity, obtruding themselves into their writing. The *Blackwood's* writers were not the first in the Romantic period to frame 'caricature' as a means of puncturing a poet's egotism: Henry Brougham's scathing review of *Hours of Idleness* (1807) in the *Edinburgh Review* (which provoked Byron's satire *English Bards, and Scotch Reviewers*) justifies its personal criticisms by remarking that the poems self-promotingly parade Byron's youth and hereditary privilege, 'allud[ing] frequently to his family and ancestors—sometimes in poetry, sometimes in notes'.[26] Romantic poetry of sentiments, when seen to exaggerate the beauties of nature and absurdly elevate the individual's powers of perception and feeling, could strike the cynical reader as being the poet's caricature of himself. Thus Anna Seward objects to lines in Wordsworth's poem 'I Wandered Lonely as a Cloud' with 'contemptuous astonishment and disgust':

> I read about his dancing daffodils, ten thousand, as he says, in high dance in the breeze beside the river, whose waves dance with them, and in the poet's heart, we are told, danced too. Then he proceeds to say, that in the hours of pensive or of pained contemplation, these same capering flowers flash on his memory, and his heart, losing its cares, dances with them too.
> Surely if his worst foe had chosen to caricature this egotistic manufacturer of metaphysic importance upon trivial themes, he could not have done it more effectively![27]

Individualist and confessional writers, addressing their readers in the first person and including biographical information in poems as well as prefaces, were vulnerable to charges of self-importance of a particular kind.

De Quincey apologises in his *Confessions* for 'breaking through that delicate and honourable reserve which, for the most part, restrains us from the public exposure of our own errors and infirmities. Nothing, indeed is more revolting to English feelings than the spectacle of a human being obtruding on our notice his moral ulcers or scars'.[28] In the first number of *The Friend*, Coleridge unabashedly calls himself 'the Biographer of my own sentiments', a Romantic self-regard that attracted the scorn of *Blackwood's*.[29] Wilson frames his 1817 review of the *Biographia Literaria* as a just retort to an improperly personal biography that 'lays open, not unfrequently, the character of the Man as well as of the Author'. Coleridge has not understood that it is the job of critics such as Wilson and Lockhart to celebrate authors: he celebrates himself, 'scatter[ing] his Sibylline Leaves around him, with as majestical an air as if a crowd of enthusiastic admirers were rushing forward to grasp the divine promulgations, instead of their being, as they in fact are, coldly received by the accidental passenger, like a lying lottery puff or a quack advertisement'. Coleridge's indecently detailed auto-characterisation contrasts, Wilson thinks, with the 'dignified deportment' of Scott, whose writing makes 'scarcely an allusion [...] to himself'.[30]

James Hogg, despite his close involvement with *Blackwood's*, came in for worse treatment when he ventured to publicise the personal history behind his literary works, beginning the third edition of his poetry collection *The Mountain Bard* with 'a Memoir of the Author's Life, written by Himself'. Like Hunt's *Story of Rimini* and Coleridge's *Biographia Literaria*, the 1821 edition of *The Mountain Bard* was published with its author's name displayed prominently on the title page. The memoir tells how Hogg, ruined by risky investments in farmland, and his reputation as a shepherd undermined by his literary pursuits, was unable to find work locally. Brandishing his rusticity as a mark of his poetry's authenticity, Hogg says that his poems were written 'to please the circles about the fire-sides in the country', that he 'had never been once in any polished society' and at the age of thirty-eight 'knew no more of human life or manners' than as a boy.[31] Candidly (and calculatedly) self-deprecating, the memoir also advertises the poet's acquaintance with important figures on the literary scene, chief among them Byron, Scott and Wilson. Hogg's apparent expectation that his book would be favourably reviewed in the magazine was insulting to Blackwood, who had been surprised to hear that the new edition of *The Mountain Bard* was being published by Oliver and Boyd. Hogg refused to consult with Blackwood about it, believing that Blackwood had no rights in the matter.[32] Wilson's and Blackwood's established friendship with Hogg did not stop them from publishing an outrageous (and anonymous) review of the new *Mountain Bard*. Focusing on the memoir, Wilson makes an ironic contribution to Hogg's self-promotion as a rustic poet:

> Well, then—this prodigy tires of the shepherd's life, and comes jogging into Edinburgh [...]. Only picture to yourself a stout country lout, with a bushel of hair on his shoulders that had not been raked for months, enveloped in a coarse plaid impregnated with tobacco, with a prodigious mouthful of immeasurable tusks, and with a dialect that set all conjecture at defiance, lumbering suddenly in upon the elegant retirement of Mr Miller's back-shop.³³

The self-styled 'Ettrick shepherd' appears here not as the next Burns but as escaped livestock. Accusing Hogg of 'self-exposure', Wilson employs an extended analogy where Hogg is the living beast, the cook, the waiter and the meat served: 'I take the liberty of sending back Hogg, which has disgusted me more severely than anything I have attempted to swallow since Macvey's Bacon.'³⁴

Editorialising the review, however, Wilson claims that 'the playful malice of this "attack"' actually conceals an advertisement for the poet and his work. The author must be a friend of Hogg – or even Hogg himself – stage-managing a public humiliation that whips the poet in order to whip up interest in his book:

> If thou art, as we believe the generality of our readers are, a person endowed with a gentlemanly portion of common sense, and can relish banter and good humour [...] thou wilt at once discover that the object of this 'deevilrie,' to use an expression of the Shepherd's, is to add to the interest which his life has excited. Indeed if the paper has not come from Altrive Lake itself, it has certainly been written by some one who takes no small interest in the Shepherd's affairs; for, in the private letter which accompanies it [...] a hope is most feelingly expressed, that by this tickling the public sympathy may be awakened, so as to occasion a most beneficial demand for his works, and put a few cool hundreds in his pocket.³⁵

On reading Wilson's anonymous review of *The Mountain Bard*, Hogg wrote to Blackwood calling him 'the worst assassin in hell' and informing him that the review had wounded his wife as well as himself: on her 'the blows that you inflict wound deeper and smart with more poignancy, nor can any palliatives that I can use heal them'. Hogg then requested that Blackwood send him the reviewer's name and address.³⁶ Receiving no response, he sought advice and sympathy from Scott: 'Shall I answer [the reviewer] in print? pursue him at law to which it will soon come if I answer him? or knock out his brains?'³⁷ Scott's reply advises philosophical reflection:

> I am very sorry to observe from the tenor of your letter that you permitted the caricature in Blackwoods magazine to sit so near your feelings. [...] If a man says that I am guilty of some particular fact I would vindicate myself if I could but if he caricatures my person and depreciates my talents I would content myself with thinking that the world will judge of my exterior and of my powers of composition by the evidence of their own eyes and of my works. [...] I know the advice to sit quiet under injury is hard to flesh and blood.[38]

As Scott points out, the personal caricature that makes Hogg a grotesque object in a comical situation does not have the satirical precision of a moral critique, as the *Blackwood's* attacks on Hunt do. But Scott's advice to Hogg – to 'sit quiet' – was likely shaped by his own attitude to Hogg as a man rising too far above his social station. Amused by the idea of a man like that participating in an 'affair of honour',[39] Scott probably appreciated the review's image of Hogg as a self-important man comically out of place. Hunt, too, was perceived as a plebeian too full of himself: in the first 'Cockney School' essay, Z describes him as 'a vulgar man [...] perpetually labouring to be genteel' and his poetry 'always on the stretch to be grand'.[40]

Indeed, Scott's novel *The Black Dwarf* (1816) and Edgeworth's novel *Castle Rackrent* (1800) show that writers could give themselves permission to relax their rules against caricaturing real people when they found good material in the lower classes. Edgeworth's notebooks, according to Butler, show 'a jackdaw-like attitude towards examples of human behaviour' and speech, particularly among servants, though her only 'conscious, systematic attempt to sketch an individual' was the narrator 'Thady Quirk'.[41] Thady's highly characteristic narration of the events in *Castle Rackrent* originated in Edgeworth's oral mimicry of her father's steward, John Langan, to entertain her family. Edgeworth developed the character by finding appropriate stories to tell in his words.[42] Edgeworth's performances may have included the physical mannerisms that she later used to characterise Thady: she describes in a letter how Langan 'shakes his head, puts up his shoulder, or changes from leg to leg which are all in him sad tokens of distress'.[43] But while Langan's peculiarities made for entertaining dramatic monologues, Edgeworth was displeased with the result of using his idiosyncratic narration for her novel. As Butler points out, Thady 'dominates the book, so that the Rackrents' various doings serve the central aesthetic purpose of revealing his character and attitudes'. Edgeworth 'found it unpalatable', Butler remarks, 'that she had made the quaint, archaic narrator more interesting than the Rackrents [...]. Her motives in taking to fiction were not to act as an amanuensis to John Langan; on the contrary, the viewpoint she wanted to adopt was English and forward-looking'.[44] The Edgeworth family publicly acknowledged that Langan was Thady's 'original', while denying that any of Edgeworth's other characters were portraits of individuals drawn from real acquaintance, despite the novels being strewn with character traits and characteristic incidents referring to the authors' acquaintances. In a letter to her aunt, Edgeworth hashed out a strategy for using their close family friend, James Corry, as the basis for her character 'King Corny' in *Ormond* (1817):

> If you recollect how we used to talk over Mr. Corry & when you used to make me laugh by the hour, we agreed that I might introduce such a character provided I did not make it too like the original—Now I am attempting this—My father [...] knows nothing of my plan—therefore I am particularly anxious to know from you how far I may go—and these are my questions—Do you think I may venture to use the handfuls of Hemlock for the gout— [...] I shall not put in the blasting—tempting almost irresistably [sic] tempting as it is nor working the goblin tapestry tho' I'd give half a finger for it. [...] The chances are that Mr. Corry himself would never read [the] thing unless he were put on the scent.[45]

None of Edgeworth's most distinctive characters were intended as detailed caricature portraits of public or prominent figures, though *Ennui*'s Lord Craiglethorpe was inspired by John Carr's authorship of *Stranger in Ireland* (1806). When characters were intended to represent public personalities with ties to the Edgeworth family, they were flatteringly idealised and often appeared in the role of mentor to the novels' protagonist.[46] However, readers still found ways to see characters as portraits of real people.

Since Thomas Love Peacock's comic symposia were first published, for example, readers have been seeing 'caricatures' in them – but caricatures of who, or what? How do we read the word 'characters' in the *Literary Gazette*'s review of *Nightmare Abbey* in 1818, which describes Peacock's writing as 'a sort of caricature of modern characters and incidents'?[47] In literary scholarship, scores of notes and keys have identified Peacock's characters with real people, until Marilyn Butler's work unsettled the established view of Peacock as a satirist of individuals. While Butler acknowledges that Peacock's symposia do allude to real people, 'his dislike of his period's taste for personality is maintained in his work, and he does not deal in character at all', Gary Dyer comments that Peacock 'avoids the error' of 'scandal-mongering "personal" satire'.[48] Figures previously assumed to be Peacock's renderings of Coleridge, Shelley and Southey as individuals – 'malicious personal portraits' – might be better interpreted,

James Mulvihill suggests, as 'criticisms of the public figure'. Mulvihill has shown that Peacock's characters are often derived from views expressed in print, arguing that 'the Peacockian novel of talk posits a popular culture in which intellectual exchange has been processed for mass consumption'.[49]

This new consensus on Peacockian 'characters' reflects the position Peacock took in the 1830s: he insists in an 1837 selected edition of his symposium novels that he has 'never intruded on the personality of others, nor taken any liberties but with public conduct and public opinions', and reiterates in his 1856 preface to a new edition of *Melincourt* that '[o]f the disputants whose opinions and public characters (for I never trespassed on private life) were shadowed in some of the persons of the story, almost all have passed from the diurnal scene'.[50] At the time Peacock wrote *Crotchet Castle* (1831), Percy Shelley's and Byron's reputations were increasingly sullied by 'tell-all' biographies such as Thomas Moore's *Letters and Journals of Lord Byron* (1830) and Leigh Hunt's *Lord Byron and Some of His Contemporaries* (1828), following Hazlitt's essay 'My First Acquaintance with Poets' (1823) and Thomas Medwin's *Journal of the Conversations of Lord Byron* (1824).[51] Hunt's memoir of Byron crossed a line – it was badly received, and effectively ended his literary career.[52] Describing Byron's physiognomy, Hunt puts together an unflattering portrait of features variously too large, too small and out of place:

> His countenance did not improve with age, and there were always some defects in it. The jaw was too big for the upper part. It had all the wilfulness of a despot in it. The animal predominated over the intellectual part of his head, insamuch as the face altogether was large in proportion to the skull. The eyes also were set too near one another; and the nose, though handsome in itself, had the appearance, when you saw it closely in front, of being grafted on the face, rather than growing properly out of it. His person was very handsome, though terminating in lameness, and tending in fat and effeminacy; which makes me remember what a hostile fair one objected to him, namely, that he had a little beard.[53]

In *Crotchet Castle*, Peacock uses a character called 'Eavesdrop' as a scapegoat for this kind of journalism. The Reverend Folliott confronts him: 'Sir, you have published a character [...] wherein you have sketched off me; me, sir, even to my nose and wig. What business have the public with my nose and wig?' Confronting Eavesdrop a second time, Folliott elaborates, 'Sir, my blood boils. What business have the public with my nose and wig? You have dished me up, like a savory omelette, to gratify the appetite of the reading rabble for gossip'.[54] The omelette figures the subject of caricature as an object of consumption, like Wilson's culinary metaphor for Hogg's mercenary 'dishing up' of himself. Eavesdrop, described by Lady Clarinda as 'a sort of bookseller's tool' who '*coins* all his acquaintances in reminiscences and sketches of character', is eventually expelled from the society of Crotchet Castle, 'a flagitious violator of the confidences of private life'.[55] While Eavesdrop has very few characteristics aside from his speaking name – he is almost totally silent throughout the text – the timing of *Crotchet Castle* suggests an identification with Hunt, as Butler has argued. Peacock certainly avoids caricaturing Hunt with the kind of detail to which Hunt had subjected Byron's memory. In 1837, Peacock echoes Folliott's words about Eavesdrop, noting that 'literary violators of the confidences of private life still gain a disreputable livelihood and an unenviable notoriety'.[56]

Earlier in his career, however, Peacock could not resist including some prosopographic elements in symposia so concerned with the modern intellectual scene. As many scholars have noted, the Scythrop–Marionetta–Celinda love triangle in *Nightmare Abbey* parallels the scandalous story of Percy Shelley, Harriet Westbrook and Mary Godwin. Peacock seems to have deliberately sprinkled the character of Celinda Toobad with physical characteristics unlike Mary Shelley's.[57] Butler sees such instances as the satirist 'careful[ly ...] blending characteristics in such a way as to frustrate identification with real people'[58] – but not carefully enough, in some cases. Attempts to deliberately frustrate identification could backfire when the identity of the real person was still apparent and personal caricature was aggravated with falsehood. When readers recognised Dickens's character 'Harold Skimpole' as a satirical portrait of Hunt, a friend of Dickens, the character was all the more offensive because Dickens gave Skimpole 'attributes quite foreign to Hunt'[59] – compounding caricature with falsehood, as Scott did with his fictionalisation of David Ritchie, which I discuss later.

There was an established market in the Romantic period for literary works with characters supposedly representing prominent members of society. The 'silver-fork' novels that offered insight into the British aristocracy accompanied by keys to the characters' real identities, were identified by Hazlitt as a distinct literary form in 1827.[60] Middle-class readers could project a 'fashionable' readership who would not need such keys, being already familiar with the 'originals' referenced: in Mary Brunton's 1814 novel *Discipline*, Lady St Edmunds 'kill[s] the time' by reading 'novels enriched with slanderous tales or caricatures of living characters' and 'fashionable sonnets, guarded to the ear of decency'.[61] Silver-fork novels like Lady Caroline Lamb's *Glenarvon* (1816) and Eaton Stannard

Barett's *Six Weeks at Long's* (1817) commodified upper-class gossip for a largely middle-class audience – or at least commodified the idea of upper-class gossip. In *Crotchet Castle*, Lady Clarinda decides to earn herself some pocket money for 'trinkets and fal-lals, which I cannot get from papa' by writing a cynical silver-fork novel that only pretends to caricature real 'originals':

LADY CLARINDA. [...] You must know I have been reading several fashionable novels, the fashionable this, and the fashionable that; and I thought to myself, why I can do better than any of these myself. So I wrote a chapter or two, and sent them as a specimen to Mr Puffall, the bookseller, telling him they were to be a part of the fashionable something or other, and he offered me, I will not say how much, to finish it in three volumes, and let him pay all the newspapers for recommending it as the work of a lady of quality, who made very free with the characters of her acquaintance.
CAPTAIN FITZCHROME. Surely you have not done so?
LADY CLARINDA. Oh, no; I leave that to Mr Eavesdrop. But Mr Puffall made it a condition that I should let him say so.
CAPTAIN FITZCHROME. A strange recommendation.
LADY CLARINDA. Oh, nothing else will do.[62]

Peacock would have known about the controversy over Benjamin Disraeli's *Vivian Grey* (1826), puffed by publisher Henry Colburn as 'the adventures of an ambitious, dashing, and talented young man of high life' and representing 'nearly all the individuals at present figuring in fashionable society'. Colburn stoked interest in the novel by telling an editor that '[t]he authorship is a great secret – a man of high fashion – very high – keeps the first society'.[63] Peacock imagines a publisher, 'Puffall', who falsely advertises Lady Clarinda's text as a modern roman à clef, when she actually intends to imagine her characters. This dilettante, though choosing to capitalise on her 'fashionable' aristocratic identity, disdains her readers' literal-minded interest in identifying real characters – an interest stoked by novels that did use elements of what was publicly known about real people.

The success in Dublin of Edgeworth's *Leonora* (1806), for example, was driven by identifications of the characters with the real individuals Lady Asgill, Lord Moira and Lady Morgan. Edgeworth could not deny that she had been inspired by stories about Lady Morgan (previously Sydney Owenson), though she was grateful to Lovell Sneyd for trying to counter the idea that the portrait was based on personal acquaintance: 'Thank you my dear brother for saying that I never saw Miss Owenson.'[64] When novelists used documentary material, they piqued the interest of literal-minded (but often insightful) readers. In Lady Morgan's own novel *Florence Macarthy* (1818), the writer Lady Clancare laments readers' literal-mindedness when she remarks that 'combine qualities as you may, to the very verge of extravagance, the world will furnish models, trace likenesses, and assign originals'.[65] – an ironic statement, given that Morgan wants readers to recognise the character 'Con Crawley' as a dig at John Wilson Croker, in revenge for his excoriating review of her 1817 account of France in the early years of the Bourbon Restoration. On the other hand, readers' identifications did sometimes make connections irrelevant to what the author could have conceivably intended. Sydney Smith erroneously took Edgeworth's clergyman character 'Buckhurst Falcolner' in *Patronage* (1814) as an offensive caricature of himself, writing in a letter that '[i]f [Edgeworth] has put into her Novels people who fed her and her odious father, she is not Trustworthy' – though Edgeworth had not known him when she wrote the novel.[66]

But with Thady, there could be no such social consequences. A comic caricature of a lowborn caretaker could not hurt feelings or damage reputations among her peers, so Edgeworth was happy to avow it.

Similarly, Scott was unrepentant about his use of David Ritchie, writing about the 'inspiration' for the character Sir Edward Mauley (or 'Canny Elshie') at length in the Magnum Introduction to *The Black Dwarf*. Scott's information about Ritchie was drawn partly from the anecdotes of Adam Fergusson, whose house was local to Ritchie's cottage and whom Scott was visiting when he had his own personal encounter with the hermit: 'The author saw this poor, and, it may be said, unhappy man, in autumn 1797.'[67] The introduction also draws on Robert Chambers's essay 'The Life and Anecdotes of the Black Dwarf, or David Ritchie' (1820), which had been published to capitalise on readers' interest in the titular character of Scott's novel. Scott's use of other people's anecdotes for the Magnum Introduction suggests that he merely 'saw' Ritchie, perhaps at a distance, and had to rely on descriptions for details such as '"his screech-owl voice, shrill, uncouth, and dissonant, [which] corresponded well with his other peculiarities'.[68] Still, Scott congratulates himself, the novel's 'personal description' of the dwarf 'has been generally allowed to be a tolerably exact and unexaggerated portrait' of the real David Ritchie.[69] This should have been recognised as an unscrupulous use of a real person to create a fictive character, and Scott's claim that 'an individual existed many years since [...] which suggested such a character' does not tally with the fact that Ritchie died only a few years before the novel was published.[70]

Scott admits that the interest stirred up by *The Black Dwarf* (which inspired several further publications about Ritchie), caused suffering to the sister who lived next to Ritchie in a cottage he built for her:

> [T]he author is sorry to learn that a sort of 'local sympathy,' and the curiosity then expressed concerning the Author of Waverley and the subjects of his Novels, exposed the poor woman to enquiries which gave her pain. When pressed about her brother's peculiarities, she asked, in her turn, why they would not permit the dead to rest?[71]

Here, Scott fails to take responsibility for his appropriation of Ritchie's life in a characterisation that uses so much detailed anecdotal material, yet combines it with fabricated episodes including Mauley's revelation of his true identity. The character is so barely fictitious that these additions become more like falsehoods than fictions. Scott might have reflected on why he never borrowed so much personal detail from a real individual, particularly one so recently living, in any of his other novels. Instead, the Introduction explicitly understates the novel's reliance on a real character – 'not altogether imaginary' – even while using anecdotes about the real 'Black Dwarf' to stoke interest in Scott's characterisation: 'The ideal being who is here presented as residing in solitude, and haunted by a consciousness of his own deformity, and a suspicion of his being generally subjected to the scorn of his fellow-men, is not altogether imaginary.'[72] Reading the anecdotes that follow, and comparing them with the descriptions in the narrative, it is hard to see the Black Dwarf as more 'ideal' than real. Scott seems unaware of the irony that his novel proves Ritchie's suspicions about society and violates the seclusion that sustained his existence: Scott actually recounts that Ritchie sought 'the least possible communication with the world' after years of wandering, finding no society where he could be free of 'disagreeable attention'. The Magnum Introduction reinscribes the novel's memorialisation of Ritchie through Mauley, effectively making sure that Ritchie will forever be 'the Black Dwarf'. Ritchie the brushmaker was not thought of as a peer: his class and his parochialism, as well as his physical differences, meant for Scott that Ritchie's peculiarities were fair game for caricature, though it was unfortunate that people got hurt.

While writers typically named their characters carefully so as to avoid strong identification with living individuals, avoiding prosopographic characterisation took on a performative aspect in realist fiction. Novelists begin using the elliptical long dash, which had been common in satires on real individuals,[73] as a way of forestalling the reader's identifying a character with a specific referent while giving the impression that there *is* a real, unmentionable referent. For example, in *Pride and Prejudice*, Mrs. Philips tells her nieces that Mr. Wickham 'was to have a lieutenant's commission in the—shire [regiment]'.[74] Dashes are used to redact the names of counties, towns and institutions entirely or in part, and also to redact digits from dates. Such redactions presumably were expedient for writers, since to plot a highly specific timeline or to map a narrative accurately onto real geography would be time-consuming, as well as inviting quibbles from pedantic readers. Elliptical punctuation could also play a role in bolstering the novel's claims to universalism.

But by performatively discouraging readers from identifying referents while hinting that such identifications might actually be possible, formal realism can have it all: specificity *and* universality, authenticity *and* fictionality. The opening lines of *The Warden* (1855) give an extended performance of this magic trick, where the particulars are made real by their concealment. Trollope sets his scene 'in the cathedral town of ————; let us call it Barchester. Were we to name it Wells or Salisbury, Exeter, Hereford, or Gloucester, it might be presumed that something personal was intended; and as this tale will refer mainly to the cathedral dignitaries of the town in question, we are anxious that no personality may be suspected'.[75] This passage can be read as both scrupulous and coy, with the narrator never stating outright that the story contains nothing personal; instead, our attention is diverted to what 'might be presumed' or 'may be suspected'. From Scott's presentation of the Black Dwarf as an 'ideal being [. . .] not altogether imaginary' to Trollope's 'let us call it Barchester', realisms take different routes to establishing an ambiguous 'originality' that insists on the writer's power to create imaginatively 'original' characters, while pretending to withhold the identity of a real being that is 'original' in the sense of pre-existing the text.

In caricature talk and anti-caricature rhetoric, readers and writers play, interminably, with the interchangeability of these 'originals'. Realism is a play space where we can both pretend to be deceived into thinking that fictions are real, and pretend to be deceived into thinking that real things are fiction. Anti-caricature rhetoric's practised denial of caricature participates in this play when it pushes resemblance towards equivalence, a controlled exertion that holds novelistic character in a state of neither real nor false.

CHAPTER 3

Caricature Talk and the Spectator

The fictitious characters created by Joseph Addison and Richard Steele in *The Spectator* (1711–12) became, over the course of the eighteenth century and more than fifty collected editions, Britain's gold standard for comic characterisation in literary prose. This chapter describes the Romantic-period novel's inheritance from the *Spectator*'s characters and their critical reception. I argue that the *Spectator*, first published a century before *Northanger Abbey* found fault with its 'improbable circumstances, unnatural characters', has a strong claim to being the text that most definitively established the terms of caricature talk about 'strong characters' – fictive non-protagonist characters who were distinctive, individualised, comic and satirically rendered – for the Romantic period.

The *Spectator*'s character-writing, I argue, sets 'diversion', 'originality' and 'realism' as key topics for the Romantic period's critical discourse about strong characterisation in the 'light literature' of novels and literary periodicals. Addison and Steele define these topics in several ways: self-reflexive comments about character-writing and character-reading, a hyperbolised distinction between satire and libel, innovative characterisation techniques in their quasi-Theophrastan 'characters', and development of individualised non-protagonist characters such as 'the Spectator' and 'Will Honeycomb'. I examine how Steele and Addison, departing from the conventions and the moral-satirical commitment of the Theophrastan character, model the characterisation of a strong character: a fictitious being that evokes, through particularity and contrast, the 'originality' of a real individual, with virtual reality offering the reader pseudo-sensory and parasocial pleasure.

Half a century after the *Spectator*'s original publishing, the critical reception of Addison and Steele's character 'Sir Roger De Coverley' became an important influence on the critical appreciation and writing of strong characters in new novels. I argue that the discourse around 'Sir Roger' in the second half of the eighteenth century was an early and formative example of the caricature talk distinctive from psychologising 'character appreciations' such as Henry Mackenzie's *Remarks on the Character of Falstaff* (1786). While Steele and Addison's collaboration on Sir Roger De Coverley was likened to literature's most famous comic knights – Don Quixote and Falstaff – it was the *Spectator* and 'Sir Roger' that offered fresh inspiration for writers seeking to enrich the modern English realist novel with non-protagonist characters both contemporary and historical. Considering a selection of examples – from Samuel Johnson's *Lives of the Poets* (1779) to Lionel Thomas Berguer's *British Essayists* (1823) – I find that the critical reception of Sir Roger not only cemented the *Spectator*'s reputation for characters, but also conventionalised and added to the existing critical vocabulary that became prevalent in anti-caricature rhetoric for the praise of strong characters. I suggest that Sir Roger's critical reception would have impressed readers and writers with the potential of non-protagonist characters to be uniquely luxurious and durable assets – a good investment for commercial authors seeking to build and sustain a readership.

Chapter 3 concludes by imagining the *Spectator*'s model for strong characters and the vocabulary and ideas generated by caricature talk about the *Spectator* as elements of character-writing that were re-purposed and re-contextualised by different novelistic realisms. The *Spectator*'s precepts and methods – and their critical reception in the 1770s–1820s – are variously refracted in the distinctive formal realisms represented over the subsequent three chapters. I end this chapter by noticing some ways in which Austen's comic moral realism, Scott's compendious historical realism and Shelley's materialist horror realism transpose elements from the *Spectator*'s precedent, taking them in new and genre-defining directions.

Diversions, Originals and Particulars

In early nineteenth-century Britain, it would have been remarkable for a leisured reader never to have picked up the *Spectator* in some form. Over the eighteenth century, dozens of collected and selected editions of the essays had capitalised on the immediate success of the periodical publication, creating an intellectual property of immense commercial value. By 1767, the *Spectator*'s market value stood at £1,228 – far exceeding prices obtained in the 1760s for other modern English texts, such as *Robinson Crusoe* (£68), *Pilgrim's Progress* (£196) and even *Paradise Lost* (£900).[1] In the Romantic period, the *Spectator*'s inclusion in publishers' series of 'English classics' with low prices and long print runs ensured that the

Spectator was read more and more widely.² The *Spectator* and *Tatler* essays headed the 'English classics', a canon of moral didactic literature extracted from periodicals including *The Tatler*, *The Rambler* and *The Mirror*. In a climate of increased worry about the dangers of reading, the *Spectator* was 'safe' – and so was its literary reputation.

Addison and Steele had explicitly targeted a female readership, and their essays became ubiquitous reading material provided to young readers and to women, even at a point when Addisonian essays of morals and manners began to show their age. In *Northanger Abbey*, Austen imagines a young lady being admired for reading the *Spectator*, rather than a novel, even though the *Spectator*'s manners are outdated:

> 'And what are you reading, Miss—?' 'Oh! It is only a novel! [. . .] It is only Cecilia, or Camilla, or Belinda'; or, in short, only some work in which the greatest powers of the mind are displayed, in which the most thorough knowledge of human nature, the happiest delineation of its varieties, the liveliest effusions of wit and humour, are conveyed to the world in the best-chosen language. Now, had the same young lady been engaged with a volume of the Spectator, instead of such a work, how proudly would she have produced the book, and told its name; though the chances must be against her being occupied by any part of that voluminous publication, of which either the matter or manner would not disgust a young person of taste: the substance of its papers so often consisting in the statement of improbable circumstances, unnatural characters, and topics of conversation which no longer concern anyone living; and their language, too, frequently so coarse as to give no very favourable idea of the age that could endure it.³

Austen had a point – sociolinguistic norms had changed, society had changed, expectations of women had changed, and young ladies were more likely to find examples relevant to their situations in novels by Fanny Burney, Maria Edgeworth or Mary Brunton than in the *Spectator* or the *Tatler*.

Nevertheless, these novelists had a considerable inheritance from the *Spectator* model of characterisation. As well as suggesting characterisation techniques for the writing of comic non-protagonist characters to enrich a plot-driven novel, the *Spectator* cultivated readers' appreciation of such characters as 'original' and 'natural'.

Post-romantic literary scholarship is suspicious of character criticism's tendency – in professing to respond to characters as though they were people and attributing characters' verisimilitude to the 'genius' of a god-like author – to elide the historical specifics of the writer's knowledge and concept of the world, and the formal ways in which characterisation conveys that knowledge to readers. In the case of the *Spectator*'s characters, modern formalist literary criticism has assigned Addison and Steele's character-writing to a particular moral didactic genre, the 'character sketch'. Theresa Shön writes that character sketches 'are containers of knowledge – social, satirical or religious, in any case moral', that 'the genre was employed to classify and thus to order the virtues and vices', and that Addison and Steele used the genre 'to convey knowledge on the moral and social nature of human beings'.[4] Deriving from the *Characters* of Theophrastus (c. 371–287 BCE), the seventeenth-century character sketch is a classically satirical genre that explicitly claims to educate and correct readers by showing portraits of imaginary individuals whose behaviours illustrate a range of moral failings and ill manners. In Joseph Healey's 1628 translation, Theophrastus's opening proem hopes 'that our children will prove the honester and better conditioned, if we shall leave them good precedents of imitation: that of good children they may prove better men'.[5] The fourth English-language edition of Jean de la Bruyère's *Caractères*, the most famous imitation of Theophrastus's *Characters*, opens with the promise that '[t]he World may view the Picture I have drawn of it from Nature, and if I have hit on any defects, which it agrees with me to be such, it may at leisure correct them'.[6] The Theophrastan characterologist assumes, or pretends to assume, that his reader needs to be taught how to recognise a bad character, so that the reader can avoid the real person who resembles it, and avoid becoming part of that person's society, with the imitation and conciliation that society involves. Thus, the *Spectator*, like de la Bruyère's *Caractères*, declares its aim 'to Cultivate and Polish Human Life, by promoting Virtue and Knowledge' – in the preface to the first collected volume, dedicated to Whig statesman John Somers (1651–1716) as 'a Person of a finished Character'.[7]

However, in the periodical publication of the *Spectator*, Addison does not describe the essays as 'instructive' until the tenth number – and there, the idea of the *Spectator* as corrective literature is comically undermined by the 'Spectator' character's baser motives. Addison presents the *Spectator*'s narrator, for the reader's amusement, as a writer pleased by the success of his own new publication. Imagining a large and deferential readership for his future writings, the Spectator attempts to flatter readers with the idea of themselves as a select group of 'Disciples'; and he assures them, in ironically elevated language, of his publication's value as a moral pharmaceutical to be taken daily:

> It is with much Satisfaction that I hear this great City inquiring Day by Day after my Papers, and receiving my Morning Lectures with a becoming Seriousness and Attention. My Publisher tells me, that there are already

Three Thousand of them distributed every Day: So that if I allow Twenty Readers to every paper, which I look upon as a modest Computation, I may reckon about Threescore thousand Disciples in *London* and *Westminster*, who I hope will take care to distinguish themselves from the thoughtless Herd of their ignorant and unattentive Brethren. Since I have raised to myself so great an Audience, I shall spare no Pains to make their Instruction agreeable, and their Diversion useful. For which Reasons I shall endeavour to enliven Morality with Wit, and to temper Wit with Morality [...]. And to the End that [readers'] Virtue and Discretion may not be short transient intermitting Starts of Thought, I have resolved to refresh their Memories from Day to Day, till I have recovered them out of that desperate State of Vice and Folly, into which the Age is fallen. The Mind that lies fallow but a single Day, sprouts up in Follies that are only to be killed by a constant and assiduous Culture. [...] I would therefore in a very particular Manner recommend these my Speculations to all well-regulated Families, that set apart an Hour in every Morning for Tea and Bread and Butter; and would earnestly advise them for their Good to order this Paper to be punctually served up, and to be looked upon as a Part of the Tea Equipage (*S* no. 10, Addison).

This is the morality of someone trying to sell something. The *Spectator* purports to serve a universally appealing combination of 'Morality', 'Civility' and 'Diversion' – rather than the 'Party' and 'Politics' that divide its potential readership. The *Spectator*'s ironical self-fashioning as an innocuously educational and non-partisan publication astutely combines Addison and Steele's underlying political concerns with a comically exaggerated portrait of non-partisanship. Neutral in all things, the Spectator character's 'exact Neutrality between the Whigs and the Tories' is one manifestation of his refusal to participate in any sphere or activity: 'I have acted in all the parts of my Life as a Looker-on, which is the Character I intend to preserve in this Paper' (*S* no. 1, Addison). He opens his mouth so seldom that he is able to quantify his spoken words with remarkable precision, claiming that 'during the Space of eight Years' at university, 'I scarce uttered the Quantity of an hundred Words; and indeed do not remember that I ever spoke three Sentences together in my whole Life' (no. 1), and confessing that he 'ha[s] indulged [his] Silence to such an Extravagance' that friends have to deduce opinions from his facial expressions (*S* no. 4, Steele). By presenting the Spectator's political neutrality not as an abstract virtue but as the comical peculiarity of an odd-mannered man, the early numbers of the *Spectator* are calculated to divert and flatter readers regardless of politics and religion.

First, the Spectator's comic auto-characterisation promises the reader – who is presumably already inundated with sermons and conduct literature – a novel narrator whose ostentatiously 'instructive' satires on manners and politics will be continually lightened with comic irony. Second, the irony of the salesman's pitch flatters the reader's critical understanding of consumerism and the commercialisation of literature, thus selling the *Spectator* more persuasively to readers who know they are being sold to. Third, the deliberately comic characterisation of neutrality flatters the knowledge of the distrustful and politically astute reader who might well have discerned, behind the pretence of non-partisanship, what the magazine's political project might be in the 1710s. The Whigs were out of favour with Queen Anne and had gone into opposition. Brian Cowan argues that the *Spectator*'s political neutrality was a pose, a strategy for a distinctively Whiggish social reform project aiming to reform and discipline practices of public sociability such as newspaper reading and political debate in coffeehouses.[8] 'The object of this reformation was not the perpetuation of a rational public sphere', writes Cowan, but the 'construct[ion of] a social world that was amenable to the survival of Whig politics during a time in which the future of Whiggery was unclear'.[9]

Part of the *Spectator*'s strategy to endear its project to a broader audience – to become a favourite with all parties – is that Addison and Steele's pretence to non-partisanship is continuous with their comic auto-characterisation of it. The *Spectator*'s characters do, of course, refract various forms of knowledge about the readers' world. But if we understand the *Spectator*'s humour merely as a pleasing cover for moral earnestness or political strategy, we risk overlooking the extent to which Addison and Steele, through comic characterisation, problematise their own claim to serve 'Morality' with 'Wit' and lower the value of doing so. The *Spectator*'s characters and auto-characterisation, I argue, make 'Diversion' a valuable good in itself. Imagining its papers as innocuous consumer objects, part of the tea service, the *Spectator* speculates a provisionally depoliticised 'civil' society where all ideas and ideals can be 'characterised' into eccentricities – where opinionated and public-minded citizens are continually diverted away from political concerns, and into good humour with each other. For the Spectator, comically peculiar characters are sport, not instruction – 'Odd and uncommon Characters are the Game that I look for, and most delight in' (no. 108, Addison) – and it is a social sport, with novel characters exchanged between friends. One fictitious 'letter to the editor' begs the Spectator, 'Give me Leave to make you a Present of a Character not yet described in your Papers' (no. 194, Steele); another letter begins by addressing him as 'the greatest Sportsman, or, if you please, the Nimrod among this Species of Writers' (no. 371, Addison).

The fictive originals of light literature thus use characterology for diversion, welcoming readers to a 'great Field of Game' (no. 131, Addison) where they can safely indulge their aggressive tendencies to sport with real people's characters. There, readers might be free both from the authority of serious moral satire, and from the risks of libellous, politically motivated satires on real individuals – so long as the sportsmen manage to confine their fire to their intended imaginary targets.

For commercial imaginative literature including the novel, the *Spectator* suggested how fictive characters could create civilised (and civilising) diversions as a compelling alternative to divisive satire and gossip. To achieve this supposed aim, characters had to be 'original' in the sense of not being copied from real people in ways that would be recognisable to readers. Here, the reader is made responsible for fictionality: they must curb any tendency to recognise real people in imaginative works and they must cultivate respect for the author's imagination. The reader must believe that 'Odd and uncommon Characters' like the *Spectator*'s (no. 108, Addison) can substantially originate in an author's mind. In other words, they must believe that in a judgement on the work's fictionality, the imagination and assemblage involved in character-writing are more significant than elements based on direct observation. Addison and Steele thus model character originality for their readers as well as for aspiring writers: they suggest that, to be safely diverted by innocently original and fictitious characters, readers must enter a compact with the writer. To accept characters' fictionality, and to admire their originality, is to be a more sophisticated reader – unlike the literal-minded man in one of the Spectator's anecdotes, who glosses the original characters of imaginative literature with his own pet hates:

> A Man who has a good Nose at Innuendo, smells Treason and Sedition in the most innocent Words that can be put together, and never sees a Vice or Folly stigmatized, but finds out one or other of his Acquaintance pointed at by the Writer. I remember an empty pragmatical Fellow in the Country, who upon reading over *the whole Duty of Man*, had written the Names of several Persons in the Village at the Side of every Sin which is mentioned by that excellent Author; so that he had converted one of the best Books in the World into a Libel against the Squire, Church-wardens, Overseers of the Poor, and all the most considerable Persons in the Parish (no. 568, Addison).

Readers, Addison suggests, can libel as badly as writers; and the *Spectator* makes a show of trusting its readers, for their intellectual sophistication, their discretion and – by association with their faith in the author's originality – their powers of imagination.

Not being Romantics, Addison and Steele do not speak of 'originality', 'imagination' or 'creativity' in positive terms; rather, these faculties are implied in statements about the importance of abstraction, generalisation, qualification and avoidance in character-writing. The Spectator, for example, 'must [. . .] intreat every Particular Person, who does me the Honour to be a Reader of this Paper, never to think himself, or any one of his Friends or Enemies, aimed at in what is said: For I promise him, never to draw a faulty Character which does not fit at least a Thousand People' (no. 34, Addison). The reader must be able to entertain the notion that a peculiar character is particular enough to belong to a real person, yet still have the status of an abstracted and generalised 'it':

> When I meet with any vicious Character that is not generally known, in order to prevent its doing Mischief, I draw it at length, and set it up as a Scarecrow; by which means I do not only make an Example of the Person to whom it belongs, but give Warning to all Her Majesty's Subjects, that they may not suffer by it (no. 205, Addison).

Steele offers more detail on character-writing as an effortful editorial process of avoidance and addition – avoiding too-particular resemblances and adding details that deliberately frustrate character-person identification:

> I believe my Reader would [. . .] think the better of me, if he knew the Pains I am at in qualifying what I write after such a manner, that nothing may be interpreted as aimed at private Persons. For this Reason when I draw any faulty Character, I consider all those Persons to whom the Malice of the World may possibly apply it, and take care to dash it with such particular Circumstances as may prevent all such ill-natured Applications. If I write any Thing on a black Man, I run over in my Mind all the eminent Persons in the Nation who are of that Complexion: When I place an imaginary Name at the Head of a Character, I examine every Syllable and Letter of it, that it may not bear any Resemblance to one that is real (no. 262, Steele).

Here, the emphasis is not on character-writing as a 'creative' endeavour, but on the necessity of examining one's 'exemplary' characters against an index of real ones.

It is not until the caricature talk of Romantic character criticism – developed in part through the critical reception of the *Spectator*'s characters – that characters' 'originality' takes a positive form. James Edward Austen-Leigh's memoir, for example, does not trouble to defend Austen's characters by claiming that she 'avoided' caricaturing real people or deliberately 'dashed' characteristics with circumstances. Instead, he trusts readers to believe that Austen could actually *originate* characters, could 'create' them and 'invest' them with qualities:

> She did not copy individuals, but invested her own creations with individuality of character. [. . .] Her own relations never recognised any individual in her characters; and I can call to mind several of her acquaintance whose peculiarities were very tempting and easy to be caricatured of whom there are no traces in her pages. She herself, when questioned on the subject by a friend, expressed a dread of what she called such an 'invasion of social proprieties.' She said that she thought it fair to note peculiarities and weaknesses, but that it was her desire to create, not to reproduce; 'besides,' she added, 'I am too proud of my gentlemen to admit that they were only Mr. A. or Colonel B.'[10]

While Austen's remark about her own writing has a note of self-deprecation, it is clear that the idea of 'originality' in character-writing has gained ground, such that it makes sense to speak in proprietary terms of '*my* gentlemen', and that originality eclipses 'observation' as a talent beneficial to characterisation technique. Whereas Addison and Steele speak of abstract characters potentially 'belonging' to real people (*S* no. 205), Romantic character criticism speaks of imaginary characters belonging securely to authors – and then to readers.

This is not to say that Augustan character-writers did not find ways of expressing pride in their 'originality'. I suggest that caricature talk's emphasis on the character-writer's creative energy is latent in early eighteenth-century literature, in moments when imaginative comic writers – Swift, Hogarth and Fielding as well as Addison and Steele – auto-characterise their satirical personae as proud of their moral rectitude. Rather than pride himself on his originality, Addison's characterologist finds self-regard in being above personal satire: 'I know very well the Value which every Man sets upon his Reputation, and how painful it is to be exposed to the Mirth and Derision of the Publick, and should therefore scorn to divert my Reader, at the Expence of any private Man' (no. 262). Sociability and civility, not queen and country, are at stake in these characterisations. In Addison's comic anecdote about *The Whole Duty of Man*, the innuendo-sniffer's marginalia is discovered and causes uproar in his village, but there is no material disturbance to the wider political or religious order. The 'Libel' only disrupts the peace of sociability, and lowers the man's value as a candidate for social acquaintance.

But while the stakes are relatively low, Augustan writers often describe the risks in strong language more suited to seditious libel than the comic characterisation of private individuals. Addison's mock-heroic language makes a joke of the Spectator's strenuous insistence on the difference between 'satire' and 'libel', transmuting the author's pride in their characters' originality into the character's excessive pride in his scrupulousness. For example, the *Spectator*'s denunciation of libellous satires and gossip, while expressed in dramatic imagery and grandiose language, boils down to some advice on how to be a good friend and not hurt people's feelings, even when they pretend to be unaffected by gossip:

> There is nothing that more betrays a base, ungenerous Spirit, than the giving of secret Stabs to a Man's Reputation. Lampoons and Satyrs, that are written with Wit and Spirit, are like poison'd Darts, which not only inflict a Wound, but make it incurable. For this Reason I am very much troubled when I see the Talents of Humour and Ridicule in the Possession of an ill-natured Man. There cannot be a greater Gratification to a barbarous and inhuman Wit, than to stir up Sorrow in the Heart of a private Person, to raise Uneasiness among near Relations, and to expose whole Families to Derision, at the same time that he remains unseen and undiscovered. If, besides, a Man is vicious into the bargain, he is one of the most mischievous Creatures that can enter into a Civil Society. [. . .] It is impossible to enumerate the Evils which arise from these Arrows that fly in the dark. [. . .] For my part, I would never trust a Man that I thought was capable of giving these secret Wounds, and cannot but think that he would hurt the Person, whose Reputation he thus assaults, in his Body or in his Fortune, could he do it with the same Security (no. 23, Addison).

And so on. Addison putatively aims this advice at publishing writers, the satirists most capable of concealing themselves from their victims – but it is also a comically overwritten and characteristic speech advertising the Spectator's own merits as an inoffensive and imaginative author. If the Spectator claims to be having 'Serious Thoughts' about the innumerable evils of libellous mockery, Addison is not presenting them seriously.

Readers might have recalled the bombastic speech in Thomas Randolph's play *The Muse's Looking Glass* (1706), where the demonic figure of 'Satyre' exults over his victims in a rapid mixing of metaphors – freezing, cutting, cooking, whipping, scarring, infecting and ulcerating:

> When I but frown'd in my Lucilius Brow,
> Each conscious Cheek grew Red, and a cold trembling
> Freez'd the chill Soul; while every guilty Breast
> Stood fearful of Dissection, as afraid
> To be anatomiz'd by that skilful Hand;
> And have each Artery, Nerve, and Vein of Sin
> By it laid open to the publick Scorn.
> I have untrussed the proudest; greatest Tyrants
> Have quak'd below my powerful Whip, half dead
> With Expectation of the smarting Jerk,

> Whose Wound no salve can cure: each blow doth leave
> A lasting Scar, that with a Poyson eats
> Into the Marrow of their Fames and Lives;
> Th' eternal Ulcer to their Memories![11]

While numerous texts of the 'Augustan' literary era condemn libellous intentions as a perversion of satire, they generally do not use the kind of overblown language and cumulative style that Randolph and Addison put in the mouths of their self-important characters. In cooler terms, writers deplore 'Invectives', 'Slander' and the 'real Names [that] turn Satyr to abuse', and they approve satire 'pointed at the *Vice* more than at the *Man*', without referring to poisoned arrows or physical assaults.[12] Contrastingly, professionals who, like the 'Spectator' character, want to foreground their own inventive talents, emphasise the supposed high-mindedness of their own satire with more sensational and more particular images like those used by Randolph's Satyre. Captioning his painting *Midnight Modern Conversation* in 1732, Hogarth advises his audience 'not to find one meant resemblance there / We lash the vices but the persons spare'. Fielding's narrator, digressing from the plot in *Joseph Andrews* (1742), describes the satirist as someone who corrects faults in private, 'like a parent', the libeller as someone who punishes them in public, 'like an executioner'.[13] These parallels are reworked from a passage in the *Tatler* where Steele's 'Isaac Bickerstaff' persona laments how the concepts of satire and libel are 'promiscuously joined together in the Notions of the Vulgar', whereas actually 'the Satyrist and the Libeller differ as much as the Magistrate and the Murderer' (*T* no. 92). Swift, in his obituary for himself, celebrates the accuracy of his aim as a satirist in jaunty rhyming couplets: 'malice never was his aim; / He lash'd the vice, but spared the name; / No individual could resent, / Where thousands equally were meant'.[14]

Are Hogarth, Swift and Fielding genuinely concerned that their comical characterisations might be taken for personal satires? Are they genuinely claiming that they create imaginary characters primarily so that their works can have more universal effect on society's morals? I read these Augustan denunciations of libel and *ad hominem* argument, with their mock-heroic imagery of lashing and stabbing and poisoning, as ironic auto-characterisations after Addison and Steele's 'Spectator' and 'Bickerstaff' characters. They celebrate the author's genius for original characterisation not with earnest condemnations of libel, but by participating in a comic tradition of hyperbolising the social evils of 'unoriginal' characters.

The caricature talk of Romantic character criticism, while writers still insist on the innocent originality of their characters, conventionally suggests that a peculiar and amusing character is so well-characterised that it must be a description of a real individual. In this permutation of the language-game of 'character talk', to use Moi's term, readers pay tribute to authors' talents for characterisation by affecting to believe that the character is *not* original. Sometimes a critic recounts how other readers have identified the character with a real person, the actual 'original' on whom the character might be based. In his essay on Austen's novels for the *Quarterly Review*, for example, Scott tells how '[a] friend of ours, whom [Austen] never saw or heard of, was at once recognized by his own family as the original of Mr. Bennet, and we do not know if he has yet got rid of the nickname'.[15]

Often for readers, however, the 'originals' of characters are ideal beings, merely imagined and 'felt' to pre-exist the author's work, as in Francis Jeffrey's review of *Waverley*. A cursory reading of the essay in the *Edinburgh Review* might suggest that Jeffrey is praising Scott for the opposite of originality in his depictions of the lower classes: after all, he notes 'the extraordinary fidelity [...] with which all the inferior agents in the story are represented' (the phrase 'inferior agents' suggesting their subordinacy in narrative as well as their socio-economic status). However, Jeffrey is also bent on persuading the reader that they can *feel*, subjectively, that this subset of Scott's characters are faithful representations without actually being familiar with the real originals that are represented:

> The way in which [manners and characters] are here represented must satisfy every reader, we think, by an inward tact and conviction, that the delineation has been made from actual experience and observation.[16]

'Inner tact' suggests a figurative application of *tact*'s original meaning in English – the sense of touch, via French from Latin *tangere*, 'to touch' – signifying a perceptive faculty that might be likened to the sense of touch. Scott's peculiar characters are tangible to the reader's mind because of 'the way in which they are here represented', independently of the sources that would verify their factual reality. The detailed texture of Scott's writing, his formal means of characterising – as Jeffrey puts it, his 'way' – creates the phenomena that satisfy the reader's 'tact' for what is real. In fact, there do exist 'records and vestiges of the more extraordinary parts of the representation', which will, Jeffrey notes, 'satisfy all who have the means of consulting them, as to the perfect accuracy of the picture' – but then, Jeffrey reaffirms his conviction that readers need no extra-textual verification to be impressed by Scott's characters' accuracy:

> No one who has not lived extensively among the lower orders of all descriptions, and made himself familiar with their various tempers and dialects, can perceive the full merit of those rapid and characteristic sketches; but it requires only a general knowledge of human nature to feel that they must be faithful copies from known originals.[17]

'Tactful' reading means the subjective experience of a virtual world with strong characters who seem real not because the reader knows their originals, but because the author's talents convince the reader that the characters are known to the author. In some cases, the reader takes satisfaction in imagining that their personal acquaintance might be the original of the fictional character – but believing that this is not actually the case.

Either way, the fictional character's accuracy is virtual. In response to realist character-writing like Scott's, fiction-readers develop a faculty of 'inner tact' such that characters' fidelity to the real can be cerebrally 'touched' and 'felt' without being known. The character-writer's talent for originality consists not in the invention of characters never seen before, but in the creation of characters that seem to have 'originals'. Romantic character talk does not use *original* to designate artistic originality in the sense of 'unconventional' or 'unprecedented'; typically, *original* is used only to mean the ideal 'real people' to which fictional characters might refer, as in 'the original of Mr. Bennet'. Nevertheless, by recognising the ideality of those originals, Romantic character talk acknowledges the author's power to originate characters through the formal realist 'way' they write, and supposes the existence of some faculty in readers that responds to it. While Romantic readers do not talk explicitly about character-writers being 'original', they do think that realist character-writers project a feeling about originality. 'Inward tact and conviction' about characters, not 'actual experience and observation', mediate for readers between realism and the real; or, to put it another way, this realism is a feeling about characters.

My analysis here falls in with a critical tradition of reading the *Spectator* and the *Tatler* as proto-novelistic, seeing Addison and Steele's characterisations as a large factor in the periodicals' success as distinctively entertaining reading material, and recognising the ways in which they deploy and develop Jean de la Bruyère's departures from the established conventions of the Theophrastan character. As Schön summarises, this criticism emphasises the differences between Theophrastan 'types' and novelistic 'individuals', arguing that the *Spectator* and its imitators provided 'examples in techniques which were later taken over as a valuable heritage by the newly emerging novel'.[18] I am interested in what the

Spectator's character-writing techniques seemingly do to replace an instructive taxonomy of moral character types with a bewildered field of characters 'not yet described' and 'not generally known',[19] seeming to trust (reasonably) that their readers would already possess knowledge of the themes and categories that had been used in the modern English 'character sketch' genre for around a hundred years, as well as being known from translations of Theophrastus and other examples from antiquity.[20]

I am also interested in how the *Spectator* arguably cultivates a desire for fictive 'reality' more generally – a realist conspiracy of setting, narrative, scenario and character – by experimenting with particularity, variety and haphazardness through the comic non-protagonist characters that comprise the Spectator's club throughout the periodical, as well as through the more briefly described (or auto-characterised) characters who appear only once in scenarios and 'letters to the editor'.

The rise of the English-language realist novel in eighteenth-century Britain has been associated with the idea that 'particularities' enhance literary works intended to divert readers because details and distinctiveness make the fiction's virtual reality more experiential and empirically credible. As Watt points out, the early British realists experimented with quotidian specificity in narrative and character decades before 'particularity' became established in critical discourse: 'For the critical tradition in the early eighteenth century was still governed by the strong classical preference for the general and universal: the proper object of literature remained *quod semper quod ubique ab omnibus creditum est.*'[21] Critics in the second half of the eighteenth century got hold of the first principle of British empiricism, that human knowledge derives from sense perception. In the discourse on the senses that introduces *Elements of Criticism* (1762), Lord Kames argues that the fine arts are part of a divine plan to decorporealise the human sensory experience of pleasure that offers mental diversion – as well as physical relief – from work:

> Our first perceptions are of external objects, and our first attachments are to them. Organic pleasures take the lead. But the mind, gradually ripening, relisheth more and more the pleasures of the eye and the ear; which approach the purely mental, without exhausting the spirits; and exceed the purely sensual, without danger of satiety. The pleasures of the eye and ear have accordingly a natural aptitude to attract us from the immoderate gratification of sensual appetite. For the mind, once accustomed to enjoy a variety of external objects [i.e. pleasure in the arts] without being conscious of the organic impression [as with pleasure in sex and eating], is prepared for enjoying internal objects where there cannot be an organic impression

[i.e. pleasure in religious devotion]. Thus the author of nature, by qualifying the human mind for a succession of enjoyments from the lowest to the highest, leads it by gentle steps from the most groveling corporeal pleasures, for which solely it is fitted in the beginning of life, to those refined and sublime pleasures which are suited to its maturity.[22]

Kames's notion of pleasure in the arts as an intermediate step between the organic satisfaction of the body and the religious exaltation of the mind – both sensory and cerebral – anticipates Jeffrey's idea of an 'inner tact' that rewards character-reading. Since the perception involved in fiction-reading has graduated from the sensory perception of material objects, readers will be more satisfied by the particular than the abstract. As Kames puts it, 'abstract or general terms have no good effect in any composition for amusement; because it is only of particular objects that images can be formed'.[23] Whereas generalities present readers with intellectual exercise, particularities produce pseudo-sensory effects in the mind of the reader, allowing them to experience a virtual reality. Kames sees this human faculty as a gift from God, 'not governed by unavoidable necessity' but 'offer[ed . . .] to us, in order to advance our happiness'.[24]

(Kames recognises that it might usually be 'the opulent [members of society], who have leisure to improve their minds and their feelings' with the pseudo-sensory pleasures of the fine arts – unsurprisingly, given his moment in history. From my own viewpoint in a different historical moment, it is over a series of economic shifts and systems – industrial revolution, de-industrialisation, neoliberalism – that the realisms available from books, film and television have become increasingly important as sources of pseudo-sensory enjoyment or 'happiness' for many of us non-opulents. 'True crime', 'reality TV', 'costume drama': as suggested by their genre monikers, the postmodern realisms co-constructed for narrative forms by media, media journalism and social media are highly self-reflexive. They extensively use techniques that encourage listeners, viewers and readers to develop scepticism about the 'reality' of narrative entertainment in order to double their pleasure in realism: both the pseudo-sensory pleasure of immersion in a virtual reality, and the humour that arises from our perception of incongruities and artifices. This faculty destabilises realism to discover the 'real' dramas behind it: complex narratives of strategic collaboration and rivalry on a petty scale among workers in the hierarchies of the media industry – producers, directors, managers, writers, researchers, performers, technicians, caterers – and beyond that, a multinational epic of production and distribution companies, studios and state censors.)

In the Romantic period, the essential link between realism and pseudo-sensory experience was often expressed in discussions about non-protagonist characters – recall Coleridge's affection for Fielding's 'characters of postilions, landlords, landladies, waiters' where 'nothing can be more true, more happy or more humorous'[25] – though it has often been implicit or repressed in modern scholarship's accounts of the realist novel, as in Watt's observation that formal realism obliges itself 'to satisfy its reader with such details of the story as to the individuality of the actors concerned, the particulars of the times and places of their actions, details which are presented through a more largely referential use of language than is common in other literary forms' (32). Is formal realism's 'satisfaction' always a feeling? Realism satisfies the reader by convincing them of a virtual reality that provides them with pseudo-sensory impressions of objects understood to be like external 'referents' – or, in Romantic caricature talk, 'originals'.

The *Spectator* tends to assume a pleasure-driven taste not only for particularity, novelty and variety but also for the ways in which these elements ironically undermine the narrator's moral authority and the text's instructiveness. Addison explicitly acknowledges the reader's innate curiosity about 'Particulars' in the first number of the *Spectator*, where the titular character introduces himself. The kind of comic auto-characterising narration pioneered by Addison and Steele, innovating on Bruyère's first-person narration of character sketches, and exemplified in the Romantic novel by Scott's pseudo-epigraphic 'editors', adds to the reader's pleasure with an additional layer of realism:

> I have observed, that a Reader seldom peruses a Book with Pleasure'till he knows whether the Writer of it be a black or a fair Man, of a mild or cholerick Disposition, Married or a Batchelor, with other Particulars of the like nature, that conduce very much to the right Understanding of an Author. To gratify this Curiosity, which is so natural to a Reader, I design this Paper, and my next, as Prefatory Discourses to my following Writings, and shall give some Account in them of the several persons that are engaged in this Work (*S* no. 1, Addison).

After the Spectator's account of himself as an extravagantly, unaccountably silent and neutral gentleman who approaches life as a spectator sport, he claims to withhold deliberately the details that would make his identity known, openly playing to the reader's hunger for particulars: 'I keep my Complexion and Dress, as very great Secrets; tho' it is not impossible, but I may make Discoveries of both in the Progress of the Work I have undertaken'. The particulars that imply an original are not, in the

Spectator, adjuncts to the illustration of a vice or a failure of manners; rather, the Spectator's eccentricity is depicted as an innocuous, bountiful source of amusement. The reader is also expected to be amused by apparent contradictions in the Spectator's character – silent yet sociable, he must 'beg People's Pardon for an odd Humour I am guilty of, [...] which is saluting any Person whom I like, whether I know him or not' (no. 454, Steele). When it comes to the 'sketched' quasi-Theophrastan characters who appear only once in the *Spectator*, their particulars and peculiarities might be understood to serve the author's moral lessons by making the scenarios more engaging.

However, the *Spectator* continually undermines the moral import of its 'character sketches', first by treating the ill effects of characters' behaviour with hyperbole, second by calling the sketched character's supposed guilt into question, and third by emphasising the appeal of variety and novelty in the presentation of characters. In no. 194, for example, Steele prefaces two 'letters to the editor' with a moralising preface by the Spectator, who laments the 'ten thousand Tortures' experienced by individuals who perceive that their companions do not make enough effort to reciprocate their affections. The first letter, from a jealous husband, complains of a wife who does not make any pro-active effort to defend the innocence of her conduct – despite being convinced of her actual innocence:

> I have a Wife, of whose Virtue I am not in the least doubtful; yet I cannot be satisfied that she loves me, which gives me as great Uneasiness as being faulty the other Way would do. [...] If my Wife does the most ordinary thing, as visiting her Sister, or taking the Air with her Mother, it is always carried with the Air of a Secret: Then she will sometimes tell a thing of no Consequence, as if it was only Want of memory made her conceal it before; and this only to dally with my Anxiety.

The Spectator gives the wife the epithet of 'Corinna', a hyperbolic comparison with Ovid's *Amores* that calls into question the letter-writer's character as a faithful, innocent husband. The poet's persona in the *Amores* is a promiscuous character who suffers from sexual impotence and is having an affair with Corinna, a married woman, whom he coaches to flirt secretly with him while her husband is present. The *Amores*'s wounded lover, despicable and self-absorbed, is certainly no less fickle than the object of his affection. In one of the poems, he grabs Corinna by the hair, hits her and scratches her face; in another, he wishes that Corinna's husband would guard her more closely, since accessibility makes her less attractive to him; in another, he elegises Corinna's parrot, referencing Catullus's verses on a pet sparrow and implying his envy of the beloved pet. By framing the husband's letter with a reference to Ovid's anxieties about Corinna, who has sex with other lovers and risks her life by terminating a pregnancy, Steele directs the reader to see the letter-writer as pathetically paranoid, eccentrically anxious about his wife merely leaving the house and not telling him immediately about everything.

No. 194's second letter is self-conscious of its novelty and variety, offering 'a Present of a Character not yet described in your Papers, which is that of a Man who treats his Friend with the same odd Variety which a Fantastical Female Tyrant practises towards her lover'. In the terminology of the 2000s, his friend is 'flaky': but that habit of 'ghosting' friends, while not consistent with the letter-writer's ideal of friendship, cannot be attributed to any conscious malice or selfishness. In fact, the letter-writer connects his friend's avoidant behaviour with his mood instability, which might be seasonal: transcribing 'some short Minutes I have taken of him in my Almanack since last Spring', the letter-writer points out that his friend's humour seems to be 'as various as the Weather'. It is hinted that the friend might be flaky because he trusts that the letter-writer will continue to love him despite his habit of avoiding his friends when it pleases his mood: 'The Rogue I know loves me, yet takes Advantage of my Fondness for him to use me as he pleases.' If the friend could be more considerate of the letter-writer, the letter-writer could also learn to take his friend's seasonality less personally. Again, the Spectator's hyperbolic description of its impact – 'the Source of utmost Unhappiness' – comically exaggerates the irritation of a letter-writer who is fortunate to enjoy, if only for part of the year, the company of 'the best Friend' and 'the sprightliest best-humoured Fellow in the World'. Addison and Steele's frequent use of the first-person 'letter to the editor', comically undermining the writer's reliability as a reporter of other characters, represents one of the *Spectator*'s biggest departures from the conventional didacticism of Theophrastan character-writing, and further comedises the 'character sketch' genre by shedding the authority of Bruyère's depersonalised I-narrator.

The *Spectator*'s haphazard accumulation of various characteristics and circumstances, dashed together and caught up in ironic comparisons, squashes the supposed 'moral' into a pretext, an occasion for diverting readers with characters. When a number of the *Spectator* begins with the moral, as in no. 194 with its 'ten thousand Tortures' and allusion to the *Amores*, it does not stabilise that moral into an authoritative pre-emption of the reader's perusal of the characters. Amid the irony of the Spectator's disapproval, and the varied particulars of the anecdotes, it becomes untenable that each character is 'an anthropomorphised social-moral theme, such as thrift or loquaciousness' or embodies a single 'social, moral, or psychological category', as Schön and Smeed respectively describe the Theophrastan character.[26] In no. 194, various elements cast serious doubt on the characters' categorisation into a type such as 'the Mercurial Person', a phrase used by the second letter-writer to mean changeable or volatile, by association with the properties of 'quicksilver' (mercury). But in fact, both characters are predictable in their behaviour, since the wife is consistently unconcerned with her husband's anxiety to know everything she is doing and thinking, while the friend changes according to the seasons. With the second letter, Steele even makes a covert pun on the word 'mercurial': keeping an eye on 'the Glass' – which might be a barometer containing mercury – the letter-writer recognises that it might be British weather, not his friend, that is fickle. In addition to these methods of frustrating a reader's efforts to make typological categorisations, the structure of the characterisations in the *Spectator*, as in the *Caractères*, does not fall in with the Theophrastan convention of beginning with formulae such as 'A Fickle Woman is the sort of woman who'. For example, the *Spectator* does not tell us how to classify William Honeycomb (*S* no. 2, Steele), in contrast with the *London Magazine*'s 1764 Bruyère-esque portrait of 'Philander', who is 'what is called the ladies' man'.[27] The reader is not instructed but rather trusted to recognise Honeycomb as a 'beau' or 'gallant'. To conclude the sketch, rather than to begin it, the Spectator twists the Theophrastan formula into a polite phrase that conceals more than reveals character: 'I find there is not one of the Company but myself, who rarely speak at all, but speaks of him as that Sort of Man, who is usually called a well-bred fine Gentlemen [sic].'

More important than putting Honeycomb's singular behaviour in a social, moral, or psychological category, is emphasising his value to the club's variety. The 'gallant Will. Honeycomb' is included so 'that our Society may not appear a Set of Humourists unacquainted with the Gallantries and Pleasures of the Age', having a 'Way of Talking [that] very much enlivens the Conversation among us of a sedate Turn'. If anything, the reader is encouraged to include gallants in their society, as amusing companions and perhaps as a means of enjoying the forthright expression of thoughts that more scrupulously polite men would leave unsaid. To illustrate this point: in no. 4, Steele includes a one-sided 'dialogue' between Honeycomb and the Spectator at the opera, where the Spectator quietly ogles the women sitting near them, and Honeycomb responds aloud to his silent friend's 'great Approbation'. No. 454 finds the Spectator chasing a young woman (whom he considers a flirt) through the streets, aided by their coachmen's hand signals, in a scene described with realist precision comparable to Defoe's in *Moll Flanders*. When the coachmen deliberately 'meet, jostle, and threaten each other for Way, [. . .] entangled at the End of Newport-Street and Long-Acre', the lady opens her window to look out, 'when she sees the Man she would avoid'. Switching in and out of the present tense, the Spectator describes how 'the Tackle of the Coach-Window is so bad she cannot draw it up again' – giving him the opportunity to watch her bumping along, 'the laced Shoe of her left Foot, with a careless Gesture, just appearing on the opposite Cushion, held her both firm, and in a proper Attitude to receive the next Jolt'. After this game of 'Blindman's Buff', the Spectator admires 'agreeable Females' with 'so many pretty Hands busie in the Foldings of Ribbands' and 'the utmost Eagerness of agreeable Faces in the sale of Patches, Pins, and Wires' – implicating him in Honeycomb's knowledge of fashionable clothing as well as his attention to women.

Thus, within a single number of the *Spectator*, a variety of characters (Honeycomb and the Spectator in no. 4; the wife, the husband and the friends in no. 194) can be played off against each other – not to make instructive contrasts between vice and virtue, between bad and good manners, but to immerse the reader in a virtual social reality where characters' various 'Particulars' prevent them from being assertively classified by a social-moral theme, as the Spectator's 'dashing' of characteristics and circumstances prevents them from being identified as portraits of real individuals. Addison and Steele's joint ownership of the Spectator and the other club members, and the periodical nature of the composition, should probably be considered as important circumstantial factors in the *Spectator*'s particular facility for 'dashing' characters with a variety of anecdotes and details. The result is a formal realism of strong characters defined by originality, particularity, variety and the seemingly haphazard entanglement of characteristics such that characters do not separately represent abstract categories.

Critical tradition has often subsumed the *Spectator*'s comic characterisations under the moral essay genre, seeing them as accessories to the conveyance of social, moral and psychological knowledge. Focusing on the *Spectator*'s precedents for Romantic caricature talk, I have argued that the periodical's character-writing techniques depart from the conventions of moral characterology, showing how it emphasises diverting characters over instructive ones, assuming that the reader already possesses the knowledge of morals and manners that is required to appreciate Addison's and Steele's irony. The 'character sketch' genre had thrived in

British literary culture throughout the seventeenth century, with sketches 'found gathered together in collections (a volume containing anything from eight to eighty [characters]), singly in pamphlet form, or scattered in the periodicals';[28] and interest in the genre was then revitalised by English translations of Jean de la Bruyère's controversial *Caractères* (1688). With each new edition of *Caractères*, readers had added to their manuscript 'keys' listing the real people that *Caractères* supposedly portrayed as quasi-Theophrastan characters – and Bruyères objected. Addison and Steele, and the British comic novelists after them, also insisted on the possibility of 'original' characters, who were carefully constructed to seem as particular as real people without having individual referents. Unseating at every turn its narrator's claim to write morally purposeful satire that aims to correct the reader and society at large, the *Spectator* offers readers a humorously ambiguous diversion where 'Morality' is always falling down on 'Wit'.

Critics and editors have tried to distinguish the *Spectator*'s wit from its wisdom, diagramming the former as a container for the latter, even to the extent of literally separating the two in an attempt to frame the *Spectator* as a set of instructive moral essays. In the late 1820s, the Rev. E. Berens split his selected edition of the *Spectator* over two volumes, one containing moral wisdom suited to the ignorant, the other containing wit intended for those already wise and well mannered. The first of these volumes, 'made with a view to readers of every description, and every rank in life' and omitting the Greek and Latin mottos, was honoured with a place on 'the Supplemental Catalogue of the Society of Promoting Christian Knowledge for the use of Parochial Libraries'. It is Berens's *Second Selection* (1828), a volume 'of a less serious character' and 'intended for readers whose literary education has been more advanced, and who have more leisure for light reading',[29] which includes the twelve numbers featuring anecdotes about the *Spectator*'s most popular character, 'Sir Roger de Coverley'. Although aspects of Addison's and Steele's writing could be read unironically and classified as 'moral essays', the complete *Spectator* could not be shoehorned into that category: its characters especially made it prone to classification as 'light reading'.

The *Spectator* and the *Tatler* emerged as precursors to the tradition of the novel luxuriant with comic characters – Fielding, Smollett, Burney, Edgeworth, Austen, Scott, Dickens – and its strong characters, particularly Sir Roger, as enduring symbols of the 'originality' required for divertingly realist characterisation.

Loving Sir Roger de Coverley

One of the first comic non-protagonist characters in English-language literature to be taken seriously by character criticism, 'Sir Roger de Coverley' was a node around which Romantic caricature talk took shape. As well as appearing in professional writing about literature, Sir Roger is a subject of readers' character talk when he is casually summoned as a virtual human presence readily recollected in humorous scenarios. A good example is Robert Burns's reference to Sir Roger's deathbed scene in a letter to the Edinburgh bookseller Peter Hill, where he uses Sir Roger for a comic reflection on his own whimsical behaviour: '[A]s Sir Roger de Coverley, because it happened to be a cold day in which he made his will, ordered his servants great-coats for mourning, so, because I have been this week plagued with an indigestion, I have sent you by the carrier a fine old ewe-milk cheese.'[30] This casual reference to a particular number of the *Spectator* suggests, I think, that Sir Roger could have featured, briefly and frequently, in oral conversations throughout the eighteenth century, for as long as speakers could assume that their interlocutors would have read the *Spectator* or at least a selection of Sir Roger's appearances. A passing reference to Sir Roger, a famously sociable and benevolent character, could powerfully signify friendship, generosity and pathos as well as providing humour.

Here I focus on how appreciations of Sir Roger practised the terms of Romantic caricature talk about strong characters in the professional literary criticism of the late eighteenth century and the Romantic period. I analyse a selection of passages about Sir Roger from essays on Steele and Addison, published between the late 1770s and the early 1820s, when perhaps professional readers' interest in formal arguments about the character is waning: excerpts from Samuel Johnson's *Lives of the Poets* (1779), James Beattie's *Papers of Joseph Addison* (1790), Nathan Drake's *Essays Biographical, Critical and Historical* (1805), Alexander Chalmers's *The British Essayists* (1808) and Lionel Thomas Berguer's *British Essayists* (1823).[31] In these passages – as well as the ideals for comic non-protagonists discussed in the first part of this chapter (diversion, originality, realism) – there are several elements distinctive of Romantic-period caricature talk. First, the critics explicitly link the character's 'originality' to the combinational power of the creative mind; and second, critics use the anti-caricature vocabulary also discussed in Chapters 2 and 4 of this book. Third, caricature talk about Sir Roger, like the critical genre of the character appreciation, takes up certain stylistic and rhetorical devices, such as the use of first-person plural pronouns and superlative constructions. Fourth, 'Sir Roger' evokes the idea of literary favouritism and of writers, as well as readers, loving fictitious characters in parasocial and/or proprietary ways.

Whereas in early eighteenth-century literature the link between the comic character's constructed 'originality' and the character-writer's imaginative 'originality' is only implied, Romantic caricature talk about strong and favourite characters praises Addison and Steele for a creative mental faculty that seems to originate the very characters that strike the reader with extra-textual 'originality'. In Johnson's *Lives of the Poets*, for example, Addison 'copies life with so much fidelity, that he can be hardly said to invent; yet his exhibitions have an air so much original, that it is difficult to suppose them not merely the product of imagination'.[32] (Here, Johnson uses the word 'merely' not as a pejorative, but in the sense of 'purely' or 'entirely'.)

Other critics followed Johnson in crediting Steele, as well as Addison, with the ability to 'originate' characters: the eight-volume edition of *The Spectator* printed in 1788 for Payne, Rivington, Davis, Longman, Dodsley et al. agrees that 'it seems most probable that the character of Sir Roger de Coverley originated in Stelee's [sic] fertile imagination, as that of Bickerstaff likewise did'.[33] After criticism misattributed no. 2 of the *Spectator* to Addison, there remained controversy over whether Addison or Steele was most responsible for Sir Roger, and critics differed on whether Steele should be given more credit for his 'outline' than Addison for his 'extension' and 'improvement' of the character, in Chalmers's words.[34] Summarising the decades of debate about Addison's and Steele's different contributions to Sir Roger, Berguer's commentary comes down on the side of inventiveness and of Steele's 'original draft':

> For the first outline, or skeleton of this character, we are indebted certainly to Steele; but Addison, after availing himself of this elementary suggestion, departs materially from the original draft, as he brings out his picture into relief. This has occasioned many critics to charge the character with inconsistency; and without question the Sir Roger de Coverley of Steele is a very altered personage in the hands of Addison. Let it, however, be always remembered, that we are *primarily* indebted to Steele for Sir Roger de Coverley, *even as we have him*: Addison finished, but Steele *invented* him.[35]

Nathan Drake, too, credits Steele with the invention of Sir Roger, using the phrase 'original character' in the sense of a character that gives an impression of authorial originality, and which requires serious effort from collaborators to 'enter [...] with perfect accuracy into the conception and keeping of a character so original as that of Sir Roger de Coverley'.[36]

For Drake, Steele's originality in character-writing creates a strong impression of 'creative energy' seemingly at odds with the convincing naturalness of characters' features and manners. Steele's comic characters in the *Spectator*, the *Tatler* and the *Guardian* are 'original' yet typical, natural yet still 'original':

> Of the oriental tale, apologue, or fable, [...] I much wish that Sir Richard had afforded us more numerous examples. [...] If in the effusions of pure imagination Sir Richard seldom indulged, he has amply compensated for the omission by the invention and originality he has exhibited in the conception and conduct of many of the various characters which enliven his productions. [... His characters] are drawn and finished in a manner which not only indicates a perfect insight into the passions and feelings of the human frame, but demonstrates likewise the possession of that creative energy which, from the numerous shades and gradations of manner, can select and associate such features as shall designate a character altogether original, though founded on the usual acknowledged motives and actions of mankind; the resemblance, in fact, is true to the species, though not to any peculiar individual. This faculty of forming natural, consistent, yet *original* character, so essential to the dramatic writer whether in poetry or prose, so rarely attainable, and so valuable when attained, Steele most assuredly possessed in a very considerable degree.[37]

Original character-writing, Drake supposes, is a process of combining and selecting from the writer's knowledge of human life, both interior and social. Like other critics, Drake contradicts the rumour that the *Spectator*'s club members were actually based on real 'originals': 'It has been supposed, though upon no firm foundation, that the personages here enumerated were intended as copies of existing characters; that Sir Roger was drawn for Sir John Packington of Worcestershire, a Tory not deficient in good sense, but abounding in whimsical peculiarities. [...] These are, however, mere conjectures, and therefore claim but little credit.'[38] Authorial originality *combines* existing materials with such novelty – contrast, irony, complexity – that the reader receives an impression of 'creative energy' capable of actually 'originating' something, rather than only copying it.

In praising both Sir Roger's 'originality' and the authorial originality of his creators, Romantic character talk fends off potential arguments that Addison's and Steele's comic characters might be unnatural or exaggerated, using the vocabulary of the anti-caricature rhetoric discussed in Chapter 2. Critics emphasise the 'delicacy', 'fidelity' and 'modesty' of Addison's character-writing – concepts that become feminised in the critical reception of Austen's characters, as I explore in Chapter 4. Johnson writes that Addison 'formed a very delicate and discriminated idea' of Sir Roger, and that he 'never outsteps the modesty of nature'; his characters 'neither divert by distortion, or amaze by aggravation'.[39] Berguer calls Sir Roger 'one of the most exquisite pieces of comic painting which English literature possesses'.[40] Beattie observes that the characterisation stops short of being 'humorous in that degree of extravagance, which Addison always avoided', and contrasts the subtle characterisation of 'Sir Roger' with the exaggerations of caricature drawing and comic theatrics:

> Many writers seem to think that humour consists in violent and preternatural exaggeration; as there are no doubt many frequenters of the theatre, who find no want of comic powers in the actor who has a sufficient variety of wry faces and antic gestures; and many admirers of farce and fun, with whom bombast and big words would pass for exquisite ridicule. But wry faces are made with little effort, caricatura may be sketched by a very unskilful [sic] hand, and he who has no command of natural expression may easily put together gigantic figures and rumbling syllables.[41]

While exaggerated 'caricatures' can make an immediate impact by playing to popular taste, they can never be lovable: only 'naturally' comic characters can inspire lasting affection, never behaving so peculiarly that the reader cannot imagine disliking their company, were they real people. 'Sir Roger has peculiarities; that was necessary to make him a comic character; but', Beattie argues, 'they are all amiable, and tend to good: and there is not one of them that would give offence, or raise contempt or concern; in any rational society. At Sir Roger we never laugh, though we generally smile; but it is a smile, always of affection, and frequently of esteem'.[42]

In this strain of anti-caricature rhetoric, avoiding caricature makes strong characters good company. Austen asks that her readers be able to enjoy, as her protagonists do, the society of peculiar yet essentially 'good' characters: Elizabeth and Mr Bennet are quietly and tolerantly amused by Mr Collins for several hours, and Emma's friends are shocked when she mocks Miss Bates to her face. Caricature talk thus imagines the reader developing parasociality with comic non-protagonist characters, a relationship comprising attentiveness, patience and affection.

While Romantic caricature talk about the *Spectator*, dominated by anti-caricature rhetoric, is distinct from the critical genre of the character appreciation as described by Lynch – 'excessive with respect to its subject matter', with an 'over-the-top effect and purple prose'[43] – there are some points of similarity with 'character appreciation' in caricature talk's rhetoric and style. Anti-caricature rhetoric uses superlative constructions to praise character and writer: Johnson writes that '[a]s a describer of life and manners, [Addison] must be allowed to stand perhaps the first of the first rank'; and Beattie thinks that 'No man on earth affects grandeur less, or thinks less of it, than Sir Roger; and no man is less solitary.'[44] Critics pretend that their opinions are controversial, using constructions like 'I beg leave to observe', 'I cannot admit' and 'I will not admit' – while also chummily assuming that other readers naturally share the critic's appreciation: 'At Sir Roger we never laugh, [. . .] we generally smile; but it is a smile,—always of affection, and frequently of esteem.'[45]

Like the character appreciation genre, caricature talk generally bases its comments on the critic's holistic remembrance of the character. The critic feels no obligation to provide evidence for specific claims with correspondingly specific textual analysis: the reader seems expected to compare the critic's claims about 'Sir Roger' not with the actual text of the *Spectator*, but with the version of Sir Roger that the reader carries around in their head. Like character appreciation, Romantic caricature talk defends or minimises the strong character's peculiarities as though their mind and ethics exist separately of the text. Johnson and Beattie, for example, feel the need to argue that Sir Roger is sound of mind. Johnson gives the opinion that Sir Roger's 'irregularities [. . .] in conduct seem not so much the effects of a mind deviating from the beaten track of life, by the perpetual pressure of some overwhelming idea, as of habitual rusticity, and that negligence which solitary grandeur naturally generates'.[46] Beattie disagrees that 'there is in this character any thing of *rusticity* (as that word is generally understood) or any of those habits or ways of thinking that solitary grandeur creates'; but he agrees with Johnson that 'it never was, or could be, the Author's purpose to represent Sir Roger as a person of disordered understanding'.[47]

However, this faith in authorial intentionality and in the author's intellectual ownership of the non-protagonist character makes a significant difference between caricature talk and the character appreciation – which, Lynch observes, continually raises the possibility that characters exceed, or somehow pre-exist, their authors' conscious control. Maurice Morgann, for example, wants to 'examine if there be not something more in the character than is shewn; something inferred'; Thomas Robertson suggests that 'Shakespeare had no particular plan laid out in his mind for Hamlet to walk by' and 'rather meant to *follow* [Hamlet]; and like an historian, with fidelity to record how a person so singularly and marvellously made up should act'.[48] In contrast, despite similar concerns with characters' 'fidelity' and 'singularity', caricature talk's anti-caricature rhetoric insists on the writer's complete control over the character, often in categorical terms: character-writers 'never' do something, and 'always' do another.

Comic characters rarely stand alone in caricature talk, even when they are identified as 'favourites'. The most fundamental difference between caricature talk and the character appreciation is the fact that appreciations focus on a single character and are relatively extended, often taking up whole essays or chapters with the character's name in the title, whereas caricature talk typically occurs in the midst of an essay on a more general topic, discussing the author and multiple works by them. Then, when fictive characters are discussed, critics usually bring multiple characters and writers into the frame, grouping them, comparing and ranking them. Berguer's remarks, in 1823, on the longevity of Sir Roger – a comic character who 'has continued without a rival for upwards of one hundred years [...and] can bear *even now* to rank unflinchingly with those masterly delineations of life and manners, which, since Shakspeare, only the Author of Waverley has been able to achieve' – exemplify the way in which Romantic caricature talk, sometimes using anti-caricature rhetoric, puts strong non-protagonist characters into competition with each other, testing their strength.[49]

This rhetorical formula is used to its fullest extent in the introduction to an 1894 edition of *Pride and Prejudice*, where George Saintsbury ranks *Pride and Prejudice*'s characters above those of Austen's other novels, and raises Austen as a comic writer even above Addison:

> I for one should put *Pride and Prejudice* far lower if it did not contain what seem to me the very masterpieces of Miss Austen's humour and of her faculty of character-creation—masterpieces who may indeed admit John Thorpe, the Eltons, Mrs. Norris, and one or two others to their company, but who, in one instance certainly, and perhaps in others are still superior to them.
>
> The characteristics of Miss Austen's humour are so subtle and delicate [...] To me this humour seems to possess a greater affinity, on the whole, to that of Addison than to any other of the humorous species of this greater British genus [...T]he likeness of quality consists in a great number of subdivisions of quality—demureness, extreme minuteness of touch, avoidance of loud tones and glaring effects.[50]

But despite Addison's reputation, Saintsbury argues, Mr Collins – 'the immortal, the ineffable Mr. Collins' – is 'really *great*; far greater than anything Addison ever did'.[51] As Addison's and Steele's work on the club members and character sketches of the *Spectator* became a benchmark for the critical reception of comic non-protagonist characters throughout the

Romantic period and the nineteenth century, it was admitted that some writers might be able to exceed Addison's comic talent while writing more up-to-date characters. According to Saintsbury, though he 'has been charged with exaggeration', though 'there is something gigantic' about him, Mr Collins 'is perfectly natural, and perfectly alive', and in Austen's realist characters, '[n]othing is false; nothing is superfluous': late nineteenth-century anti-caricature rhetoric uses the same absolutes to praise Austen that late eighteenth-century caricature talk uses to praise Addison.[52]

These last pages of Chapter 3 investigate Romantic-period critics' expressions of love and possessiveness about 'Sir Roger' and 'Mr Collins'. The critical receptions of these two characters illustrate how, in Romantic caricature talk, the comic non-protagonist characters most vulnerable to being 'charged with exaggeration' are capable of eliciting – by means of superior realism – a pseudo-sensory pleasure interpreted as 'love' and involving simulated feelings of anxiety, loss and relief. James Beattie exemplifies Romantic caricature talk's declared feelings about the *Spectator*'s most popular character when he writes of 'lov[ing] with that fondness with which every heart is attached to Sir Roger'.[53]

The most prominent trope in late eighteenth–century character talk about *The Spectator* is an anecdote that establishes Sir Roger's lovability and his status as a favourite. Every critic and editor refers to Eustace Budgell's claim, in the first number of *The Bee*, that Addison wanted to kill off Sir Roger before anyone else got the chance – identifying Sir Roger not only as Addison's 'favourite' but as everyone's favourite, and thus vulnerable to becoming an unauthorised literary franchise. The debate over whether Addison or Steele was most responsible for 'Sir Roger' also highlights the possibility of feeling possessive and protective of a fictive character, with Chalmers suggesting that Addison, 'charmed with his colleague's outline of Sir Roger, [...] might probably determine to make it in some measure his own, by guarding with a father's fondness, against any violation that might be offered'.[54] Johnson imagines Addison's fatherly fondness of Sir Roger, referring both to 'the killing of Sir Roger' and to Addison's displeasure with Steele's episode of Sir Roger and the prostitute, which Addison did not know of until it was published:

> It is recorded by Budgell, that of the characters feigned or exhibited in the *Spectator*, the favourite of Addison was Sir Roger de Coverley, of whom he had formed a very delicate and discriminated idea, which he would not suffer to be violated; and therefore when Steele had shown him innocently picking up a girl in the Temple and taking her to a tavern, he drew upon himself so much of his friend's indignation, that he was forced to appease

him by a promise of forbearing Sir Roger for the time to come. The reason which induced Cervantes to bring his hero to the grave, *para mi solo nacio Don Quixote, y yo para el*, made Addison declare, with an undue vehemence of expression, that he would kill Sir Roger; being of opinion that they were born for one another, and that any other hand would do him wrong.[55]

The love of an author for his character is a relationship between gentlemen, as Johnson sees it: Addison 'kills' Sir Roger – ensuring authorial control of the circumstances and manner of the character's death – not merely to do honour to a textual character but as though to preserve the honour of an extra-textual character. Johnson's version of the 'killing Sir Roger' anecdote imagines that the focus of Addison's love is not the text characterising 'Sir Roger' but 'a very delicate and discriminate idea' of Sir Roger residing in his mind. Because for Addison any textual addition or sequel that seems to modify the character, or show it in a different light, is not an extension of the character but a 'violation' of it, Sir Roger acquires a quality of extra-textuality.

Critics differ on how proprietorial Addison's love of Sir Roger was, with Chalmers claiming that 'he neither immediately laid hold on what he considered as Steele's property, nor did he wish to monopolize the worthy Knight'.[56] However, the anecdote about Addison killing Sir Roger out of love consistently recurs in the introductions and footnotes to successive editions of the *Spectator*: readers experiencing Sir Roger's death for the first time would typically have encountered it with footnotes referring to Budgell's anecdote in the *Bee*. For example, in Payne's 1788 edition of the *Spectator*, the page looks like this ('departed' is the catchword):

> We last night received a piece of ill news at our club, which very sensibly afflicted every one of us. I question not but my readers themselves will be troubled at the hearing of it. To keep them no longer in suspence, Sir ROGER DE COVERLEY *is dead*.* He
> departed
> * 'Mr. Addison was so fond of this character, that a little before he laid down The Spectator, (foreseeing that some nimble gentleman would catch up his pen the moment he quitted it) he said to an intimate friend, with a certain *warmth* in his expression, which he was not often guilty of, *By G—, I'll kill Sir Roger, that nobody else may murder him*. Accordingly the whole *Spectator*, N° 517, consists of nothing else but an account of the old knight's death, and some moving circumstances which attended it.'[57]

This anecdote, reiterated in edition after edition, and cited in numerous critical essays on Addison and Steele, would have impressed generations of *Spectator*-readers with the notion of Sir Roger as an 'idea' separate from the text, animated by an authorial love that demands the primacy of authorial intention.

From the second half of the nineteenth century onwards, and after the *Spectator* as a whole ceased to be regularly recommended reading, Sir Roger's continued recognition as a favourite character was reinforced by selected editions of 'the Sir Roger de Coverley papers'. Thus, the *Spectator* endured as a model of comic characterisation. The first *Sir Roger De Coverley Papers* appeared in 1850, and successive editions of *The Sir Roger de Coverley Papers from "The Spectator"* came out in the 1890s, in Britain and the United States – often alongside other 'classics', such as in *Longmans' English Classics*, the American Book Company's *Eclectic English Classics* and *Riverside Literature Series*. In Britain, Joseph Meek's edition of *The De Coverley Papers from The Spectator* (London: J. M. Dent, 1920), part of *The Kings Treasuries of Literature* series, went through several printings.

Meek's introduction suggests an unbroken critical tradition of caricature talk and anti-caricature rhetoric about Sir Roger – though it adopts an idiom that deploys more similes than the 'sentimental' caricature talk of the Romantic period (and which is perhaps, depending on your taste, a more affectedly sentimental or 'twee' mode of criticism). Meek of course makes references to Scott and Dickens, as well as Shakespeare: 'There is no original for Sir Roger or Falstaff or Mr. Micawber.' The tropes, rhetoric and stylistic devices of anti-caricature rhetoric in Romantic caricature talk about Sir Roger are all present in Meek's introduction. The first-person pronouns, superlatives, ranking of comic characters, comparisons with Shakespeare and other literary touchstones, emphasis on authorial originality, on the author's possessiveness and the reader's love, are all trotted out as dependable clichés of popular literary criticism:

> No character in our literature, not even Mr. Pickwick, has more endeared himself to successive generations of readers than Addison's Sir Roger de Coverley: there are many figures in drama and fiction of whom we feel that they are in a way personal friends of our own, that once introduced to us they remain a permanent part of our little world. It is the abiding glory of Dickens, it is one of Shakespeare's abiding glories, to have created many such [...]. We are brought into the society of a fine old-fashioned country gentleman [...] with just those touches of whimsicality and those lovable faults which go straight to our hearts. [...]
>
> 'Addison's' Sir Roger we have called him, and be sure that honest Dick Steele, even if he drew the first outlines of the figure, would not bear us a grudge for so doing. Whoever first thought of Sir Roger, and however many little touches may have been added by other hands, he remains Addison's creation: and furthermore it does not matter a snap of the fingers

whether any actual person served as the model from which the picture was taken. Of all the bootless quests that literary criticism can undertake, this search for 'the original' is the least valuable. The artist's mind is a crucible which transmutes and re-creates.[58]

The belief that Sir Roger belongs to Addison, his supposed creator, not only frames the 1920 *Papers* but actually alters the reader's encounter with Sir Roger. Meek opts not to include Steele's episode of Sir Roger inviting a prostitute to the countryside, 'which is wholly out of keeping with Sir Roger's character'.[59] Meek does not reveal what happens in the omitted episode and does not inform the reader about which number of the *Spectator* is concerned. Thus, Meek's most significant editorial decision is driven by Romantic caricature talk's concept of Sir Roger being Addison's, both as an intellectual property and as an object of love. Favouritism gives editors like Meek a special sense of duty. In Meek's interpretation of this duty, the selected Sir Roger is more authentic than the complete 'Sir Roger' – resulting in an edition that is textually incomplete but which honours Addison's supposed feelings about Sir Roger as an extra-textual personage.

Scholarship on the novel, when it considers the fictitious characters most prone to being seen as 'caricatures', has often defined their 'minorness' or 'subordination' in terms of narrative or plot. Caricature talk, however, as it evokes favouritism for strong non-protagonist characters, is well-placed to argue for their importance to the narrative form of the realist novel, where plots might emerge 'naturally' out of collisions between diverse characters in a social space. In the last pages of this chapter, I argue that Romantic caricature talk was able to think that comic and eccentric non-protagonist characters were inceptive to realist novels because it reckoned the intellect and creative energy that authors seemed to have disproportionately invested in such 'favourites'. From a 1904 edition of the *Sir Roger De Coverley Papers*, via Watt's observations about character and narrative in *Tom Jones* in 1957, I wend to Coleridge's commentary on Mercutio as one of 'Shakspere's favourite characters'. Coleridge's analysis of the narrative importance of favouritism represents with great intellectual clarity a facet of Romantic caricature talk's faith that readers forge especially 'real', parasocial connections with certain characters, the ones who might possibly be considered 'caricatures' – and that fondness for strong characters has a crucial role in readers feeling themselves convinced by literary constructions of reality.

As I have discussed, highly particularised non-protagonist characters were more readily conceptualised as extra-textual entities who exist prior to narrative; and this was reinforced by the literal extraction of Sir Roger from his textual context in publications like *The Sir Roger De Coverley Papers* and indexes in selections from Addison's and Steele's writings.[60] In one such edition, C. T. Winchester argues using anti-caricature rhetoric that since strong characters like Sir Roger have 'living' presence that pre-exists narrative, they are crucial to the process of realist plot-writing:

> The Sir Roger de Coverley papers are often said to be the precursor of the modern English novel. And in a very real sense they are. There are, to be sure, crude specimens of prose fiction in the preceding century. [...] But these romances, while they supply the element of plot and adventure most liberally, were deficient in genuine characters. There are no real men and women in them. Moreover, they made no attempt to depict contemporary life as it was. But Sir Roger de Coverley is no personage of romance. He is a hearty, red-blooded, Tory gentleman who lives in Worcestershire. And he has no adventures more striking than might naturally befall a country squire who comes up to London for the season once a year. There were scores of just such men in every shire in England. His speech, his habits, his prejudices, are all shown us with simple truth. And yet this is done with so much art and humour that Sir Roger is one of the most living persons in our literature. He is as immortal as Hamlet or Julius Caesar. We know him as well as we know our nearest neighbour; and we like him quite as well as we like most of our neighbours.
>
> Now this was something new in English literature. Sir Roger is the earliest person in English imaginative prose that is really still alive. There are men and women in our poetry before his day – in the drama there is, of course, a great host of them; but in prose literature Sir Roger is the first. Furthermore, the men and women of the drama, even in that comedy of manners which professed to reflect most accurately contemporary society, were almost always drawn with some romantic or satiric exaggeration; but there is no exaggeration in the character of Sir Roger. Here was the beginning of a healthy realism. It was only necessary for Richardson and Fielding, thirty years later, to bring together several such characters into a group, and to show how the incidents of their lives naturally ran into plot or story – and we have a novel.[61]

There are language and ideas here that are familiar from early nineteenth-century caricature talk such as in the critical reception of Austen's characters, which I discuss in Chapter 4.

Winchester's explicit subordination of narrative to character is less typical of caricature talk, however, and interests me by the way it contradicts Watt's argument in *The Rise of the Novel* that 'minor characters' are generally incidental to the plots of realist novels. Strong characters are free to provide humour and sociological interest because they have little to do with the central narrative:

> *Tom Jones* [...] would seem to exemplify a principle of considerable significance for the novel form in general: namely, that the importance of the plot is in inverse proportion to that of character. [... T]he organisation of the narrative into an extended and complex structure will tend to turn the protagonists into its passive agents, but will offer compensatingly greater opportunities for the introduction of a variety of minor characters, whose treatment will not be hampered in the same way by the roles which they are allotted by the complications of the narrative design. The principle and its corollary would seem to lie behind Coleridge's contrast of the 'forced and unnatural quality' of the scenes between the protagonists in *Tom Jones* and Fielding's treatment of the 'characters of postilions, landlords, landladies, waiters' where 'nothing can be more true, more happy or more humorous'. These minor characters figure only in scenes which require exactly the amount of psychological individuality which they are possessed of; relieved of any responsibility for carrying out the major narrative design, Mrs. Honour can get herself dismissed from the Western household by methods which are at once triumphantly comic, sociologically perceptive and eminently characteristic.[62]

In Watt's schema of plot and character, every plot device, and every new setting or social interaction involved in the progression of the plot, is an opportunity for the writer to introduce a new 'minor character', or to tell an anecdote about an already established one; and the non-protagonist character's power to divert is bound up with its status as a digression. Romantic character talk, however, has a long-standing alternative perspective on the eighteenth-century British novel's supposed innovations in plot-construction: Winchester's caricature talk about 'Sir Roger' in 1904 resonates with Coleridge's remarks about 'Mercutio', his seventh lecture on Shakespeare, in linking the amiability of the non-protagonist character to the impact of narrative realism.

Coleridge's commentary on the strong characters in *Romeo and Juliet* somewhat resembles the 'character appreciation' genre, in that he is ready to appreciate character eccentricities in terms of the complexity of the human mind. He celebrates characteristic comic dialogue for its 'truth' in distinctly representing different operations of the human mental faculty. Coleridge also acknowledges that peculiar or 'irregular' characters can serve to make plots more plausible and emotionally interesting (Mercutio, and the narrative consequences of Romeo's friendship with him), as well as indirectly characterising protagonists (the nurse, and her contrast with Juliet). The plot's structure may not require the non-protagonists' interesting peculiarities, but the plot's significance and realism can rely on them. Coleridge points out that the plot of *Romeo and Juliet*, in the inciting action of Tybalt's killing, depends not just on Mercutio's death, but on his character. Peculiarity of character renders Mercutio's death interesting, important and a plausible cause of Romeo's switch from self-absorbed lover to vengeful friend:

> Shakspere's favourite characters are full of such lively intellect. Mercutio is a man possessing all the elements of a poet: the whole word was, as it were, subject to his law of association. Whenever he wishes to impress anything, all things become his servants for the purpose: all things tell the same tale, and sound in unison. This faculty, moreover, is combined with the manners and feelings of a perfect gentleman, himself utterly unconscious of his powers. By his loss it was contrived that the whole catastrophe of the tragedy should be brought about: it endears him to Romeo, and gives to the death of Mercutio an importance which it could not otherwise have acquired.
>
> I say this in answer to an observation, I think by Dryden (to which indeed Dr. Johnson has fully replied), that Shakspere having carried the part of Mercutio as far as he could, till his genius was exhausted, had killed him in the third Act, to get him out of the way. What shallow nonsense! As I have remarked, upon the death of Mercutio the whole catastrophe depends; it is produced by it. The scene in which it occurs serves to show how indifference to any subject but one, and aversion to activity on the part of Romeo, may be overcome and roused to the most resolute and determined conduct. Had not Mercutio been rendered so amiable and so interesting, we could not have felt so strongly the necessity for Romeo's interference, connecting it immediately, and passionately, with the future fortunes of the lover and his mistress.[63]

Put another way, 'we' understand that Romeo kills Tybalt because Mercutio is Romeo's particular favourite, and we find the action convincing because Mercutio is our favourite too. Romantic character criticism insists that fictive characters can be the objects of our love, and occasion our sense of loss when they fictitiously die. While Coleridge does not address how favouritism for Mercutio might interact with emotional responses to the lovers' deaths at the close of the narrative, it is implicit in his commentary that the more one cares about Mercutio, the more one will be convinced of the tragic necessity of the play's final events, which represent Romeo and Juliet's failure to overcome the separation imposed by Romeo's revenge for Mercutio. One's emotional response to the lovers' deaths might be intensified and complicated by the textual and diegetic 'precedence' of the stronger 'favourite' character.

For readers familiar with the caricature talk that mediated the *Spectator* in the Romantic period, the death of Sir Roger was famously affecting.

While the character's appearances in the *Spectator* did not form a novelistic plot, 'killing' Sir Roger offered something like a sense of narrative closure. The character's death acted as emotional punctuation, inviting readers to reflect on the pleasure they had taken in Sir Roger, to contemplate his finitude and experience a semblance of loss; asking readers to feel satisfied by a 'natural ending' to Addison and Steele's papers, and to feel the twinge of one emotion accompanying another, when amusement at Edward Biscuit's letter and Sir Roger's marginalia is swiftly displaced by grief:

> This Letter, notwithstanding the poor Butler's Manner of writing it, gave us such an Idea of our good old Friend, that upon the reading of it there was not a dry Eye in the Club. Sir Andrew opening the Book, found it to be a Collection of Acts of Parliament. There was in particular the Act of Uniformity, with some Passages in it marked by Sir Roger's own Hand. Sir Andrew found that they related to two or three points, which he had disputed with Sir Roger the last time he appeared at the Club. Sir Andrew, who would have been merry at such an Incident on another Occasion, at the sight of the old Man's Hand-writing burst into Tears, and put the Book into his Pocket (no. 517, Addison).

In *The British Essayists*, Chalmers claims that 'it is universally agreed that [the killing of Sir Roger] produced a paper of transcendant [sic] excellence in all the graces of simplicity and pathos. There is not in our language any assumption of character more faithful than that of the honest butler, nor a more irresistible stroke of nature than the circumstance of the book received by Sir Andrew Freeport'.[64] Readers committed no. 517 to memory, able to recall details of incident: Sir Roger writing his will on a cold day and leaving warm clothing to everyone in the parish, Sir Andrew Freeport putting the book in his pocket. The description of Sir Andrew weeping openly over Sir Roger's handwriting in the *Acts of Parliament* prompts the *Spectator*'s readers to recognise their own emotional sensitivity to such mundane and characteristic textual details in a context of mortality and loss. Finalising its characterisation of Sir Roger with his fictitious death, rather than with a more arbitrary textual truncation, the *Spectator* invites readers to discern the full extent of their love for Sir Roger, now that he exists both as 'such an Idea of our good old Friend' – particularised, static, immortal – and as a real departed presence, here and gone. By reading, re-reading and remembering Sir Roger's life and death in the *Spectator*, the Romantic character-reader experiences a cycle of love, loss and relief, ultimately reassured by the permanence of their idea of Sir Roger as much as his permanence in the pages of the *Spectator*.

The continued reading of Addison's and Steele's essays in the Romantic period, and the emergence of Romantic character criticism about Sir Roger, established the *Spectator* as a gold standard for realist characterisation, a centennial 'favourite' against which nineteenth-century novelists might test their own strong characters. While the *Spectator*'s critical reception primed readers (and would-be writers) to think that memorable non-protagonist characters were unique assets to novelistic realism, the durability of the character-centric *Spectator*'s critical acclaim and high market value made it clear that 'favourite' characters were a good commercial investment for authors seeking to attract and sustain a readership.[65]

Caricature talk continued to insist on 'originality' throughout the nineteenth century in large part because readers continued to speculate on characters' 'originals' – after all, as discussed in Chapter 2, it was possible to discover extra-textual evidence that a writer had based a strong character on a real person. Saintsbury, in 1920, decries 'this search for "the original"' as 'the least valuable' of 'the bootless quests that literary criticism can undertake' – and yet the quest was a popular one. In 1884–85, Lord Brabourne's edition of previously unpublished correspondence by Jane Austen raised a flutter of curiosity among literary journalists and Janeites. T. E. Kebbel imagines that Austen, her writing process continually interrupted by neighbours, would have been 'rewarded for her self-possession by finding that many of her morning visitors were qualified to serve as models; and that, while she seemed to be listening with ready politeness to the gossip of some village bore, she was quietly taking his likeness, and forming in her own mind a Mr. Collins or a Miss Bates'.[66]

But readers' concern with 'real characters' was not necessarily, as Saintsbury implies, an unsophisticated reading that devalued an author's originality. When an article in the *Standard* stokes interest in Brabourne's edition, the emphasis is just as much on Austen's 'humour at work' as the identification of originals. Readers, the *Standard* implies, are interested in these letters because they preserve a trace of Austen's mental process in a singular originative moment. The letters might offer not an insight into the extended process of writing a novel, but a glimmer of creativity itself, the fantasised moment when a character comes into the world:

> Will these Letters display Miss Austen's humour at work upon real character, and exhibit her in the act of filling in a Mrs. Norris or a Mr. Elton from among her own acquaintances? To judge from some of the published Letters, we should say this is very likely. And if the anticipation is well founded, the promised volume should be one of the most delightful in the language.[67]

It is easy to misrepresent such remarks as the idle curiosity of readers with a simplistic understanding of literature. However, through the lens of Romantic caricature talk described in this chapter – its concepts of originality, realism and favouritism – the nuances of this language-game come into focus. The *Standard* reviewer anticipates Austen's letters being superlatively 'the most delightful' not, I argue, because readers in the 1880s were interested in Hampshire folk who lived a hundred years ago, but because they might witness the inception of their favourite characters. As the *Spectator*'s ideal of character-creation contains the necessity of an author who, like the Spectator, excels in observing and listening, so – conversely – the quest for 'the original' contains the desire to see the first textual trace of pure creative energy invisibly meeting raw materials.

My aim is not to argue that the *Spectator*'s comic non-protagonist characters directly influenced the distinctive Romantic-period realisms that I analyse in this book. My point is that the *Spectator* – its characterisation techniques, its ideals of character-writing and its critical reception as a model for strong characters starting in the late eighteenth century – is powerfully representative of the Romantic-period novel's inheritance from eighteenth-century literature's diverse combinations of character-writing with formal realism.

Part II explores how that inheritance is selectively re-purposed and recontextualised by caricature talk combining with characterisation technique in the realisms of Jane Austen, Walter Scott and Mary Shelley. As compared with the *Spectator*'s realism of character, Scott substitutes history for contemporaneity; moves from the *Spectator*'s limited social variety to a compendium of ethnic, regional, religious and professional characteristics; and plans, especially in the Magnum Opus editions, for the impending obsolescence of strongly historical characters.

Shelley might not seem to inherit much from the *Spectator*'s model of character realism: *Frankenstein* and 'Transformation' lack comic non-protagonist characters, and resemble Gothic tales more than 'English classics' by Fielding or Smollett. No source from the Romantic period admits to acquiring a 'favourite' from *Frankenstein*. But it is significant that Shelley's experiments in horror fiction develop writing techniques for a 'horrid realism' that happens to invert the concept of using particularised and varied characters to create pseudo-sensory pleasure – eliciting pseudo-sensory revulsion by continually drawing legible 'character' into tension with the heterogenous particulars of the material body.

For Austen, on the other hand, the fat body is legible within a concept of caricature as the aesthetic effect of self-indulgence. Under the aegis of this ethics of caricature, Austen carries techniques for strong characterisation: her realism is put forward as accurate narration of a social phenomenon of people who 'really' think, speak, look and occupy space in 'caricatured' ways. Touting the new comic realism of Burney and Edgeworth, *Northanger Abbey* openly names the *Spectator* as the dotard of the genre, now coasting on a reputation for 'wit and humour' combined with 'knowledge of human nature' and the 'delineation of its varieties'. Austen seems unimpressed by decades of praise for the *Spectator*'s characters. Others might claim that Sir Roger is immortal; Austen recognises that strong characters must be reconceived for a new age.

PART II

Novel Caricatures

Caricature Talk and Characterisation Technique

What does the caricature talk of the Romantic period have to do with literary criticism's persistent notion of 'caricature' as a technique or style of characterisation in an author's work? Does caricature have a formal existence, a set of stylistic markers, which can be identified in fictive characters across literary works?

Most of the time, this book keeps 'caricature' shut up in inverted commas to remind us that authors and critics have different concepts of caricature, rather than caricature being a discrete genre, technique or other object of analysis. But this is not to say that caricature talk has no relationship with novelists' characterisation techniques; on the contrary, when novelists use the language-game of character talk, use caricature talk and anti-caricature rhetoric in their writings – as they often do – caricature talk helps constitute literary character for realism.

There is no 'caricature-writing' technique or style without a corresponding 'caricature-reading' method dictated by caricature talk. The incorporation of caricature talk into novels recognises that exaggeration, humour and satire are contingent on cultural specifics (regional, historical, linguistic) and that responsibly 'real' (realist) fiction might find ways to tell readers when, how and why exaggeration, humour and satire are happening in the text. With caricature talk being necessarily always about things other than caricature (gender, ethnicity, nation, class, morality, civility), in the realist novel it recommends particular characterisation techniques and styles as just and accurate representations of such things. Whereas some realisms are quite ready to assume that the reader shares, to a greater or lesser extent, the author's view of real people's characters, other realisms scrupulously provide terms of caricature talk for the reader. Caricature talk puts the -ism in character realism. Caricature talk 'tells' us about the characterisation techniques with which the author supposedly 'shows' us characters.

Chapter 4 in particular illustrates this principle, analysing how caricature talk co-operates with characterisation technique in Austen's novels.

We are told in *Sense and Sensibility* that John Dashwood's new wife is a 'strong caricature of himself'; and in *Pride and Prejudice*, when Mr Bennet is compared with his wife, that '[*h*]*er* mind was less difficult to develope'. We are told, in *Emma*, that Miss Bates is humorous to imitate; we are told, in *Sanditon*, that Charlotte can 'scarce keep her countenance' around Arthur Parker. Austen's moral concept of caricature participates in such moments that tell the reader how to read characters. In Chapter 5, I turn my attention to Scott's use of caricature talk to construct historical characters for compendious realism. Chapter 6 looks at Shelley's and Scott's use of literalised caricature in 'horrid realism', contemplating the effacement of character by physical peculiarity. Wherever caricature talk tells us how to read characters, framing them as comic, historical or grotesque, fiction manipulates and manufactures the reader's sense of a social reality shared with the author.

CHAPTER 4

Jane Austen and Anti-caricature

Critics have often claimed that Jane Austen 'never stooped to caricature',[1] and that avoidance of caricature made her fiction superior and distinctively 'natural' in its realism. The first part of this chapter traces the development of a critical tradition which, in the nineteenth century and beyond, insisted on Austen's 'delicacy' and 'accuracy', and posited caricature as the antithesis of her literary achievement. More than any other novelist of the period, Austen has been seen as fundamentally 'anti-caricature'. I argue that the critical tradition's tendency to deny caricature in Austen's works has substantially helped to secure the reputation of her realism: critics continually use anti-caricature rhetoric to express the author's exemplary femininity and promote a homogeneous Englishness – picking up on the vocabulary and imagery of the 'snug' aesthetic that the novels themselves present as metonymic of their distinctive reality. Moving on to twentieth-century criticism and recent studies more sceptical of the anti-caricature consensus, I consider how the critical tradition has used 'caricature' to distinguish Austen's early works from the mature novels and to position *Sanditon* as an outlier.

I offer a new definition of Austen's 'anti-caricature' in the second part of this chapter, refocusing the discussion on the moral concept of caricature that operates within Austen's novels, and showing how caricature talk works in concert with characterisation techniques. I examine how the narrator's 'character appreciations' take the word 'caricature' for ethical criticism, modelling the language-game of talking about fictional characters as though they were real people and vice versa. I argue that in Austen's realism, caricature is the aesthetic effect of self-interestedness, is self-reflexive and self-inflicted. Austen's textual styling of character is bound up with her moral concept of caricature, so that the writer's comic and satirical characterisation techniques can pretend to be ethical criticism of real people. Thus Austen's characters are 'explained caricatures'; by this sleight of hand, realism substitutes humour and satire for reportage and analysis.

To look in detail at this co-operation of caricature talk and characterisation technique, I explore how Austen's moral concept of self-reflexive caricature interacts with characterisation techniques in Austen's depictions of fat bodies. I argue that Austen deploys an ethics of fatness in conjunction with formal techniques that represent fat bodies as comic, making 'corpulence' representative of the 'real' or 'explained' caricature. Discussing the key stylistic features Austen typically uses in dialogue to characterise the explained caricature – prolonging, repeating, reiterating – I demonstrate that the third-person narrator shifts into that same formal pattern when she talks about fatness and fat bodies. This stylistic resonance between narrator and caricature, I suggest, makes openings for the reader to identify Austen's fat-hating as an eccentricity and subject it to ethical or psychological criticism.

While Austen's reputation as a superlatively feminine and English realist has insisted on her refusal to caricature, in fact her novels present their own characterisation techniques under the aegis of a moral concept of caricature, telling readers what 'caricature' means in the social world that Austen's realism purports to show them. Through caricature talk, Austen's realism offers readers the pleasure of comic and satiric characterisations packaged as accurate, instructive and morally principled, where 'explained caricatures' are supposed to pre-exist the text as objects of ethical or psychological criticism. My broader argument about caricature talk's constitution of realism responds to Jane Stabler's provocative insight that Austen's novels show how 'our notion of realistic characterization needs to include caricature, not exclude it'.[2]

Looking beyond Austen, the 'anti-caricature' of nineteenth-century realism has less to do with the avoidance of caricature through 'restraint' or 'simplicity' of technique or style, than with the appropriate framing of characterisation techniques through caricature talk. The artifice of a writer's comic or satiric characterisation can be naturalised, rationalised and moralised into the 'explained caricatures' of a reality supposedly already populated by caricatures, where distortions of character are attributed to the external and internal forces that shape people.

Austen in the 'Age of Caricature'

The phrase 'the Age of Caricature' has done some heavy lifting where critics have wanted to align the characterisation techniques of Austen's writing with the distinctive features of late-Georgian satirical prints. Asking for Austen to be recognised and admired as a 'caricaturist',

Donald Greene writes: 'One needs to remember that she grew up in the great age of English caricature, when Hogarth's engravings were on every wall, and Gillray, Rowlandson, and the Cruikshanks were producing their twisted, grotesque distortions of the human frame.'[3] Though it is reasonable to assume that Austen would have come across single-sheet satirical prints (perhaps pasted to a wall or screen, or interleaved with cuttings and drawings in a borrowed portfolio), it is more difficult to ascertain what 'caricature' her writing could have gained from satirical prints that it did not gain from elsewhere. As yet, we have no concrete evidence – textual or material – of Austen's engagement with the single-sheet satirical print, a genre with socio-economic contexts and formal properties that should complicate our assumptions about how late-Georgian graphic caricature parallels contemporaneous comic and satirical literary works. 'Hogarth and Gillray' is itself a problematic pairing for the Romantic period; so too, I think, is 'Gillray and Austen'.

Later in this chapter, I briefly refer to John Kay's caricature portraits and to Diana Beauclerk's and Lavinia Spencer's caricature drawings of Edward Gibbon as a counterpoint to Austen's characterisation of fat bodies as explained caricatures; I suggest some nuances in the ways that late-Georgian parliamentary satirical prints use fatness and thinness; and I point the reader to new studies of fatness in Georgian culture. So, I do address the 'visualising' aspects of Austen's representation of fat bodies as caricatures – without fully exploring parallels in contemporaneous graphic caricature or visual culture more broadly. Readers looking for analyses of Austen's writing alongside particular satirical prints might start with Rachel Brownstein's 2015 article 'Character and Caricature: Jane Austen and James Gillray' and Jane Stabler's 2007 article 'Jane Austen and Caricature'. Readers who want to know about possible links between Austen and graphic caricature might consider Cassandra Austen's portrait of her sister, and their collaborative *History of England*, in relation to the amateur caricaturing I discuss in Chapter 1.

I am cautious of relying on the 'Age of Caricature' as a context for literature's caricature as it existed during roughly the same historical period. But the phrase has enabled, in Austen's case, some scepticism of the 'anti-caricature' rhetoric in the critical tradition and some willingness to contemplate how caricature might be constructive in literary texts. This is because print historians' work and consequent increased scholarly interest in Georgian satirical prints has made *caricature* a less dirty word in eighteenth- and nineteenth-century literary studies. 'Fifty years ago',

Brownstein points out, 'it would have been unthinkable to speak in the same breath, or the same paper, as Jane Austen and [graphic] caricature'.[4] Analysing Austen's writing alongside prints by James Gillray, Brownstein suggests that Austen 'saw caricature as a mode of characterization'.[5] We need not establish direct influences or shared contexts, to gain insights from the comparison of textual and pictorial characterisation.

While my approach does not put Austen and graphic satirists on parallel tracks, for reasons discussed here and in Chapter 1, I share other critics' interest in stepping away from the debate over which of Austen's characters are 'caricatures' and when – to think instead about caricature in terms of forms and concepts, in ways facilitated by exploring what caricature means in different media and contexts of the late-Georgian period.

Austen and Anti-caricature

Before surveying the longer critical tradition on caricature in Austen's novels, I want to consider a manuscript that registers Austen's interest in how her comic and satirically rendered characters were received by her first readers. The text, untitled by Austen, is known as 'Opinions of Mansfield Park and Opinions of Emma' (British Library, Add. MSS. 41253A). 'Opinions' ostensibly transcribes the opinions of other people, but inevitably it is Austen's reception of her reception: at least partly a subjective interpretation of the opinions' content, and probably using some of Austen's own vocabulary and linguistic constructions. For one thing, the Opinions are written in the third person, suggesting that verbatim transcription was not Austen's overriding priority. It is impossible to know either how closely the Opinions reflect the readers' original responses, or how spontaneous or authentic those opinions were to begin with. Did they come to Austen via letters, or in conversation? Did Austen actively elicit them, and did she question friends and family on particular topics? In the absence of evidence on such issues, I understand the Opinions as 'belonging' to their author. This is literally true of the manuscript – but the opinions also belong to Austen in the sense that she believed them worth shaping into a private document for (presumably) some combination of self-reflection and self-congratulation on her authorship. Seen this way, the Opinions are all the more helpful as a document for understanding how Austen might have used caricature talk for comic and satiric characterisation in anticipation of the reception of her novels by contemporary readers.

The Opinions pay ample attention to the comically and satirically rendered characters in *Pride and Prejudice*, *Mansfield Park* and *Emma*. In this respect, the Opinions present *Emma* – a novel that twentieth-century critics have often seen as Austen's subtlest, most restrained and 'mature' work – as relatively slim pickings after *Pride and Prejudice*. Austen notes her friends and family apparently seizing on Mrs Elton and Miss Bates as highlights, with one reader 'delighted with Miss Bates, but thought Mrs Elton the best-drawn Character in the book'. One declares that 'Miss Bates is incomparable'; another that, on reading *Emma* a second time, they 'liked Miss Bates much better than at first'. Phrases evocative of 'strong' characters, and familiar tropes from anti-caricature rhetoric, appear in words and phrases such as 'rather too much', 'highly-drawn', 'strongly marked' and 'interesting', as opposed to 'natural' – without using the words 'overcharged' or 'caricature', which would judge unequivocally that Austen had gone too far. References to comic exaggeration and satirical emphasis are carefully understated and balanced by praise in opinions such as 'Miss Bates excellent, but rather too much of her' and a diplomatic statement attributed to Anna Lefroy, that the characters in *Emma* are 'perhaps less strongly marked than some, but only the more natural for that reason—Mr Knightley Mrs Elton & Miss Bates her favourites'. Austen records a blunter opinion about the effect of the characterisations in *Emma*: Mrs Guiton apparently 'thought her [Emma] too natural to be interesting'. Austen's mother similarly finds *Emma* 'not so interesting as P. & P.', a judgement recorded in proximity to her remark that there are 'no characters in it equal to Ly Catherine & Mr Collins'. This disappointment with *Emma*'s characters is echoed by a contemporaneous review in the *Gentleman's Magazine*, that the latest novel 'has not the highly-drawn characters' of *Pride and Prejudice*.[6]

When it comes to *Mansfield Park*, the Opinions seem to dwell on readers' reactions to the character most emphatically presented as comic and satirical, Mrs Norris. One reader 'admired [the novel] very much—particularly Mrs Norris'; other opinions are: 'Delighted with Mrs Norris', 'Enjoyed Mrs Norris', 'Mrs Norris is a great favourite of mine'. Did Austen seek opinions about Mrs Norris specifically, because Mrs Norris was a great favourite of *hers* or because she was concerned that she might have gone too far in creating such a 'strongly marked' character? At any rate, the Opinions suggest an author conscious that 'favourites' are a crucial part of her literary achievement; and if we own that Austen's novels might have been shaped by anticipating and responding to feedback from family and friends, she was not under pressure to excise all 'caricature' from her novels – quite the opposite.

This chapter argues that Austen's 'anti-caricature' is not, and has never been, the mere avoidance of techniques that could be described as 'caricaturing'. In the critical tradition, anti-caricature is the strategic insistence on Austen's understatement and her supposed avoidance of caricature; in Austen's writing practice, 'anti-caricature' is the strategic overstatement of literary understatement, and the framing of 'explained caricatures' as referential to a real social world. While my account, in the next few pages, of how literary critics have insisted on the femininity and 'delicacy' of Austen's satire, might give the impression that 'anti-caricature' was a set of ideas *imposed* on her work, I will be arguing later that anti-caricature was – as the Opinions suggest – intrinsic to Austen's realism.

Anti-caricature and Femininity in the Early Critical Tradition

From the 1820s to the mid-twentieth century, critics frequently complimented Austen on her avoidance of caricature. Sometimes they did so with relatively gender-neutral language. *The Retrospective Review* refrains from many tropes of femininity that would become associated with Austen's anti-caricature, when it positions the author – who by 1823 had been dead for several years – as a contemporary cultural touchstone: 'In the lively and spirited caricatures of Evelina and Cecilia, we may see the style of portrait-painting relished by our fathers. Turning from them to the soberly coloured and faithful likenesses of Jane Austen, we may behold that approved by ourselves.'[7] Most of the time, however, anti-caricature was bundled up with femininity and domesticity. Richard Whately, in 1829, uses a range of phrases linking anti-caricature and femininity that would become clichés in later nineteenth-century criticism on Austen: he praises the author's 'accurate and unexaggerated delineation of events and characters', her 'minute fidelity of detail' and 'minute fidelity to nature'.[8] George Henry Lewes, in 1859, maintains that in *Emma*, Mrs Elton's vulgarity is never tainted 'by caricature of any kind'.[9] Julia Kavanagh approves Austen's 'most delicate portrait of character [...] no caricature, no exaggeration'; Margaret Oliphant approves her 'finesse' and 'self-restraint' in creating works so 'softly feminine and polite'.[10] Words such as 'gentleness', 'softness', 'delicacy', 'minuteness', 'neatness', 'nicety', 'precision', 'exactness', 'faithfulness' – referring to literary works by women – insistently cluster together, fabricating a femininity for anti-caricature.

Based on the claim that she avoided caricature, Austen was favourably contrasted to other women novelists, as in *The Retrospective Review*'s opposition of Fanny Burney's 'caricatures' to Austen's 'likenesses'. Anna Laetitia Barbauld, who was generally wary in her *British Novelists* essays of the potential vulgarity of literary caricature, notes Burney's use of different linguistic registers for 'vulgar characters'; and *The Retrospective Review* deprecates Burney's 'exaggeration of nature' and 'everlasting sameness of character', reprising the theme of Horace Walpole's observation that Burney 'never lets [characters] say a syllable but what is to mark their character, which is very unnatural'.[11] This contrast with Burney's 'caricatures' continued to feature in Austen's reception throughout the nineteenth century. In 1843, Thomas Babington Macaulay contrasts Burney's 'extravagantly overcharged' characters to Austen's 'touches so delicate [...] that we know them to exist only by the general effect to which they have contributed'.[12] In 1862, Julia Kavanagh notes Burney's 'turn for caricature', supposing that her ability to 'verg[e] on caricature' secured her more popularity than Charlotte Smith, whose best characters are 'wholly free from caricature or exaggeration'.[13] A reviewer for *The Standard* judges Austen's work, with its 'rarest delicacy and refinement of mind [...] more subdued and subtle than Miss Burney's', in 1884.[14] Susan Ferrier and Maria Edgeworth were also perceived as less womanly for the 'breadth' and 'force' of their fictional characterisations. Edgeworth is accused of caricature as early as 1815, when a writer for *The Edinburgh Review* observes that Edgeworth's characters 'are all caricatures [...] distinctly marked'.[15] In 1834, praising Austen's 'delicate mirth [...] gently hinted satire [...] feminine decorous humour', Sara Coleridge writes that 'Austen's works are essentially feminine, but the best part of Miss Edgeworth's seem as if they had been written by a man'.[16] Mary Ward, in 1884, comments that in Ferrier's novels, 'everything is done to death [...] everything superabundant and second-rate'.[17]

Austen herself would have recognised the rhetoric in this gendering of delicacy, which reveres and belittles simultaneously. In a much-quoted letter to her nephew, Austen compares her writing to a bird's building of a humble nest, and to a miniature-painter working on a 'little bit (two Inches wide) of Ivory [...] with so fine a Brush, as produces little effect after much labour'.[18] It was a short step from the miniaturist's two inches of ivory – small, delicate, private – to the hinged sets of ivory tablets (polyptychs) where women's memoranda were pencilled and effaced. One example of a simple two-leaf ivory memorandum tablet, made in London circa 1760, was kept in an agate mounted dressing case or necessaire among toiletries and other personal items.[19] Ivory memorandum tablets and miniatures were, to pun on Austen's phrase, 'little effects', kept close to the body, their contents concealed by hinged lids. By the time Austen described her work this way, in 1816, she had published several novels. Her self-deprecating imagery in this letter – 'a Nest of my own' – can be read both as humorously exaggerated humility and as appropriately feminine self-effacement, in a personal missive that depends on the existing understanding between sender and receiver for the (in)stability of its meaning. Critics in the nineteenth century take these images seriously as fitting metaphors for the supposed domesticity, simplicity and finitude of Austen's work, as when R. H. Hutton locates her appeal in 'the reduced scale [...] of her exquisite pictures', their 'delicate touches' and 'lightest tracing' made by a 'fine feminine sieve'.[20] Many refer to her novels as miniatures, while James Edward Leigh in 1869 and Anne Thackeray in 1871 compare a novel to a nest 'which some little bird builds of the materials nearest at hand [...] curiously constructed out of the simplest matters', imagining Austen's literary work as a confined yet cosy habitation.[21]

When we date these metaphors of homemaking and handiwork that appear in anti-caricature rhetoric about Austen's novels, it seems that they were facilitated by posthumous accounts of Austen's domestic and feminine virtues: the 'dear Aunt Jane' of Austen-Leigh's 1869 memoir. Thus, in an essay responding to the memoir, Richard Simpson links Austen's novel-writing to her domestic offices: 'Her handwriting was beautiful, her needlework delicate. She was neat-handed in any operation that required steadiness and precision.'[22] The critical tradition associates Austen's anti-caricature with the respectable labours permitted to gentility – pencil-drawing, letter-writing, needlework – using imagery and idioms relating to hands, or which imply the action of fingers, such as the word 'touches'. Critics' references to genteel femininity and respectability, both explicit and implicit, dovetail with defences of Austen's reputation against accusations of 'caricature'. As discussed in Chapter 1, pictorial caricaturing was associated with the social and political elite; it was primarily through the novel, where writers seemed often to slip into 'caricature' when focusing on lower-class, provincial or criminal characters, that textual caricature became strongly associated with vulgarity. When E. M. Forster recognises, in 1927, the century-long consensus that Austen 'never stooped to caricature', his choice of image – physical abasement – captures the critical tradition's suspicion of the ways literary works seemed to lower themselves to the level of the 'vulgar' people whom genteel writers represented in caricatured ways. Austen did not deal in such 'vulgar' characters; nor did she deal in foreign ones.

'Pure English': Anti-caricature in Austen's Novels

In 1818, after twenty years of commercial success and critical attention for novels set in European, Irish and Scottish locations, *The Edinburgh Magazine* looks forward to a new cycle in literary fashion: unmixed Englishness. In an essay on *Northanger Abbey* and *Persuasion*, the writer admits to being wearied of the national peculiarities of vulgar characters exhibited in some contemporary novels. Austen's novels, plainer and simpler, 'have fallen [...] upon an age whose taste can only be gratified by the highest seasoned food'. Austen will only be fully appreciated once readers return to the fictional English characters – 'the Partridges and the Trullibers [...] the Clementinas and Clarissas', that made them laugh 'while [they] could enjoy a work that was written all in pure English, without ever dreaming how great would be the embellishment to have at least one half of it in the dialect of Scotland or of Ireland'.[23] Indeed, Austen's characters typically return from their travels beyond England's borders apparently 'uncoloured' by their experience, literally and figuratively. Austen's Colonel Brandon, blandly 'not unpleasing', returns from India with no peculiarities, no talk of '"nabobs, gold mohrs, and palanquins"'; whereas Scott's nabob Touchwood in *Saint Ronan's Well* is full of his acquired knowledge, his face 'burned to a brick-colour' and 'seamed by a million of wrinkles'.[24] In 1818, readers were still avidly consuming art and literature set in strange times and exotic places with characters to match, and Austen's novels could easily be seen as lacking interest because they exclude foreign picturesque and peculiarity.

Austen's choice to set every one of her novels in England – a deliberate, even contrarian, choice for the time – fits with her self-reflexive presentation of her writing as adhering to an aesthetic of cultivation and habitation. This 'snug' aesthetic specifically idealises rural southern England, as a cultivated and productive yet tidy and comfortable landscape, organised by working estates, farms and dwellings. In *Sense and Sensibility*, Elinor's future husband delivers a manifesto of the snug:

> '"I like a fine prospect, but not on picturesque principles. I do not like crooked, twisted, blasted trees. I admire them much more if they are tall, straight, and flourishing. I do not like ruined, tattered cottages. I am not fond of nettles, or thistles, or heath blossoms. I have more pleasure in a snug

farmhouse than a watch-tower—and a troop of tidy, happy villagers please me better than the finest banditti in the world.'"[25]

The land is beautiful because it is worked, because it is good and useful. Walking purposelessly around an unproductive landscape is, for Austen's characters, a dangerous sign: we are told that Catherine Morland is not a sedentary person, and that she is not industrious, in the same breath. Weighing up Catherine's 'defects of that sort', Mrs Morland 'could not but perceive them now to be greatly increased. [...] In her rambling and her idleness she [was] a caricature of herself'.[26] Her mother tells her, '"there is a time for work"' and '"now you must try to be useful"'. Since Catherine Morland lacks the mountains or moorland that would necessitate real 'rambling' and make a fitting backdrop for the feelings of a romantic heroine, she wanders sadly around her family's comfortable house and productive orchard. In her purposeless, twisting and circular path, 'caricature' Catherine is out of step with the order and practicality of her surroundings.

Edward Ferrars's descriptions of English landscape in *Sense and Sensibility* can be read as the kind of satire on eighteenth-century picturesque conventions that had itself become conventional and even affected. Elinor says as much (jokingly) to Edward and Marianne: '"Because he believes many people pretend to more admiration of the beauties of nature than they really feel [...] he affects greater indifference and less discrimination in viewing them himself than he possesses"'. Edward, however, positively asserts his preference for the snug aesthetic, his right to discriminate in favour of neatness, utility and comfort:

> 'I shall call hills steep, which ought to be bold; surfaces strange and uncouth, which ought to be irregular and rugged; and distant objects out of sight, which ought only to be indistinct through the soft medium of a hazy atmosphere. I call it a very fine country—the hills are steep, the woods seem full of fine timber, and the valley looks comfortable and snug—with rich meadows and several neat farmhouses scattered here and there. It exactly answers my idea of a fine country because it unites beauty with utility.'[27]

The aesthetic includes preferences for language as well as for landscape: preferences for specific items of vocabulary, and also high tolerance for repetition of general terms of approbation. Edward forgoes 'bold' for 'steep', 'rugged' for 'strange' and 'indistinct' for 'out of sight'; he uses the word 'fine' four times and 'snug' twice in the space of a few sentences. His contentedness with unpoetic and unpretentious language aligns the snug aesthetic with 'plain English', disdaining the artifice that 'caricatures' nature by striving for great effects.

The English landscape is aligned in *Northanger Abbey*, too, with a nature enclosed and made safe and useful. Henry Tilney ironically invites Catherine to imagine 'a piece of rocky fragment and [...] withered oak' to romanticise the summit of Beechen Cliff; he then transitions to instructing Catherine and Eleanor on 'forests, the inclosure of them, waste lands, crown lands and government'. Following this discussion of land management issues, Tilney's speech aimed at dispelling Catherine's Gothic illusions ('"Remember the country and the age in which we live. Remember that we are English, that we are Christians"') maps out a landscape of enclosed fields, open roads and watchful neighbours. To the south, to the north, and to the west, the landscapes might be mountainous and the people monstrous – these are for other writers to exploit. Austen sets out her plot in a snugly enclosed 'midlands', all the more real for being in the middle, which still – as Catherine learns – has cruelty and inequality enough to furnish plots for a thousand and one English novels:

> Charming as were all Mrs. Radcliffe's works, and charming even as were the works of all her imitators, it was not in them perhaps that human nature, at least in the midland counties of England, was to be looked for. Of the Alps and the Pyrenees, with their pine forests and their vices, they might give a faithful delineation; and Italy, Switzerland, and the South of France, might be as fruitful in horrors as they were there represented. Catherine dared not doubt beyond her own country, and even of that, if hard pressed, would have yielded the northern and western extremities. But in the central part of England there was surely some security. [...] Among the Alps and Pyrenees, perhaps, there were no mixed characters. [...] But in England it was not so; among the English, she believed, in their hearts and habits, there was a general though unequal mixture of good and bad.[28]

The professed anti-caricature of Austen's work is perhaps most obviously spelled out here in *Northanger Abbey* and *Sense and Sensibility*, the first two full-length novels she completed, through the future husbands' pragmatic attitudes to rural landscape and to England. Contemporary readers could have recalled numerous examples of the sublime massifs in foreign lands that feature in Catherine and Isabella's favourite Gothic novels.

That kind of scenery, and its associations with 'horrors' and 'vices', are taken to the extreme in Matthew G. Lewis's *The Monk* (1796), John Thorpe's preferred reading material and the most notorious Gothic fiction of the 1790s. The story, set in Spain, chronicles the protagonist-villain Ambrosio's swift transformation from angelic to demonic. He signs his soul over to the Devil, writing in his own blood with an intravenous iron pen. In exchange, the Devil rescues Ambrosio from the Inquisition – but flies him straight from Madrid to the steepest part of the Sierra Morena. The novel culminates in a fantastic scene where the Devil drops the monk from 'a dreadful height'[29] onto the top of a mountain peak, and Ambrosio then dies slowly over the course of seven days, giving him full opportunity to experience sharp rocks, oppressive temperatures, bloodthirsty animals and torrential rain. In Lewis's enthusiastic parody of the Gothic sublime, the natural features that would usually impress the protagonist with exhilaration or dread become literally painful and deadly. Whereas a protagonist in a Radcliffean Gothic novel might be awed, yet excited, to see eagles at a distance, Ambrosio becomes their prey: as he lies paralysed with 'broken and dislocated limbs', '[t]he Eagles of the rock tore his flesh piecemeal, and dug out his eyeballs with their crooked beaks'.[30] Whereas a protagonist in a realist novel might become ill after being caught in the rain, in *The Monk* Ambrosio's body is carried away when a river burst its banks in a lightning storm. It can be read as a parody of the Gothic, as totally ridiculous; but read dramatically, with reverence, it could be Biblically serious; and staged and filmed as horror, it could be a straight-faced torture scene. In Austen's novels, injuries are incurred more by people's risk-taking than by the obstacles themselves: dangerous driving (e.g. *Northanger Abbey*, *Persuasion*) and attempting bad roads (*Sanditon*), jumping off steps onto hard pavements (*Persuasion*), sitting in wet grass and running at full speed down hills (*Sense and Sensibility*) are all dangerous enough. Austen's anti-caricature landscapes participate in the snug aesthetic while providing realistic dangers to move plots along.

By explaining and regularly emphasising the distinctive 'Englishness' of their aesthetic and subject matter, by setting themselves in opposition to the perceived exaggerations of the sentimental, the romantic and the Gothic, Austen's novels lay claim to their own representation of the real, one that is emphatically *not* the inclusively 'full and authentic report' of Watt's formal realism. There is much that the novels leave out – and these limitations and enclosures are explicitly part of the novels' anti-caricature reality, of their supposedly unmixed Englishness. Thus, Austen provides the vocabulary and the oppositions by which she wishes her novels to be defined. Scott's essay in the *Quarterly Review*, analysing the determined ordinariness of Austen's novelistic reality, uses language that might have come straight from Ferrars's manifesto: Austen's novels, he explains, 'bear the same relation to that of the sentimental and romantic cast, that cornfields and cottages and meadows bear to the highly adorned grounds of a show mansion, or the rugged sublimities of a mountain landscape.'³¹ *Sanditon* provides a comic dramatisation of this difference, in the Parkers' 'bad exchange' of a snug rural setting for a windswept coast. Their ancestral home is a 'moderate-sized house, well fenced & planted, & rich in the Garden, ~~Ground~~ <Orchard> & ~~Orchards~~ <Meadows>', situated in a 'sheltered Dip' which Tom describes as a '"contracted Nook, without Air or Veiw"' [sic]. His wife looks back at 'such an excellent Garden' as a paradise lost.³² Like Ferrars's manifesto, the novels are so consistent and unabashed in their purported aesthetic, that those who most disparage the snugness of Austen's fictional world are those who have seen its distinctive character most clearly. If Austen had heard of a reader's dislike for her 'carefully-fenced, highly-cultivated garden, with neat borders [...] no open country, no fresh air' (in Charlotte Brontë's phrase), she might have thought it a kind of compliment to her novels' declared differences to other novels.³³ Actually the novels' settings and aesthetic effects are more diverse than this – recall the Portsmouth scenes in *Mansfield Park*, or even the winding glen in Mr Darcy's Derbyshire estate in *Pride and Prejudice* – but Brontë has taken up Austen's own rhetoric and selection of imagery as metonymic for a novelistic reality that relies on limitations and exclusions.

Limitations placed on the English language – on a version of Southern Standard English, specifically – is another key facet of Austen's characterisation techniques interacting with caricature talk. The figures who would presumably speak most differently from the genteel characters on which the novels focus – servants, farmers, itinerants, the working poor – never speak even when named, as in *Mansfield Park* and *Emma*. For example, Austen avoids direct reportage of the speech and writing of two minor but key characters in *Emma*, the tenant farmer Robert Martin and Mr Knightley's bailiff William Larkins. Although Knightley's relative intimacy with these men helps characterise him as a responsible and kind landlord, their voices are not allowed to interrupt the novel's 'pure English' style. Austen's linguistic narrowness helps to avoid drastic switches between styles for characterisation, an effect that was criticised in Scott, whose interactions between 'high' and 'low' characters struck some readers as jarring mixtures of history, tragedy and comedy. At the same time, the linguistic homogeneity of Austen's novels increases readers' sensitivity to irony created through structural and quantitative variations in language (a technique long used in the writing of comic dialogue).³⁴ Rather than widely varying characters' vocabularies, or using orthographic difference to render characters' different phonetic realisations of the same words,

Austen uses 'disorganised' syntax, oral punctuation and repetition. W. F. Pollock, in 1860, contends that 'there are no catch words or phrases perpetually recurring from the same person' in Austen's novels, which is not true – but I agree with Mary Lascelle's statement that Austen individualises her characters in relatively 'low relief'.[35] Marilyn Butler, in her response to J. F. Burrows's findings that Austen's 'pure narrative' is interspersed with 'character narratives' more divergent and heterogenous than in the novels of Henry James, E. M. Forster and Virginia Woolf, points out that when Austen is compared with her contemporaries and with eighteenth-century novelists, her characters' dialogue actually appears relatively homogenous. Austen's dialogue, Butler argues, represents a change in the novel's well-established trade in peculiar characters: 'Minor characters become more vivacious, eccentric, linguistically distinctive as the 18th century wears on. [...] Novelists go on portraying the social panorama through minor characters' diversity until this dispersed, atomistic emphasis is superseded by a generalizing one.'[36]

Austen's writing in particular might be seen as a decisive move in that gradual shift towards linguistic generality in narrative fiction. As well as limiting linguistic variation in reported dialogue with speech tags, she famously uses a formal technique that encloses characters' voices and (incompletely) assimilates them to the narrator's voice: free indirect discourse has become nearly synonymous with Austen's name in anglophone literary criticism. I see Austen's version of free indirect discourse less as a method for ironically and subtly introducing characters' differences, more as a method of conservation for the purity of the narrator's style. As Frances Ferguson observes, 'the novel of free indirect style has characters and society speaking the same language',[37] whether that speech be 'real' and its rendering in the novel 'realistic' or not. The linguistic errors and tics of Austen's comic characters are actually more descriptive of spoken language, more realistic than the implausibly fluent speech of the serious characters – but in anti-caricature's contract with realism, linguistic features that are actually realistic and natural are prescriptively framed as distortions of the English language.

Many other factors can account for the qualities of Austen's English that I have discussed here: some critics have wondered, for example, whether Austen could reasonably have felt unable to represent 'low' characters convincingly, or politely. I have shown that her homogenisation of English – through the formal limits she places on text's capacity to represent linguistic variety, and through the techniques of free indirect discourse and free indirect style – aligns with her commitment to an aesthetic and a rhetoric of English anti-caricature. Austen's characterisations, I argue, are conscious of their tactical exclusions and assimilations. As incorporated in Austen's novels, anti-caricature strategically overstates realism's understatement.

Sanditon and Caricature's Threat to Permanence

Anti-caricature rhetoric has played a significant part in the critical tradition's efforts to justify a permanent place for Austen in English Literature. Macaulay contends, in his 1843 essay on Burney, that 'the chief seats' among the literary classics, 'the places on the dias and under the canopy, are reserved for the few who have excelled in the difficult art of portraying characters in which no single feature is extravagantly overcharged'.[38] Earlier reviewers trust that Austen's understated Englishness represents a return to the imagined timelessness of 'English classics'. In the *Edinburgh Magazine*, Austen's characters will join those of Fielding and Richardson as a source of 'permanent delight' and 'pure English' to be enjoyed by an intergenerational readership; in the *Retrospective Review*, Austen's characters surpass those 'spirited caricatures' beloved merely by 'our fathers'. Austen is both legitimised by a connection to the literary past and projected into the future, kept current by a readership that will always circle back to uncaricatured works of literary permanence while satirical 'temporary characters' and 'originals' grow ever less intelligible and amusing – at best, puzzling embellishments and textual hangers-on to a work still worth reading. Posterity is not kind to literary 'caricatures', as I discuss further in Chapter 5.

Towards the end of the nineteenth century, and on into the twentieth, critics increasingly concede to the presence of caricatures or 'caricature touches' in Austen, but typically contextualise them within the development of Austen's art over time. In 1870, Richard Simpson identifies a tendency to caricature in the early novels that is then surpassed: 'Miss Austen in her later novels has given us new and improved versions [of these characters ...] Sir Walter is a character constructed in the same way as Mr. Collins, with simpler means and less caricature.'[39] I disagree with this view of Sir Walter: it seems necessary to misconstrue or misremember characterisations in order to place the novels on what Donald Greene has described as the 'generally descending' curve on a graph of Austen's supposed 'caricaturing', a curve that *Sanditon* has seemed to disrupt.[40] With anti-caricature rhetoric, *Emma* and *Persuasion* have been elevated as the mature and 'mellowed' works. Barbara Thaden, for example, suggests that in *Emma* Austen 'attempts to broaden the sphere of her characterisation' by taking for her protagonist a rich young snob whose shortcomings she might otherwise have 'painted with the bold, harsh, and spare strokes of the caricaturist'. By giving so much of the novel from Emma's perspective, 'the quality of all other caricatures is softened [...] they must be painted with a softer brush because they are the heroine's friends'. Thaden speculates that Austen 'perhaps realized by this time that her unsympathetic characters were mere caricatures, entertaining but unconvincing'.[41]

On the basis of the thesis that Austen's satire softened over time, *Sanditon* – the work most susceptible to being accused of caricature – has often been grouped with Austen's early manuscripts: as Anne Toner warily observes, 'the style of the juvenilia is most commonly thought to re-emerge in the caricatures of Austen's last work *Sanditon*, especially in its improbable hypochondriacs'.[42] Austen's last novel, the unfinished work of fiction conventionally titled *Sanditon*, has been the most serious obstacle for the anti-caricature school of Austen criticism. As it exists only in manuscript form, however, its 'caricature' can be seen as provisional, its forms unstable. Critics have not found it easy to reconcile *Sanditon* with a literary career defined by maturity, consistency and permanence. R. W. Chapman seems shocked by the manuscript's 'roughness and harshness of satire [...] which at its worst amounts to caricature', and assumes that a later draft would have 'smoothed these coarse strokes, so strikingly different from the mellow pencillings of *Persuasion*'.[43] Michelle Levy argues that *Sanditon*, in its unfinished state, provides evidence for a composition process whereby Austen softened and relegated her 'satirical renderings of minor eccentric figures' before sending a final version to print.[44] On the other hand, B. C. Southam observes that the revisions Austen made to the manuscript do not (yet) 'mellow' or 'soften' the caricatures – 'she was not toning down but heightening their traits and eccentricities' – and asks whether *Sanditon*'s excess might have been 'the product of an imagination stimulated in ill-health'.[45] In Southam's view, caricature is so essentially uncharacteristic of Austen that its seemingly deliberate practice can be taken for a symptom of disease. Kathryn Sutherland sees *Sanditon*'s eccentric formal properties in more positive terms, as 'the imprint of a peculiar imagination' and 'the vivid emergence of imagination and perception from the decay of form'.[46]

A fun and fascinating document in itself, *Sanditon* is also an opportunity to revisit our opinions about caricature in Austen's published novels. I have argued that key elements of the anti-caricature rhetoric that so dominates Austen's critical reception can be derived directly from the novels themselves. In the following pages, I argue that Austen's snug aesthetic and anti-caricature rhetoric cooperate with a moral concept that frames and exculpates the author's use of characterisation techniques that might be accused of caricature. In the final section of the chapter, I focus on Austen's depictions of fat bodies in *Persuasion* and *Sanditon*, aiming to challenge the notion that Austen's 'caricature' of Mrs Musgrove is inconsistent with her approach to satirical characterisation elsewhere in the novels, and likewise to problematise the idea that *Sanditon*'s 'caricatures' are atypical of Austen's oeuvre.

Austen's Moral Concept of the Self-Reflexive Caricature

In modern literary studies, the first critic to enthusiastically acknowledge literary caricature's relationship with ethics in Austen's novels was D. W. Harding, in his 1940 lecture on 'Regulated Hatred' and the less known essay 'Character and Caricature'. However, Harding's detailed account of Austen's satirical characterisation is underpinned by the faulty assumption that textual caricature was perceived as 'innocuous' by Austen and her contemporaries, and thus was an acceptable means of 'regulating hatred'. Harding writes that Austen's caricatures relied on 'one of the most useful peculiarities of her society [...] its willingness to remain blind to the implications of caricature', and that caricature in Austen becomes 'a means not of admonition but of self-preservation'.[47] While this book contradicts a key aspect of that idea, the essence of Harding's thesis – that Austen's caricature must be innocuous – is borne out by the methods Austen used to frame her characterisations, and those which her readers used to promote the idea of her 'anti-caricature'.

Austen's characterisation techniques – both the content of what characters do and say, and the formal presentation of their dialogue, actions and bodies – operate not only in the frameworks of anti-caricature rhetoric and the snug aesthetic, but also under the aegis of a moral concept of caricature. By this concept, caricature is moralised as an effect of self-interest: absorption in one's individual experiences and in one's social and material wants, acted out through the distribution of social and material goods (information, food, affection, money and so on).

Stabler engages with this moral concept of caricature when she 'recognize[s] a pervasive role of caricature as an extreme, necessarily truncated expression of self – a psychological peculiarity [...] that might be unleashed when the interests of the self override the almost instinctive self-surveillance that preserves the interest of the general' in Austen's novels.[48] In *Sense and Sensibility* and *Northanger Abbey*, Austen uses the word 'caricature' in pre-emptive analyses or 'character appreciations' of the self-interested Dashwoods and the self-absorbed Catherine as though they were real people. I have already touched on Mrs Morland's character analysis of her daughter in *Northanger Abbey*, which portrays Catherine as idle and selfish. Returned from Northanger, Catherine's character is not matured as her mother hoped: 'In her rambling and idleness she [was] a caricature of herself.'[49] This passage should be read alongside the double portrait of Mr and Mrs John Dashwood in *Sense and Sensibility*, where the word 'caricature' is also used to represent a character who fails their family by being too much themselves: more selfish, less helpful, more oblivious to other people's disapproval or disgust than they have hitherto proved themselves capable of. Elinor and Marianne's already 'rather cold hearted and rather selfish' brother takes a wife who, far from being his better half, is 'a strong caricature of himself:—more narrow-minded and selfish'.[50]

The self-reflexive grammatical constructions in both passages – 'caricature of himself', 'caricature of herself' – position caricature almost as an uncanny aesthetic effect, where familiar people behave in ways so typical of themselves that they actually become strange. The description of the Dashwoods has an interesting pronoun mismatch: 'she was a strong caricature of himself' technically should be 'she was a strong caricature of *him*', as 'himself' would ordinarily pair with 'he'. The disjuncture in the grammar makes each partner in the marriage both the subject and the object of the sentence, that is, John Dashwood and the new Mrs John Dashwood are both 'more narrow-minded and selfish' than the original John Dashwood. The woman's name is revealed later to be 'Fanny', but the convention of using the man's first name for both partners happens to underline the idea of John Dashwood doubling his self-interest. This kind of narcissism by relationship, crossing the boundaries of gender and rank, is redescribed in the patronage of Mr Collins by Lady Catherine de Bourgh, where Collins makes the self-absorbed aristocrat an extension of his own self-importance. Collins's dialogue recurs to Lady Catherine so that the reader often encounters the two 'caricatures' simultaneously, while Collins's sense of entitlement to the Bennet daughters and the legal entailment of Bennet estate complements the *droit de seigneur* outlook of the entitled Lady Catherine.

In this 'explained caricature' – explained as an effect of psychological self-indulgence – the 'true' self is conflated with the self-interested distortion 'of himself' or 'of herself'. The characterisation simultaneously manages to tell us what a particularised fiction character is 'really like now', through the intensification, doubling or extension of their self as a 'caricature', *and* to estrange them (to a lesser or greater extent) from that caricature as a distortion of their better self. This ontological claim does not seem odd once contextualised in precepts about self-reflection and self-regulation that are familiar from studies of ethics and religion in Austen's writing. As a term in Austen's character talk, and a concept in ethical criticism about fictive characters, 'caricature' posits the existence of a better self that remains essentially flawed – 'rather selfish', 'not very industrious' – but with less pernicious material effect. Her moral concept of caricature evokes a 'moral realism' lacking in puritanical fervour: it does not imagine human beings able to free themselves from sin; it describes people who cannot be made ideal (or evil), cannot be made radically or even qualitatively different, but who might be improved (or worsened) in some measure.

The Greedy Caricature: Austen's Morally Meaningful Fatness

Austen's association between caricature and quantitative increase participates in the meanings generated in the process of abstracting *caricatúra* from its equivalence with graphic portraiture. As discussed in Chapter 1, by the time Austen was writing, *caricatúra* and 'caricature' were well established in the English lexicon such that they could be freely used to describe representation in any medium or art form. Once British readers could be expected to know what Browne's '*Caricatura* Draughts' were, writers increasingly used the word independently of references to pictorial art, and in ways that played on the associations the Italian word *caricatúra* derived from its grammatical elements and the idioms in which it figured. For Austen, caricature's fundamental meaning of overstated peculiarity, while abstracted from the concrete techniques of *ritratti carichi*, remains grounded in *caricatúra*'s etymological associations with corporeality, size and force. In Austen's moral concept, caricature involves the increase of weight, defined as a body or object's relative mass as it occupies space and produces downward force.

Giuseppe Baretti's Italian–English dictionary, as discussed in Chapter 1, contextualises the definition of *caricatúra* in its linguistic constituents and the phrases in which these were used. Among these, a common theme is material objects – including objectified human bodies and body parts – being filled and laden, heavier and bigger. This would be inconsistent with an understanding of caricature as the shrinking of smaller things as well as the enlarging of bigger things, of 'exaggeration' as comprising extreme understatement as well as overstatement. However, the prevailing concept of caricature is biased to giganticism, to addition and enlargement. *Cárica* (weight, freight, load, charge, burden) is an object defined by being added to, or pressed on, something else. Among Baretti's illustrations for the verb *caricare* is the figurative usage of *caricare* for speech and writing: 'accrescere in parlando la cosa più che veramente sia' (to make something bigger, in the telling, than it really is), which Baretti translates as 'to enlarge, to be more vehement than it is need [sic], to exaggerate'. Other examples register caricature's semantic associations, via *caricare*, with gluttony and other forms of surfeit: 'Caricar l'orza (mangier molto) *to eat one's belly full*. A vulgar expression', 'Carico di vino, *drunk*'.[51] Moral concepts of caricature are thus etymologically underpinned by ideas about aggrandisement and by idioms that use *caricare* more literally, to describe the filling of the stomach.

Austen's moral concept of caricature refers to *caricare*'s suggestion that full satisfaction is vulgar: to eat or drink one's fill, to have as much as you can hold, is to alter oneself for the worse. Austen's caricature talk attempts to circle back from the figurative usage of *caricare* (*accrescere in parlando*) for an increase created 'in the telling', to the literalised meaning of a real increase in the mass, the downward force, of a person's social and material existence. Crucially, when Austen thus moralises caricature as an effect of self-interested satisfaction, caricature's increase becomes self-inflicted: not something the author does to the character, but something the character does to themselves. 'Caricature' becomes something real and ordinary, taking up space in the world – and taking up more space than it should: in *Persuasion* and *Sanditon*, Austen depicts fat bodies in ways that link corporeal fatness, more than any other physical attribute, with the moral failings of the self-made caricature. The characterisation of Arthur Parker's sisters in *Sanditon* – 'slender', 'delicate', 'thin & worn by Illness & Medecine' – suggests a more general sizeism that points out a family resemblance between too fat and too thin, and moralises them both as failures to self-regulate.[52] In practice, with the special attention that Arthur Parker's and Mrs Musgrove's bodies receive and the textual space that they are made to occupy, the novels construct 'too fat' and 'too thin' as inequal failures. Fatness is a special occasion for anti-caricature rhetoric's pretence to moral criticism.

We might be tempted to read Austen's emphatically comic and satirical characterisations of fat bodies – which moralise corpulence as the outward attribute of an inwardly 'fat self' – as an almost unintended consequence of the bias to enlargement in concepts of caricature. I would argue, however, that the etymological underpinnings of *caricare* (to weight, to enlarge) and *exaggerare* (to unrestrictedly heap up) are simply convenient to the decided antipathy to fatness that exists in Austen's novels. It is because the fat body, for Austen, is a particular target for humour and satire that the fat character becomes a special occasion for anti-caricature's claims to accuracy and moral rectitude.

Ideas about 'corpulence' or 'fatness' contemporary with Austen's novels are constructed by historically specific concepts of race, gender, sexuality, beauty, health, affluence and so on. Texts and images that might seem, to us, to represent or comment on fatness, do so through different media and genres. Georgian-period fatness can too easily be read through any and every idea about fatness that might occur to modern readers, while phenomena such as the wearing of false stomachs or the gravitas of the 'power paunch' require explanation.[53] While graphic satire, for example, might play a particularly important role in our understanding of Georgian fatness and fat-hating, the depictions of fat bodies in satirical prints are perhaps also particularly fraught with interpretive pitfalls. Is corpulence meaningful by default, in these images; to what aspect of the satire does it belong; and what are its precise meanings in the depiction of individuals? I would argue that while satirical prints do make fatness part of a moral commentary on an individual's particular vices sometimes, most prints use fatness for more general satirical purposes. Fat bodies are often in dyads with thin bodies, in straightforward visual gags and in claims about modern statesmen generally falling short of classical ideals. Well-fed fatness is apparently linked with nationalism and masculinity in propagandist satirical prints where John Bull's body represents British prosperity in contrast with scrawny *sans coulottes* and an emaciated 'French liberty'. Does this reflect ideas about fatness in the period, and how far did such ideas extend beyond the elites and gentility who consumed satirical prints? When – and to what extent – can we read fatness as a moral critique of an individual, for example in graphic caricatures of the Prince Regent? New scholarship on late-Georgian representations of fatness is adding to our knowledge and transforming our understanding of the various ways in which graphic satire, among other forms of visual and material culture, has historically constructed fatness.[54]

The problematic status of fatness in graphic caricature can help us to begin contextualising and relativising the attitude to fatness in *Persuasion* and *Sanditon*. Are Austen's depictions of fat bodies and fat characters in *Persuasion* and *Sanditon* typical of her period, or in some way anomalous? Could satirical prints or caricature drawings have influenced the way she looks at fat bodies in her novels? Austen did not belong to the West-End world that primarily drove the production and consumption of commercial single-sheet satirical prints, but she was a member of the genteel classes that had adopted the aristocracy's leisure pursuit of drawing caricature portraits without commercial motives, a practice that predated and outlasted the 'Age of Caricature'. Because such portraits were occasions for polite amusement confidentially shared between the artist, the subject and their circle, we would expect them to be relatively polite and tactful about fatness, as about all physical features subject to framing as 'peculiarities'. It is fair to suppose that many amateur caricaturists, with intimate knowledge of their subjects' sensitivities, and with relationships to maintain, would have deliberately avoided the exaggeration of particular characteristics – trying to achieve a balance of flattery and honesty that could be acknowledged as 'more like' the subject than an idealising painting or miniature would be, while still participating in portraiture's sociability.

Many surviving examples of amateur *rittrati carichi* are not at all recognisably satirical to us – at least not by comparison with the single-sheet prints, which have political points to score. Notwithstanding the techniques for parsing and exaggerating physiognomy that Mary Darly's and Francis Grose's manuals attempted to teach, many of the amateur drawings that contemporaries understood to be 'caricatures' – like the portraits of the Edinburgh caricaturist John Kay discussed in Chapters 1 and 5 – do not follow the conventions of visual exaggeration that we might expect to find in something described as a caricature portrait. There are graphic caricatures in which it is difficult to detect pointed satire, and where any deliberate visual exaggeration is far from the grotesqueness of the single-sheet prints. Frequently it is the size and shape of *clothing* that is most obviously exaggerated for comic effect. Frequently in caricature prints and drawings, the physical attributes that modern readers might identify as 'fat' lack physiognomic meaning, and it is far from clear that all such depictions disapprove of fatness in itself.

Arguably, fatness is even valorised in pictorial caricature when it is key to a celebrity's real physical presence and recognisability. In the ink and graphite drawings of Edward Gibbon by the noblewomen Diana Beauclerk and Lavinia Spencer, for example, the subject's fatness is not made to say anything about a 'fat character', and fatness is not depicted as repellent. If we were to insist that these drawings involve fatness in graphic *satire*, our claims about these *ritratti carichi* – which do not depict actions or use text to make fat something of moral consequence – would speak to the culturally and historically specific ways that we read fatness and its cultural meanings into portraits. I argue that these high-society caricatures, like many others, allow the viewer opportunities for some acknowledgement of body mass that need not be forced into a meaningful 'fatness', but which simply is there.

Not so, I think, in Austen's writing. Turning our attention to the realist novel, we do not have to look far for characters whose fatness is made physiognomically meaningful. In these cases, we might be able to distinguish at least two types of culturally constructed fatness: first, the application of physiognomic principles that deplore fatness as a violation of classical proportions and make it one of many indices to a generally bad character; second, the forging of semantic and/or causal links between the character's fatness and their individual flaws or failures. There is an example of the former in Fielding's *Amelia* (1751), where initially Mrs Ellison's fatness seems incidental to her character: Amelia's first impression is of a woman 'short and immoderately fat', a 'good woman' whose 'good humour and complaisance [...] were highly pleasing'.[55] When Amelia discovers that Mrs Ellison is a pimp, the fatness that was framed as merely superficially unappealing retrospectively becomes a minor physical manifestation of her fundamentally unappealing character. Here, Fielding ascribes fatness to the character's enemy in a way that makes fat physiognomically meaningful, yes – but as one of several qualities judged to be aesthetically unpleasing. The text describes Mrs Ellison's body only briefly and does not use fatness to make a particular ethical point by linking it with specific character traits. In *Persuasion* and *Sanditon* on the other hand, Austen frames fatness both as aesthetically unpleasing in itself *and* as symbolic of an individual's specific flaws and failures. Austen's view of fatness as the literalised caricaturing of the body describes the fat body not simply as a reflection of the character's general moral imperfection, but as the physical manifestation of a 'fat character', a self that makes too much of itself.

In developing this argument, I have encountered some pushback on my claim that Austen's writing is fat-hating. Working on an earlier draft of the material in this chapter, I was advised to alter phrases that 'might sound as though you are saying that Austen is fatphobic'. My response is to make it clear that I *do* see Austen's writing as dehumanising people by moralising fatness, and that I am suspicious of attempts to distance this writing from Austen herself. I argue that Austen's novels despise fatness, not fleetingly or trivially, but consistently and substantially; and I would suggest that Austen engages with fatness in ways that anticipate mainstream moral panic about an 'obesity epidemic', where preconceptions about fatness – and the consequent medical and social treatment of individuals perceived as 'overweight' – can have significant impacts on people's health and happiness.

Here, I propose that Austen's novels engage with fatness in ways that were distinctive within British literary culture of the eighteenth century and Romantic period, and which would have been objectionable to some of her contemporaries. In *Persuasion*, for example, we can read the narrator's pre-emptive justification of her disdain for the fatness of a fictive character as a kind of insurance against the negative reactions that Austen must have anticipated from some readers. 'There are unbecoming conjunctions, which reason will patronize in vain' is a statement explicitly precluding a rational response to fatness, explicitly naturalising fat-hating as an inevitable response to something intrinsically distasteful and ridiculous. I see no harm in contemplating the question: if the author herself possessed no negative emotions, no animus towards fatness, why would she write passages that call on readers to accept as normal certain emotional responses to fat bodies?

I have tried to analyse the role of fatness in Austen's textual styling of caricature without dismissing the complexity of her writing about bodies, or forgetting that fat-hating can be just as focused on one's own body as on other people's. To be plain, however: 'Austen was fatphobic' is a valid enough shorthand for what I describe in this chapter. I think that the word 'fatphobia', while certainly anachronous, is more helpful for placing Austen's depictions of fat characters in the history of moral panics about body size and shape than more scrupulously historical phrasing might be. However, for the purposes of this chapter, I have settled for 'fat-hating', another term not used by Austen's contemporaries. This is an attempt both to recognise the distinctiveness of new concepts of 'fatphobia' (a term coined in the 1990s), and to convey the intensity of the anxious aversion to fatness which, I argue, comes out through what Austen's novels say about fat bodies, and how they back it up through caricature talk expressing the idea that a fat individual is already a caricature of themselves.

The Exceptional Caricature of Fat Bodies in Austen's Novels

It has become a truism that Austen avoided the description of character's physical bodies. Lewes suggests that, by having to visualise Austen's fictive characters for themselves, readers are unfortunately 'missing many of the subtle connections between physical and mental organisation'. He regrets this particularly in the case of a satirically rendered character such as

Mr Collins, whose caricature might have been given a physiognomic dimension:

> [W]e might imagine that this was a purblind world, wherein nobody saw anybody, except in a dim vagueness that obscured all peculiarities. It is impossible that Mr. Collins should not have been endowed by nature with an appearance in some way heralding the delicious folly of the inward man. [...] Balzac and Dickens would not have been content without making the reader *see* this Mr. Collins [...]. It is not stated whether [Austen] was shortsighted, but the absence of all sense of the outward world – either scenery or personal appearance – is more remarkable in her than in any writer we remember.[56]

In this respect, Lewes seems not to remember Austen's writing very well: he has come away from the novels with no lasting impression of the many settings that are described there, even in *Pride and Prejudice* alone. He is far from the only reader to claim that Austen did not visualise characters.

This may be true as a rule – but not when it comes to fat characters. Fat bodies are exceptionally caricatured by Austen, compared with other physical attributes mentioned in the novels. To start with, in *Pride and Prejudice* there is the richly vague description of Mr Collins as 'heavy-looking'.[57] This is a physiognomic clue to individual character, associating a visualised heaviness with the self-involvement of a 'fat self', which is echoed in *Sanditon*'s description of Arthur Parker, '<heavy in Eye as well as figure> He had in every respect a heavy look'.[58] The negative associations of fatness come to the foreground in *Mansfield Park* and *Persuasion* as well as in *Sanditon*, where fat bodies visualise the selfishness of self-made caricatures who indulge themselves without restraint. Brownstein suggests that Austen's 'satire on selfishness' is particularly conspicuous in her depictions of self-interested relationships with food: '[w]hen Mr Woodhouse refuses to serve enough food to guests, when Dr Grant dies of gluttony, when Mrs. Norris steals away from Southerton with a cream cheese for her own consumption, the dining room and the table are identified as the arena where gobblers give themselves away'.[59] (Mr. Woodhouse's selfishness around food has to do with hypochondria, self-superiority and the tyranny of the invalid rather than the greed of a gourmand.) In *Sanditon*, Arthur Parker fits the pattern Michael Parrish Lee discovers in Austen's published novels, of social maturity being constructed against the desire for food. There is a lot of not eating in *Sense and Sensibility*: Parrish points out, for example, that when the prepubescent Margaret Dashwood regrets missing her dinner, her 'un-blunted appetite signals a social immaturity that contrasts with the deeply sympathetic feelings of the older Dashwoods'.⁶⁰ *Sanditon* discounts Arthur Parker as a marriage prospect almost as soon as he is introduced: he is more concerned about dinner than he is about Charlotte.

Not only making fatness metonymic of psychological self-indulgence and self-involvement, Austen's oeuvre also frames fatness as the direct result of self-indulgent overeating. Among the published novels, it is in *Mansfield Park* that Austen puts fatness in a cause-and-effect narrative: first, the moral character faults of idleness and selfishness; second, fatness; third, ill health and premature death. Dr Grant's inactivity and gustatory self-indulgence are discussed in third-person narration and in several characters' dialogue: for example, Tom Bertram, who hopes for the clergyman's speedy death, describes him as '"a short-necked, apoplectic sort of fellow [. . . who], plied well with good things, would soon pop off"'. Throughout *Mansfield Park*, Dr Grant's appetite provides a series of small comic moments, with some detail about what he is eating and drinking: goose, pheasant, turkey or mutton, raids on the sandwich tray and claret every day. He suffers from 'gouty symptoms', and in the novel's dénouement he is said to have 'brought on apoplexy and death, by three great institutionary dinners in one week'. In a humorous conversation about '"slovenly and selfish"' clergymen, his sister-in-law Mary Crawford describes Dr Grant as '"an indolent, selfish bon vivant, who must have his palate consulted in everything; who will not stir a finger for the convenience of any one; and who, moreover, if the cook makes a blunder, is out of humour with his excellent wife"'. Whereas Fanny attempts to defend Dr Grant on the grounds that he '"would have been in a greater danger of becoming worse in a more active and worldly profession"', since weekly sermons '"must make him think"' and '"restrain himself"', Edmund holds the opinion that Dr Grant has caricatured himself, by '"a great defect of temper, made worse by a very faulty habit of self-indulgence"'. When Mary accuses him of '"preferring an income ready made, to the trouble of working for one [. . .] doing nothing all the rest of his days but eat, drink, and grow fat"', Dr Grant's fatness is causally linked with unrestrained eating and drinking.⁶¹

Sanditon likewise draws a causal link between fatness and self-indulgence: in the context of its satirical focus on invalidism, the text positions Arthur's fatness as the natural product of gourmandism, hypochondria and reluctance to undergo the discomforts of abstinence and activity.⁶² The character of Arthur combines the self-interest of a gourmand such as Dr Grant with that of a valetudinarian such as Mr Woodhouse. Observing Arthur closely, Charlotte gathers details of a self-indulgent lifestyle:

> Certainly, Mr. Arthur P.'s enjoyments in Invalidism were very different from his Sisters – by no means so spiritualized. – A good deal of Earthy <Dross> hung about him. ~~He seemed of haveing~~ [sic] ~~chosen~~ <Charlotte could not but suspect him of adopting that line of Life,> ~~cheifly~~ [sic] <principally> for the indulgent of an indolent Temper – & to be determined on having no Disorders but such as called for warm rooms & good Nourishment.[63]

Arthur enjoys heavily buttered toast, strong cocoa and wine every day, for his nerves. Charlotte presses him to take '"daily, regular Exercise, – and I should recommend rather more of it to you than I suspect you are in the habit of taking"', then questions the efficacy of his existing exercise regime.[64] As in *Mansfield Park*, the fat person is lazy and vulgarly debased in their habit of making food the centre of their social life.

The fat character's supposed obstructiveness and inertia in society links Austen's fat gourmands Dr Grant and Arthur Parker with the 'Mrs Musgrove' character in *Persuasion*. In *Sanditon*, when Arthur is absorbed in food he loses interest in Charlotte, 'turning completely to the Fire' and saying nothing but 'a few broken sentences of <self->approbation ~~of his own Doings & prosperity~~ >& success'.[65] When Arthur finally turns back to Charlotte, she finds that his bulk comes in useful, and repositions herself 'to have all the advantage of ~~him for~~ <his Person as> a screen'.[66] Struck through and replaced by 'his Person' as Austen was writing, the fat character is experienced more like the surface of an object than an individual. In *Persuasion*, Mary Elliot complains to Anne that her new in-laws, the Musgroves, '"are both so very large, and take up so much room"',[67] anticipating Anne's experience of the fat body as an inconvenient object later in the novel, when Mrs Musgrove obstructs the developing relationship between Anne Elliot and Captain Wentworth:

> They were actually on the same sofa, for Mrs Musgrove had most readily made room for him; they were divided only by Mrs Musgrove. It was no insignificant barrier, indeed. Mrs Musgrove was of a comfortable, substantial size, infinitely more fitted by nature to express good cheer and humour, than tenderness and sentiment; and while the agitations of Anne's slender form, and pensive face, may be considered as very completely screened, Captain Wentworth should be allowed some credit for the self-command with which he attended to her large fat sighings over the destiny of a son, whom alive nobody had cared for.[68]

Here, corporeal fatness associates with the self-affliction of emotional pain. While Mrs Musgrove's body takes up too much space, she grieves for 'a thick-headed, unfeeling, unprofitable Dick Musgrove, who had never done any thing to entitle himself to more than the abbreviation of his name, living or dead', her 'large fat sighings' exceeding her proper feelings. It was Wentworth who induced Dick to write 'the only two disinterested letters' he ever sent to his parents, whom he was always asking for money.[69] That last phrase – 'whom alive nobody had cared for' – implies that not even Mrs Musgrove cared for her son while he lived. Her fat body and its 'fat feelings' are positioned as barriers to more genuine social connection and introspection.

Marvin Mudrick points out that *Persuasion*'s satirical portrait of a grieving fat woman echoes humorous remarks about self-indulgent mourners in Austen's letters: Austen refers to a Mrs Bromley as 'a fat woman in mourning', and seizes on the idea that excessive mourning betrays self-absorption: 'Dr Hall in such deep mourning that either his mother, his wife, or himself must be dead'.[70] Disproportionate, self-absorbed and self-stimulated grief is similarly characterised in *Sense and Sensibility*. When Henry Dashwood dies and the new Mrs John Dashwood arrives, immediately and unannounced, to move into the property occupied by his widow, Mrs Henry Dashwood abandons herself to her feelings – 'in sorrow [...] carried away by her fancy' – and encourages Marianne to do the same:

> Elinor saw, with great concern, the excess of her sister's sensibility; but by Mrs. Dashwood it was valued and cherished. They encouraged each other now in the violence of their affliction. The agony of grief which overpowered them at first, was voluntarily renewed, was sought for, was created again and again. They gave themselves up wholly in their sorrow, seeking increase of wretchedness in every reflection that could afford it, and resolved against any consolation in future.[71]

This is a critique, in a form suited to the realist novel, of the unchecked sentimentality that Austen parodies in *Edgar and Emma* (1787), where the heroine literally never stops crying: 'having no check to the overflowings of her greif [sic], she gave free vent to them, & retiring to her own room, continued in tears the remainder of her Life'.[72] In *Persuasion*'s satirical characterisation of Mrs Musgrove's 'large fat sighings', Austen's consistent attention to the comic potential of tears and sighs combines with the disapproving, even hostile attitude to fat bodies in *Mansfield Park* as well as *Sanditon*. I have argued that fatness is exceptionally visualised compared with other physical attributes in Austen's novels; that there are several precedents in Austen's oeuvre for the comic and satirical portraits of Mrs Musgrove and Arthur Parker as 'fat characters'; and that the 'fat character' is presented as a self-inflicted 'explained caricature' that pre-exists textual characterisation.

Next, I investigate the textual styling of caricature in Austen's depictions of Mrs Musgrove and Arthur Parker. I show that, while Austen's narrator claims in *Persuasion* that distaste for fat bodies is universal and inevitable, the stylistic features of the passages about Mrs Musgrove and Arthur Parker – which prolong, repeat and reiterate with variations what they have to say about fatness – suggest an author implicated in her own moral concept of caricature.

Fat-Hating and Narrative Style in Persuasion and Sanditon

Austen's textual styling for explained caricature, in *Persuasion*'s and *Sanditon*'s passages about fat characters, makes openings for the reader to identify the text's fixation on fatness. The narration palpably makes too much of the fat characters – 'goes on' about them for too long, too digressively and too emphatically – as if we have been cornered by an eccentric who wants to lecture us about fat people. In these passages, Austen's third-person narrator takes on key stylistic features that she ordinarily uses to render characters comically and satirically through dialogue, creating a resonance between narrator and caricature. The style becomes more discursive and cumulative, seemingly to accommodate a compulsion to describe fat characters and moralise fatness.

In *Sanditon*, third-person narration prolongs the scenes where Arthur interacts with Charlotte, with minutiae, redundancy and variations on themes. Charlotte sums up Arthur's vices as indolence and self-indulgence – but only once the scene has accumulated several pages of evidence for this judgement, using a series of examples to position his invalidism, again and again, as a form of hedonism. Arthur's dialogue is styled as explained caricature, with dashes, exclamation marks, hyperbole and a tic of emphasis: 'very fond of standing at an open window', 'very nervous', 'a very poor creature', 'very fond of exercise', 'a very good Toaster', 'very bad for the Stomach', 'very bad indeed'.[73] The satirical import and comic effect of the dialogue's content – which all revolves around Arthur's body – is pointed up by these formal features. Repetitive use of an intensifier such as 'very' or 'really' is not unusual in natural speech, but in literary language it conventionally signifies unsophisticated, unselfconscious and recursive thought patterns. While Arthur's dialogue – itself characterised by detail, redundancy, repetition and variation – takes up considerable space in the scene, much of its content is replicated by the third-person narration, in Charlotte's minutely observed running commentary on Arthur's activities. The account of Arthur making toast and cocoa, then talking to Charlotte about toast, then eating his toast with butter, goes on for pages of the manuscript. Charlotte watches him closely enough to notice him, after having 'scrupulously scraped off <almost> as much butter as he put on [. . .] seize an odd moment for adding a great dab just before it went into his Mouth'.[74] Watching Arthur sneak butter this way, Charlotte 'c^{d.} hardly contain ~~himself~~ <herself>'. Despite her supposed distaste for the 'Physics' of a body which, Arthur shares, is 'very subject to Perspiration',[75] Charlotte's disapproval of fatness involves some self-gratification, for which she keeps Arthur under continuous surveillance. The pleasure that Arthur self-administers through food, warmth and rest becomes 'food' for Charlotte's own self-gratification.

One of Austen's own favourite meals was cheese on toast, a recipe which in the Austen household called for careful measuring of quantities: Martha Lloyd's method was to '[g]rate the Cheese & add to it one egg, & a teaspoonful of Mustard, & a little Butter'. A more indulgent recipe in Hannah Glasse's cookbook gives instructions to soak toast in red wine, 'then cut some cheese very thin and lay it very thick over the bread, and put it in a tin oven before the fire', a lengthier process closer to Arthur's fireside 'coddling' of his meal.[76] Charlotte, who prefers her own toast with a 'reasonable quantity of butter spread over it',[77] can support and supplement any self-denial she might need with the self-satisfaction she derives from quantifying what Arthur eats and drinks.

In *Persuasion*, too, the fat body is described redundantly, through synonyms, intensifiers and variations. 'Mrs Musgrove was of a comfortable, substantial size', we are told, 'no insignificant barrier' between Wentworth and Anne, who is 'very completely screened' by Mrs Musgrove and her 'large fat sighings': 'comfortable' and 'substantial' are synonyms for 'fat', Mrs Musgrove is both a 'screen' and a 'barrier', and her sighs are immediately 'large' and 'fat'.[78] Then, in *Persuasion*'s notorious three sentences about the 'unbecoming conjunction' of fatness and feelings, Austen justifies her characterisation of Mrs Musgrove with a statement couched as a universal aesthetic principle:

> Personal size and mental sorrow certainly have no necessary proportions. A large bulky figure has as good a right to be in deep affliction, as the most graceful set of limbs in the world. But, fair or not fair, there are unbecoming conjunctions, which reason will patronize in vain, —which taste cannot tolerate, —which ridicule will seize.[79]

I see no irony here, no indication that this straight-faced statement should be attributed to anyone but the narrator, and every indication that the author expects the rational and tasteful reader to share her opinion – as long as they have a sense of humour. In these three sentences, where action, dialogue and setting are dropped completely, Austen uses several rhetorical devices (concession, variation, repetition) as well as intensifiers to get her point across. In the first two sentences, there are three ways of expressing the same concession: there are 'certainly [...] no necessary proportions' between body mass and mental suffering; larger bodies have the same 'right to be in deep affliction'; and it is 'not fair' for a fat person's suffering to be ridiculous. As in the description of Mrs Murgrove, fatness is conveyed through an immediate pair of synonyms, 'large bulky'. In the third sentence, Austen's aesthetic principle of 'unbecoming conjunctions' takes the form of a distinctive rhetorical device (isocolon) whose serious tripartite structure is punctuated with long dashes that ask the reader to pause and consider each clause as a separate facet of the argument that a fat person's suffering is aesthetically unpleasing. The digression into aesthetic principles reframes Mrs Musgrove's 'large fat sighings': even if her grief were in proportion to its object (if her true feelings were deeper, if Dick better deserved them), she still would be ridiculous.

Some critics have found here an acid antidote to the innocuously pleasant 'Aunt Jane'; others have ascribed the 'unbecoming conjunctions' statement to someone other than Austen, for example by arguing that the narrator is ventriloquising a conventional opinion that Austen might actually disapprove.[80] Marvin Mudrick has called the passage 'a savage caricature' that 'serves as a pretext for abusing Mrs. Musgrove'.[81] Reflecting on parallels with Gillray's prints, Brownstein suggests that: 'At their most disturbing, [Austen and Gillray] pair the organic with the elaborately artificial, the beautiful with the disgusting. As either Anne Elliot or the narrator reflects, some people – physically and/or morally – are sometimes simply comical.'[82]

But interpreting the 'unbecoming conjunctions' passage either in very specific terms (as 'abuse of Mrs Musgrove' as an individual) or in very general terms (as a remark about 'some people, sometimes') might gloss over the fact that Austen's theory of unbecoming conjunctions refers to fat (specifically) people (generally). It states that they are unbeautiful, and comical when they express sadness or distress. In her picturing of characters' personal appearances, Austen makes an exception for fat bodies: fatness is a special occasion for characterisation. This exceptionalism plays out in the narrative voice, which loses the stylistic concision and proportion that seem to contribute so much, elsewhere, to its composed, rational impersonality – laying its author open, like her own characters, to questions of ethical or psychological criticism like the ones I have asked here. There are other such passages, on different topics: the ones I have analysed here are relatively conspicuous due to the theme of fat-hating. For the duration of these lapses in style, the narrator might seem to share the formalised and framed 'eccentricity' of her satirically rendered characters. Throughout, Austen's characterisation techniques operate under a moral concept of caricature as self-inflicted, which works (not always successfully) to present us with a narrator who is essentially likeable and believable, and to show us people as they really are.

There is a tendency to judge the 'realism' of Austen's novels – to distinguish Austen's 'caricatures' from her 'characters' or one character's 'roundness' from another's 'flatness' – according to the reader's own conceptions of what is plausible or realistic. 'Most often', Woloch notes, 'readers have understood Austen's flat characters as a reasonable imitation of actual life. If there are round and flat characters in Austen, this is an accurate representation of the real social universe [...]. Other critics take an opposite tack, noting the way that Austen's minor characters are *clearly* distorted and, therefore, cannot be interpreted as the transparent reflections of credible persons'.[83] Woloch's identification of Mr Collins as a minor character must still assume that one can discern a writer's 'simple exaggeration' of what could be more credibly represented, as well as recognising the formal elements of caricaturing. The (in)credibility of the character's *content*, Woloch suggests, is fundamental to the caricature: 'Collins's caricatured personality, the symptom and sign of his minorness, emerges through three interrelated registers: the simple exaggeration of his faults, his incessant repetition of these faults, and the continual annoyance or disruption that these faults provoke.'[84] Perhaps we cannot avoid, when engaging in (anti-)caricature talk about Austen's novels, participating in 'naive realism' by implying the existence of some actual person or people like Mr Collins, whom it might be possible to extricate from the text's caricaturing. In this chapter, I have shown that caricature talk is crucial to Austen's realism, not only in the critical tradition but also because her co-operations of caricature talk with characterisation techniques work so hard to persuade us that her comic and satirically rendered characters are 'real' or 'explained' caricatures, pre-distorted, made ridiculous by what they are and not by how the writer presents them.

Perhaps we must, to be sceptical of that strategy, assume our familiarity with *what* has been 'simply exaggerated' or 'clearly distorted', and believe ourselves capable of making ethical judgements about it. For example, if we agree with Woloch that writing one character's negative reaction to another – contradicting what they say, or laughing at them – can be a 'caricaturing' technique, our character talk will probably have to make some reference to our real social universes; that is, we believe there are real people like Mr Collins, who are actually annoying, and thus that the other characters are reasonably annoyed.

In this chapter, where I describe how Austen's caricature talk interacts with her characterisation techniques, I have tended to emphasise the *how* of characterisation (formal and rhetorical devices) over the *what* of characterisation (the content of a character's history, actions and dialogue). This is not because I want to attempt reading fictive characters as purely formal constructions that can be understood independently of assumptions about their imitation and distortion of actual life. In fact, our tendency to assume the *what* of caricature, as well the impulse to question our assumptions, is a necessity for full, interminable and shared caricature talk that participates in writers' self-conscious realisms.

We use caricature talk when we discuss fictive characters that have what McKeon calls 'the concrete particularity of probabilistic "realism"',[85] and particularly to examine the moments when we might lose faith in the fiction's heightened or selective reality. In these discussions, the anti-caricature claim that humorous or satirical characterisations accurately reflect the distorted forms of people in the real world can be strongest where the fictional text provides its own compelling rules for understanding 'explained caricatures' with underpinning concepts of morality, psychology, society or history that explain how such 'caricatures' come to be. George Lukács describes how Goethe, in *Wilhelm Meister's Apprenticeship*, 'draws characters in whom the specialization, brought about by the capitalist division of labour, ossifies one feature of their personality to the point of caricature, leaving the rest of their humanity to atrophy completely'.[86] The artifice of the writer's characterisation technique is caught up and partly concealed in a realism that attributes caricature to the structures and forces that externally and internally shape people – away from what they might have been, into what they are.

CHAPTER 5

Walter Scott and Historical Caricatures

Walter Scott was open to the concept of caricature's potential for accuracy, particularly for documenting the varied textures of historical reality. In his novels and other writings, Scott explores *caricatúra*'s possible associations with particularity, accuracy and actual reference, as opposed to distortion, oversimplification and misrepresentation.

To begin this chapter, I contextualise Scott's individual concept of caricature in his knowledge of *ritratti carichi* and his admiration for John Kay's 'caricatures' of eighteenth-century Edinburgh, analysing passages in *The Heart of Mid-Lothian* and *Rob Roy*. I argue that Scott looked to Kay's caricature prints as a model for comically and satirically rendered non-protagonists to populate a compendious historical realism. In the second part of the chapter, I look at how compendious realism attracted accusations of 'caricature' for its perceived artificiality and heterogeneity – drawing on *caricatúra*'s meanings of effort and contrast – and how Scott anticipated and responded to those accusations. I consider the connection Scott makes between caricature and the picturesque in *Guy Mannering* and *Rob Roy*, which offer justifications for 'caricature' as an effect of artificial combinations that cater to readers' mixed tastes with a synthetic compendious realism. I describe how, in the later part of his novel-writing career, Scott imagined that romance-readers were becoming bored and sceptical of characterisations that luxuriated in peculiarity and contrast. I analyse his efforts – in an 1821 essay on Tobias Smollett for the *Novelist's Library* and in a selection of Magnum Opus editions – to explain these characters' historical accuracy and to come to terms with their literary obsolescence. Caleb Balderstone (*The Bride of Lammermoor*) and Sir Piercie Shafton (*The Monastery*) exemplify the problem of the 'historically explained caricature' whose literary value is especially dependent on readers' understanding of a specific historical context.

While some of Scott's historically peculiar characters were criticised for being superficially different 'temporary characters', in other cases he develops figures of romanticised 'deep peculiarity' extending through historical time periods. In the third part of the chapter, I argue that Scott romanticises dwarfism and gigantism in order to perform the factualisation of these supposedly legendary figures, with the extraordinary bodies of Sir Edward Mauley and Rob Roy MacGregor being based on accounts of real individuals. (The techniques in Scott's grotesquing descriptions of dwarf characters – used across *The Black Dwarf*, *Rob Roy*, *The Pirate*, *The Talisman* and *Peveril of the Peak* – are discussed further in Chapter 6 alongside Shelley's 'horrid realist' depictions of dwarf and giant characters.)

The last part of the chapter returns to the idea of the explained caricature, looking through the lens of 'sympathy' at Scott's characterisations of national and ethnic minorities, where sympathy is extended to Scots and withdrawn from Jews. First, I close-read Scott's sympathetic account of the Scots 'body-corporate' in *The Heart of Mid-Lothian* against unsympathetic representations in *Rob Roy* and Hazlitt's essay 'On the Scotch Character'. Then, I look at Scott's version of the 'self-inflicted caricature' in *Ivanhoe*'s anti-Semitic characterisation of 'Isaac of York' (with reference to the real person 'Abraham of Bristol'), making comparisons with Edgeworth's references to Abraham's torture in her 1817 novel *Harrington*. On the one hand, the rhetorical strategy of explained caricature can participate in national prejudices 'more rationally' and 'more sympathetically', by identifying historical points of origin for unpleasant traits and behaviours perceived as national characteristics, and assigning those characteristics noble or pragmatic motives – which is what happens in *The Heart of Mid-Lothian* and *Rob Roy*. In *Ivanhoe*, on the other hand, the same rhetorical strategy is used both to intellectualise racism – rationalising it and bestowing an intellectual character on it – and to shift blame for historical anti-Semitism and persecution onto Jews. 'Historical caricature' is latent in Scott's compendious realism that extensively (and self-consciously) relies on readers acquiring and being complicit in a shared understanding of history. The historical romance, its diverse characterisations concerned with how people really were, seems to generate a disturbingly accelerated process of realism being disintegrated by sceptical readers.

Kay's Caricatures

When Scott sets the scene in the second chapter of *The Heart of Mid-Lothian*, he aligns his recovery of historical characters with the artist John Kay's first-hand attention to the details that might escape dignified historiographies or flattering painted portraits. Scott embellishes the historical background to the Porteous riots with a description of Edinburgh's city guard, a civic militia originally formed in 1513 in response to the violent unrest following the Battle of Flodden.[1] The City Guard was eventually rendered unnecessary by the passage of the 1805 Edinburgh Police Act and the formation of a new police force – but the Guard was not disbanded until 1817, when the medieval Tolbooth was demolished.[2] Writing in 1818, with the knowledge that the Guard would soon pass out of living memory, Scott records the peculiar appearance of the militia men who were still employed in the later decades of the eighteenth century, many of them Highlanders, with the intended purpose of keeping order on Edinburgh's streets. Scott's epigraph to the chapter quotes the last stanza of Robert Fergusson's poem 'The Daft-Days' (1772), which praises drinking and music in Edinburgh during the twelve days between Christmas and the new year, and ends with an ominous reference to 'that black banditti, / The City Guard'; Scott also refers to Fergusson's 'Hallow-Fair' (1772), which warns of 'this black squad'. Fergusson's poems are particularly well qualified to evoke the City Guard, Scott notes, because they are based on the poet's first-hand drunken encounters with the militia when they were on duty during public holidays.[3]

Scott imagines Fergusson's poetic record of personal experience, together with his own childhood memories, becoming a textual accompaniment or 'illustration' to John Kay's pictorial 'caricatures' of the City Guard:

> A spectre may indeed here and there still be seen, of an old grey-headed and grey-bearded Highlander, with war-worn features, but bent double by age; dressed in an old fashioned cocked-hat, bound with white tape instead of silver lace; and in coat, waistcoat, and breeches, of a muddy-coloured red, bearing in his withered hand an ancient weapon, called a Lochaber-axe; a long pole, namely, with an axe at the extremity, and a hook at the back of the hatchet. Such a phantom of former days still creeps, I have been informed, round the statue of Charles the Second, in the Parliament Square, as if the image of a Stuart were the last refuge for any memorial of our ancient manners; and one or two others are supposed to glide around the door of the guardhouse assigned to them in the Luckenbooths, when their ancient refuge in the High Street was laid low.
>
> But the fate of manuscripts bequeathed to friends and executors is so uncertain, that the narrative containing these frail memorials of the old Town Guard of Edinburgh, who, with their grim and valiant corporal, John Dhu (the fiercest-looking fellow I ever saw), may, perhaps, only come to light when all memory of the institution has faded away, and then serve as

an illustration of Kay's caricatures, who has preserved the features of some of their heroes.[4]

Pictorial caricature is construed here as a uniquely evocative witness to history: it is visually particular, unflatteringly accurate and concerned with actual reference such that it can substitute for personal memories of people in all their regional and individual peculiarity.

The caricature of *ritratti carichi* might find a place in Nancy Armstrong's 'prehistory' of visual realism,[5] with portraits like Kay's seen by his contemporaries as material traces able to preserve the actual living qualities of the dead, rather than paying tribute to idealised versions of the person. In this concept of caricature, accuracy and particularity are supposed to derive from the artist's personal familiarity with his or her subject, whether through an on-the-spot encounter or continual acquaintance. Kay, supported by an annuity from Sir William Nisbet of Dirleton (who had employed Kay as a body-servant), was known to draw most of his subjects from life, opportunistically. Hugh Paton's testimony that people rarely posed for Kay to draw them helps explain why so many of his portraits, particularly the 'society caricatures', show people in the street, in profile, conversing with their peers or passing by the artist's viewpoint.[6] Quick, on-the-spot drawings, attempting to capture the distinguishing features of individuals as seen in action, are described admiringly by Scott as 'caricatures'. Scott owned a copy of the anonymous Scots English poem *The Unwelcome Guest* (1799), which praises Kay as the 'wonderfu true visage taker'.[7] In *Redgauntlet*, drawing inspiration from Lockhart's penchant for caricaturing as a law student, Darsie Lattimer's law school notebook is '"filled with caricatures of the professors and my fellow students"'.[8] Such drawings held out the possibility of a visual representation approximating how people appeared when physically encountered in a social setting. Because they put unflattering emphasis on the distinctive features that other portraits would minimise or leave out, even the caricature portraits in deliberately disapproving single-sheet prints could be judged good likenesses – as in the *Dublin Literary Gazette*'s claim about the satirical prints of the Duke of Wellington produced around the time of the Roman Catholic Relief Act, mentioned in Chapter 1: 'Those who judge of the Duke of Wellington's countenance by the highly finished prints sold in the shops, judge erroneously; the caricatures give much more accurate resemblances, and some of them possess an exactness of similitude to the original [such that] one forgets that it is a caricature, and feels as if one were actually looking at the Duke.'[9]

Caricatúra was often used to suggest that a portrait focused too exclusively on accuracy, however, particularly when it was at the expense of the subject's feelings. Scott's journal entry for 1 March 1826 records how his bankrupt drawing master, George Walker,[10] effaced a portrait of himself by a well-known artist:

> [Archibald] Skirving made an admirable likeness of poor Walker; not a single scar or mark of the small-pox which seamd [sic] his countenance but the too accurate brother of the brush had faithfully laid it down in longitude and latitude. Poor Walker destroyd [sic] it (being in crayons) rather than let the caricatura of his ugliness appear at the sale of his effects.[11]

The offensive *caricatúra* here is 'faithful', only 'too accurate', an 'admirable likeness'. In *Rob Roy*, Scott suggests the difficulty of separating the supposedly 'unjust' caricature from genuine likeness, when *caricatúra* possesses its own perverse realism. When Frank overhears Andrew's 'perverted account of my temper and studies', he admits that 'my self-love, while revolting against it as a caricature, could not, nevertheless, refuse to recognise it as a likeness'; later in the novel, Frank relies on distinct meanings of 'caricature' and 'likeness' to protest Rashleigh's remarks about his father: '"Mine was a likeness, Rashleigh; yours is a *caricatura*."'[12] Accurate pictorial 'caricatures' – Skirving's drawing of Walker and Kay's portraits of the Edinburgh city guard – demonstrated for Scott the power and perverse realism of the unflattering *caricatúra*.

Scott owned at least one Kay print relevant to the City Guard passage in *The Heart of Mid-Lothian*, the 1796 etching *James McKean at the Bar Edin^r* (NPG D31984), where the accused McKean is guarded by two soldiers with smart uniforms, grim faces and sharp swords. He must also have seen one or more of Kay's several prints that portray members of the City Guard as individuals, and carrying Lochaber axes. John Dhu features in at least three of these, appearing in *Three Edin^r Bucks* (1784) and *The Old City Guard of Edinburgh* (1786) as well as being the subject of *Shon Dow* (1784).[13] A comparison with David Allan's numerous prints of the City Guard clarifies why Scott would allude to Kay's portraits, with their individualising and particularising qualities. Kay depicted many other individuals who were fixtures of Edinburgh street life in the late eighteenth century: the fops and 'bucks' of the volunteers, members of the aristocracy, shopkeepers, hawkers and beggars. Local 'eccentrics' portrayed by Kay include James Robertson of Kincraigie, continually thwarted in his ambition to be hanged as a martyr to the Stuart cause, and Jamie Duff, an 'idiot boy' who attended all the funeral processions that took place in the city.

Many others practised traditional occupations that were becoming 'picturesque' in the aesthetic taste of the Romantic period, or whose advanced age made them objects of historical interest: John Steele, a Perthshire beggar; Geordie Syme, official Piper of Dalkeith; John Tait, a broom-maker; Margaret Suttie, a salt hawker; and William Wilson, 'Mortar Willie', a chemist's assistant who lived to be over a hundred years old. Ancient, antiquated or parochial: these were individuals perceived to make Edinburgh more 'interesting', and for whose portraits Kay often adopted more detailed, individualising and realist styles than for his portraits of lawyers, ministers and academics. Whereas some of his portraits are polite 'society caricatures', minimally individualised and holding little interest for anyone not acquainted with their subjects, Kay's 'romantic' portraits present minute details, such as the texture of a heavy cloak, or the wrinkles round the eyes, as a documented reality that substitutes for really encountering the person. Whereas the society caricatures give an overall impression of sameness, these present an array of distinctive, heterogeneous elements – various professions, classes, regions and even historical periods – all existing compendiously in a single part of Scotland.

Scott's admiration for 'Kay's caricatures' suggests a parallel with how his novels' compendious realism uses non-protagonist characters not only to provide humour and facilitate plots, but also to immerse the reader in a wealth of minute historical differences, presenting a world of visual and aural variety where it is worth attending to the different ways people look and speak.

Anti-caricature and Compendious Realism

By offering this concept of caricature as a tool for compendious realism, Scott's novels anticipate readers' objections to their deliberately contrasting characters, settings, moods and language. In anti-caricature rhetoric objecting to compendious realism, 'caricature' denotes an unpleasant effect resulting from the artist's or writer's labour to synthesise in one work the disparate things that readers might expect of it. Such realism squashes things together in ways readers might find implausible or distasteful. They might like comedy to be kept separate from tragedy, or a modern Glasgow separate from a romantic Scottish Highlands, or a garrulous smuggler from a dignified lady, or Lallans from 'pure English'. Scott works to bring these disparate things together, in the knowledge that such synthesis can be read as failure to conceal the novel's artificiality – a belaboured 'caricature' that strikes the reader with too many effects and contrasts.

Scott's concept of caricature's realism collides with anti-caricature rhetoric in *Guy Mannering* (1815), where a landscape sketch exemplifies caricature's association with conspicuous artistic labour and artificial combination, but from which emerges a remarkable likeness of reality. The novel's central character, Henry Bertram alias Vanbeest Brown, was kidnapped by smugglers as a child, and conveyed from his native Scotland to Holland. Bertram experiences the 'levels of the isle of Zealand' as a flat 'blank' conspicuously lacking in glens and mountains. Scott had not seen this flatness for himself at the time of writing *Guy Mannering*, but may have read published accounts of the Walcheren campaign that include descriptions of the island. *Letters from Flushing* (1809) observes that while 'there are some elevations which the people are pleased to call hills [. . .] the island has a very near resemblance to a billiard-table; so level, that a ball rolled from one side, would pass without impediment to the other'.[14] Leaving flat Holland behind, Bertram catches his friend Delaserre's 'Swiss fanaticism for mountains and torrents' while retaining an 'indelible impression' of Scotland. Returning to Britain and travelling through Cumbria on his way to his estate in Galloway, Bertram is struck by the peculiarities of the hilly landscape. Like a good tourist of the picturesque, he tries to capture them on paper.[15] When he compares his drawings with a friend's, he realises that in trying to render the heterogeneity of a landscape characterised by contrasts, he has exaggerated it: '"Some drawings have I attempted, but I succeed vilely—Dudley, on the contrary, draws delightfully, with a rapid touch that seems like magic, while I labour and botch, and make this too heavy, and that too light, and produce at last a base caricature."'[16] Bertram attributes the 'caricature' of his drawing to lack of skill in pictorial art. The better artist cultivates restraint, compromising between peculiarity and plausibility – as a connoisseur says of Tyrell's landscape drawing in *Saint Ronan's Well* (1824), '"[h]ere is both force and keeping."'[17] In Bertram's landscape, as elsewhere, caricature is visible in the effort of artificially recreating the picturesque: Hazlitt, in his essay on the Elgin Marbles, remarks that lesser artists' representations of mountains 'lose probability and effect by striving at too much'.[18]

However, in *Guy Mannering*, the 'base caricature' of northern landscape is not a complete failure. Bertram's exaggerations have a fidelity of their own, evoking the exile's palimpsestic view of landscape: the drawings are Cumbria viewed through a childhood memory, indelible though perhaps dreamlike and distorted, of Scotland; they are Cumbria viewed through his difficult travels through mountain ranges in Europe. The drawings are 'a vile success', as Bertram suggests. Their deformities implicitly created by the pressures of the past, they fail to represent Cumbria but succeed in representing something else. Whereas Dudley's talent and training enable him to draw accurately what is in front of him, Bertram's aesthetic sensibility is synthetic, preoccupied with what is not there, and seeing all landscapes in a compendium of memory and desire. By juxtaposing Bertram's bad drawing with his impressions of the landscapes he has passed through, *Guy Mannering* quietly offers a counterpoint to grumbles about picturesque artists 'caricaturing' the natural world.

It was understood in the Romantic period that the picturesque tips easily into a caricature of itself.[19] Writing about John Martin's popular landscape paintings,[20] Hazlitt complains that 'his mountains are piled up one upon the back of the other, like the stories of houses', striving for sublime effects through multiplication and elevation. Thus caricatured, nature acquires a manufactured quality. 'A landscape', Hazlitt says, 'is not an architectural elevation. You may build a house as high as you can lift up stones with pulleys and levers, but you cannot raise mountains into the sky merely with the pencil'.[21] Hazlitt refers to the topographical features in Edinburgh's Royal Park, mentioned in James Hutton's *Theory of the Earth* (1788), to illustrate nature's superior creative powers:

> We defy any landscape-painter to invent out of his own head, and by jumbling together all the different forms of hills he ever saw, by adding a bit to one, and taking a bit from another, any thing equal to Arthur's seat, with the appendage of Salisbury Crags, that overlooks Edinburgh. Why so? Because there are no levers in the mind of man equal to those with which nature works at her utmost need. No imagination can toss and tumble about huge heaps of earth as the ocean in its fury can. A volcano is more potent to rend rocks asunder than the most splashing pencil.[22]

Reality tips into fantasy when an artist attempts to heighten our view of a topographical structure made by violent mechanisms which have already gone to the edge of what is materially impossible, and whose every creation is completely and original. The landscape artist should observe and copy, not improvise and fantasise. In 'caricature', the industrious hand of the artist is too conspicuous.

Non-protagonist characters in Scott's novels have sometimes been seen as too miscellaneous and as conspicuous in ways that make the author's labour visible and shake the reader's illusion of reality. A novelist desperately in want of novelty could also be tempted into overworking familiar materials, and mixing them in unlikely new combinations. In his

1822 essay for the *Quarterly Review*, Nassau Senior cautions writers against 'introducing something of overcolouring and caricature, into figures, in his endeavours to render striking, the representations of a well-known class. A painter may be tempted to put horses and cows into some studied attitude, or group them too artificially, who would not thinking of anything more than an unaffected resemblance of a hippopotamus'.[23] Senior is concerned with Scott's comic and satirically rendered characters, disapproving the 'fools and bores [...] from Monk Barns down to the Euphuist' (Sir Piercie Shafton) as an expedient means of mixing humour with tragedy: 'an artificial effort after the contrasts of tragi-comedy, to have the broadest and most extravagant caricature continually dragged into studied opposition to the tragic characters and incidents'.[24] Picturesque landscape gardening becomes a helpful analogy both for Scott's seemingly artificial contrasts of mood and for the diversity of the social panorama in his novels: 'It is the old mistake', writes Senior, 'of the first landscape gardeners, who, in their rage to imitate nature, used to plant dead trees, and build ant-hills, close to a house' – an allusion to William Kent, who was accused of inserting incongruous objects into his picturesque garden designs.[25] Senior singles out Caleb Balderstone, an important character in *The Bride of Lammermoor* (1819), as 'the most pertinacious, the most intrusive' of Scott's attempts to create comic diversions with characters.[26] Perhaps as a result of such criticisms, Scott himself came to wonder (according to Lockhart's *Memoirs*) that with Caleb, 'he might have sprinkled rather too much parsley over his chicken'.[27] When artists and writers are seen deliberately to select, combine and present miscellaneous products – rather than seeming to present what already exists contiguously in nature – they become builders, planters, cooks, caricaturists.

Such caricature talk about over-seasoned and out-of-place non-protagonist characters is already anticipated by Scott's own gestures at the artificiality of novelistic realism in his novels. Scott is often explicit about picturesque landscapes, characters, customs and objects as supplies for a reader, viewer or consumer whose appetite simultaneously demands novelty and variety, yet also consistency. Novel-readers are like Andrew Fairservice's lady clients, '"aye crying for apricocks, pears, plums, and apples [...] without distinction o' seasons"' – wanting this *and* that, and all the time.[28] *Rob Roy* provides the terms for Senior's objections to eccentric characters as the excrescences of an over-enthusiastic landscape gardener, where Andrew's preoccupation with the delicious fruits of his horticulture ironically parallels Frank's taste for the picturesque. Mocking his employer's preference for untended landscape, Andrew claims that

"'[Frank]'ll glower at an auld warld barkit aik-snag as if it were a quiz-maddam in full bearing, and a naked craig wi' a burn jawing out ower't is unto him as a garden garnisht with flowering knots and choice pot-herbs.'"[29] Andrew's juxtapositions, of a broken tree stump with a fruit tree imported from France, and a rock formation with a herb garden, supplant the picturesque nature of the 'romanticist' with the productive nature of the 'realist'. Andrew's taste has a proprietorial, as well as a pragmatic, dimension: when he visits Andrew's cottage, Frank notices his jargonelle pear tree, nicknamed *cuisse-madame* in reference to the fruit's bulge, the same prized 'quizmaddam' Andrew contrasts with Frank's preferred oak tree later in the novel.[30] Fruits and vegetables are substituted for feminine beauty again in Andrew's remark that when "'a kail-blade, or a colliflour, glances sae glegly by moonlight—it's like a leddy in her diamonds'".[31] Andrew's appreciation of the beautiful is just as partial as Frank's: one would rather look at a crag, the other a cauliflower. When we first see Diana Vernon, she is not a lady in diamonds, but something much more exciting to Frank, a lady in masculine riding clothes. By the time of the novel's setting, that fashion had been around for a while: Samuel Pepys wrote of 'Ladies of Honour dressed in their riding garbs, with coats and doublets with deep skirts, just, for all the world, like mine [...] which was an odde [sic] sight, and a sight did not please me.'[32] The style is 'perfectly new' and pleasing to Frank, however, and he is struck by 'the wild gaiety of the scene, and the romance of her singular dress and unexpected appearance'.[33] Frank wants to see what he has not seen, and what exceeds his control – novelty, romance, wildness, female masculinity – the opposite of Andrew's well-kept garden. Thus, *Rob Roy*'s comedy of tastes suggests the problem that compendious realism proposes to solve: how to satisfy readers with such different preferences, without offering variety and incongruity? You cannot please everyone all the time – but put Andrew Fairservice by Die Vernon, a cabbage in moonlight by a lady in coat skirts, and you might increase your chances. Compendious realism anticipates a mixture of readers, and hopes for readers with mixed taste. Like Henry Bertram's perversely realist 'caricature' of Cumbria, Scott's compendious realism is a fixed viewpoint on a labour-intensive assemblage of people and things that might strictly belong to different layers but which appear to be present in the same place and moment.

The earliest readers of Scott's novels were keenly interested in his highly individualised fictive characters, many of whom became household names. At the same time, early readers' objections to Scott's compendious realism as artificial, aesthetically inconsistent and/or empirically implausible often focus on the most comic, satirically rendered and peculiar characters in the novels. In the 1820s, Scott began to see these characters as particularly vulnerable to changing tastes. More than landscapes, these characters determined readers' opinions of how successfully compendious realism seemed to comprehend different genres and to gratify taste. Non-protagonist characters strongly differentiated by historically specific national, religious, ethnic and professional traits also became targets for readers' scepticism about the novels' claims to combine the real with the romantic. The first chapter of *Saint Ronan's Well* pre-emptively defends its characterisation of Meg Dods – a character, Scott's narrator admits, 'somewhat overcharged in the features' – as belonging to 'a peculiar class' whom the narrator's contemporaries north of the border will remember. The novel's opening portrays Meg's peculiarities of physique, temper and manners, introducing her catchphrase 'and what for no?'.[34] Scott felt the need to justify peculiar characters as accurate of particular nations, classes and historical periods. When readers rejected these historically specific characters, would they soon reject the novels altogether, refusing credit for Scott's speculative combination of history with romance? In his review of *Frankenstein*, Scott imagines the novel-reader as a bank, advancing the author credulity: 'The author opens a sort of account-current with the reader; drawing upon him, in the first place, for credit to that degree of the marvellous which he proposes to employ.'[35] This connection between the author's creative liability and the author's financial liability became personal for Scott in the depressing atmosphere of the 1820s.

In an essay written for the *Novelist's Library* in 1821, and his revisions to that essay in 1827, Scott responds to the accusations of 'caricature' in the critical reception of Smollett's novels, and justifies his own peculiar characters by proxy. This defence of Smollett seemed necessary because in the early nineteenth century Smollett's place in the canon was threatened by an association with 'caricature'. Previously, it had been generally accepted that Smollett's depictions of sailors, based on his personal experience of working as a naval surgeon, were true to life. John Dunlop refers to this consensus in his *History of Fiction* (1814): 'No one wishes to be told, for the twentieth time, that [Smollett] is distinguished for his delineation of [. . .] naval characters.'[36] But taste was turning against Smollett and his sailors, and Dunlop ventures that the characters in *Peregrine Pickle* (1751) are 'a little caricatured'.[37] An essay in *The Retrospective Review* contrasts Smollett's peculiar sailors with Defoe's naval characters, who possess an 'air of truth and reality', and pairs Smollett with Fielding as writers whose imaginative talents have 'unfitted them to be the humble copyists of nature, and the faithful historians of human life'.[38] Later, Smollett's comic rendition of eighteenth-century naval life was given short shrift by a new generation with experience of the professionalised nineteenth-century navy. A passage on Allan Cunningham's novel *Paul Jones* (1826) in the *Noctes Ambrosianae* compares Cunningham not with Smollett, but with 'the truly naval author of the Pilot', James Fenimore Cooper.[39] William Glascock, who served in the Royal Navy between 1800 and 1855, describes Smollett in his essay on 'naval novels' as 'not [...] a painter of real life [but] a caricaturist'.[40] When *The North American Review* pits Scott against Smollett in a fantasy tournament of British novelists, Smollett's defeat is down to 'the coarse caricature of his pencil'.[41] Anna Letitia Barbauld, in 1810, is an early voice of opposition to Smollett's 'caricatures': she describes Commodore Trunnion, in her essay on Smollett for *The British Novelists*, as 'scarcely like anything human [...] the Caliban of Smollett', and Trunnion's wife as 'still more overcharged'.[42]

Reissued in 1820 and foundational to the canonisation of the English-language novel, Barbauld's popular series was a model for Scott's *Novelist's Library*. Her treatment of Smollett put Scott on the defensive. Whereas Barbauld includes only *The Expedition of Humphry Clinker* (1771) in her thirty-volume series, Scott makes room for Smollett's entire oeuvre in the much smaller *Novelist's Library*: a move that was part of the series's 'remasculinisation' of the novel, with only two women among the fourteen writers represented.[43] The *Novelist's Library* also addresses Barbauld's critique of Smollett's sailors as 'caricatures', a judgement that may well have played a part in her decision to include *Humphry Clinker* but not *Roderick Random* (1748) or *Peregrine Pickle* in her series. Scott's approving remarks on Smollett's peculiar characters could also be applied to his own. His defence of Smollett's 'striking' yet 'accurate' characters was presented to the public in 1821, the same year as the essay for the *Quarterly Review* where Nassau William Senior gives his opinion that eccentric characters are blots on all the novels Scott had written since 1817; and in 1817, Francis Jeffrey had criticised some of Scott's characters as 'caricatures [...] after the fashion of the caricatures in the novels of Smollett'.[44] While Scott acknowledges the grounds for seeing Smollett's sailors as caricatures, he insists that their extravagance does not make them inaccurate. There are sailor characters in *Peregrine Pickle*, he thinks, which 'border on caricature' (Trunnion, Pipes and Hatchway); others in *Roderick Random* are 'truth and nature itself' (Lieutenant Bowling and Jack Rattlin).

Into the established consensus on the verisimilitude of Smollett's sailors, Scott incorporates the idea that proximity to 'caricature' actually makes a character more vividly real: they are 'striking', 'characteristic' and 'historic', perhaps like Kay's caricatures of the Edinburgh city guard. The peculiarities that make a character liable to be seen as a caricature, especially by later generations, can serve as a record of characteristics that might not be tasteful or even credible, but which give the reader a window on the past as a many-textured combination of distinctive elements, whose looks and manners do not conform to the dignity of Tragedy or History:

> Smollett's sea characters have been deservedly considered as inimitable; and the power with which he has diversified them [...] we have noticed as his chief advantage over Fielding [...]. These striking portraits have now the merit that is cherished by antiquaries—they preserve the memory of the school of Benbow and Boscawen, whose manners are now banished from the quarterdeck to the fore-castle.[45]

Scott concludes his essay on Smollett with a redemption of the naval 'caricatures' on aesthetic grounds, praising their vividness and diversity by comparison with the paintings of Rubens.[46] Leigh Hunt, in *Table-Talk*, would agree with Scott's view that Smollett incorporated truth in extravagance, allowing the novelist to have been 'a masterly observer' as well as 'the finest of caricaturists': one whose 'caricatures are always substantially true: it is only the complexional vehemence of his gusto that leads him to toss them up as he does, and tumble them on our plates'.[47] Here, Smollett's energy, his tossing and tumbling, makes him conspicuous as a cook of characters – but, Scott and Hunt insist, strong seasoning and varied combinations do not interfere too much with the substance.

In the 1821 essay, Scott states his special admiration for Smollett's comic character Obadiah Lismahago, the Scottish lieutenant who appears in *Humphry Clinker* as the Don Quixote of eighteenth-century British imperialism. Smollett explicitly presents Lismahago to the reader as a mixture and an 'original', pointing out his peculiar and heterogeneous traits. Physically, Lismahago is a *cadaver exquis* of odd body parts: a skull scalped, 'patched and plastered', joined to a face 'half a yard in length, brown and shrivelled', on top of a figure 'very narrow' in places and 'very thick' in others.[48] Other characters in the novel relish Lismahago as a 'high flavoured dish' whose peculiarities fascinate them,[49] and who is caught in farcical incidents. When he is forced to climb out of a window in his nightshirt, 'long lank limbs and posteriors [...] illuminated by the links and torches which the servants held up', an onlooker laughs: '"O, what a subject!—O, what *caricatura*!"'[50] Lismahago's most continually accentuated peculiarity is his patriotism, which leads him into specious reasoning, 'undertak[ing] to prove that poverty was a blessing to a nation; that *oatmeal* was preferable to *wheat-flour*'.⁵¹ When Scott argues that Smollett's characterisation of Lismahago is grounded in historical reality, he holds out the possibility of an actual referent:

> Captain Lismahago was probably no violent caricature, owing for the manners of the time. We can remember a good and gallant officer who was said to have been his prototype, but believe the opinion was only entertained from the striking resemblance he bore in externals to the doughty captain.⁵²

Scott employed this kind of authentication technique again when he revised the essay on Smollett for his *Miscellaneous Prose Works*. To the paragraph on Smollett's sailors, he added a final sentence that addresses criticisms of Smollett's characters based on ignorance of eighteenth-century naval manners:

> The naval officers of the present day, the splendour of whose actions has thrown into shadow the exploits of a thousand years, do not now affect the manners of foremast-men [...]. <But these, when memory carries them back thirty or forty years, must remember many a weather-beaten veteran, whose appearance, language, and sentiments free Smollett from the charge of extravagance in his characteristic sketches of British seamen of the last century.>⁵³

As in his defences of Lismahago and Meg Dods, Scott refers to personal memory as the best way to authenticate characters whose peculiar appearances and ways of speaking are not recorded anywhere else.

But how to rehabilitate these characters for readers who do not possess the memory to carry themselves back sixty or more years since? Smollett, his novels riddled with historical 'caricatures', would need advocacy for inclusion in the canon of the English-language novel. New processes of literary canonisation took place not only in the expert judgements of men and women of letters, but also in the selling of new editions to new generations of readers. Senior might disparage Scott's 'fools and bores' as unnecessary additions to narratives involving more dignified characters – but since the eccentric characters, being enjoyed by so many of the novels' first readers, were often integral to plots and to the characterisation of the other characters, they could not possibly be excised. Perhaps it would do, rather than toning them down or abridging them, to justify them by explaining their historical accuracy. The sentence Scott added to his essay on Smollett, to defend the accuracy of his historical 'caricatures', belongs with the material Scott chose to include in the Magnum Opus edition of his novels between 1829 and 1833.

Defending Historical 'Caricatures' in the Magnum Opus

By the 1830s, there was a widespread sense that Scott's reputation, and the immense popularity of his works, was insecure.[54] In the decade that closed with the publication of the Magnum Opus edition of his novels, and even as he was assured of the profits from *Woodstock* (1826) and his *Life of Napoleon* (1827), Scott anticipated falling out of favour. He wrote in 1826 that 'fashion changes and I am getting old and may become unpopular'. In 1827, he comforted himself, '[t]he public favour may wane indeed but it has not yet faild [sic] as yet and I must not be too anxious about that possibility'.[55] Scott's speculation on his writing as an increasingly risky investment – the apprehensive repetition of 'it has not yet faild as yet' – chimes with Angela Esterhammer's description of 'a climate of speculation that reached its peak in 1824 [...] when British culture was profoundly affected by a rapid and severe boom-and-bust cycle'.[56] The 1825 crash, and the financial collapse of the publishing enterprise in which he had heavily and profitably invested, had left Scott owing over £120,000. While this immense personal financial obligation loaded him with stress and depression, he was troubled by the idea of himself as a boom-and-bust author:

> I should mention that the plan about the new edition of the novels was considerd [sic] at a meeting of trustees and finally approved of. Yet, who can warrant the continuance of popularity? Old Corri [...] entered into many projects and could never sett [sic] the sails of a windmill so as to catch the *aura popularis* [...]. I have had better luck to dress my sails to every wind. And so blow on, God's wind, and spin round, whirlagig.[57]

Recording the trustees' assent to the Magnum Opus edition, Scott has windmills in his head. Reminiscent of Don Quixote's most famous adventure, the windmill spun by popular taste corresponds with his view of chivalry as a problematic intersection of fantasy and reality in *Ivanhoe*, and about the mixed reception of the knight Sir Piercie Shafton, a comic character in *The Monastery*.

Scott's Magnum Introduction to *The Monastery* devotes whole pages to defending this single character, a disproportionate attention that suggests a chain of associations in Scott's speculation on the Magnum Opus: that chivalry might resolve the contradiction between history and romance; that the 'chivalrous' Sir Piercie is a synecdoche for the inherent absurdities of historical romance; and that readers' ambivalence about Sir Pierce is, therefore, cause for worry. Once taken as a ridiculous caricature of Euphuism, Sir Piercie appears to represent the unravelling of historical romance's contract between author and reader. Scott's emphasis in the Magnum Introduction on apologising for 'characters formed on the extravagances of temporary fashion'[58] echoes his sense of himself in the 1820s as dependent on specific literary fashions and tastes. His novels would remain giants only as long as public favour blew in the right direction.

When Constable first suggested a new edition of the novels in March 1823, he put it to Scott that a set of authoritative notes would secure the novel's reputation as romances about real things, for which plausible – if not actual – referents could be found:

> There will be attempts at illustrations and notes of all sorts, kinds and designations, full of absurdities and blunders—and in my opinion it is the Author only who could do anything at all acceptable in the way of genuine illustration—the Characters Incidents and descriptions in which all of them so fully abound have either originated in what may be termed reality or are drawn from sources but little known.[59]

Among the volumes of annotations already being sold, the most notable was Robert Chambers's *Illustrations of the Author of Waverley: Being Notices and Anecdotes of Real Characters, Scenes, and Incidents, Supposed to Be Described in His Works* (1822), a second edition being issued in 1825. William Chambers published an invasive biography uncovering the 'real' identity of Scott's character Sir Edward Mauley, *The Life and Anecdotes of the Black Dwarf, or David Ritchie* (1820). The public's bankable interest in such characters meant that Scott, like other authors, was frequently in the position of needing to deny that his more peculiar or satirically rendered characters were portraits of real people. This was the case from the very beginning: the last chapter of *Waverley* assures the reader that its 'Lowland Scottish gentlemen and the subordinate characters are not given as individual portraits, but are drawn from the general habits of the period.'[60] At the same time, the perceived popularity of highly individualised comic characters may partly explain the accretive and amplifying revisions Scott made, in the process of bringing new editions of *Waverley* and *Guy Mannering* to press, to the characterisations of Dominie Sampson, Paulus Pleydell, Dandie Dinmont and the Baron of Bradwardine. The Magnum adjusts these characters' idiolects with attention to their professional vocabularies and the orthographic representation of non-standard pronunciations; and, as J. H. Alexander notes, the Magnum Introductions posit the most memorably eccentric characters as inceptive to Scott's early novels with Scottish settings.[61]

Scott thus resists Nassau Senior's view of peculiar non-protagonist characters as superfluous additions to the novel. As well as claiming that the peculiar characters are foundational to the Scottish novels, the Magnum Introductions work hard to establish the historical reality of Scott's subordinate eccentric characters more generally. This is clearest in the Magnum Introduction to *The Monastery* (1820), which devotes several pages of caricature talk to apologising for Sir Piercie Shafton. Scott seems to have observed that this character was underappreciated by the novel's first readers. The first edition of *The Monastery* was no commercial or critical failure, but coming on the heels of *Ivanhoe*, its reception was relatively disappointing.

In the Magnum Introduction, Scott focuses his defence of the novel on its most remarkable characters, not to dispute their extravagance or implausibility, but to assert their basis in reality *despite* extravagance and implausibility. Historical facts, he insists, include things that are peculiar, implausible, fantastic, absurd. This fictive historical 'reality' does not necessitate actual referents, he reminds us, taking Robert Chambers to task for mistakenly identifying *The Monastery*'s pseudoepigraphic narrator, Captain Clutterbuck, as a 'Mr. O—n of Melrose', a neighbour and friend of Scott's. Clutterbuck is like Susan Ferrier's Mrs Gawffaw and Mrs Macshake: individualised enough to suggest that a real person might exist, but all the more historically real for Scott's and Ferrier's framing them as representatives of larger populations. It is only as fictive characters that they are individualised: while they are artificially made singular within the text of the novel, they are reproducible under a particular set of historical conditions. Without knowledge of those conditions, however, readers might understand the character as the novelist's fanciful or downright absurd invention. This applies also to supernatural characters: Scott justifies the White Lady of Avenel as not only an imitation of literary example, but also a superstition local to the novel's historical setting in the Scottish Borders, and a figure of some historical substance. Implicitly, the White Lady is excused from the charge of artificiality both by the fact of general belief in such phenomena, and by the idea that this general belief is confined to a time and place: elsewhere, at another time, she would not exist. She is not, like some other ghostly figures in other novels of the Romantic period, an example of the 'explained supernatural' – but her historical and regional credentials lend her the concrete particularity of literary realism. Lockhart recalls that while readers were scornful of Sir Piercie's 'grotesque absurdity', it was actually the White Lady who was criticised as the 'primary blot' in *The Monastery*, with Sir Piercie 'loudly, though not quite so generally, condemned'.

Despite the public's more decisive judgement against the White Lady, however, the Magnum Introduction offers a much longer justification for

Sir Piercie, perhaps suggesting that Scott was substituting Sir Piercie for more engrossing problem that stretched beyond this single character. If Clutterbuck could be generally real, and the White Lady contingently real, could Sir Piercie not be like Smollett's sailors, styled as a 'caricature' but real in substance? Such 'historical caricatures', Scott recognised, might seem especially well suited to his historical fiction, since they would seem bizarre in a novel with an imprecise or contemporary setting. Literary 'caricatures' might be ultra-historical when they exaggerated temporal differences over 'timeless' human qualities, creating a strong effect of period authenticity. A caricature might be more 'historically real' than a serious and subtle character – more artefactual, a thing more palpably *made* by history – because the caricature's reality is more exclusive to its precise historical context. But deprive the reader's knowledge of that context, or lose the reader's memory of the referent, and the character might become obnoxiously unreal.

Scott appears convinced in the Magnum Introduction to the 1830 edition of *The Monastery* that Sir Piercie fails as a character because readers' knowledge of Euphuism is insufficient. While the Introduction attempts to correct that, it also risks prejudicing new readers against Sir Piercie by presenting him as a weak point in the novel and implying that his eccentricities are not adequately contextualised or explained within the novel itself. Scott's rendering of euphuistic speech was regarded as absurd by several generations of readers, many of whom would have encountered him through the Magnum Opus's apologies for him. Moreover, in its effort to defend Sir Piercie against the charge of absurdity, the Magnum Introduction and footnotes to *The Monastery* accuse Euphuism itself of being absurd. Within a few decades, Scott came to be seen as chiefly responsible for widespread misunderstanding of historical Euphuism, and Sir Piercie was notoriously a caricature. George Lillie Craik's *Pictorial History of England* (1841) calls Sir Piercie 'rather a caricature than a fair sample of Euphuism'.[62] In a lecture first given in Edinburgh in 1870, Trollope identifies Scott's over-dressed knight as the foremost example of courtly euphuism for modern readers: 'We know it best in the caricature of Sir Piercie Shafton, "the Euphuist."'[63] The *OED* mentions the character in its prescriptive note on 'loose uses' of *euphuism*, apparently 'chiefly suggested by the absurd bombast which Scott puts into the mouth of Sir Piercie Shafton (who is described as a "Euphuist") in *The Monastery*; this caricature, however, bears very little resemblance to the genuine "euphuism"'.[64] No wonder that when John Dover Wilson wrote a critical biography of John Lyly, author of *Euphues*, in 1970, he felt that Scott had already been 'sufficiently called to account for his caricature of Lyly [...] a historical *faux pas*'.[65] Reactions to the character were likely influenced by Scott's attack on Lyly, 'a clever but conceited author', his mental powers 'deformed by the most unnatural affectation that ever disgraced a printed page'.[66] I will discuss two excerpts from the Magnum Introduction's long and recursive passage inspired by Sir Piercie – characterised by continual repetition of the words *extremity*, *peculiarity*, *affectation*, *extravagance* and *absurdity* – which both defends and admits the limitations of the characters Scott calls 'temporary pieces'.[67]

Reckoning with the built-in obsolescence of characters whose leading features must be historically explained, Scott appeals to his reader's supposed familiarity with Jonson's and Shakespeare's satirically rendered courtiers, on whose dialogue he based Sir Piercie's. Even 'Shakspeare himself', Scott pleads, drew characters too fashionable to retain either their realism or their entertainment value:

> With the whole sum of idolatry which affects us at his name, the mass of readers peruse, without amusement, the characters formed on the extravagances of temporary fashion; and the Euphuist Don Armado, the pedant Holofernes, even Nym and Pistol, are read with little pleasure by the mass of the public, as portraits of which we cannot recognise the humour, because the originals cease to exist. In like manner, while the distresses of Romeo and Juliet continue to interest every bosom, Mercutio, drawn as an accurate representation of the finished fine gentleman of the period, and as such received by the unanimous approbation of contemporaries, has so little to interest the present age, that, stripped of all his puns and quirks of verbal wit, he only retains his place in the scene, in virtue of his fine and fanciful speech upon dreaming, which belongs to no age, and as a personage whose presence is indispensable to the plot.[68]

As a work whose subordinate yet indispensable characters bring comedy into close proximity with tragedy, *Romeo and Juliet* is a good model for the problem Scott identifies: that the satirising of peculiarities closely based on the manners, costume and other 'temporary' signifiers of a particular historical period will inevitably, sooner or later, leave readers with intermittent gaps in their comprehension of the literary work. The very characters initially intended as light entertainment might require the densest critical apparatus to explain why they were originally funny. All this amounts to an argument against Sir Piercie, since Scott is admitting that most early nineteenth-century readers coming to *The Monastery* would not have the knowledge to understand a satirical rendering of Euphuism even in the works of Shakespeare.

Scott was at disadvantage here, of course: whereas Jonson, Shakespeare and Smollett had depicted the absurd fashions of their own times, Scott had taken his from times and places with which many contemporary readers were unfamiliar. They might come to Scott's novels with some idea, from history books, of the moral characters of famous historical figures, but they were learning the minutiae of historical texture largely from the novels themselves. For *The Monastery*, this texture included *Euphues*, something very few readers would have read. It was a considerable burden for the novel to be responsible for educating its reader into understanding its jokes – and was it worth it, if the (con)temporary characters that were intended to spark recognition and spontaneous amusement were actually, for most readers, wearying homework assignments? Nor would footnotes and critical introductions do anything to mend some readers' perceptions that Scott gave peculiar characters too many appearances and too much dialogue in his novels. In his review of *Tales of My Landlord*, Francis Jeffrey complains that:

> [Scott's] most striking and highly coloured characters appear rather too often, and go on rather too long. It is astonishing, indeed, with what spirit they are supported, and how fresh and animated they are to the very last;—but still there is something too much of them,—and they would be more waited for and welcomed, if they were not quite so lavish of their presence.[69]

Jeffrey might have recommended that Scott abridge Sir Piercie's presence in a new edition of *The Monastery*, not make him a main subject of its introductory pages.

The worrying concept of a temporary 'historical caricature' was the counterpart of the comic type seen to stretch continuously through the ages. Scott's 'Essay on the Drama' (1819), first published as a supplement to the *Encyclopaedia Britannica*, quotes the antiquarian Joseph Cooper Walker's writing on *commedia dell'arte* characters: descended from the types of the Roman New Comedy yet with new peculiarities belonging to the districts, towns and professions of sixteenth-century Italy, commedia characters seemed to inhabit both categories.[70] *Il Dottore* spoke, as Richard Andrews describes it, 'Bolognese interlarded with Latin and outright garbled nonsense', reflecting Bologna's status as the university city.[71] The specificity of a (con)temporary character can give audiences pleasure in their shared knowledge and narcissism of small differences. In the long eighteenth century, when Scott and other British writers made their Latin-quoting pedantic characters Scottish – Smollett's Maclaymore in *The Reprisal*, Scott's Cleishbotham in *Tales of My Landlord*, Peacock's

Mac Quedy in *Crotchet Castle* – they were playing on readers' notions that socially obtrusive learning and specious reasoning often had Scottish accents. Smollett has his Irish character 'Oclabber' tell Maclaymore, 'You're a man of learning Honey [...] I am always happy when you are spaiking, whether I'm asleep or awake'.[72] Coleridge includes 'presumptuous sciolism' in his list of vices that '*caledonianize* the human face'.[73] Scott's consciousness of the Scottish pedant being a temporary character, like his predecessor the Dottore, ties in with his conviction that comic characters, once fixed in print, were liable to pass quickly from the circulating library into the cabinet of curiosities. Typological 'systems' on which peculiar characters could be based, such as the physiological theory of cardinal humours, were themselves historically specific and could not be relied on to carry a character forward indefinitely:

> [T]he comedies of Ben Jonson, founded upon system, on what the age termed humours [...], in spite of acute satire, deep scholarship, and strong sense, do not now afford general pleasure, but are confined to the closet of the antiquary, whose studies have assured him that the personages of the dramatist were once, though they are now no longer, portraits of existing nature.[74]

As readers begin to require corroborating sources for character's seemingly improbable peculiarities, the critical apparatus of the antiquary's closet prolongs temporary characters beyond their natural lives. A Magnum footnote to *The Bride of Lammermoor*, for example, acknowledges that Caleb's method of providing dinner for Ravenswood and his guests 'has been universally considered on the southern side of the Tweed as grotesquely and absurdly extravagant'.[75] Scott insists that, while the scenario may not be plausible, it must be accurate because it can be likened to an actual historical referent, preserved in memory and conveyed vividly through oral storytelling:

> The author can only say, that a similar anecdote was communicated to him, with date and names of the parties, by a noble Earl lately deceased, whose remembrances of former days, both in Scotland and England, while they were given with a felicity and power of humour never to be forgotten [...] were especially valuable from their extreme accuracy.

The strategic phrase 'date and names' begs the reader to accept the authenticating move of specifying, without actually giving specifics.

Inevitably however, such footnotes cannot substitute for the reading experience of recognising, unmediated, the reality conveyed through the power of caricature. Caleb, like Sir Piercie, is founded on 'some forgotten model' and is 'more likely to awaken the disgust of the reader, as unnatural, than find him food for laughter'.[76] There is too much parsley, Scott concedes – but removing it would compromise the novel's design, would diminish the artificial combinations of high and low, tragic and comic, ideal and real, timeless and historical, which define its compendious realism. In the Magnum Introduction to *The Monastery*, Scott puts himself in the role of a waiter extolling an exotic sprig or mysterious purée. He feels the difficulty of countering readers' distaste for characters they do not recognise or believe, 'the formidable objection of *incredulus odi*'.[77] When readers cannot be reconciled to the unlikeliness of the real, then the conjunction of history and romance is a bad investment.

Temporary and Deep Peculiarity in the Historical Romance

Scott was concerned anew with balancing peculiarity and credulity when he decided to novelise English history, a challenge he addresses in *Ivanhoe*'s 'Dedicatory Epistle' and in the Magnum Introduction to the second edition of *Ivanhoe* ten years later. To Scott's mind, seeking new material might help him avoid over-egging familiar materials, but basing novels on English history ran a new risk: that English readers, complacent in long-established modernity, would balk at highly differentiated characters and social peculiarities.

Ivanhoe's 'Epistle' and Magnum Introduction explain this trade-off. Turning to English subjects will be a refreshing change for both author and readers: to a writer 'employed in catering for public amusement, a fresh topic [. . .] is the untasted spring of the desert'. Returning to Scottish subjects, the author will struggle to provide readers with something new: 'in order to obtain the indispensable charm of novelty, he is forced upon caricature, and, to avoid being trite, must become extravagant'.[78] But English readers, Scott thinks, are less willing to believe the peculiarities of their own country's history – England being a place where 'civilization has been so long complete' and where 'all that gives verisimilitude to a narrative and individuality to the persons introduced' is forgotten.[79] Due to the 'uneven development' of the two countries, Scotland's peculiar characters – Edinburgh's city guard, for example – are still within living memory. In the dedication to *Ivanhoe*, the antiquarian Dryasdust compares the author of the Scottish novels to the legendary witch Erichtho, who reanimates corpses 'whose limbs had recently quivered with existence' whereas Templeton – the fictive narrator presented as the author of *Ivanhoe* – must dig for material in 'dry, sapless, mouldering and disjointed bones'.[80] These dry bones are history stripped of its distinctive textures, its conflicting energies. Everyone looks the same. Scott must differentiate these characters, strongly enough that they seem historically real, but not so extravagantly that their peculiarities seem artificial – silly outfits and quaint language making ordinary people temporarily ridiculous.

In *The Monastery*, Scott illustrates this point with Sir Piercie's character. The courtier's peculiarities are mere fashions, silly and shallow. A devotee of Euphuism and Italian conventions of swordsmanship,[81] his over-elaborate dialogue – the 'embroidery of his conversation'[82] – is repeatedly pulled before the reader. At the end of novel, Sir Piercie's whole identity is unravelled: he is revealed as the son of a tailor's daughter, in an ironic twist on his penchant for fine clothing; and he himself takes a miller's daughter, rather than a high-born lady, for his wife. This connects with the skeptical view of chivalric character as a foreign affectation in *Ivanhoe*, where Cedric the Saxon speaks dismissively of '"the fantastic fashions of Norman chivalry"'; and with the idea that chivalry is acquired through copying other people and following formulae in the 1832 Magnum Introduction to *The Talisman*, where Scott describes Richard I as 'a pattern of chivalry, with all its extravagant virtues, and its no less absurd errors'.[83] The first edition of *The Monastery*, attempting to inoculate the characterisation of Sir Piercie, to make him a historically explained caricature, blames the knight's ability 'to *parler Euphuisme*' on Lyly's being 'at the very zenith of his absurdity and his reputation', his influence 'a fashion as rapid as it was momentary'.[84] Sir Piercie's historical peculiarities are costume drama, exhumed from the closet, not genuine flesh reanimated. Whether or not this deliberate irony was lost on readers, their reactions to the Euphuist's sartorial and linguistic flourishes are echoed in more general criticisms that Scott's appeal was due to the superficial attractions of 'colour' and 'costume'. Comparing Scott's historical fiction with Defoe's *Memoirs of a Cavalier* (1720),[85] pitting a romantic realism against a realism of reportage, the *Retrospective Review* praises the ordinariness of Defoe's fictional cavalier. A romance-reader might find him dull and commonplace, but to the discerning reader he is satisfyingly like reality. Captain Delgatty, the inspiration for Scott's character in *A Legend of Montrose* (1819), may have been 'an infinitely more amusing personage than any cavalier who ever served in Flanders or elsewhere, but it is precisely because he is more amusing that we lose our confidence in his reality'.[86] The critic expresses a classical preference for the general, recalling a line from Shaftesbury's *Essay on the Freedom of Wit and Humour* (1709): 'The variety of nature is such, as to distinguish every thing she forms, by a *peculiar* original character;

which, if strictly observed, will make the subject appear unlike to anything extant in the world besides.'[87] Jeffrey had made a similar point about some characters in Scott's fiction being 'pictures, at best, of individuals who must always have been unique and extraordinary'.[88] There is no one like Delgatty, regardless of the fact that he actually existed, whereas Defoe's cavalier is historically real because he represents other cavaliers like him. Founded on particular historical facts, Scott's most peculiar historical characters seem like inventions 'called into existence by the hand of a mighty magician, and presented to the wondering eyes of the present curious generation, man and horse, in full costume'.[89] Scott's allusions to actual referents – to the real Captain Delgatty or the real followers of Lyly – do not excuse the ways in which highly individualised characters interfere with literary realism.

Sir Piercie, the costumed knight Scott intended to be a timelessly pretentious character with historically specific pretensions, converges with the unsympathetic view of Scott's antiquarian details as merely decorative. The historical peculiarities of the character are a superficial texture antiquating familiar things in order to make them novel; the Euphuist is 'really' nothing but a fop or dandy in old-fashioned clothing. Lukács distinguishes the historical richness of Scott's novels – his characters real 'historical-social types' – from the luxury of the 'false historicism' endemic to lesser fiction:

> [T]he German Romantics, in particular, place extreme emphasis upon the historical faithfulness of every detail. They discover the picturesque charm of the Middle Ages and produce it with 'nazarene' accuracy: everything, from medieval Catholicism to antique furniture is reproduced with craftsmanlike [sic] precision, which often becomes mere decorative pedantry. [...] This decorative caricature of historical faithfulness was firmly rejected in Germany by the great champions of progress in literature and culture, Goethe and Hegel.[90]

Whereas Lukács stresses that 'local colour' is only one of many features in Scott's 'artistic demonstration of historical reality',[91] others have seen it as crucial to readers' taste for – if not Scott's actual composition of – the novels' historical representations.

Readers' taste for this kind of period costuming will prove as temporary as the sartorial fashions themselves, Thomas Carlyle suggests, reviewing Lockhart's *Memoirs* a few years after the publication of the Magnum Opus:

> Much of the interests of [Scott's] novels results from what may be called contrasts of costume. The phraseology, fashion of arms, of dress and life,

belonging to one age, is brought suddenly, with singular vividness before the eyes of another. A great effect this; yet by the very nature of it, an altogether temporary one. Consider, brethren, shall we not too, one day be antiques, and grow to have as quaint a costume as the rest? The stuffed dandy, only give him *time*, will become one of the wonderfullest [...] mummies.

What then is the result of these Waverley romances? Are they to amuse one generation only? One or more. As many generations as they can, but not all generations: ah no, when our swallow-tail has become fantastic as trunk-hose, they will cease to amuse![92]

Sartorial fashions were not only new or strange in themselves, but were also signs of the accelerating newness and strangeness of modernity, whose cast-offs would soon join Scott's historically 'costumed' characters in the dust. Timothy Campbell argues that eighteenth-century Britons' 'increased sensitivity to cycles of fashion – and to now-familiar dynamics of currency and obsolescence in everyday commercial life [...] both shaped and vexed the period's projects of historical representation'.[93] Campbell reveals in *Kenilworth* (1821) a 'commercializing pastiche' of Elizabethan fashion viewed through the consumer culture of the Romantic period.[94] While Scott used sartorial fashion as a system of historical representation across the Waverley novels, as Campbell demonstrates, it seems appropriate that Scott wrote *Kenilworth* – with its heightened consciousness of fashion as a means of sorting and marketing history – shortly after *The Monastery*'s satirical rendering of an Elizabethan courtier seemed to have disappointed readers. Rather than sartorial consumerism being attributed exaggeratedly to a single character, and made part and parcel of that character's silliness, commercialised fashion is woven throughout *Kenilworth*. This has the effect of giving a sense of the peculiarities – superficial though they might be – of a historical milieu, immersing the reader in an old-fashioned 'fashionable' world.

The methods of compendious realism opened Scott up to charges of 'caricature' not only on the grounds that historical romance's heightened peculiarities and contrasts were artificial, but also on the grounds that its historical representations were often superficially concerned with 'costume' and 'colour'. Characters with dwarfish and gigantic physical features, on the other hand, were an opportunity to incorporate 'deep peculiarity' in the novels' historical realism. By including references to the credulity of older generations and children, and quoting from their folklore, while using actual referents to factualise the fantastic beings of myth and legend, Scott romanticises and historicises non-normative bodies in such a way that readers can both indulge in the '"auld-warld stories"' and reserve their distance from the original scene of storytelling, with its participants '"sitting on the broomy knowe and cracking about Black Dwarfs, and siccan clavers, as was the gate lang syne, when the short sheep were in fashion"'.[95] Whereas Sir Piercie's and Caleb Balderstone's manners are 'temporary', absurdly peculiar because of the historical reality that shapes them, the physically disproportioned Rob Roy MacGregor and Sir Edward Mauley are fantastic in spite of their historical reality. Whereas historical fashions are quickly changed, put on and taken off, dwarfish and gigantic figures supply a deeper peculiarity that connects real, historical people to the figures of storybook romance and oral legend. Whereas Sir Piercie Shafton is a 'historically explained caricature' made peculiar by Euphuism and Elizabethan court manners, Scott's novels present dwarfish and gigantic figures as *deeply* peculiar: 'caricatures' who embody the most fantastic qualities of romance in historical characters appropriate to particular times and places.

Scott's dwarfs are invariably connected with necromancy and supernatural beings, often with reference to popular beliefs. Sir Edward Mauley, the titular character of *The Black Dwarf* (1816), is first seen as a witch, then as a ghost, before being likened to 'a giant in a romance' and finally accepted as 'a being of blood and bone' yet 'in close league with the invisible world', a wizard.[96] In *Kenilworth*, the 'gigantic porter' enlisted to play the part of Hercules in Dudley's courtly entertainments 'represented excellently one of those giants of popular romance, who figure in every fairy tale or legend of knight-errantry'.[97] In *The Pirate* (1822), Nick Strumpfer is the real version of 'Trolld', the saga-famed inhabitant of the Dwarfie Stone; Magnus Troil likens him to 'Pacolet', a character in the Carolingian romance *Valentine and Orson*, and he is described as 'the hideous mis-shapen figure of Pacolet'; Triptolemus, taking him for a goblin, addresses him in Latin; and he is associated with dragons, being seen to emerge from behind a stone 'like some overgrown reptile' and (unreliably) reported as flying on a dragon.[98] 'Sir' Geoffrey Hudson, in *Peveril of the Peak* (1822) is associated with 'the fraternity of gnomes, or fairies, whom he resembled so much in point of size', and likened to 'an alchemist, or [...] necromancer'.[99] Dwarfism also has romantic connections in *The Talisman* (1825), where the female court dwarf calls herself 'Guenevra' after the queen of Arthurian legend, while the male court dwarf has taken on the identity of 'Nectabanus', referring to the 'Nectanebus' character of Egyptian legend (based on the real pharaoh Nectanebo II) who disguises himself as a dragon and fathers Alexander the Great in the

Alexander Romance. Looking on the two dwarfs 'as if spellbound', Sir Kenneth remembers 'the popular creed … concerning the gnomes or earthly spirits which make their abode in the caverns of the earth'.[100] Additional tropes in Scott's representation of dwarfs include emerging from rocks or subterranean passages, supernatural strength (for moving rocks), being illuminated by lamps or moonlight, unearthly voices, outlandish clothing, overgrown facial hair, and disproportioned, even gigantic, physical features. (I discuss the gigantism of Scott's dwarfs in Chapter 6, alongside my commentary on the dwarf character in Mary Shelley's story 'The Transformation'.) Overall, Scott frames physiological dwarfism as a deep peculiarity, specifically located in history yet with a consistent aesthetic that recalls the supernatural and necromantic beings of old romances and rumours.

Dwarfs, in Scott's novels, can be objects of fun. However, bodies perceived to combine 'dwarfish' and 'gigantic' qualities easily become objects of apprehension, recalling tales supposedly more widely believed in ancient times. Scott repeatedly professes feelings of revulsion and pity towards the dwarf characters, an attitude which he frames as enlightened by contrast with amused contempt or credulous fear. *The Talisman*, for example, contextualises the historical phenomenon of employing court dwarfs as jesters by referring to the unenlightened mindset of an earlier age: Sir Kenneth 'could not, from their language, manners, and appearance, doubt that they belonged to the degraded class of beings whom deformity of person and weakness of intellect recommended to the painful situation of appendages to great families, where their personal appearance and imbecility were food for merriment to the household'; and the knight, '[s]uperior in no respect to the ideas and manners of his time, [. . .] might, at another period, have been much amused by the mummery of these poor effigies of humanity'.[101] Unable to sympathise with the view of court dwarfs as amusing, Scott asks the reader to share in his feelings of disgust and pity, the words 'poor' and 'unhappy' occurring in all his characterisations of dwarfs.

By far the most complex and humanised of Scott's dwarf characters is 'Sir' Geoffrey Hudson, in *Peveril of the Peak* (1822), who is described as 'rather ludicrous than disagreeable to look upon', having 'nothing positively ugly in his countenance, or actually distorted in his limbs'.[102] Geoffrey combines the role of a court dwarf with the Quixotic fanaticism of a romance-reader, the pretensions of a cavalier and the comedy typical of a garrulous servant character. The novel suggests that the court's treatment of him is a kind of abuse, even while hypocritically partaking in some scenes as 'food for merriment'. As well as the more dramatic humiliations, Geoffrey is subject to quotidian ableism: '"Confusion to the scoundrel Clink, he has put the spice-box out of my reach!–Will you hand it to me from the mantelpiece?"'[103] In varying its language for continual references to Geoffrey's size, the narrative uses phrases such as 'little Knight', 'dwarfish hero' and 'this diminutive person', as well as the term 'pigmy' (from the Greek *pugmaios*, 'dwarf'), rather than likening him to an animal. Scott's relatively measured and sympathetic accounting of Hudson's physique, atypical of descriptions of dwarfs elsewhere in his novels, has techniques in common with the description, in *Rob Roy*, of the hero's disproportioned body: Geoffrey's body is 'much thicker than was consistent with symmetry', while Rob's shoulders and arms exceed 'the rules of symmetry'.[104] Rob's body is a deep peculiarity, connecting him with the beings in the tales of 'ancient times' told by Frank's Northumbrian nurse: 'according to her traditions, [...] a sort of half goblin half human beings, distinguished, like this man, for courage, cunning, ferocity, the length of their arms, and the squareness of their shoulders'.[105] *The Black Dwarf*, having recounted the discovery of the Black Dwarf's true identity of Sir Edward Mauley, concludes with a reassertion of the common beliefs and tales, among the local people, about 'the Man of the Moors, whose feats were quoted by Mrs Elliot to her grandsons'. Over time, Mauley's association with the malignant supernatural has only increased, such that 'the evils most dreaded and deprecated by the inhabitants of that pastoral country, are ascribed to the agency of the Black Dwarf'.[106] Scott qualifies this in the Magnum Introduction to the novel with a note that 'some of the poor and ignorant, as well as all the children, in the neighbourhood, held [David Ritchie] to be what is called *uncanny*', and that 'even in a rude Scottish glen thirty years back, the fear of sorcery was very much out of date'.[107] The novels make 'interest' out of the 'deep peculiarity' they ascribe to dwarf characters – presenting their bodies for reader's awe and amusement – while also consigning that attitude to the past.

While the texts of the novels inhabit the credulity of local, common and ancient attitudes to dwarfs generally, the Magnum editions of *The Black Dwarf*, *Rob Roy* and *Peveril of the Peak* ground the novels' 'personal descriptions' in anecdotes about specific historical people. The Magnum Opus *Rob Roy* repeats words from Frank's description in the form of a historical anecdote, changing Frank's phrase 'I afterwards heard' to 'it was said', and giving a measurement in inches (something also done in the Magnum notes on the other dwarf characters):

> His stature was not of the tallest, but his person was uncommonly strong and compact. The greatest peculiarities of his frame were the breadth of his shoulders, and the great and almost disproportioned length of his arms; so remarkable, indeed, that it was said that he could, without stooping, tie the garters of his Highland hose, which are placed two inches below the knee.[108]

Giving evidence for the character Sir Geoffrey Hudson in the Magnum Opus notes to *Peveril*, Scott begins by clarifying that this is the name of a real individual: 'Geoffrey or Jeffrey Hudson is often mentioned in anecdotes of Charles I.'s time'.[109] The Magnum notes specify Jeffrey Hudson's height in feet and inches at different times of life, substantiate the character's own tales of the pie and the duel, and allude to 'many squabbles with the King's gigantic porter' (suggesting an echo with *Kenilworth*'s 'gigantic porter' who finds a '"dwarfish auxiliary"' in Dickie Sludge), who is mentioned in the novel as a '"tall fellow"' who '"carried you about in his pocket, Sir Geoffrey, as all the world heard tell"'.[110] Scott refers the reader to Van Dyck's painting *Queen Henrietta Maria with Sir Jeffrey Hudson* (1633) and to Hudson's clothes, 'said to be preserved as articles of curiosity in Sir Hans Sloan's [sic] Museum'.[111] The Van Dyck painting, which physically idealises both subjects and registers the queen's favouritism for Hudson (who became valued as an advisor as well as an entertainer) makes an ironic contrast with Scott's description of Geoffrey – equipped with a simmering pot and a massive codex 'well-nigh and tall and bulky as himself' – as fit for a more 'romantic' sort of painting, where the sitter takes on an exotic character:

> The singularity of his features, and of the eyes, armed with spectacles [...] now directed towards his little cauldron, would have tempted Rembrandt to exhibit him on canvas, either in the character of an alchymist, or of a necromancer, engaged in some strange experiment, under the direction of one of the huge manuals which treat of the theory of these mystic arts.

In fact, Scott's narrator reveals, Geoffrey is making soup for breakfast.

Fleshing out anecdotes of a historical person of whom little is known, Scott builds a relatively sympathetic many-sided portrait that nevertheless has dwarfism at the centre of it, as the shaping force of Geoffrey's character. There is a touch of Lismahago's perverse arguments in Geoffrey's obsession with proving 'the superiority of men of little stature', a topic 'so great a favourite with him, that [...] the dwarf had collected almost all the instances of their victories over giants, which history or romance afforded'.[112] *Peveril*, like *Dwarf*, attempts a sympathetic view of the misanthropy expressed by the persecuted dwarfs, imagining through the character of Geoffrey that the real Jeffrey Hudson must have possessed 'great jealousy of being despised, on account of the peculiarity of his outward form'.[113] Following Francis Bacon's notion of 'a perpetual Spur' within the deformed person,[114] Scott speculates that dwarfism engenders 'restless desire' for importance, framing Geoffrey's Piercie-like vanity for lavish clothes and large moustaches as the result of 'the unhappy taste which frequently induces those whom nature has marked by personal deformity, to distinguish, and at the same time to render themselves ridiculous, by the use of showy colours, and garments fantastically and extraordinarily fashioned'.[115] Geoffrey first appears to Peveril as 'a small bundle of crimson cloth' and the court dwarfs in *The Talisman* also wear red cloth, luxurious 'samite, fantastically cut and flounced'.[116] Scott's dwarf characters are rendered either ridiculous or repulsive by their clothing, with 'the richness of [Nectabanus's clothing] render[ing] his ugliness more conspicuous', and the Black Dwarf's 'cap made of badger's skin, or some other rough fur, [. . .] add[ing] considerably to the grotesque effect of his whole appearance, and overshadowed features'.[117] This was a romantic departure from the existing anecdotes about Ritchie, with Robert Chambers's essay for the *Scots Magazine* (1817) noting 'nothing very uncommon about his dress'.[118] The Magnum Introduction to *The Black Dwarf* is Scott's most extensive grounding of a character in a recently living person – breaking the taboo against creating particularised portraits of contemporary individuals.

The Body-Corporate: National Caricatures

In this final part of the chapter, I consider a selection of 'explained caricatures' of national and ethnic minorities in Scott's novels. First, I look at how Rashleigh's caricature of a Scottish national character in *Rob Roy*, like Hazlitt's essay 'On the Scotch Character', views the Scottish character as a self-inflicted caricature of itself. I suggest a link with Austen's moral concept of caricature as an effect of self-importance and self-interest, here applied to a national character distinguished primarily by its 'corporate' self-regard for national character and national interests. Scott uses Rashleigh's cynical voice to theorise that individual self-love is the psychological complex underlying clannishness and beyond that a 'selfish nationalism'. I analyse how *The Heart of Mid-Lothian* uses Jeanie Deans's interactions with fellow Scots to agree with Rashleigh's essential premise, as part of a sympathetic account of Scots' conflation of self and nation. The last pages of the chapter examine Scott's hateful account of Jewish character in *Ivanhoe*. I show how Scott offers a historical explanation for Jewish character being an actual and self-inflicted caricature of itself, and how he uses the story of Abraham of Bristol to illustrate his idea that Jewish self-defence under international persecution was self-demeaning in ways that perpetuated anti-Semitism. Scott's idea that a group of people can 'distort' and 'dwarf' itself into a literal caricature through adapting to cope with oppression echoes the rhetoric from Wollstonecraft's comparison of women with the English Dissenters, as groups self-caricatured through a combination of passiveness and energy expended in a restricted sphere. In contrast to these histories of excluded groups resorting to evasive, reactive tactics, the self-interested wariness of the Scottish national character – made so offensive by Rashleigh's and Hazlitt's characterisations – is framed by Scott as an active strategy, taken independently of other groups.

In Rashleigh's characterisation of Scottish nationalism, the Scotsman is the architect and defender of a fortified castle, a castle that represents the limitations placed on the individual's humanitarian impulses by a nationalism that is merely an extension of self-interest. The castle simultaneously prevents outsiders from entering and prevents inhabitants from leaving. Mixing metaphors, Rashleigh also imagines the Scottish national corporation as a failing circulatory system, unable to pump blood far from its heart. He describes:

> [A] narrow spirited, but yet ardent patriotism, which forms as it were the outmost of the concentric bulwarks with which a Scotchman fortifies himself against all the attacks of a generous philanthropic principle. Surmount this mound, you find an inner and yet dearer barrier – the love of his province, his village, or, most probably of his clan; storm this second obstacle, you have a third – his attachment to his own family, his father, mother, sons, daughters, uncles, aunts, and cousins, to the ninth generation. It is only within these circles that a Scotchman's social affection expands itself, never reaching those which are outermost, till all means of discharging itself in the interior circles have been exhausted. It is within these circles that his heart throbs, each pulsation beating fainter and fainter, till, beyond the widest boundary, it is almost unfelt. And what is worst of all, could you surmount these concentric outworks, you have an inner citadel, deeper, higher, and more efficient than them all – a Scotchman's love for himself.

Terms such as 'philanthropic', 'attachment' and 'social affection' only partly conceal that Rashleigh is talking about love in order to talk about money. When Diana objects that the caricature '"is *not* true"' – Rashleigh retorts that '"*is* true, [. . .] because you cannot deny I know the country and people intimately, and the character is drawn from deep and accurate consideration'".[119] He speaks from experience, he says, when he accuses Campbell (really Rob MacGregor) of being too efficient a businessman, hesitating to help Frank due to '"seeing no prospect of personal advantage, but, on the contrary, much hazard of loss of time and delay of business'". Diana is forced to concede the point when Rashleigh points out Campbell's business concern in the matter.[120] The 'discharging' and 'pulsation' of the heart's blood is an expenditure that must be strictly rationed, and must be spent in ways that will yield some personal return. Rashleigh's Scotsman is like Austen's John Dashwood on a national scale, extending help to others only so far as his generosity guards his own interest, his selfishness doubled by the joining of others' interests to his own.

The satirical characterisation of the Scots corporation in *Rob Roy* draws somewhat on the common perceptions, frequently expressed by English natives throughout the long eighteenth century, that England was overrun with Scots 'placemen'; that Scots were conspicuously partial to working with each other; and that Scots advocated too much for Scotland (and, directly or indirectly, for themselves). In his essay 'On Scotch Character' Hazlitt holds up Smollett's character Lismahago as a humorously exaggerated portrait of Scottish patriotism – pointing out, however, that in everyday life this patriotism might be unpleasantly militant and take hostile forms. Whereas Rashleigh's self-interested Scot is a besieged and isolated castle – a Scot in Scotland – Hazlitt's is one of many mobile mercenaries prepared to go anywhere for what he can get:

> The Scotch nation are a body-corporate. They hang together like a swarm of bees, I do not know how it may be among themselves, but with us they are all united as one man. They are not straggling individuals, but embodied, formidable abstractions – determined personifications of the land they come from. A Scotchman gets on in the world, because he is not one, but many. He moves in himself a host, drawn up in battle-array, and armed at all points against impugners. His is a double existence – he stands for himself and his country. Every Scotchman is bond and surety for every other Scotchman [...]. Lismahago in Smollett is a striking and laughable picture of this national propensity. He maintained with good discretion and method that oat-cakes were better than wheaten-bread, and that the air of the old town of Edinburgh was sweet and salubrious. [...] In general his countrymen only plod on with the national character fastened behind them, looking around with wary eye and warning voice to those who would pick out a single article of their precious charge.[121]

In the Scots body-corporate, the nation and the individual are one and the same, patriotism a means of self-importance and self-interest. Hazlitt's image of the Scots as 'a swarm of bees' recalls satirical prints representing Scots as locusts and bringers of plague to England,[122] a prejudice ironically reversed in *Rob Roy* when Andrew complains about new British taxmen with references to the spoiling of Egypt in Exodus 12:36.[123] As in Rashleigh's caricature, the characterisation of Scots as stingy with their love, trust and assistance barely conceals the anxiety about how well Scots might be 'getting on in the world' financially.

Scott, himself named in Hazlitt's essay as a self-interested member of the Scots body-corporate,[124] joins Smollett in the role of cosmopolitan Scotsman professing a good-humoured, self-deprecating attitude to English characterisations of Scottish patriotism. Commenting on the propagandistic characterisations of the French, the Scots and the Irish in Smollett's 1757 farce *The Reprisal*,[125] Scott opines that '[t]he Scotchman and Irishman are hit off with the touch of a caricaturist of skill and spirit'.[126] An exiled Highlander turned ensign in the French service, the Latin-spouting Jacobite is obsessed with his family connections. The Englishman 'Heartly' and his clever English servant 'Brush' play on Maclaymore's clannishness to secure his assistance against the French: 'I won his heart', says Brush, 'with some transient encomiums on his country. I affected to admire his plaid, as an improvement on the Roman toga [...] and in order to clinch my remonstrance, told him that my master's great grandmother's aunt was a Scotchwoman of the name of Mackintosh, and that Mr. Heartly piqued himself on the Highland blood that ran in his veins'.[127] Playing to an English crowd, Scott and Smollett acknowledge the truth of the body-corporate and use it to flatter and entertain readers.

Scott was well aware that national 'caricatures' of the Scots and Irish were popular among English audiences – and the less they knew about Scotland and Ireland, the more exaggerated the characters had to be. Writing to London friends in June 1821, Scott urged them to attend a one-night performance of *Rob Roy* featuring a Scots actor, a 'Monsieur Mackay', who played the role of Baillie Nicol Jarvie – 'the purseproud [sic] consequential magistrate humane and irritable in the same moment' – 'with a degree of national truth and individuality which makes the part equal to any thing I have ever seen on stage'. Scott supposed that Mackay's acting would be underappreciated by the majority of the audience, 'doubt[ing] whether the exhibition will prove as satisfactory to those who do not know the original from which the resemblance is taken', and 'observ[ing that] the English demand (as is natural) broad caricature in the depicting of national peculiarities' and Mackay's Baillie is 'not sufficiently caricatured for their apprehensions'.[128] Scott does his bit to secure Mackay a Scottish reception at Covent Garden. Writing to Lord Montagu, he supposes that Mackay will be 'like a cow in a fremd loaning and glad of Scots countenance'. Writing to Baillie, he encourages her 'to collect a party of Scotch friends' to see Mackay: 'let it not be said that a dramatic genius of Scotland wanted the countenance and protection of Joanna Baillie'. Without 'broad caricature', Mackay's performance of a distinctively Scottish character relies on Scottish patronage. Despite making a great success of the part in Edinburgh, he will be at Covent Garden for one night only. Scott hoped that by expanding his English readers' knowledge of Scotland, and by providing historical explanations for 'substantially true' renderings of national peculiarities, he could help to nuance appetites for 'caricature' and problematise antagonistic characterisations like Rashleigh's, which could scarcely ameliorate relations between inhabitants of the two countries. Since the writing of *Rob Roy* overlapped with the planning of *The Heart of Mid-Lothian*,[129] the second novel's depiction of the Scots corporation can be seen as Scott's immediate response to Rashleigh's caricature of stingy sympathy.

In *Heart of Mid-Lothian*, Scott takes the concept of Scottish self-interest expressed unsympathetically by the outsiders Rashleigh and by Hazlitt – and turns it around, revealing the intimacy on the other side of exclusivity. Passages about Scots 'intimacy' in *The Heart of Mid-Lothian* use very different language and imagery to describe what is essentially the same concept of the Scots body-corporate, countering Rashleigh's satirical tone while agreeing with the premise of his caricature. Where Rashleigh's vocabulary focuses on what the Scots body excludes by means of 'bulwarks', 'barrier', 'obstacle' and 'boundary', *The Heart of Mid-Lothian*, acknowledging the diversity of Scottish society, focuses on how the body-corporate can include Scots people of different classes and regions. Where Rashleigh depicts a Scots sympathy soon 'exhausted', *Heart of Mid-Lothian* sees it 'extended'. Concrete metaphors of 'bulwarks' and 'barriers' are switched out for more abstract 'connections', 'bonds' and 'associations'. Scott considers from an insider's perspective how the Scots body-corporate morally – rather than materially – benefits its members, particularly those who might find themselves at a socio-economic disadvantage. Because members of the corporation see themselves as representatives of larger units, they are more personally involved in a larger range of moral events. This is explored when Scott depicts Jeanie Deans struggling, self-consciously, with her part in the Deans family corporation. The narrator states even-handedly that Scots' 'intimacy' with each other has positive as well as negative effects: the self-interest and self-importance of the body-corporate can have self-improving effects on individuals, encouraging them to value their good qualities more highly, and to imagine more far-reaching consequences for their misdeeds. Being self-involved may be morally suspect in itself, but it has the effect of making the individual more deeply involved overall, increasing their total investment in the qualities they value, and raising the importance of the education and guardianship that members might extend to each other. These bonds, Scott suggests, are strongest within families, and most intense where the family lacks shared assets of more material worth:

> It is well known, that much, both of what is good and bad in the Scottish national character, arises out of the intimacy of their family connections. 'To be come of honest folk,' that is, of people who have borne a fair and unstained reputation, is an advantage as highly prized among the lower Scotch, as the emphatic counterpart, 'to be of a good family,' is valued among their gentry. The worth and respectability of one member of a peasant's family is always accounted by themselves and others, not only a matter of honest pride, but a guarantee for the good conduct of the whole. On the contrary, such a melancholy stain as was now flung on one of the children of Deans, extended its disgrace to all connected with him, and Jeanie felt herself lowered at once, in her own eyes, and in those of her lover. It was in vain that she repressed this feeling, as far subordinate and too selfish to be mingled with her sorrow for her sister's calamity. Nature prevailed; and while she shed tears for her sister's distress and danger, there mingled with them bitter drops of grief for her own degradation.[130]

By illustrating the principle of Scots intimacy with Jeanie's tears, shed for herself as well as her sister, Scott disarms the body-corporate that bristles with masculine energy and military fortification in Rashleigh's and Hazlitt's imagery. By exemplifying the Scots corporation in a powerless and impoverished family, Scott distances the concept from nepotism and ill-gotten upward mobility, cleansing words such as 'prized', 'valued', 'accounted' and 'guarantee' of pecuniary associations.

When Jeanie encounters the Duke of Argyll later in the novel, Scott suggests that Scots intimacy can also connect the most disadvantaged families with the highest ranking, thus lending the body-corporate an ideal of nobility. Again, an insider's perspective is required to appreciate that from exclusivity and meanness to non-Scots, the body-corporate derives its strengths of inclusivity and generosity:

> Perhaps one ought to be actually a Scotchman to conceive how ardently, under all distinctions of rank and situation, they feel their mutual

connexion with each other as natives of the same country. There are, I believe, more associations common to the inhabitants of a rude and wild, than of a well cultivated and fertile country; their ancestors have more seldom changed their place of residence; their mutual recollections of remarkable objects are more accurate; the high and the low are more interested in each other's welfare; the feelings of kindred and relationship are more widely extended, and, in a word, the bonds of patriotic affection, always honourable even when a little too exclusively strained, have more influence on men's feelings and actions.[131]

Scots intimacy is romanticised, here, as an effect of a static society that retains historic identifications of people and place. The corporation seems to preserve the ghost of an ancient 'honour' that was not merely a code of behaviour, but an intense and authentic sensitive response to perceived wrongs. Scott invites English readers to reconceive the Scots body-corporate as an ancient kinship natural to all peoples, lost to civilization – not a self-defensive construction peculiar to the Scots.

The Heart of Mid-Lothian addresses the moral problem of the body-corporate most directly, and counters Rashleigh's and Hazlitt's arguments most explicitly, in the scene where the Scottish landlady of an English inn presses Jeanie to accept her assistance. Here, Scott acknowledges the hostility towards the 'prejudice', 'narrowness' and 'partiality' of the Scots body-corporate. Once more, he asks the reader to shift their perspective: rather than judge the Scottish character against an ideal of universal beneficence, they might understand the corporation as an honour system enabling individuals to deploy their finite resources in targeted, effective ways. The landlady's ability to feel personally involved in the interests of a countrywoman she has never met before is not merely a 'feeling' or 'sentiment', however. Her honour consists both in her acceptance of the national 'guarantee' for Jeanie's character, and in her belief that Jeanie sees her in the same way. Mutually assured, each woman owes to the other the good conduct for which their common national character stands surety:

> [T]he eagerness with which Scottish people meet, communicate, and, to the extent of their power, assist each other, although it is often objected to us, as a prejudice and narrowness of sentiment, seems, on the contrary, to arise from a most justifiable and honourable feeling of patriotism, combined with a conviction, which, if undeserved, would long since have been confuted by experience, that the habits and principles of the nation are a sort of guarantee for the character of the individual. At any rate, if the extensive influence of this national partiality be considered as an additional tie, binding man to man [...] we think it must be found to exceed, as an active and efficient motive to generosity, that more impartial and wider

principle of general benevolence, which we have sometimes seen pleaded as an excuse for assisting no individual whatever.[132]

Hazlitt's essay uses the phrase 'bond and surety', a synonymising that sharpens the words' financial associations, in describing Scots' 'double existence' of national and individual character. Scots' reliance on each other for material advantage, for 'getting on in the world', presents outsiders with a debt-based economy of characters: commodities are continually dissolving into promissory notes, and notes into commodities; every asset is mortgaged, collateral for another enterprise. Scottish characters seem, like paper money, infinitely interchangeable and possessing no intrinsic value. In *The Heart of Mid-Lothian*, on the other hand, Scott's repeated use of the word 'guarantee' (as well as 'bonds' and 'binding') describes a national network of Scots honourably and mutually indebted, such that individual characters secure credit for themselves by advancing it to others. The system enables even the members of society with fewest material advantages to incur debts of assistance and repay them in another form. Because it is impractical to try to assist everyone in an entirely disinterested and impartial way, 'general benevolence' is of less market value than an honour system where different benefits are more readily exchanged and nebulous sympathies made 'efficient'. Thanks to a collective feat of imagination, tangible benefits convert easily to intangible ones, and vice versa. The Scottish economy of national character is, as *The Heart of Mid-Lothian* presents it, a virtuous cycle of the intrinsic value of individuals adding to the extrinsic value of the national character which is invested back into individuals. Hazlitt admits, 'I do not know how it may be among themselves'. The body-corporate that presents outsiders with the effect of a self-constructed 'national caricature', Scott claims, will necessarily seem more exclusive, prejudiced and political – not just a character but an *identity* – the more that its solidarity, maintained by mutual self-interest, is strong and effective.

In *Rob Roy* and *The Heart of Mid-Lothian*, the 'national caricature' effect emerges from the strength and activity of a self-interested and self-identifying Scots body-corporate engaging in a virtuous cycle of giving and receiving. Scots' supposed propensity to help each other is imagined as a debt-based economy facilitated by the abstraction of national character. In *Ivanhoe*, on the other hand, Scott's description of a Jewish self-caricature – though it contains a measure of sympathy in its emphasis on the history of hated and oppression of Jews by 'Norman, Saxon, Dane, and Briton'[133] – presents financial instruments for exchange of foreign currencies both as an adaptive response to persecution and as a mechanism for exacerbating detestable national peculiarities. Jews, Scott claims, are a self-made caricature emerging from a vicious cycle, where channelling the moral defect of materialism into survival tactics exacerbates an obsession with money:

> In spite of [...] a special court of taxations, called the Jews' Exchequer, erected for the very purpose of despoiling and distressing them, the Jews increased, multiplied, and accumulated huge sums, which they transferred from one hand to another by means of bills of exchange—an invention for which commerce is said to be indebted to them, and which enabled them to transfer their wealth from land to land, that when threatened with oppression in one country, their treasure might be secured in another.
>
> The obstinacy and avarice of the Jews being thus in a measure placed in opposition to the fanaticism and tyranny of those under whom they lived, seemed as it were to increase in proportion to the persecution with which they were visited; and the immense wealth they usually acquired in commerce, while it frequently placed them in danger, was at other times used to extend their influence and to secure them a certain degree of protection. On these terms they lived, and their character, influenced accordingly, was watchful, suspicious, and timid—yet obstinate, uncomplying, and skilful in evading the dangers to which they were exposed.[134]

This first introduction of the 'Isaac of York' character, though it emphasises the hatred directed at Isaac, also assumes the reader's agreement about physical and ethical peculiarities of a Jewish 'national character'. The narrator shifts from complimenting Isaac on his individual physiognomy, to claiming that his face was inevitably read as a signifier of ugliness:

> His features, keen and regular, with an aquiline nose, and piercing black eyes, would have been considered as handsome, had they not been the marks of a physiognomy peculiar to a race, which, during these dark ages, was alike detested by the credulous and prejudiced vulgar, and persecuted by the greedy and rapacious nobility, and who, perhaps, owing to that very hatred and persecution, had adopted a national character, in which there was much, to say the least, mean and unamiable.

Scott's sympathetic framing of Isaac's appearance at Cedric's court – 'an outcast in the present society, like his people among the nations, looking in vain for welcome or resting place' – sits alongside the strong insinuation that Jews are complicit in anti-Semitism: that they did not have the moral character to withstand unjust persecution, and thus are responsible for a national character that provokes a now *righteous* persecution.[135]

While Scott makes the beauty of Isaac's physiognomy a contrast with anti-Semitic hatred of Jewish faces, he still locates elements of 'national caricature' in Isaac's body. He gives the evasiveness and passiveness of the 'national character' a physical dimension, following the logic used by Wollstonecraft in her argument that Dissenters were physically diminished by the tactics to which they habitually resorted and by self-imposed limits, 'shap[ing] their persons as well as their minds in the mould of prim littleness'.[136] Isaac of York is first pictured 'advanc[ing] with fear and hesitation, and many a bow of deep humility', through which practice he has permanently altered his stature: 'a tall, thin old man, who, however, had lost by the habit of stooping much of his actual height'.[137] An explained caricature not completely unlike Hazlitt's Scotsman 'armed at all points against impugners' and Rashleigh's Scotsman fortified against philanthropy, Scott's characterisation of Isaac claims that the Jew's offensiveness arises from the amplification of moral failings by his own defensive tactics. The narrative acknowledges the Jew's vulnerability among racist opportunists, reasoning that Isaac's 'doubts [about Ivanhoe, disguised as a pilgrim] might have been indeed pardoned; for, except perhaps the flying fish, there was no race existing on the earth, in the air, or the waters, who were the object of such as unintermitting, general, and relentless persecution as the Jews of this period'.[138] Isaac seeks the safety of Sheffield, a town with a substantial Jewish community where he can '"harbour with [his] kinsman Zareth, and find some means of travelling forth with safety"'.[139] He directs Ivanhoe to Leicester, where his 'kinsman' Kirjath Jairam will lend the knight gear for the tournament. Having promised Ivanhoe credit to secure a horse and armour, Isaac does not withdraw his offer in spite of the knight's warning that he may not be able to repay the debt – but '[t]he Jew twisted himself in his saddle, like a man in a fit of the cholic', a physical convulsion that betrays self-interest so chronic that it distorts the body.[140] Ivanhoe smiles on him with amusement and contempt. The Jewish national character is demeaned by prejudice – but that character then really is diminished, Scott claims, with Isaac physically diminished by his own fearfulness. Scott implies that an upright posture of bravery and dignity would have allowed the Jews to adopt a better national character. Key passages in *Ivanhoe* thus intellectualise, through historical explanations, the early nineteenth-century suspicions about 'wandering commercial Jews' also expressed in Scott's personal writings.[141] In this 'historically explained caricature', Jews are supposedly complicit in the diminishing and deforming of character to fit the outlet granted to it.

Complicity is a factor in Jewish national caricature also in Edgeworth's relatively sympathetic *Harrington* (1817). After her correspondence with an American reader, Rachel Mordecai, Edgeworth wrote a novel focused on Jewish characters and with a plot revolving around a fictional history painting titled *The Dentition of the Jew*. One of the characters purchases and destroys this painting, to prevent its being purchased by an engraver and thus '"seen and sold in every print-shop in London"'.[142] The painting depicts the much-chronicled story of King John's torture of a Jewish merchant, named Abraham of Bristol in some accounts. In 1210, John extorted money from England's wealthier Jewish families by imprisoning important male family members and demanding massive ransoms. Abraham was held in Bristol Castle, where torturers removed one of his molars on each of the seven days that he refused to pay the ten thousand marks King John demanded. In *Harrington*, Montenero wants to destroy *The Dentition* because it causes painful disgust to those who see it. Glimpsing the framed painting in Montenero's hands, the protagonist is 'struck [...] with such associated feelings of horror' that he physically recoils from the image, shouting '"I cannot bear it! I cannot bear that picture!"' Montenero suggests that the painting made Harrington feel '"sick"'.[143] When Montenero tears it up and burns the pieces, he explains that he would destroy, if he could, '"every record of cruelty and intolerance"': *The Dentition* is one such record '"that can keep alive feelings of hatred and vengeance between Jews and Christians!"'[144] Harrington ironically refers to the painting's destruction as an '*auto-da-fé*'. Edgeworth thus shows a Jewish character taking responsibility for repairing Jewish–Christian relations by attempting to erase the most sadistic acts of anti-Semitism from the historical record.

While Edgeworth's depictions of a Jewish family differ greatly from Scott's in *Ivanhoe*, in this respect they are singing from the same hymn sheet: Montenero represents Scott's ideal Jew, who would take a particular kind of active role in rapprochement – not only forgiving Christians' cruelty, but attempting to remove the need for forgiveness by preventing Jews' and Christians' knowledge of it. My view of the novel's ideal of Jewish heroism is supported by the fact that Montenero destroys a painting inspired by historical chronicles, rather than speaking against textual caricatures of Jews of the kind that occur in Harrington's reading material:

> And here I must observe, that not only in the old story books, where the Jews are sure to be wicked as the bad fairies, or bad genii, or allegorical personifications of the devils, and the vices in the old emblems, mysteries, moralities, &c.; but in almost every work of fiction, I found them represented as hateful beings; nay, even in modern tales of very late years, since I have come to man's estate, I have met with books by authors professing candour and toleration—books written expressly for the rising generation,

> called, if I mistake not, Moral Tales for Young People; and even in these, wherever the Jews are introduced, I find that they are invariably represented as beings of a mean, avaricious, unprincipled, treacherous character. Even the peculiarities of their persons, the errors of their foreign dialect and pronunciation, were mimicked and caricatured, as if to render them objects of perpetual derision and detestation.

Edgeworth is clearly reflecting on the ways in which her own fiction participates in the caricaturing of Jews, and acknowledging that 'the indisputable authority of *printed books*' enables such caricatures to reinforce readers' anti-Semitism.[145] However, like Scott in *Ivanhoe* two years later, Edgeworth also insists on Jews proving themselves undeserving of persecution by minimising the impact it has on them and by re-forming their character as though the violence never took place. Scott, too, refers to the dentition of Abraham of Bristol in *Ivanhoe*, where the formulation of the character's name 'Isaac of York' is the first allusion to the historical narrative. In *Ivanhoe*, Abraham of Bristol is used to illustrate both the extreme cruelty of the Jews' oppressors and the extremity of the Jewish self-caricature. Abraham's capacity to withstand torture and tolerate mutilation seems to prove, for Scott, the depth of his avarice:

> It is a well-known story of King John, that he confined a wealthy Jew in one of the royal castles, and daily caused one of his teeth to be torn out, until, when the jaw of the unhappy Israelite was half disfurnished, he consented to pay a large sum, which it was the tyrant's object to extort from him. The little ready money which was in the country was chiefly in possession of this persecuted people, and the nobility hesitated not to follow the example of their sovereign, in writing it from them by every species of oppression, and even personal torture. Yet the passive courage inspired by the love of gain induced the Jews to dare the various evils to which they were subjected, in consideration of the immense profits which they were enabled to realize in a country naturally so wealthy as England.[146]

The implication is that only a man obsessed with money would lose teeth rather than pay a ransom. Scott's assumption here – that his British readers would be willing to accept Abraham's dentition as a story illustrating Jewish just as much as English greed – perhaps sheds light on the fact that the characters in *Harrington* perceive Edgeworth's fictive painting *The Dentition of the Jew* as both a record of anti-Semitic persecution and a derogatory caricature of 'the Jewish character', because it seems to represent materialism extreme enough to justify anti-Semitism. Whereas Edgeworth proposes that the painting be destroyed, the history effaced and the vicious cycle of national caricature broken, Scott makes his history of the Jews indispensable to explaining what Jews are 'really like'. *Harrington* speculates on a world where the historical caricature of Jewish materialism and 'passive courage' is perceptible as rotten, sickening.

This chapter has explored how Scott's admiring concept of historical 'caricature' was beset, in practice, by readers' objections to compendious realism's non-protagonist characters as artificial, incredible and temporary. Characters such as Caleb Balderstone and Piercie Shafton, Scott realised, might fail to convince a broad and multi-generational readership that historical 'caricatures' – characterisations identifying absurdity and peculiarity in historically specific manners, mental processes and ways of life – were key to his novels' varied and highly textured realism. On the other hand, the characters whose bodies can be compared with graphic caricatures – such as Edward Mauley, Rob MacGregor and Geoffrey Hudson – afford a 'deep peculiarity' intersecting romance and actual reference. The Magnum Opus editions work hard to substantiate all these characters with historical sources, giving a sense of such potential 'caricatures' – peculiar to the point of implausibility – as especially vulnerable to time passing and literary tastes changing, despite all the apparatus that a critical edition can provide. In *The Heart of Mid-Lothian*, when Scott gives a historical explanation for the 'national caricature' of the Scots body-corporate, he imagines Scots being able to share highly peculiarised realities: 'mutual recollections of remarkable objects are more accurate' between them. In this imagining of histories intimately shared by living Scottish people – a minutely textured and folkloric knowledge of things past – there is a natural and vernacular precursor to his own compendious, historical and romantic realism. In novels for a broad readership, however, historical 'caricature' carries within it the nightmare of a tapestry rotting before the author's eyes: this is the many-coloured fabric of knowledge and assumptions about historical reality that his readers share with him and with each other, disintegrating at an accelerated rate. Other realisms might deteriorate more slowly. Austen's realism has been able to make relatively strong claims to literary immortality, first because it prides itself on the author's complete knowledge of a limited time and place, and second because it retains a readership whose understanding of that moment has been shored up by adaptations and cultural heritage.

For Scott's compendiously historical novels, however, as readers' knowledge (including their assumptions and prejudices) about the novelist's subjects becomes vaguer, realism becomes less assured. The scope of readers' caricature talk contracts, with characters' peculiarities generally less subject to detailed debate and instead dismissed as unintelligible, extraneous or offensive. Through the historically explained caricatures in Scott's romances, we can experience an acute, even exaggerated, anxiety about the contingency of literary realisms: they might seem to forecast the fragility and obsolescence of *all* realisms, as they present us with an extreme case of realism's betrayal by readers who know differently.

CHAPTER 6

Mary Shelley, Flesh-Caricature and Horrid Realism

The disproportioned and distorted bodies in Mary Shelley's horror writing have a legacy from the 'flesh-caricatures' of eighteenth-century writing descriptive of the body, where social critique and moral counsel often give way to materialist, detail-oriented fascination with the physical 'caricaturing' of the human body in vulnerable transitional states. From Thomas Browne's *Letter to a Friend* (1690) to J. P. Malcolm's *Historical Sketch of the Art of Caricaturing* (1813): in the century before *Frankenstein*, the *troppo caricato* meaning of *caricatúra* lends itself to lurid descriptions that not only speak on the subject of 'deformity' but offer grotesque representations of bodies partitioned into proportions and contrasts. Shelley and Scott use 'flesh-caricature' tropes as occasions for a 'horrid realism' of descriptive and narrative techniques that work to disrupt political and moral allegories of monstrosity. In *Frankenstein* (1818) and in Shelley's short story 'Transformation' (1831), horrid realism's literalising and fragmenting effects reify and 'de characterise' deviant bodies into collections of material facts. This strain of horror writing dismantles character's place in formal realism, eliciting pseudo-sensory revulsion by continually drawing legible 'character' into tension with the mixed particulars of the material body. In horror writing's legacy from Romantic caricature talk, representation becomes flesh: caricature is made real, 'character' put in quotation marks.

I begin by countering the argument that in *Frankenstein*'s descriptions of the creature's 'disproportion', Shelley's vocabulary is non-technical, and the narrators' accounts unreliable. Highlighting the understanding of corporeal disproportion and distortion in the Shelleys' editorial decisions, I argue that *Frankenstein* describes the creature's body consistently and reiteratively, making his physical being static and factual, rather than an impression that alters depending on the viewer, or according to changes in moral or psychological 'character'. Examining the ways in which Shelley's concept of disproportion carries over to her story 'Transformation', I show

how both narratives open the potential of a formal realism for horror writing through the 'gigantic dwarf', an aesthetic type associated with a compulsive rhythm of looking and not looking. Repeatedly presented as a disturbing combination of divergent physical characteristics and aesthetic effects, gigantic/dwarfish bodies are chronically partitioned and detailed, providing opportunities for a 'horrid realism' prosaically concerned with material bodies. I analyse the tropes and techniques Shelley uses to represent physical disproportion as grotesque in *Frankenstein* and 'Transformation', making comparisons with Scott's grotesques in *The Black Dwarf*, *Rob Roy*, *The Pirate* and *The Talisman*. Exploring how these de-characterisation techniques continually destabilise critical readings that abstract the body into an 'image' or signifier, I address how horrid realism exists alongside idealising physiognomic portraiture and the mind-body equation in Shelley's novels, close-reading key passages in *Frankenstein* and indicating variants in the novel's textual history that establish the grotesque body as an exception to physiognomic analysis.

In the last section of the chapter, I point out some concrete links between Shelley's flesh-caricatures and their non-fiction precedents, collating passages about the physical disproportioning of growing and dying bodies in texts such as John Locke's *Thoughts Concerning Education* (1728), Rousseau's *Émile* (1762) and William Buchan's *Domestic Medicine* (1769), as well as Browne's description of the Hippocratic face and Malcolm's theory of flesh-caricatures. To conclude Chapter 6, I suggest that the horrid realism developed through the depiction of 'gigantic dwarfs' in fiction – influentially by Scott, Hugo and Dickens as well as Shelley – can be seen to provide techniques, tropes and vocabulary for a tradition of flesh-caricatures in the 'body horror' subgenre.

Gigantic Dwarfs: Shelley's Vocabulary of Disproportion

It has been argued that *Frankenstein*'s descriptions of the creature's body do not use the term 'deformity' consistently, nor in accordance with Burke's attempt at a technical definition of deformity. Denise Gigante's focus on *ugliness* in *Frankenstein*, where ugliness 'precedes and predetermines [...] monstrosity', finds a gap where conceptions of ugliness might fit in eighteenth-century aesthetics, arguing that Shelley's monster represents an 'aesthetic impossibility: the positive manifestation of ugliness'.[1] This analysis separates ugliness from a particular conception of deformity, which refers to a *disproportioned* form. Thus, the monster, Gigante argues, is not actually 'deformed', quoting Burke's precept that '[t]hough ugliness be the opposite of beauty, it is not the opposite to proportion':[2]

> Certainly, the Creature is not 'opposite to proportion'. [...] As Burke explains, it is not ugliness but 'deformity' that is opposed to proportion: 'deformity is opposed, not to beauty, but to the *compleat, common form*' (*E*, 102; emphasis in the original). One must keep in mind that Burke is working from an aesthetic tradition that he feels has been unsystematic in its use of terms and inexact in mapping the terrain of the non-beautiful. Even the Creature refers to the 'deformity of [his] figure,' despite the fact that, although large, he is not technically deformed' (*F*, 142). When he sees himself in a transparent pool for the first time, he laments, 'the fatal effects of this miserable deformity' (*F*, 142). Yet, as his creator seems to know better than himself, deformity is a distinct category not to be confused [...] with the ugly.[3]

This argument refers to Victor's description, on the night of the creature's animation, of how he constructed the creature 'in proportion'.[4] Since Gigante's compelling distinction between the monster's deformity and his ugliness, scholarship on Shelley's fiction seems not to have re-examined the key point that the creature is well-proportioned, excepting Essaka Joshua's mentioning that '[p]roportionality is an important element in the description of the creature, though the accounts of it [in the novel] are inconsistent'.[5] Looking at descriptions of the creature in the 1818 *Frankenstein*, alongside the Shelleys' manuscript revisions and the treatment of a physically grotesque character in 'Transformation', I will argue that the creature *is* technically deformed and consistently described as such. In this chapter, I am interested in the creature's disproportion because of the fundamental role it might play in readings of the novel, not as a political, social or moral allegory, but as a literary pioneer in the development of a 'horrid realism' whose descriptions and narrative techniques insist on the body as a material fact that defies abstraction.

The creature is identified most positively with proportion in Victor's narration of the candlelit scene where he animates the creature and it takes its first breaths. We are told, indeed, that '[h]is limbs were in proportion' – but these five words, excerpted from the scene, and dislocated from the following scene of Victor's dream, give an incomplete description of the creature's general shape. It is necessary to re-examine some of the most quoted passages in the novel, starting with the moment of animation:

> [I]t breathed hard, and a convulsive motion agitated its limbs.
> How can I describe my emotions at this catastrophe, or how delineate the wretch whom with such infinite pains and care I had endeavoured to

form? His limbs were in proportion, and I had selected his features as beautiful. Beautiful!—Great God! His yellow skin scarcely covered the work of muscles and arteries beneath; his hair was of a lustrous black, and flowing; his teeth of a pearly whiteness; but these luxuriances only formed a more horrid contrast with his watery eyes (39).

Four points stand out here, with regard to the creature's proportions. First, that Shelley's paragraph contextualises the past tense of the limbs being 'in proportion' with Victor's pluperfect statements 'I *had* endeavoured' and '*had* selected'. When the phrase 'his limbs were in proportion' is quoted out of context, the past tense appears to belong in the first layer of the third-person past-tense narration, and to take on a continuous aspect: in other words, it seems that the creature was continuously well proportioned, before and after animation. In the text, however, the words are sandwiched between two pluperfect statements, imparting the sense of the limbs *having been* in proportion. After Victor's exclamation – 'Great God!' – we return to the first layer of the narrative's past tense, describing how the creature looks post-animation. My interpretation is that this passage ascribes the creature's proportion to his pre-animation state and to an earlier phase of Victor's process (perhaps even before the limbs were actually joined together).

The second point is that the creature's proportions are associated with Victor's attempted and unsuccessful process of *forming* – 'endeavoured to form' – not ascribed to a final, accomplished form; with the work of *choosing* – grouped with the features 'I had selected' and with the creature's multiple limbs rather than with the assembled whole of his body. Earlier in the novel, proportions are included in Victor's plan – 'I resolved [...] to make the being of a gigantic stature; that is to say, about eight feet in height, and proportionably large' – and so associated explicitly with the first stages, of the months spent 'successfully collecting and arranging my materials' (35–6). The third point is that the narration reiterates several times the distorting effect of animation on the creature's arms and legs. The moment when 'a convulsive motion agitated its limbs' is echoed in the following scene, where Victor wakes from a nightmare with 'every limb convulsed' (39). Then the pluperfect returns: 'I had gazed on him while unfinished; he was ugly then; but when those muscles and joints were rendered capable of motion, it became a thing such as even Dante could not have conceived' (40). Once the creature's body is made capable – its muscularity tense and its joints flexible – the ideal of proportion is unachievable. This could be interpreted as Victor's failure, when selecting pieces of the appropriate dimensions, to account for the impact of mobility and plasticity on the entire figure's final proportions. We might imagine the creature's limbs (or segments of his limbs) as disproportioned not because they are the wrong length but because some segments of his body, like the 'shrivelled' and readily 'wrinkled' skin on his face (39, 119, 138), have failed to fatten over 'the work of muscles and arteries beneath' (39). Fourth, when Victor's 'Beautiful! —Great God!' signals a switch from before to after, from a selection of beautiful features and proportioned limbs to a body whose different parts generate an effect of 'horrid contrast', Shelley introduces the idea of mismatch and disparity into her descriptions of the creature's physique. After Victor's stated intention to create a being 'proportionably large', the creature is never again depicted as gigantic yet well proportioned.

Quite the opposite. Walton's last letter describes the creature as 'gigantic in stature, yet uncouth and distorted in its proportions' (186–87), and Victor sees 'the distorted proportions of a well-known form' (176), aligning with the animation scene's representation of the creature's proportions as a failed project. While the word 'deformity' occasionally refers generally to the creature's form, when linked with more precise descriptions of the body it occurs with the words 'shape' and 'figure', suggesting a disproportioned outline. This association of the creature's deformity with his shape is reinforced in Shelley's draft notebooks of 1816–17, where Percy's revisions add the words 'shape', 'distorted' and 'proportions', and in one case attribute deformity to the creature's 'aspect'. This word, 'aspect', suggests a general 'look' or 'appearance', such that Percy's phrase 'deformity of its aspect' can also be consistent with a more technical definition, as in Burke, of a deformed body as internally disproportioned: the creature's 'aspect' is its general 'shape'. Mary's original draft reads:

> A flash of lightning illumined the object, and discovered to me its gigantic stature, deformity more hideous than belongs to humanity instantly informed me who it was.[6]

Percy adds a semi-colon that syntactically nudges the creature's 'deformity' away from its stature and towards the new word 'aspect'. He also adds the phrase 'human shape', amplifying Mary's original suggestion that there is something bestial or demonic about him, which exceeds the ugliness possible in a human, living or dead. Misshapenness, more than gigantic stature, is what disallows the creature's humanity. Edited by Percy, the passage reads:

> A flash of lightning illumined the object and discovered to me its gigantic stature; and the deformity of its aspect, more hideous than belongs to humanity, instantly informed me who it was. Nothing in human shape could have destroyed that fair child.

In the first published edition, this last sentence is moved later in the paragraph, but retained. The 1818 text also commits to 'shape', repeating the word in an addition to the first sentence:

> A flash of lightning illuminated the object, and discovered its shape plainly to me; its gigantic stature, and the deformity of its aspect, more hideous than belongs to humanity, instantly informed me that it was the wretch, the filthy daemon to whom I had given life (56).

Percy again adds the word 'shape' in another scene where the creature's body is illuminated, and also suggests the word 'distorted', a pairing that most explicitly aligns the creature's technical 'deformity' with disproportion. In the notebook draft, Mary writes:

> When suddenly the broard [sic] disk of the moon arose and shone fully upon the daemon who fled.[7]

With Percy's edits, this becomes:

> Suddenly the broard [sic] disk of the moon arose and shone fully upon his ghastly & distorted shape.

Anne K. Mellor has suggested that 'Percy Shelley on several occasions actually distorted the meaning of the text'[8] – here we see Percy actually adding the word 'distorted' to Mary's description of the creature.

The textual history of *Frankenstein* should not, however, credit Percy's revisions with introducing the novel's emphasis on the creature's proportions or its insistence on a technical definition of 'deformity' as disproportion or misshapenness. The key words and phrases in Mary's original descriptions of the creature's body, as just discussed, assume an educated reader's technical understanding of 'deformity', also assumed by Burke in his *Enquiry*. For example, in *Gulliver's Travels* (1726) – which Mary had been rereading – Gulliver's meticulous accounting of new worlds continually distinguishes size from proportion, and ugly imperfections from 'actual' deformity. In Brobdingnag and Lilliput, extraordinarily large and small things are nevertheless 'all in proportion', 'all in the same proportion', 'of proportionable Magnitude', 'of a size proportionable', 'a proportionable quantity', 'an exact proportion', and so on. When Gulliver describes a Brobdingnagian nurse, he is careful to differentiate the ugliness of a magnified human being from grotesque disproportion, 'lest the Reader might think those vast Creatures were actually deformed'.[9] While it is generally true that Percy 'tended to see the creature as more monstrous and less human than did Mary',[10] the chain of revisions between Mary's notebooks and the 1818 text show wife and husband collaborating on descriptions of the creature's 'actual deformity'. This is clearest in the textual history of the novel's final pages. In the scene where Victor spies the creature crossing the ice in a sledge, Mary's original draft reads:

> I strained my sight to view what it could be & uttered wild cry of extacy [sic] when I distinguished a sledge dogs & a hideous form moving away[11]

Percy alters this, substituting for the vaguer word 'hideous' a phrase corresponding with words – 'shape', 'proportion', 'deformity' – used earlier in the novel to describe the creature's physique more technically. As well as adding the word 'distorted' for the second time, he refers to the creature's 'proportions', a word not used since the account of Victor's plans for the creature's size. The draft becomes:

> I strained my sight to discover what it could be & uttered a wild cry of extacy [sic] when I distinguished a sledge dogs & the distorted proportions of a wellknown [sic] form within.

Continuing her notebook draft, in the scene of Walton's encounter with the creature, Mary reiterates the word 'distorted' (which now appears in the text for the third time) and re-uses the formula of distinguishing the extraordinary size of gigantism from the disproportion of technical deformity. The creature is huge *yet* deformed:

> Over him hung a form – which I cannot find words to describe, gigantic in stature – yet uncouth & distorted.[12]

In the fair copy, Mary further tweaks Walton's phrase, adding the word 'proportions' suggested by Percy for Victor's earlier remark about the creature's 'distorted proportions':

> Over him hung a form which I cannot find words to describe gigantic in stature, yet uncouth & distorted in its proportions.[13]

The 1818 text contains three further references to the creature's deformity in relation to his proportions, two of which use the word 'figure' as a synonym for 'shape'. The creature hopes that learning language will 'enable me to make [the cottagers] overlook the deformity of my figure; for with this also the contrast perpetually presented to my eyes had made me acquainted' (90); and he acknowledges that he possesses 'a figure hideously deformed' (96). The phrase 'this miserable deformity' (90), used when the creature recounts seeing himself reflected in a pool, and coming soon after the phrase 'deformity of my figure', incorporates the Burkean definition of deformity as 'an unusual figure' and 'the want of common proportions'.[14] The creature then recalls, 'From my earliest remembrance

I had been as I then was in height and proportion' (97), corroborating the implication that Victor's statement '[h]is limbs were in proportion' does not refer to the creature's body once assembled and animated, and affirming the consistency of the many descriptions of his body as deformed in the sense of being disproportioned.

While there is no record of whether these phrases were in Mary's original draft or were Percy's edits adopted by Mary in later versions – the draft notebooks for these chapters do not survive – their account of the creature's deformity as a matter of shape, figure and proportion is consistent with the definition of deformity agreed and reiterated by the Shelleys in the textual evolution discussed previously. Changes suggested by Percy, and agreed and re-applied by Mary in later drafts, create a consistent picture of the creature as being deformed, in Burke's technical sense of the word, because he is distorted in his proportions.

Shelley goes on to link the term 'deformity' consistently with misshapenness and disproportion in 'Transformation', a short story written in 1830 for the 1831 issue of the literary gift annual *The Keepsake*, around the time that she was preparing the third revised edition of *Frankenstein*. Whereas Frankenstein's creature is a disproportioned giant, the object of horror in 'Transformation' is a disproportioned dwarf. Shelley's descriptions of the dwarf's body participate in the 'gigantic dwarf' of nineteenth-century literature, a grotesque type that Scott influentially adapted to the realist novel – first in *The Black Dwarf* (1816), then in *The Pirate* (1822) and *The Talisman* (1825), and to a lesser extent in *Peveril of the Peak* (1823) and *Rob Roy* (1818). A keen reader of Scott, and influenced by him in her historical romance of *The Fortunes of Perkin Warbeck* (1830), Shelley had the opportunity to notice the emphasis on disproportion in Scott's evocative descriptions of characters strongly associated with folklore and the supernatural, and to contribute to a new novelistic tradition of visualising these characters. In the next section of the chapter, which focuses on the descriptive techniques of the 'horrid realism' used in nineteenth-century literature to present disproportioned bodies as grotesque, I will look in more detail at the language and imagery that Shelley and Scott use in characterising 'gigantic' and 'dwarfish' bodies. Here, I define the aesthetic type of the 'gigantic dwarf', whose physical disproportion is grotesqued as a chimerical combination of gigantic with dwarfish features, and where the author imagines the disturbing co-existence of the beautiful, the sublime, the ugly and/or the ludicrous. I show how authors' efforts to describe this aesthetic type generate a particular way of seeing, one that repeatedly drains the power of reason and sympathy, and which creates the conditions for the obsessive, objectifying focus of horrid realism. Shelley and Scott fantasise the gigantic/dwarfish being, with its disruptions to scale and proportion, as a test object for a realist mode that is concerned with the repetitive subdivision and detailing of material objects, and conscious of these descriptive techniques as horror writing.

Human gigantism and dwarfism were important cases in eighteenth-century aesthetics for thinking about perceptions of size, scale and proportion. In his inscription for *The Bench* (1758), Hogarth takes 'a Giant or a Dwarf' as a metaphor for the *outré* in art. Whereas a 'caricature', for Hogarth, is an inadvertently and comically simplistic drawing of the human form, resembling 'the early scrawlings of a child', a figure *outré* is an artistic distortion that still represents the human body accurately: *outré* 'signifies [...] the exaggerated outlines of a figure, all the parts of which may be in other respects, a perfect and true picture of nature. A Giant or a Dwarf may be called a common man *Outré*. (The phrase 'or a Dwarf' is added in superscript, an afterthought, suggesting the bias towards gigantism in our concepts of exaggeration.) Hogarth does not distinguish the aesthetic effects of the giant versus the dwarf, or discuss the internal proportions of these figures: being extraordinarily small or extraordinarily large is enough for either the giant or the dwarf to serve as an illustration of the *outré*. Theorising the distinct aesthetic effects of giants and dwarfs, however, Burke's *Enquiry* (1757) separates the extraordinarily large from the extraordinarily small figure, and makes room for the type of the 'gigantic dwarf', which combines smallness of stature with gigantism of feature. Gigantism is sublime, smallness more or less neutral – but a combination of the two creates an effect of deformity that repulses and discomfits rather than terrify the viewer.

The gigantic dwarf illustrates both Burke's definition of deformity as disproportion (82) and his association of beauty with 'gradual variation' and 'no sudden protuberance through the whole' (93–4). In delineating his ideal dwarf – extraordinarily small yet well proportioned – Burke may have had in mind particular court dwarfs such as Nicholas Ferry (1741–64) and Józef Boruwłaski (1739–1837), who was said by contemporaries to be 'perfectly straight, upright, well formed and proportioned'.[15] These curious miniatures of humanity, according to Burke, are outnumbered by dwarfs whose body parts are not proportionately small:

> Littleness, merely as such, has nothing contrary to the idea of beauty. The humming bird both in shape and colouring yields to none of the winged species, of which it is the least; and perhaps his beauty is enhanced by its smallness. But there are animals, which when they are extremely small are

rarely (if ever) beautiful. There is a dwarfish size of men and women, which is almost constantly so gross and massive in comparison of their height, that they present us with a very disagreeable image. But should a man be found not above two or three feet high, supposing such a person to have all the parts of his body of a delicacy suitable to such a size, and otherwise endued with the common qualities of other beautiful bodies, I am pretty well convinced that a person of such stature might be considered as beautiful; might be the object of love; might give us very pleasing ideas on viewing him (126).

Nineteenth-century fiction featuring dwarf characters devotes considerable space to visualising disproportion and explaining its aesthetic effect on an imagined viewer. In *Peveril of the Peak*, Scott's fictionalisation of Jeffrey Hudson (1619–82), the court dwarf of Queen Henrietta Maria, includes a detailed description that searches through the dwarf's physical features for potential sources of beauty, ugliness and the grotesque. Scott fixes on disproportion as the factor that dehumanises the character, supposedly undermining the attractiveness of his face and making him an object of wonder and ridicule:

Geoffrey Hudson [...] although a dwarf of the least possible size, had nothing positively ugly in his countenance, or actually distorted in his limbs. His head, hands, and feet were indeed large, and disproportioned to the height of his body, and his body itself much thicker than was consistent with symmetry, but in a degree which was rather ludicrous than disagreeable to look upon. His countenance, in particular, had he been a little taller, would have been accounted, in youth, handsome, and now, in age, striking and expressive; it was but the uncommon disproportion betwixt the head and the trunk which made the features seem whimsical and bizarre—an effect which was considerably increased by dwarf's moustaches, which it was his pleasure to wear so large, that they almost twisted back amongst, and mingled with, his grizzled hair.[16]

Geoffrey is one of Burke's gigantic dwarfs, 'gross and massive in comparison of their height'. Asymmetry and disproportion prevent him from being taken seriously, either in valour or in virility: he inspires neither love nor fear. In Burke's *Enquiry*, it is implied that the disproportioned dwarf's gigantism of feature does not share the sublimity of gigantism of stature. 'It is impossible', claims Burke, 'to suppose a giant the object of love. When we let our imaginations loose in romance, the ideas we naturally annex to that size are those of tyranny, cruelty, injustice, and every thing horrid and abominable' (126).

The creature in *Frankenstein*, originally designed to be 'proportionately large', is doubly impossible to love: a figure that combines distortion and disproportion with terrifying stature and strength. In 'Transformation', the immensely powerful dwarf necromancer is similarly suspended between ugliness and sublimity. The body associated with both dwarfism and gigantism – a gigantic dwarf, or a dwarfish giant – emerges as a special aesthetic type, exceeding the human form *outré*. It possesses elements of ugliness and deformity alongside elements of beauty and/or sublimity, which destabilise but do not eclipse each other. The defining characteristic of the gigantic dwarf is the confounding of aesthetic categories by a body not in scale with its size.

The aesthetic type of the gigantic dwarf is applied many times over in Scott's descriptions of grotesque characters. The first is the fictionalisation of David Ritchie, who is portrayed on his first appearance in *The Black Dwarf* as an object 'nearly as broad as long, or rather of a spherical shape, which could only be occasioned by some strange personal deformity' (21). A few pages later, this description is filled out with the disproportion of specific features: a head 'of immense size', a body 'thick and square', arms 'long and brawny', and legs 'so very short as to be hidden by the dress which he wore' (29). Scott explicitly assigns the Black Dwarf to the gigantic dwarf category, summarising the aesthetic impression of his size and disproportion: 'It seemed as if nature had originally intended the separate parts of his body to be the members of a giant, but had afterward capriciously assigned them to the person of a dwarf, so ill did the length of his arms and the iron strength of his frame correspond with the shortness of his stature' (29). (Dickens uses a similar formula in *The Old Curiosity Shop*, describing Quilp as 'so low in stature as to be quite a dwarf, though his head and face were large enough for the body of a giant'.[17]) In *Rob Roy*, Scott elaborates the anecdote about Rob's being able to tie his garters without stooping into a detailed account of how his body evocatively combines the dwarfish with the gigantic:

> Two points in his person interfered with the rules of symmetry—his shoulders were so broad in proportion to his height, as, notwithstanding the lean and lathy appearance of his frame, gave him something the air of being too square in respect to his stature; and his arms, though round, sinewy, and strong, were so very long as to be rather a deformity.[18]

The disproportioned 'squareness' of the dwarfish body is remarked in several of Scott's characterisations, from the Black Dwarf being 'thick and square', to Trolld and Nick Strumpfer in *The Pirate* – respectively a 'square and mis-shaped bulk' and 'a square-made dwarf'[19] – to Rob Roy's 'air of being too square', like the marauding Picts known for 'the length of their arms, and the squareness of their shoulders' (187). Long arms are another recurring feature: as well as Rob's arms and the Black Dwarf's, we have the 'long, skinny arm' of the court dwarf in *The Talisman*. Overlong arms are particularly marked as a non-human attribute, associated with goblins in *Rob Roy* and with apes in *The Black Dwarf*, where Sir Edward Mauley describes his body as 'more odious, by bearing that distorted resemblance to humanity which we observe in the animal tribes that are more hateful to man because they seem his caricature' (104). Shelley, in 'Transformation', assigns the dwarf necromancer 'two long lank arms, that looked like spider's claws' (28). The disproportion of the gigantic dwarf confronts the viewer simultaneously with an animal's form becoming uncomfortably close to human and a human's form becoming uncomfortably close to animal. Resemblance, not difference, is the source of disgust. In the *Frankenstein* notebooks of 1816–17, the creature muses that 'God in pity made man beautiful & alluring – I am more hateful to the sight than the bitter apples of Hell to the taste.'[20] At some point in the revision process this sentence was altered to focus on the creature's relation to an ideal human form, so that the 1818 text reads: 'God in pity made man beautiful and alluring, after his own image; but my form is a filthy type of yours, more horrid from its very resemblance' (105). Echoing Sir Edward Mauley's self-loathing in *The Black Dwarf*, the creature accuses Frankenstein of caricaturing corporeal humanity. Disproportion carries the gigantic/dwarfish body beyond the merely ugly and into an ugly uncanny, alike yet not alike.

The gigantic/dwarfish body generates a particular rhythm of seeing, where the body is pulled close by description then suppressed from view repeatedly throughout the text. In the narrative, a strong compulsion to look away allows characters to escape the most intense reaction of disgust and hatred – but they are then compelled in some way to look again, in a cycle of revulsion and fascination. There is a compressed version of this cycle in 'Transformation', where Guido sees 'a misshapen dwarf, with squinting eyes, distorted features, and body deformed, till it became a horror to behold' (27–8). Detailed examination of the dwarf's separate features gives way to revulsion, the desire not to look and not to touch. Persuaded by the necromancer's sublime power, however, the ambitious young cavalier overcomes one compulsion with another – '[a]we, curiosity, a clinging fascination, drew me towards him' (28) – and Guido makes further observations on the dwarf's physical features and 'contortions' (29). In an echo of Victor repulsing his creature's physical touch (*F* 79), Guido rejects the dwarf's physical advances – 'he held out his hand; I could not touch it' – but then closes the distance again: 'I drew near him' (29). When Guido is himself transformed into the dwarf's body – 'a shape of horror' (31) – he suppresses the sight, 'turn[ing] my face to the sun, that I might not see my shadow' (32). Victor's first rejection of the creature, rushing from his laboratory '[u]nable to endure the aspect of the being I had created' (*F* 39), similarly begins a pattern of seeing the creature, then banishing the sight of him, then seeing him again. Individual characters' interactions with the creature in the narrative create, through repetition, the reader's rhythmic experience of fascinated seeing that is continually interrupted by moments of suppression and abjection. Passages of detailed description, analysing the aesthetic effects of the body's various attributes, are swiftly followed by suppression or removal, sometimes accompanied by emphatic not-looking: 'Oh! no mortal could support the horror of that countenance' (40), 'almost too horrible for human eyes' (76), '"Begone! relieve me from the sight of your detested form' (79), 'contortions too horrible for human eyes to behold' (119), 'I shut my eyes involuntarily' (187). The tension between looking and not looking at the creature is acted out with violence when the creature forces William Frankenstein to look at him: 'I seized on the boy as he passed, and drew him towards me. As soon as he beheld my form, he placed his hands before his eyes, and uttered a shrill scream: I drew his hand forcibly from his face' (117). In another scene, Victor's narration spells out the fact that the aesthetic effect of the creature's physical appearance overpowers sympathy and moral reasoning, making him impossible to love even in the mildest sense of pity: 'I compassionated him, and sometimes felt a wish to console him; but when I looked upon him, when I saw the filthy mass that moved and talked, my heart sickened, and my feelings were altered to those of horror and hatred. I tried to stifle these sensations' (121). Real horror freezes the mental faculties along with the blood, counteracting the essentially imaginative work of compassion, as in Radcliffe's meditation on the difference between sublime, expansive terror and earthly, prosaic horror: '"They must be men of very cold imaginations," said W——, "with whom certainty is more terrible than surmise. Terror and horror are so far opposite, that the first expands the soul, and awakens the faculties to a high degree of life; the other contracts, freezes, and nearly annihilates them."'[21]

Shelley's cynicism about the possibility of loving a disgusting 'mass' in this scene contrasts with the episode in Matthew G. Lewis's *The Monk* (1796) where the heroine cuddles the body of her dead baby even as it rots: 'It soon became a mass of putridity, and to every eye was a loathsome and disgusting Object; To every eye, but a Mother's. [...] I endeavoured to retrace its features through the livid corruption, with which they were over-spread' (412–13). There is no such suggestion, in *Frankenstein*, that parents might possess superhuman powers of loving, or that deformity and distortion might be overlooked. Some readings of the novel point to the framing of Victor's narrative within Walton's, and the creature's narrative within Victor's, to argue that descriptions of the creature's body are unreliable: that Walton sees the creature through Victor's eyes, for example. There is no inconsistency or change in the creature's body throughout the novel; he has the same effect on everyone who sees him, even an inexperienced child, and the only hope of breaking the cycle lies in De Lacey's blindness. The pragmatic solution would be to find or make blind companions for the creature, as Victor Hugo arranges for the facially disfigured Gwynplaine in *L'Homme qui rit* (1869). That this does not occur to Victor Frankenstein might be rationalised by the idea that, having once seen the creature, it is impossible to imagine *not* seeing him.

In 'Transformation', horrid realism is a representation technique used within a romantic tale, a narrative in which the bond between self and body is tenuous, magical: Guido and the dwarf exchange bodies, and re-exchange them when their blood mingles in a duel. In *Frankenstein*, the realism of the creature's body extends beyond descriptive technique, to the narrative and to our sense of the novel as a 'world' or a 'reality'. Shelley's novel insists on the prosaic materiality of the creature's body, consistently described and universally hated. Forbidden the transformative power of imagination, the creature's body is caught in a realism that extends through the novel's narrative structure to its existential propositions: 'I was in reality the monster that I am' (90).

The Prosaic Grotesque: Against Critical Readings of *Frankenstein*

The grotesquing of disproportioned bodies serves, for Shelley and for Scott, as a site of innovation for a realist mode conscious of its potential for horror writing. Techniques and tropes developed from this horrid realism have become more universally deployed in modern realist fiction, across the genres of crime, thriller, fantasy and science fiction as well as in works conceived and marketed as horror fiction. While these tropes and techniques can be, and are, applied to the description of any object – landscapes, food, human-made objects – and to descriptions of the ordinary human body, they are most strongly associated with the extreme grotesques of the 'body horror' subgenre, and in other fictive works with localised moments of body horror, highly visually realised.

In Scott's fiction, horrid realism is localised to the description of dwarf characters and associated very specifically with hostility to the kinds of non-normative bodies that Scott's grotesques are intended to represent. In *Frankenstein*, the tropes and techniques of horrid realism are deployed more often and more generally, though still primarily in association with the creature's body, such that they constitute a sustained mode of representation – granular, vivid and prosaic – alongside the modes of narration and description that otherwise dominate the text. Romanticising, idealising, psychologising, moralising and reasoning: these modes offer frameworks through which the creature's body can emerge as something other than itself: a symbol, an example, a moral. As George Levine observes, *Frankenstein* 'exercises its appeal in part because it fails to explain so much. The narrative has a plausibility of images, and the images themselves, not really reflective of a world divinely ordered and intelligible or susceptible to the mind, lend themselves to proliferating and unrestricted interpretations, and can be assimilated to almost any powerful mythology'.[22] Accordingly, as Joshua points out, '[m]uch of the commentary on monstrosity in *Frankenstein* centres on the idea that [physical] monstrosity is in some sense a projection of something else'.[23]

Here, pulling comparisons from Scott's horrid realist descriptions of dwarf characters, and from Shelley's story 'Transformation', I argue that *Frankenstein*'s moments of 'body horror' use a distinctive set of tropes and techniques that work to literalise the monstrous body; and which, being reiterated throughout the text, continually puzzle, interrupt and destabilise critical readings of the novel.

Horrid realism is repetitive because it describes the grotesque body every time it appears in the narrative, suggesting that the reader, like Victor Frankenstein, should never lose sight of the character's ugliness and inhumanity for too long. Rather than being described when they are first introduced and then referred to simply as 'the monster' or 'the dwarf' in subsequent scenes, such characters are continually re-visualised, often using the same words repeated from previous descriptions. In horror realisms, writers regularly take the opportunity to provoke a shudder, a moment of disgust and hatred that interrupts any more coherent thoughts and sympathetic feelings that the reader might be developing about the character. *Frankenstein* not only carries out that strategy, but also thematises it by having the creature literally read Victor's 'minutest' written description of his body. Earlier I discussed the consistency of descriptions of the creature's body in *Frankenstein*, with the Shelleys' revisions to the text repeating, with variations and elaborations, words and ideas from Victor's original description. Midway through the novel, the reader is asked to imagine reading a fuller and more detailed account of that first experience, when the creature reads Victor's journal: 'the minutest description of my odious and loathsome person is given, in language which painted your own horrors, and rendered mine ineffaceable. I sickened as I read' (105).

This language might be interpreted as implausibly similar to the language that different characters (Victor, Walton, the creature) use to describe the creature's body, and/or as a sign of Victor's and Walton's unreliability as narrators; it might be seen as bad writing on Shelley's part. It is the language of horror writing: I attribute its consistency to a realism that uses repetition to maintain the visual impact of the horror object. The conventionality of horror writing's 'flesh-caricatures' is especially obvious in Scott's writing, with its many dwarf characters. In extended and brief descriptions that grotesque dwarfs' bodies, Scott uses the same words again and again. 'Misshapen' occurs five times in *The Black Dwarf*, six times in *Pirate*, once in *Talisman*, and twice in the Magnum Introduction to *Dwarf* – as well as 'unshapely', 'ill-shaped' and 'shapeless' in *Pirate*. 'Discordant' is used in *Dwarf*, *Pirate* and *Talisman*, as well as 'dissonant', 'loud' and 'shrill', which is used four times in *Dwarf*, three times in *Talisman*, once in *Peveril* and once more in the Magnum *Dwarf*: for example, the 'harsh and dissonant sounds of the dwarf's enunciation' in *Peveril*.[24] Dwarf characters are described as having dark 'shaggy' hair or 'beetle-brows' overhanging deep-set and dark yet brilliant eyes in *Dwarf*, *Kenilworth*, *Pirate* and *Talisman*. In *Talisman* and *Peveril*, dwarfs have 'shrivelled' features. Dwarf characters are likened to animals, including primates (*Dwarf*, *Peveril*), a bulldog and a reptile (*Pirate*) and a toad (*Talisman*). The phrase 'wretched abortion of nature' occurs in *Peveril*, and 'abortion-seeming' in *Talisman*. As in *Frankenstein*, variants of the words 'disproportion', 'distortion' and 'deformity' – as well as 'absurdity', 'extravagance', 'peculiarity', 'ugliness', 'bizarre', 'fantastic' etc. – appear in numerous descriptions of dwarf characters, and in other characters' dialogue about the dwarfs. This descriptive mode, generally characterised by reiteration, consistency and repetition to the point of conventionalising, reifies the grotesque body as a horror object.

Pressuring critical readings of the creature, horrid realism insists on the impact of what is 'really there', in spite of what the being might think or feel, in spite of what else it might represent. After reading Victor's journal, the creature asks a question that no character in the novel ever answers: 'My person was hideous and my stature gigantic. What did this mean?' (104). Every possible critical reading of the creature's body – what his person 'really means' and how it fits in the world as it is 'really like' – struggles with horrid realism's 'really there', a continually renewed representation of pure, meaningless horror.

Clarity is one of the more conspicuous tropes in horrid realist descriptions of grotesque bodies, aligning them with the fear of the known rather than the terror of darkness. Monsters are lit up so that they can be seen, either because a character is deliberately illuminating them (by lamplight or candlelight) or because horrid realism requires the character's body to be vividly re-described even when the plot would require only a statement that another character sees and recognises them. In *Talisman*, for example, Sir Kenneth first sees the court dwarfs by lamplight, and when he reencounters one of them, 'there stepped from the shadow into the moonlight, like an actor entering upon the stage, a stunted, decrepit creature, whom, by his fantastic dress and deformity, he recognized, even at a distance'.[25] There are several such instances in *Frankenstein*, starting with 'the glimmer of the half-extinguished light' (38) and the 'dim and yellow light of the moon' (39) that are sufficient to discern the creature's appearance at close range. On the next meeting with the creature, '[a] flash of lightning illuminated the object, and discovered its shape plainly to me' (56). Later, Victor sees the creature's face, again at close range, 'by the light of the moon' (138) and 'the pale yellow light of the moon' (166); and when the creature escapes him in Geneva, 'the broad disk of the moon arose, and shone full upon his ghastly and distorted shape' (172). The titular character of *The Black Dwarf* is first seen by the 'doubtful and occasional light' of the moon and mistaken for a ghost (20), but not revealed as a gigantic dwarf until a daylight scene, where his physical appearance is described fully (29).

Scott's and Shelley's grotesque characters thus violate one of Burke's key criteria for the sublime, obscurity. Whereas supernatural beings are seen imperfectly, monstrous humans are seen in unmysterious detail. In *The Pirate*, Norna recounts seeing the 'indistinct form' of Trolld, a demon dwarf featuring in a saga 'through the dim light which the upper aperture admitted'; contrastingly, every physical feature of Norna's servant, the dwarf Nick Strumpfer, is described, including his exact height in feet and inches.[26] Burke reasons that terror and apprehension rely not just on literal darkness but on uncertain visualisation more generally. He considers 'ghosts and goblins, of which none can form clear ideas' (48), and praises Milton's description of Death for its 'significant and expressive uncertainty of strokes and colouring' (49). Rather than being misshapen, Death has no certain form: 'If shape it might be called that shape had none

/ Distinguishable, in member, joint, or limb; / Or substance might be called that shadow seemed, / For each seemed either.' In contrast, the gigantic/dwarfish beings of Scott's and Shelley's horror writing – grotesquely opposed to both the sublime and the beautiful – are sized and shaped in every limb and feature. Their deformity, paradoxically, gives them more certain forms than the other characters.

In these clear views of the grotesque body, 'distinctly pictured forth' to produce 'positive horror' rather than imaginative suspense,[27] horrid realism divides its objects into parts (limbs, hands, heads, torsos, mouths) and details (colours, textures, measurements). Shelley and Scott both seem to reflect on the relative precision of physical description in the horror realism they are developing, in *Frankenstein* when the creature 'sickens' at the 'minutest description' of his body in Victor's journal (105), and in *The Talisman* when the court dwarfs, ordered by Queen Berengaria to make an attack on Sir Kenneth's 'nerves' by displaying their bodies to him, repeatedly illuminate themselves with lamps. Rather than holding his lamp in a fixed position, Nectabanus moves it to display each part of his body in turn. This deliberate attempt to horrify Sir Kenneth dramatises horrid realism's technique of partitioning the grotesque body into features and details, which are gradually revealed through extended descriptions:

> So soon as he had stepped from the aperture through which he arose, he stood still, and, as if to show himself more distinctly, moved the lamp which he held slowly over his face and person, successively illuminating his wild and fantastic features, and his misshapen but nervous limbs. Though disproportioned in person, the dwarf was not so distorted as to argue any want of strength or activity.[28]

The slow movement of the dwarf's lamp, and his gradual ascent from the chapel's subterranean vault, dramatise the descriptive technique that is used in the scene, of focusing on the grotesque body piece by piece. First we hear the dwarf's 'shrill whistle', then see 'a long, skinny arm' rising from the aperture, then 'a large head, a cap fantastically adorned'. The performance is repeated by the dwarf's wife:

> [I]t was a female form, much resembling the first in shape and proportions, which slowly emerged from the floor. Her dress was also of red samite, fantastically cut and flounced, as if she had been dressed for some exhibition of mimes or jugglers; and with the same minuteness which her predecessor had exhibited, she passed the lamp over her face and person, which seemed to rival the male's in ugliness.[29]

As well as being detailed and repetitious, the exhibition highlights two features that form horrid contrasts – first, the dwarfs' elaborate clothing, 'the richness of which rendered [their] ugliness more conspicuous'; second, their eyes, which have an element of beauty. Like the 'luxuriances' of Victor's creature – 'his hair was of a lustrous black, and flowing; his teeth of a pearly whiteness' (*F* 39) – the dwarfs' eyes are represented as visually appealing, yet submerged in ugliness:

> But with all this unfavourable exterior, there was one trait in the features of both which argued alertness and intelligence in the most uncommon degree. This arose from the brilliancy of their eyes, which, deep-set beneath black and shaggy brows, gleamed with a lustre which, like that in the eye of a toad, seemed to make some amends for the extreme ugliness of countenance and person.

A single trait – shining hair, shining eyes – might promise the viewer some relief from the other parts of the grotesque body.

This suggestion is undercut, however, by the dwarfs' next action. They successively illuminate their bodies' features once more, 'so as to allow him distinctly [...] to observe' the feature that might offset or diminish the unpleasant impact of the rest:

> [P]lacing themselves side by side, directly opposite to Sir Kenneth, they again slowly shifted the lights which they held, so as to allow him distinctly to survey features which were not rendered more agreeable by being brought nearer, and to observe the extreme quickness and keenness with which their black and glittering eyes flashed back the light of the lamps.[30]

Masters of horrid realism, the dwarfs draw closer to Sir Kenneth and use light to enhance the feature with the best claim to beauty – or perhaps sublimity, given the eyes' rapid and potentially threatening movements. This fragment of 'lustre' actually heightens the horror-impact of the whole. Unable to appreciate the dwarfs' eyes or the creature's teeth in isolation from the grotesque body's succession of parts, the viewer experiences the jarring of aesthetic dissonance. It is not pleasurable to see a fragment of beauty joined to ugliness, supposedly. Scott could have borrowed this idea from *Frankenstein*'s first description of the creature's body, a description that spells out its own deliberate aesthetic incoherence: a 'horrid contrast' of gleaming black hair and white teeth – presenting a high contrast of dark and light – with 'watery eyes, that seemed almost of the same colour as the dun white sockets in which they were set' – presenting a lack of contrast (39). Scott's earlier portrait of the Black Dwarf does not use aesthetic dissonance in this way, describing how Elshie's 'eye-brows, shaggy and prominent, overhung a pair of small, dark, piercing eyes, set far back in their sockets, that rolled with a portentous wildness, indicative of partial insanity' (29), making the eyes coherent with the rest of the portrait rather than exploring, as in *Frankenstein* and *Talisman*, how a fragment of beauty or sublimity might create ambivalence in the viewer.

These techniques and tropes of horrid realism – repetition, clarity, partition, minute details and aesthetic dissonance – are obsessed with specifics, taking the post-classical preference for particularity to the extreme. Ian Watt points to Shaftesbury and Kames as advocates for the two opposing schools of thought, the former on the side of the general and universal in art and literature, the latter for particularity.[31] Shaftesbury's *Essay on the Freedom of Wit and Humour* (1709) expresses the opinion that artists and writers should take impressions of general forms rather than trying to copy real, singular objects accurately in every detail:

> Now the Variety of Nature is such, as to distinguish every thing she forms, by a *peculiar* original Character; which, if strictly observed, will make the Subject appear unlike to anything extant in the World besides. But this Effect the good Poet and Painter seek industriously to prevent. They hate *Minuteness*, and are afraid of *Singularity*.[32]

Kames, on the other hand, claims that 'abstract or general terms have no good effect in any composition for amusement; because it is only of particular objects that images can be formed'.[33] In their descriptions of grotesque bodies, Shelley and Scott experiment with details so 'strictly observed' that they could attract the now well-established criticisms of realist horror: 'gratuitous', 'sensational', 'in bad taste', 'leaving nothing to the imagination'. The dwarf Nick Strumpfer is not simply 'mute' or 'silent'; instead Scott describes how 'in the immense cavity of his mouth, there only remained the small shrivelled remnant of a tongue, capable, perhaps of assisting him in swallowing his food, but unequal to the formation of articulate sounds'.[34] Rather than a poetic prompting of the reader's ability to think and feel without visualising every detail, horrid realism offers a prosaic anatomy of sights, sounds and physiological sensations, from the bruises on the dead Frankensteins' necks (*F* 52, 166) to the unseen movement of fluid around Victor's body, 'the blood trickling in [his] veins and tingling in the extremities of my limbs' (165). When Victor exclaims, 'Oh! With what a burning gush did hope revisit my heart!' and describes the 'burning drops' of his 'warm tears' (176), the association with body heat and liquid movement associates the abstract 'hope' with the heart as a physical organ. This kind of physiological drama has become so commonplace in literary realisms that it is easy to overlook its importance in Shelley's writing: as well as an artefact of the nineteenth-century popularisation of vivisectional interest in the body's vascular system, it is remarkable as a writing technique.

In Elizabeth's death scene, instead of suggesting enough that the reader could form a mental concept of the tragedy – without needing to visualise it – Shelley tells 'every thing'. Victor quickly moves on from abstract and general terms such as 'destruction' and 'lifeless'. Not stopping at telling us that Elizabeth was dead, he describes the appearance of the dead body, its parts and qualities, the location of the body and the position of the limbs: he sees 'her head hanging down and her pale and distorted features half covered by her hair'; he sees 'her bloodless arms and relaxed form flung' and 'thrown across the bed' (165). The reader is not allowed the freedom of abstractly contemplating Elizabeth's death, or idealising her body as a peacefully reclining form – we are shown, instead, how the body 'really' looks in death. When Victor runs back to the body, the people of the inn have repositioned it to give the comforting illusion that Elizabeth is resting. Again, Shelley specifies the arrangement of the limbs; and rather than suggesting that Elizabeth's face has been concealed, she makes the reader visualise a particular object covering it. It is also worth noting Shelley's choice to have Victor actually embrace Elizabeth, in a completed action. Rather than using suggestive and relatively indeterminate phrases such as 'rushed to embrace her' or 'rushed to her', Shelley provides a more highly visualised and detailed picture of a man holding a corpse closely enough to feel the slack muscles and cold skin in multiple limbs of the dead body:

> She had been moved from the posture in which I had first beheld her, and now, as she lay, her head upon her arm and a handkerchief thrown across her face and neck, I might have supposed her asleep. I rushed towards her and embraced her with ardour, but the deadly languor and coldness of the limbs told me that what I now held in my arms had ceased to be the Elizabeth whom I had loved and cherished. The murderous mark of the fiend's grasp was on her neck (165–66).

The unnamed and unlovable 'what' that Victor finds in Elizabeth's bed is characterised by prosaic details, creating an impression of a thing heavy with separable parts that recalls his destruction of the half-made female monster. There, the abstract phrase 'destroy the creature' is coupled with an account of Victor physically shaking and dismembering a fully objectified 'thing': 'trembling with passion, [I] tore to pieces the thing on which I was engaged' (139). In the following pages, Shelley follows through on the practical consequences of Victor's act: he has to re-enter the room, clean his tools, pick up the separated flesh and dispose of it (142). He puts the 'scattered' and 'mangled' pieces in a basket, loads it with stones, and drops it into the sea, where it sinks with a 'gurgling sound' (142–43). This is the 'what if' of realist horror and crime fiction, following through on its premise with prosaic detail.

Such exactness might be readily associated, by readers, with actual experience of situations and observation of objects described in the work, as opposed to the 'invention' and 'design' of imagination. The gruesome details in Shelley's and Scott's portraits of grotesque bodies, either congenitally deformed or distorted in death, prioritise the close-up detail in a way that recalls the popular (and spurious) anecdote about the Ottoman sultan Mehmet II and the painter Gentile Bellini. In Burke's telling, the sultan's 'exact knowledge' of the physical appearance of dead bodies and severed body parts suggests his advice to the painter:

> A fine piece of a decollated head of St. John the Baptist was shewn to a Turkish emperor; he praised many things, but he observed one defect; he observed that the skin did not shrink from the wounded part of the neck. The sultan on this occasion, though his observation was very just, discovered no more natural Taste than the painter who executed this piece, or than a thousand European connoisseurs who probably never would have made the same observation. His Turkish majesty had indeed been well acquainted with that terrible spectacle, which the others could only have represented in their imagination (*Enquiry* 20–1).

Burke leaves out the second half of the anecdote, where the sultan has a slave beheaded so that Bellini can observe the shrinking skin for himself. The important thing, for Burke, is that aesthetic judgement of the painting as a representation of John the Baptist and the story of his beheading does not require evaluation of the painting as a representation of a severed head. Horrid realism admits (or pretends) that the author has intimate knowledge of the body's flesh and its injuries, and calls on readers to recognise the material details of dead, diseased and wounded bodies, knowable through such common experiences as childbirth, stillbirth, miscarriage, surgery and wounds from accidents or deliberate violence. Horrid realism does not negate the body's claim to signify and symbolise, but it does pressure those meanings, continually and often repetitiously, with an excess of material detail; with a prosaic this-then-that of what is physically happening and how bodies and body parts move in relation to each other; with the body's thingness as most emphatically revealed by deformity, injury and death.

The short story 'Transformation' has a compressed version of the tension between the grotesque body's literalism and critical readings in which deformity serves as an image or projection of something else. Shelley begins with an epigraph from Coleridge's *Ancient Mariner*, framing

Guido's narrative as a confession, and explicitly associating the tale's 'horrors' with his 'excess of fiendly pride' (18). The story concludes with Guido speculating that the dwarf necromancer was 'a good rather than an evil spirit, sent by my guardian angel, to show me the folly and misery of pride', satisfied that he has learned his 'lesson' (39). This pat conclusion, where the story provides its own moral, retrospectively casts the necromancer's gigantic/dwarfish body as an incarnation of the handsome young knight's moral decrepitude. The dwarf addresses him in words echoing lines from Keats's 'La Belle Dame Sans Merci' – 'O what can ail thee, knight-at-arms, / So haggard and so woe-begone? [...] And this is why I sojourn here, / Alone and palely loitering' – 'Something does please me in your well-proportioned body and handsome face, though you do look a little woe-begone [...] And now [...] tell me why, young and gallant as you seem, you wander thus alone and downcast on this wild sea-shore' (29). A hedonist who has wasted his family's fortune, exchanging land for fine clothes, and who destroys his relationships and his reputation by attempting to abduct a young woman, Guido has betrayed the ideals of chivalry – and when he exchanges bodies with the dwarf, tempted by the prospect of returning to the city rich and powerful, he loses the external appearance of gentility and valour.

However, the story's attempted moral and its romantic literary antecedents are at odds with the literalism of the narrative. First, the shipwrecked dwarf has a history and an individualist motive: far from being a good or evil 'spirit' concerned with Guido's soul, he is a necromancer with his own agenda, tricking the knight into giving up his 'comely face and well-made limbs' to achieve his own goals, not to teach or punish Guido (30). The knight's fate is incidental to what the dwarf wants. Second, Shelley fully literalises the dwarf's body by demonstrating the practical consequences of Guido being grotesquely disproportioned. He has difficulty walking with 'distorted limbs [...] so ill adapted for a straight-forward movement' (33); and like Frankenstein's creature, he attempts to hide his ugliness, worried that 'mere boys would [...] stone me to death as I passed' (33). Third, the means of reclaiming Guido's body, the mingling of 'warm life-blood' in a simultaneous murder-suicide, is incoherent with moral allegory. By attempting to strangle the necromancer before stabbing him – 'I threw myself on him [...] I *felt* only my enemy, whose throat I grasped, and my dagger's hilt' – the dwarf-shaped Guido re-enacts an incident that happened when he was eleven years old, an attack on an older cousin who proposed marriage to Guido's eight-year-old friend Juliet: 'I threw myself on him—I strove to draw his sword—I clung to his neck with the ferocious resolve to strangle him' (20, 37). Shelley's description of the 'death-blow' is detailed and relatively prosaic: 'We fell together, rolling over each other, and the tide of blood that flowed from the gaping wound of each mingled on the grass' (37). It is dwarf-Guido's quick thinking and physical effort that save him. Rather than reforming his character in order to shed the dwarf's deformed limbs, Guido learns his lesson *after* getting his body back, in the process of healing under Juliet's care: 'the work of my bodily cure and mental reform went on together' (38). Guido's encounter with the dwarf is only indirectly the cause of his reform, which actually results from the material fact of a near-fatal wound and the resulting physical weakness. With Guido rendered harmless and forced to convalesce in a domestic setting, Juliet's father has the opportunity to 's[i]t beside' him and convey 'such wisdom as might win friends to repentance' (38). In comparison with *Frankenstein*, 'Transformation', explicitly framed by the epigraph and Guido's talk of a 'guardian angel', might seem to be a relatively straightforward allegory where the grotesque body substitutes for moral deformity. Nevertheless, I argue, 'Transformation' revisits the techniques of *Frankenstein*'s horrid realism to present horrors for their own sake. The literalism of the gigantic/dwarfish body, and the incoherence between the prosaic narrative and Guido's 'lesson', tend to destabilise the story's 'moral' into an attempt, after-the-fact, to spiritualise bodies into souls.

In *Frankenstein*, the horrid realism used primarily to describe grotesque bodies exists alongside a romantic adaptation of physiognomic discourse to evoke the idealism of the Frankenstein family and the De Lacey family. The idealising language of these physiognomic portraits makes a contrast with Shelley's descriptions of grotesque bodies, not because the latter use demonising language, but because their horrid realism excludes physiognomic analysis. It is only late in the novel that the wrinkles in the creature's skin begin to settle into signs of his passions. Otherwise, the creature's body is unreadable, like the dead bodies of Elizabeth and of Victor's mother, infested by 'grave-worms crawling in the folds' of her shroud in Victor's dream (39). The creature's overall appearance often strikes Victor as demonic, certainly – but the details of his distinctive body exceed moral physiognomy's links between corporeal ugliness and moral evil. With the creature's skin, hair, eyes and disproportioned limbs consistent throughout the novel, the only physical characteristic explicitly linked with moral corruption is his facial expression. When Percy altered one of Victor's remarks on the creature's face to suggest that his physical appearance might not accurately reflect his moral or psychological self – 'his countenance appeared to express the utmost extent of malice and barbarity' – Mary reinstated her original phrase.[35] The 1818 text accepts Percy's elevation of 'face' to 'countenance', but rejects the pivotal change from 'expressed' to 'appeared to express', instead unequivocally stating that 'his countenance expressed the utmost extent of malice and treachery' (139). On the other hand, we are never told that the creature's mummy-like skin *means* anything about his character.

This is a significant exception to the portrayals of ideal and ordinary non-ideal bodies across Shelley's novels, where she is adamant that body and mind are mutually constituted. Descriptions of the creature's facial expressions, later in *Frankenstein*, do fit with Shelley's physiognomic mode of description where physical details reliably convey what someone is thinking and feeling. In her later novels, Shelley uses the wrinkles in the human face as an index of violent and physically convulsive emotions.[36] A physiognomic system is applied xenophobically in *Lodore* (1835), where the passionate Neapolitan Clarinda has a face 'too pantomimely expressive [...] not to impress disagreeably one accustomed to the composure of the English', and in a moment of jealous rage her beauty is 'vanished, changed, melted away and awfully transformed into actual ugliness'.[37] *Falkner* (1837) has an extended physiognomic description of the protagonist's face, his forehead 'high and expansive, though somewhat distorted by various lines that spoke more of passion than of thought [...] his mouth, rather too large in its proportions, yet grew into beauty when he smiled'.[38] The static aspects of the creature's grotesque, misshapen body are not readable like Falkner's '*somewhat* distorted' forehead and his mouth '*rather* too large in its proportions' (my emphases). Only once the creature begins to experience other people's reactions to him, and to react violently, does his face become subject to the physiognomy applied to the other characters. In this, Frankenstein's creature conforms to two key ideas in Bacon's 'Of Deformity' theory, applied by Scott to the Black Dwarf and Geoffrey Hudson: that 'deformed persons' are inclined to misanthropy and driven to avenge the contempt they experience from others; and that deformity should thus be considered 'not as a sign, which is more deceivable, but as a cause, which seldom faileth of the effect'.[39] The creature's original and consistent deformity is the literal 'cause' of his later wrongdoing – neither a retrospective nor predictive 'sign' of it.

While the horrors of the creature's body exceed physiognomic analysis, the physiognomic portraits in *Frankenstein* do help to secure the literalism of that grotesque body, in one respect. For Shelley, the body is neither an arbitrary signifier of character, nor an unreliable image that might conceal or misrepresent character; rather, there is an essential relationship between the two. She does not apply that interpretive framework in depicting the static aspects of the creature's body; outwith these localised deployments of horrid realism, however, she insists that body and mind share a single form. The unreadability of the creature's body exists in a fictional universe where bodies are people. The 1831 edition of *Frankenstein* adds a scene where Caroline Frankenstein retrieves Elizabeth from the family of Italian peasants who adopted her. Idealising physiognomic portraiture contrasts Elizabeth with the peasant children:

> She appeared of a different stock. The four others were dark-eyed, hardy little vagrants; this child was thin and very fair. Her hair was the brightest living gold, and despite the poverty of her clothing, seemed to set a crown of distinction on her head. Her brow was clear and ample, her blue eyes cloudless, and the lips and moulding of her face so expressive of sensibility and sweetness that none could behold her without looking on her as of a distinct species, a being heaven-sent, and bearing a celestial stamp in all her features.[40]

We might tie Shelley's evident credulity about physiognomic principles to *Frankenstein*'s fascination with the 'what' of a horrific, unmeaning body. I suggest that Shelley's mind-body equation – to which she makes the creature's static deformity an exception – supports horrid realism's literalisation of the creature, obstructing interpretations of the novel that understand the creature's body as a symbol, or as a deviation from a socially constructed norm, and/or as an 'image' or 'stereotype'.

David Mitchell and Sharon Snyder see the creature's narrative as 'an allegorical moment in literary history where those constructed as physically deviant assail those who would create them in that image', and Paul Youngquist argues that the creature takes 'vengeance on the bodies that the norm so invisibly advantages'.[41] Lee Sterrenburg interprets Shelley's narrative as an allegory of political 'monstering': written in 'a postrevolutionary era when collective political movements no longer appear viable', the novel 'asks what it is like to be labelled, defined, and even physically distorted by a political stereotype'.[42] We can imagine Shelley's sympathy with her parents' experience of being targeted by anti-jacobin discourse.

Alternatively, we can read the creature's body as symbolic of political 'deformity', looking to the variety of monstrosity imagery in Wollstonecraft's and Godwin's writings, as well as in Burke's *Reflections* and Paine's *Rights of Man*.[43] Such readings of *Frankenstein* resonate with the political satirical prints of the 1790s, not because the novel was directly influenced by them, but because Gillray and the Cruikshanks were participating in a common stream of spectral and monstrous imagery, some of which originated in literary and classical texts,[44] as well as textual sources such as Burke's *Reflections*, Barruel's *Mémoires* and the Austrian ambassador Count von Starhemberg's satirical pamphlet on Bonaparte, *Le Grand Homme*, printed by the *Anti-Jacobin* in 1801. Gillray's print *German-Nonchalence, or the Vexation of little-Boney* (1803), for example, depicts an undersized Bonaparte consumed with Rumpelstiltskin-like rage on the steps of the Palais de Tuileries as the ambassador speeds past in a carriage. Thereafter dwarfism, often coupled with disproportion, became common in the British satirical prints' depictions of Napoleon. Taken out of context, some of my observations about gigantic/dwarfish bodies might be subordinated to theories that the body of Frankenstein's creature contains an allegory of republicanism as political monstrosity, or that aspects of the creature's body encode Shelley's anxiety about the abolition of slavery in the West Indies. I am interested here in the ways that such perceptive readings of the creature's body as a constructed, symbolic or specious 'monstrosity' – valid readings essential to our understanding of *Frankenstein*'s unrestricted complexity and powerful legacy – stumble across *Frankenstein*'s bodies: both the essentialism of Shelley's mind-body equation, and the literalism of the prosaic grotesque body.

Straight Clothes and Mortal Faces: Non-fiction Precedents for Horror's Flesh-Caricatures

Frankenstein broke new ground for modern 'genre fiction' with a distinctive realist mode for representing a familiar premise – the Promethean creation of a human being – and the consequent events as though they were physical facts open to minute observation. Scholarship on *Frankenstein* has examined the scientific texts and theories influential on the novel's representation of Victor animating his creature with an electrical 'spark of being' (38); vivisections and experimental surgeries, perhaps including John Hunter's auto-transplants of the 1760s, would also have made *Frankenstein*'s premise seem more plausible to Shelley's first readers. In the last section of this chapter, I look at several non-fiction precedents for Victor's construction of a disproportioned, distorted and discoloured body, quoting from texts that created 'flesh-caricatures' as objects of lurid description between 1690 and 1818. Literature about the medical care of infants and the education of children popularised concepts of the human body's plasticity, explaining how the body could be literally 'caricatured' through constant physical pressure. Parents and caregivers were advised that the physical convulsions caused by strong emotions could, with repetition, distort children's faces. General reference works as well as specialised medical texts conveyed Hippocrates's famously graphic description of diverse symptoms seen to distort the face of a person close to death. Thus grounded in medical and advice literature whose images are presented to readers as facts, the flesh-caricature cannot be safely bracketed as an extraordinary 'freak' or exiled to the realm of the fantastic. *Frankenstein*'s descriptions of distorted bodies and faces, I argue, would have activated nineteenth-century readers' awareness of swaddled, convulsed and moribund bodies as prosaic horror.

Up to the eighteenth century, it was common practice in Britain, as elsewhere in Western Europe, to bind new-born children tightly in 'swaddling cloths' and 'stay bands', primarily with the intention of making the limbs grow straight. Physicians began to caution that swaddling actually caused physical deformities when done improperly, and that it prevented infants from exercising their limbs – but opinion was slow to change. John Locke, in *Some Thoughts Concerning Education* (1693), was one of the first publicly to advocate abandoning the practice altogether. Locke refers to 'straight clothes', grouping swaddling cloths with the highly structured and constrictive undergarments that in Britain were commonly worn by children as well as adults, and at all levels of society, to shape the upper body's proportions and posture: bodices, stays, jumps and (by the end of the eighteenth century, following French fashion) quilted waistcoats without bones, corsets. Cosmetological foundation garments, Locke warns, causes respiratory problems by compressing the chest, and by restricting blood circulation, make a person misshapen and disproportioned. Presenting his reader with the exotic image of 'a pair of China shoes', Locke seeks to defamiliarise the foundation garments then known in Britain as 'bodies':

> Narrow breasts, short and stinking breath, ill lungs, and crookedness, are natural and almost constant effects of hard bodice, and clothes that pinch. That way of making slender wastes, and fine shapes, serves but the more effectually to spoil them. Nor can there indeed but be disproportion in the parts, when the nourishment prepared in the several offices of the body cannot be distributed as nature designs. And therefore what wonder is it, if, it being laid where it can, on some part not so braced, it often makes a shoulder or hip higher or bigger than its just proportion? 'Tis generally known, that the women of China [. . .] by bracing and binding them hard from their infancy, have very little feet. I saw lately a pair of China shoes, which I was told were for a grown woman: they were so exceedingly disproportion'd to the feet of one of the same age among us, that they would scarce have been big enough for one of our little girls. Besides this,

'tis observed, that their women are also very little, and short-liv'd; whereas the men are of the ordinary stature of other men, and live to a proportionable age. These defects in the female sex in that country, are by some imputed to the unreasonable binding of their feet, whereby the free circulation of the blood is hinder'd, and the growth and health of the whole body suffers. And how often do we see, that some small part of the foot being injur'd by a wrench or blow, the whole leg or thigh thereby lose their strength and nourishment, and dwindle away? How much greater inconveniences may we expect, when the thorax, wherein is placed the heart and seat of life, is unnaturally compress'd, and hindr'd from its due expansion?[45]

Over the eighteenth century, and influenced by Locke's and Rousseau's criticism of swaddling bands and foundation garments, physicians begin to express the idea that the bracing and binding of growing bodies is inevitably harmful. William Cadogan, in his *Essay upon Nursing* (1748), not only rejects swaddling cloths but recommends loose clothing – 'a little Flannel Waistcoat without Sleeves, made to fit the Body' – and no stockings or shoes until the child is three years old. Like Locke, Cadogan reasons that circulation, 'restrained by the Compression of any one Part, must produce unnatural Swellings in some other; especially as the Fibres of Infants are so easily distended' – hence 'the many Distortions and Deformities we meet with every where'.[46]

Later in the eighteenth century, the horrid specifics of straight clothes' impact on growing bodies continue to fascinate writers in philosophical and political arguments where physical monstrosity serves to make a point about something else. In *Émile*, while the British mania for swaddling clothes and foundation garments illustrates Rousseau's argument that 'human nature' is distorted by 'irrational' customs and institutions, Rousseau is fascinated, in the first place, with the material facts of neonatal swaddling, and how the practice constricts the body to the point of moribundity:

> A new-born infant requires to be at liberty to move and stretch its limbs, to shake off that numbness in which, moulded together in a heap, they have remained so long. They are stretched out, it is true, but they are prevented from moving: Even the head itself is rendered immoveable by stay-bands: So that one would imagine the nurses were afraid the poor creature should have the appearance of being alive. [...] More compressed, more confined, and less at ease in his swaddling-cloaths than its mother's womb, I see not what it has gained by its birth (20).

Since, Rousseau observes, 'to live is not merely to breathe; it is to act, to make a proper use of our organs, our senses, our faculties, and of all those parts of the human frame which contribute to the consciousness of our existence', swaddling imposes a kind of living death. He compares the child 'bound up in swaddling-cloaths' to a dead man 'nailed down in his coffin' (19). By immobilising the infant, the caregiver frustrates its physical efforts, congests its physiological processes, dampens its sensations and generally limits its corporeal experiences. Rousseau moves on to discuss the lasting physical deformities that result from swaddling and straight clothes:

> This state of inaction, and constraint, in which the limbs of infants are confined, cannot fail to prevent the free circulation of the blood [...]. In countries where no such extravagant precautions are taken, the people are tall, robust, and well-proportioned: [...] those where infants are thus treated, swarm with hunch-backed, crooked-legged, lame, rickety, and deformed persons of every kind.[47]

As he points out, in some countries, swaddling does not end with infancy: adults wear fashionable clothing that is supposed to improve the body's shape and posture, but which might actually deform their bodies. English women, says Rousseau, are notorious in Europe for their 'Gothic fetters [...] numerous ligatures, which check the circulation, and confine the different limbs'.[48] By the mid-eighteenth century, it was recognised that women typically wore more compressing foundation garments, with Cadogan noting that '[w]omen [...] suffer more in this Particular than the men';[49] and later in the century, Wollstonecraft, picking up Locke's reference to Chinese foot-binding customs, laments that '[t]o preserve personal beauty, woman's glory! the limbs and faculties are cramped with worse than Chinese bands' (*Vindication* 41).

Thus, in the Romantic period, foundation garments could readily be seen by intellectuals and the well-read as an outdated practice of 'abortive' cosmetology with horrific effects.[50] Godwin's claim that a government 'fettered' by individual interests and failings produces a society 'distorted in every joint, abortive and monstrous' might seem to mix metaphors about chains and childbirth, presenting the reader with vague imagery and abstracted 'distortion' and 'monstrosity'.[51] But for readers familiar with Locke's and Rousseau's graphic passages of body horror about straight clothes, such language would have evoked the straight-laced body. Breathing but not living, it is immobilised by bands, bones and laces, reshaped by the blockage of vital fluid.

In terms of practical advice to parents and caregivers, one of the most authoritative voices on the physical care of children in the mid- to late eighteenth century was the Scottish physician William Buchan. His book

Domestic Medicine (1769) was in its seventeenth edition by 1800, and was followed by a sequel focused on childcare, *Advice to Mothers* (1804). Echoing Locke and Cadogan on the plasticity of the body, Buchan describes the infant as 'a bundle of soft pipes, replenished with fluids in constant motion'.[52] Whereas Rousseau imagines the womb as a confined space, Buchan instructs his reader that the womb actually protects the developing body from 'unequal pressure' by 'surround[ing] the foetus every where with fluids' (9). Swaddling does the opposite:

> Even the bones of an infant are so soft and cartilaginous, that they readily yield to the slightest pressure, and easily take on a bad shape, which can never after be remedied. Hence it is, that so many people appear with high shoulders, crooked spines and flat breasts, who were born with as good a shape as others, but had the misfortune to be squeezed into monsters by the application of stays and bandages.
>
> Pressure, by obstructing the circulation, prevents the equal distribution of nourishment to the different parts of the body, by which means the growth becomes unequal. One part of the body grows too large, while another remains too small, and thus in time the whole frame becomes disproportioned and misshapen (9–10).

According to Buchan, swaddling clothes also cause dangerous fevers (by making the infant too hot), respiratory diseases (by constricting the lungs), and convulsions (by piercing the child with pins used to secure the cloths). Buchan describes a horrific instance of pins 'found sticking above half an inch into the body of a child after it had died of convulsion-fits' (11). Whereas in *Domestic Medicine*, Buchan blames infant deformity on midwives, accusing them of promoting swaddling as a valuable professional skill (8), it is no coincidence that *Advice to Mothers* plays on maternal anxiety by blaming female parents for a remarkable 'ninety-nine' per cent of 'all cases of dwarfishness and deformity'.[53] Buchan claims that the majority of women in London are 'of a diminutive stature' and 'distorted either in body or limbs', deformed by 'the tightness of their dress [. . .] and the artificial moulding or pretended improvement of their shape when young' (262–63): women, themselves especially deformed, must be kept from passing on that deformity to the next generation.

It was also thought that children could become disproportioned when mothers sustained physical injuries or undertook certain physical activities. The Quaker-educated engraver James Peller Malcolm, in his *Historical Sketch of the Art of Caricaturing*, supposes that Quakers are 'well-made people' because Quaker women avoid 'mixing in the usual amusements of the world' and escape 'those accidents which would cause caricatured lineaments in their offspring' by interfering with the infant's physical formation:

> Nature [. . .] being interrupted, makes a forehood too high or too low [. . .]. The causes of the interruptions alluded to cannot be inquired into at present: they more properly belong to the Surgeon; but they may safely, in most cases, be attributed to the want of due care and circumspection in the mothers of those persons whose features or limbs are thus distorted.[54]

Sexual intercourse is one of the 'interruptions' Malcolm alludes to. Buchan's *Advice to Mothers*, addressed to a general audience, refers delicately to mothers' 'folly and misconduct' causing physical deformity.[55] This idea is discussed more explicitly in medical texts: Walter Harris's *A Full View of All the Diseases Incident to Children* (1742) correlates rickets – a disease that distorts the bones of the legs – with the mother's having 'indulg[ed] herself in Indolence while with child' or 'an intemperate use of Venery, during the Time of Pregnancy'.[56] As David Turner has shown, eighteenth-century prescriptive writing about child-rearing was generally 'saturated with notions of parental guilt and blame, which began even before conception itself'.[57] The notion of Victor as parent to a deformed child, an 'abortion', can be made coherent with Ellen Moers's reading of the novel as 'a birth myth' representing 'the trauma of afterbirth' through 'the motif of revulsion against newborn life',[58] or with Anne K. Mellor's argument that '*Frankenstein* is a book about what happens when a man tries to have a baby without a woman.'[59] My analysis of *Frankenstein*'s horrid realism, as the set of tropes and techniques whereby Shelley presents grotesque bodies, offers a somewhat different interpretation: that in minutely exploring the prosaic ramifications of creating an exceptionally deformed being, Shelley re-purposes language, imagery and ideas from the 'flesh-caricatures' of influential prescriptive texts that imagine swaddling and straight clothes distorting and deadening the human body.

Shelley's descriptions of the creature's face, grimacing and wrinkled, suggest another commonly held idea about the physical deforming of children by parents and caregivers, that faces were permanently distorted by facial contortions in excited emotional states. As Malcolm puts it, by failing to subdue children's emotions, 'parents and guardians are too frequently Caricaturists'. More interesting, however, is the way that the creature's face – his original features as well as his impassioned grimaces later in the novel – might be physiologically associated with the dead or dying body. Echoing Rousseau's notion of the swaddled child as suspended between life and death, Malcolm describes the body of a child exhausted by unchecked anger: 'the blood stagnating, the eyes flare, and the face becomes black, the body convulsed—and this is the caricature of Vexation'.[60] Lifeless, distorted and discoloured: the child flesh-caricatured by emotions recalls Browne's metaphorical association of caricature portraiture with the Hippocratic face. As described in the *Prognosticon* or *Book of Prognostics*, the dying face was supposed to appear misshapen by concavities, as well as discoloured: 'hollow eyes, the temples collapse, the ears cold and contracted, the lobes inverted, the skin about the forehead hard, tense, and dry, with the whole face of a palish green, black, livid, or leaden hue'.[61] It is to the prognosis of the Hippocratic face that Shakespeare refers in Mistress Quickly's account of Falstaff's face on his deathbed: 'his nose was as sharp as a pen' (*Henry V* act 2, scene 3). Browne elaborates on Hippocrates's description with an analogy to the graphic caricature portrait, emphasising changes in the body's proportions, as well as the shape and colour of the face, as presages of death:

> Some are so curious as to observe the depth of the Throat-pit, how the proportion varieth of the Small of the Legs unto the Calf, or the compass of the Neck unto the Circumference of the Head: but all these, with many more, were so drowned in a mortal Visage and last Face of *Hippocrates*, that a weak Physiognomist might say at first eye, This was a face of Earth, and that Morta had set her Hard-Seal upon his Temples, easily perceiving what *Caricatura* Draughts Death makes upon pined faces.[62]

In physical descriptions of the creature and of Elizabeth's dead body, Shelley's horrid realism substitutes the speaking faces of moral physiognomy with the diverse, incoherent details of mortal physiognomy, whose only meaning is death. While the creature has 'yellow skin', some of Shelley's readers, noticing the creature's 'straight black lips', would have associated his appearance with the Hippocratic face (*F* 39), partly explaining Thomas Cooke's choice of green or blue face paint when he played the creature onstage in the 1820s. The symptoms of the 'facies Hippocratica' or 'Hippocratic countenance' – also referred to as the 'moribund' or 'cadaverous face' – were common knowledge and were described in several general reference works, including the *Encyclopaedia Britannica*, as well as specialised medical dictionaries, which usually transcribed a translation of the relevant passage in the *Prognostics*. Bartholomew Parr's *London Medical Dictionary* (1809), for example, describes a 'countenance pale, greenish, or dark'.[63] Shelley's descriptions of the creature's 'clouded eyes' *F* (154) refer to another of Hippocrates's prognostics of death, the cornea's loss of transparency: Moffat's 1788 translation describes eyes 'of a nasty, dry, dull appearance'.[64] Overall, Shelley draws on numerous aspects of the *facies Hippocratica* by detailing the grotesque mortal face as an incoherent combination of still-beautiful features (hair, teeth), a distorted expression, unnatural and contrasting colours, and skin that is dry in texture and stretched over bone.

Victor and Walton both remark that the creature appears mummified, Frankenstein claiming that '[a] mummy again endued with animation could not be so hideous as that wretch' (*F* 40) and Walton noticing hands 'in colour and apparent texture like that of a mummy' (187). Might this reference to mummies, wrapped in layers of linen to preserve the body's shape and upright posture, have recalled the distorting pressure of straight clothes? Noticing how Victor 'collected bones from charnel houses' (36) – presumably bones from which flesh has already rotted – and that the creature's 'yellow skin scarcely covered the work of muscles and arteries beneath' (39), might readers have visualised skin pulled tight like swaddling bands? In Shelley's horrid realism, the prosaic horrors of straight clothes, physical convulsions and the Hippocratic face form a mesh of incoherent details that literalise the grotesque body into a flesh-caricature, continually pulling on the critical readings that would abstract it. Repetitively using highly visualised moments of fear and disgust, Shelley's techniques of horrid realism – and the horror realisms that followed – baffle the reader or viewer's ability to imagine the body as other than what it materially is.

In Shelley's fiction, as in Scott's, tropes and techniques of horrid realism are localised to descriptions of grotesquely distorted bodies. But whereas Scott's gigantic dwarfs – David Ritchie, Rob Roy MacGregor, Jeffrey Hudson and other court dwarfs – are historicised and subordinated to the novels' compendious realism, Shelley centres the grotesque body and its de-characterising power such that *Frankenstein* and 'Transformation' pioneer horror writing as a distinct genre. Shelley's creature and Scott's dwarfs, followed by Dickens's Quilp and Hugo's Quasimodo, provided key concepts, tropes and techniques for a horror tradition of disproportioned and partitioned characters. The narrator of H. G. Wells's *The Island of Doctor Moreau* (1896), for example, describes Moreau's creations as 'grotesque caricatures of humanity' and 'horrible caricatures of my Maker's image', echoing phrases from *The Black Dwarf* and *Frankenstein*; and in addition to graphic descriptions that partition the monsters into divergent features, Wells uses the words 'disproportion', 'misshapen' and 'distorted': the same shorthand Shelley and Scott use for their depictions of grotesque bodies.⁶⁵ *Frankenstein*'s combination of horrid realism with a speculative narrative made another major contribution to the subject matter of 'body horror' fiction: the idea of flesh-caricatures being literally manufactured through human creativity, skill and perversity. 'Manufactured monster' narratives ground their premises in 'real' or historical precedents, sometimes fictionalised or sensationalised. The premise of *L'Homme qui Rit* (1869) is the fictional history of a nomadic society – the 'Comprachicos' – who make a living from buying and kidnapping children whom they physically deform and display for entertainment. Inspired by the Chinese practices of foot-binding and of miniaturised *penjing* (or *penzai*) trees, Hugo invents the practice of 'croissance en bouteille', whereby a growing infant is stunted and deformed by being confined, day and night, to a vase. 'C'est commode', the narrator comments sarcastically, 'on peut d'avance se commander son nain de la forme qu'on veut'.⁶⁶ Dr Moreau, in a one-sided dialogue with the novel's protagonist, gives a long list of precedents for the novel's flesh-caricaturing, including John Hunter's cock-spur experiments and 'those mediaeval practitioners who made dwarfs and beggar-cripples, show-monsters [...]. Victor Hugo gives an account of them'.⁶⁷ In twentieth-century body horror, flesh-caricatures can be explained by the redistribution of atoms (such as in George Langelaan's mystery-horror story 'The Fly', first published in *Playboy* in 1957) or the manipulation of DNA (such as in David Cronenburg's 1986 film interpretation of Langelaan's premise).

This strain of body horror follows *Frankenstein* in its convention of revealing the methods of flesh-caricaturing, explained and described prosaically rather than presented as an unsystematised magic. The first of many horror realisms in narrative fiction, Shelley's horrid realism assembles distinctive tropes and techniques in an effort to visualise grotesque bodies and flesh-caricatures, rather than leave the reader to imagine them (or not). In these bold moments of representing fictional characters' bodies more prosaically and literally, caricature is made flesh and 'character' is put in quotation marks. Whereas comic, compendious and historical realisms are understood, in the Romantic period, to elicit pseudo-sensory and parasocial pleasure through particularised and varied characters, Shelley's 'horrid realism' models a formal realism that elicits pseudo-sensory revulsion in ways new to novelistic fiction, through flesh-caricature's de-characterisation of the human.

Afterword

This book tells a history of literature's caricature in the Romantic period, investigating caricature talk's legacies in the self-reflexive realisms of comic, historical and horror fiction. By shifting the focus to 'caricature talk' – the varied yet well-defined ways in which 'caricature' and associated terms were used to talk about art and reality – I have reconceived 'caricature' as a concept substantially concerned with text, literature and the novel. I extricate the 'caricature' of Romantic-period Britain from the late-Georgian satirical print of 'the golden age of caricature', while illustrating its ties with the etymology and idioms of *caricatúra* that first entered British consciousness with *ritratti carichi* in the seventeenth century. David Taylor has called for caricature to be thought of in 'more rigorously intermedial terms', wondering whether 'the golden age of caricature' might 'become a way of thinking about a moment in literary history as much as in art history'.[1] This study has suggested that caricature's importance to literature in the Romantic period is clearest in the criticism, canonisation and self-reflexive writing of novelistic realisms. And perhaps 1817–18 was a 'golden year' for the concept of caricature in the novel, with the publication of texts that furnish many of the examples in this study: *Northanger Abbey*, *Persuasion*, *Rob Roy*, *The Heart of Mid-Lothian* and *Frankenstein* – and *Sanditon* left unfinished. Was there any consciousness, among critics and writers in the Romantic period, that their texts participated in some special 'age of caricature'?

Inevitably, given the Romantics' consciousness of 'the spirit of the age' illuminated by James Chandler's study of Romantic historicism,[2] my research has uncovered a handful of statements reflecting on the possible causes of a 'taste for caricature' in the current historical moment. Some critics use anti-caricature rhetoric simply to express the idea that society is becoming progressively jaded in its tastes. A writer for the *Morning Chronicle* in 1796 regrets that '[t]he taste of the day leans entirely to caricature' and 'we must have something grotesque and disproportioned, cumbrous with ornament and gigantic in its dimensions'.[3] E. J. Clery has observed that in the 1790s 'the French Revolution was being written, and consumed by a paranoid British public, like a gripping romance translated from the German'.[4] Commentators of the time did make this connection between news and novels, venturing to find a basis for contemporary culture's seeming 'caricature of nature' in the reality of their own specific historical period. A review of Austen's novels in the *Edinburgh Literary Miscellany*, and Walter Scott's review of *Frankenstein* in the *Scots Magazine* – both published in the spring of 1818 – theorise that the 'wondrous and gigantic' scenes, events and characters of the Napoleonic era have raised readers' expectations for entertainment. The reading public is ready for *Frankenstein*, 'one of the productions of the modern school in its highest style of caricature and exaggeration', while neglecting English classics of the eighteenth century. Anti-caricature rhetoric is here turned on reality itself, with the war years seen as a period of magnified character and eventfulness:

> There never was a wilder story imagined [than *Frankenstein*], yet, like most of the fictions of this age, it has an air of reality attached to it, by being connected with the favourite projects and passions of the times. The real events of the world have, in our day, too, been of so wondrous and gigantic a kind,—the shiftings of the scenes in our stupendous drama have been so rapid and various, that Shakespeare himself, in his wildest flights, has been completely distanced by the eccentricities of actual existence. Even he would scarcely have dared to have raised, in one act, a private adventurer to the greatest of European thrones,—to have conducted him, in the next, victorious over the necks of emperors and kings, and then, in a third, to have shewn him an exile, in a remote speck of island, some thousands of miles from the scene of his triumphs. [...] Our appetite [...] for every sort of wonder and vehement interest, has in this way become so desperately inflamed, that especially as the world around us has again settled into its old dull state of happiness and legitimacy, which we can be satisfied with nothing in fiction that is not highly coloured and exaggerated; we even like a story the better that is disjointed and irregular, and our greatest inventors, accordingly, have been obliged to accommodate themselves to the taste of the age [...]. The very extravagance of the present production will now, therefore, be, perhaps, in its favour, since the events which have eventually passed before our eyes have made the atmosphere of miracles in which we most readily breathe.[5]

The *Edinburgh Literary Miscellany* strikes a similar note to Scott by attributing readers' new preferences for strong characters not to vitiated taste but to the fascinating qualities of real-life characters. Looking forward to a time when readers will settle down again with English classics, the reviewer hopes that 'our sons and daughters will deign once more to laugh over the Partridges and the Trullibers, and to weep over the Clementinas and Clarissas of past times, as we [did] ourselves before we were so entirely engrossed with the Napoleons of real life, or the Corsairs of poetry'.[6]

Yet, eschewing anti-caricature rhetoric, this review celebrates the novelists and poets of the Romantic period – with their 'striking', 'powerful' and peculiar characters – for giving literary form to the 'strong character' of their own times:

> This [taste] ... may be partly owing to the wonderful realities which it has been our lot to witness. We have been spoiled for the tranquil enjoyment of common interests, and nothing now will satisfy us in fiction, any more than in real life, but grand movements and striking characters. A singular union has, accordingly, been attempted between history, and poetry. The periods of great events have been seized on as a ground work for the display of powerful or fantastic characters: correct and instructive pictures of national peculiarities have been exhibited; and even in those fictions which are altogether wild and monstrous, some insight has been given into the passions and theories which have convulsed and bewildered this our 'age of Reason.' In the poetry of Mr Scott and Lord Byron, in the novels of Miss Edgeworth, Mr Godwin, and the author of *Waverley*, we see exemplified in different forms this influence of the spirit of the times,—the prevailing love of historical, and at the same time romantic incident,—dark and high-wrought passions,—the delineations, chiefly of national character,—the pursuit of some substance, in short, yet of an existence more fanciful often than absolute fiction.[7]

Caricature, I have shown, played its own distinctive part in the critical tradition of the realist novel that emerged in the Romantic period, and became especially bound up with novelists' self-consciously realist characterisation techniques in the early nineteenth century. Rather than being *about* caricature in any deliberately conceptual way, caricature talk is always concerned with art and literature's 'substance' and 'originality' as weighed against the 'realities' of people, places and times. I end this book with the *Edinburgh Literary Miscellany* and the *Scots Magazine*'s irresistible suggestion that the novelists and poets of the Romantic period formed their literary realisms in competition with reality, proving literature's own imaginative strength and substance against the gigantic character of the age.

Notes

Chapter 1

1 *The Scots Magazine* (1 November 1797), p. 796.
2 *Johnson's Dictionary of the English Language, in Miniature* (Edinburgh: for W. Creech, Peter Hill, Ogle & Aikman and J. Thomson, Jun. & Co.; Glasgow: for Brash & Reid, 1808), p. 33. This definition appears in other pocket editions such as *Johnson's Dictionary of the English Language with Walker's Pronunciation of all the Difficult or Doubtful Words* (London: C. Corall and Thomas Hurst, Edward Chance, & Co., 1827).
3 Walker's recommended pronunciation for the last syllable is 'tshure', suggesting that of the two currently attested pronunciations in Standard English with RP, |ˈkarɪkətjʊə| and |ˈkarɪkətʃɔː|, the latter is the more conservative.
4 Giuseppe Baretti, *A Dictionary of the English and Italian Languages* (London: for C. Hitch and L. Lawes, R. Baldwin, W. Johnston, W. Johnston, W. Owen, J. Richardson, G. Keith, T. Longman, S. Crowder and Co., P. Davey and B. Law, and H. Woodgate and S. Brookes, 1760).
5 Thomas Browne, *Letter to a Friend, Upon Occasion of the Death of His Intimate Friend* (London: Brome, 1690), pp. 3–5.
6 John Hughes, *The Spectator*, 537 (15 November 1712), p. 1.
7 Walter Scott, *Rob Roy*, edited by David Hewitt (Edinburgh: Edinburgh University Press, 2008), p. 95'.
8 'Letter to the Editor, March 20', *Morning Post and Daily Advertiser*, 774 (20 April 1775), p. 1; Wollstonecraft, *A Vindication of the Rights of Woman*, ed. Janet Todd (Oxford University Press, 2008), pp. 282, 274; 'The Mirror of Fashion', *Morning Chronicle* (August 1796), p. 7; *Morning Post and Gazetteer*, 9177 (6 June 1798), p. 1; *Morning Star*, 191 (23 September 1798), p. 4; *Cobbett's Weekly Political Register*, 24 (12 December 1807), p. 18; *The Morning Post*, 13619) (14 September 1814), p. 3; 'Frankenstein; or the Modern Prometheus', *Scots Magazine*, 2.3 (March 1818), pp. 249, 253.
9 Reproduced in 'Account of George Steevens, Esq. the Celebrated Commentator on Shakespeare', *The Edinburgh Magazine and Literary Miscellany* (April 1800), p. 293.
10 *The Spectator*, 537 (15 November 1712), p. 1.

11 Francis Grose, *Rules for Drawing Caricaturas* (London: Bagster, 1788), p. 5.
12 Wollstonecraft, *Vindication*, p. 117.
13 Jane Austen, ['Opinions by various people of Jane Austen's work'] Add MS 41253, British Library, London; Thomas Babington Macaulay, 'Madame D'Arblay', *The Edinburgh Review*, 76 (January 1843), p. 562.
14 *Morning Post and Daily Advertiser*, 1129 (7 June 1776), p. 4.
15 *Morning Herald*, 5668 (17 November 1798), p. 2.
16 Michael O'Neill, 'Mournful Ditties and Merry Measures: Feeling and Form in the Romantic Short Lyric and Song', in *A Companion to Romantic Poetry*, ed. Charles Mahoney (Hoboken, NJ: Wiley-Blackwell, 2010), p. 20.
17 David Taylor surveys the field of scholarship on Georgian satirical prints in 'The Practice of Caricature in 18th-Century Britain', *Literature Compass* (2017); https://doi.org/10.1111.lic3.12383. On caricature prints later in the nineteenth century, see David Kerr, *Caricature and French Political Culture, 1830–1848* (Oxford University Press, 2000) and Brian Maidment, *Comedy, Caricature, and the Social Order, 1820–50* (Manchester University Press, 2013).
18 See David Taylor, *The Politics of Parody: A Literary History of Caricature, 1760–1830* (New Haven, CT: Yale University Press, 2018).
19 This print was one of Cruikshank's multiple publications on behalf of the state lotteries, 'presented gratis to every Purchaser of a Ticket or Share at Martins Lottery Office' and advertised in *The Morning Post* for 28 April 1814. It is possible that Shelley saw the print, though she later professed to dislike lotteries – 'demoralising gambling', 'the destruction of the savings of the poor' (see *Rambles in Germany and Italy*, vol. II, 1844, pp. 23–6) – and was largely absent from Britain between 1814 and the writing of *Frankenstein*.
20 *Morning Herald* (26 January 1781), p. 2; 'Art. XVI. A Treatise on the Lues Bovilla, or Cow-Pox', *The Monthly Review* (August 1805), pp. 428–29; 'The Peace', *Morning Post* (12 December 1815), p. 2.
21 Anthony Ashley Cooper, *The Moralists: A Philosophical Rhapsody* (London: John Wyat, 1709), p. 24.
22 'Ode, On the Success of His Majesty's Arms', *London Evening Post* (9–11 December 1777), p. 14.
23 Ian Haywood, *Romanticism and Caricature* (Cambridge: Cambridge University Press, 2014), p. 6.
24 E. H. Gombrich, 'Imagery and Art in the Romantic Period', in *The Essential Gombrich*, ed. Richard Woodfield (New York: Phaidon, 1963), p. 533.
25 Robert L. Patten, 'Conventions of Georgian Caricature', *Art Journal*, 43.4 (1983), p. 331.
26 'The Mirror of French Manners. On Caricatures', *La Belle Assemblée; Or, Bell's Court and Fashionable Magazine*, 76 (1 October 1815), p. 189.
27 Donald Posner, *Annibale Carracci: A Study in the Reform of Italian Painting around 1590* (New York: Phaidon, 1971), p. 69.
28 E. H. Gombrich and Ernst Kris, *Caricature* (London: Penguin, 1940), cited in Donald Posner, *ibid*.

29 Ann Summerscale (ed. and trans.), *Malvasia's Life of the Carracci* (University Park, PA: Penn State University Press, 2000), p. 123.
30 *Ibid.*, p. 278 n. 83.
31 See Clare Robertson, *The Invention of Annibale Carracci* (Milan: Silvana Editoriale, 2008) and Claude Douglas Dickerson, *Raw Painting: The Butcher's Shop by Annibale Carracci* (New Haven, CT: Yale University Press, 2010).
32 For example, Ghezzi's portrait of the Jacobite Lord Southesk in exile in Rome, PG 2452, National Gallery of Scotland, Edinburgh.
33 Mary Darly, *A Book of Carricaturas* (London: Darly, 1762), p. 2.
34 Grose, *Caricaturas*, p. 10.
35 D 5057.92 B, National Galleries of Scotland. See also Clerk's drawings catalogued as *Caricature of a Hedgehog Dressed as a Woman* (D 5057.79.A), *Woman Wearing a Fancy Bonnet* (D 5057.94.A) and *Caricature of a Man in a Wig* (NGS D 5057.73 A), which has been tentatively identified as a portrait of his friend Grose, whose own efforts include a drawing catalogued as *Caricature of Gluttons at Table* (NGS D 5057.69.A). For further examples of amateur caricature drawings, see photographer John Muir Wood's calotype of an unattributed drawing, *The Professor* (NGS PGP.W.113); Charles Kirkpatrick Sharpe's *The Music Room, Oxford, 1802* (NGS D 4800.H) and *Caricature of Fanny Persiani, Italian Soprano* (NGS D.2381); Lavinia, Countess Spencer's *Gallant and Gay Lothario* (Tate T10114); and portraits of Edward Gibbon by Spencer (BM Binyon 1898–1904 4) and by Lady Diana Beauclerk (BM Binyon 1898–1907 1). On caricatures by elite women, see Cindy McCreery on *The Satirical Gaze: Prints of Women in Late Eighteenth-Century England* (Oxford University Press, 2004), p. 23.
36 Unsigned review of *English Caricaturists and Graphic Humourists of the Nineteenth Century*, The Athenaeum, 3064 (17 July 1886), p. 85.
37 *The Letters of Sir Walter Scott*, edited by Herbert Grierson, 12 vols. (London: Constable, 1932–37), vol. IX, p. 463.
38 Jonathan Henry Christie, 'Life of Lockhart', *The Quarterly Review*, 116 (1864), p. 447.
39 Walter Scott, *Redgauntlet*, eds. G. A. M. Wood and David Hewitt (Edinburgh: Edinburgh University Press, 1997), p. 3.
40 William Makepeace Thackeray, *Vanity Fair: A Novel without a Hero*, ed. Helen Small (Oxford University Press, 2015), pp. 576–77; William Makepeace Thackeray, 'Life and Genius of George Cruikshank', *The Monthly Magazine*, 15.86 (February 1833), pp. 131–47.
41 One of Taylor's drawings depicts her presentation to Queen Victoria by Princess Mary (1869, Royal Collection Trust, RCIN 918861); she sketched quick caricatures of Isidore Brasseur, French teacher to the Prince of Wales and Princess Mary (Royal Collection Trust, DM 5263), Count B. Chotek, Secretary to the Austrian Embassy in London (DM 4262) and Count Kielmansegge, Hanoverian Envoy Extraordinary at the Court of St James's (DM 5266). Her other drawings include *Four Caricatures of Dr Quin's adventures on his way to Cambridge Cottage* (1860, RCIN 918820),

A celebrated noble Lord in sporting dress (1859, DM 5288), and *Sketches made at the Opening of Parliament* (1861, RCIN 918824).
42 Draper Hill's estimate, that this constituted over three quarters of Gillray's output in 1795–96, is cited in Taylor, *Politics of Parody*, p. 184; Taylor, *Politics of Parody*, pp. 181–209. The print is BMC 10019.
43 Add MS 27337, British Library, London.
44 *Ibid.*, pp. 92–3.
45 'James Gillray, and His Caricatures', *The Athenaeum*, 205 (1 October 1831), p. 633.
46 Eirwen E. C. Nicholson, 'Consumers and Spectators: The Public of the Political Print in Eighteenth-Century England', *History*, 81.261 (1996), p. 6.
47 Nicholson, 'Consumers and Spectators', p. 25.
48 Baker, *The Business of Satirical Prints in Late-Georgian England* (London: Palgrave Macmillan, 2017), pp. 149–67.
49 H. T. Dickinson, *Caricatures and the Constitution 1760–1832* (Cambridge: Chadwyck-Healey, 1986), p. 15
50 See for example Thomas Rowlandson, *The Covent Garden Night Mare* (1784, BM Satires 6543), *Dutch Night-Mare or the Fraternal Hug Returned with a Dutch Squeeze* (1813, BM Satires 12105); George Cruikshank, *The Night Mare* (1816, BMC 12817); and James Gillray, *The Apotheosis of Hoche* (1798, BM Satires 9156).
51 Mary Brunton, *Self-control*, 2 vols. (Edinburgh: Manners and Miller; London: Longman, Hurst, Rees, Orme, and Brown, 1811), vol. I, pp. 137–38, 13–14, 28; vol. II, p. 7.
52 Mary Brunton, *Discipline*, 3 vols. (Edinburgh: Manners and Miller; London: Longman, Hurst, Rees, Orme, and Brown), vol. I, pp. 49–50.
53 *Ibid.*, vol. I, p. 174.
54 See Taylor, 'Edgeworth's *Belinda* and the Gendering of Caricature', *Eighteenth-Century Fiction* 26.4 (2014): 493–624.
55 Maria Edgeworth, *Ennui*, ed. Marilyn Butler (London: Penguin, 1992), p. 209. The print is *English Fire-side*, published by J. Le Petit in Dublin, which depicts a gouty man asleep in a chair and two fashionably dressed men standing by the fireplace. One lounges across the mantlepiece while reading the Racing Calendar. Paintings on the walls show a boxing match and a cock-fighting pit, in addition to a portrait of Chesterfield. There is no copy of *English Fire-side* in the British Museum's Departments of Prints and Drawings, but one can be consulted in the Abbotsford Collection: see 'Portfolio of caricatures, coloured', Advocates Library, National Library of Scotland.
56 Edgeworth, *Helen* (London: Pandora, 1987), p. 232.
57 See Olivia Ferguson, 'Wellington's Rats in the Illustrated *Devil's Walk*', *Notes and Queries*, 61.1 (2014), pp. 54–6.
58 Letter 345 (29 August 1798), to Thomas Southey, in *The Collected Letters of Robert Southey: Part Two: 1798–1803*, eds. Lynda Pratt, Tim Fulford and Ian Packer: https://romantic-circles.org/editions/southey_letters/Part_Two/index.html.

59 Letter 356 (6 November 1798), to Charles Biddlecombe, *ibid*.
60 Letter 348 (18 September 1798), to George Dyer, *ibid*.
61 Taylor, *Politics of Parody*, p. 30. On Canning's acquaintance with Gillray, see Draper Hill, *Mr. Gillray: The Caricaturist* (New York: Phaidon, 1965), pp. 57–63.
62 See for example Thomas Hood, *The Progress of Cant* (1815, BMC 14815), Robert Isaac Cruikshank, *The Great Unknown Lately Discovered in Ireland* (1825, BMC 14825) and *The Great Unknown Cutting Up Napoleon the Great* (1827, BMC 154167), Henry Thomas Aiken, *Calves' Heads and Brains or a Phrenological Lecture* (1826, BMC 15158) and John Doyle, *The Balance of Public Favor* (1827, BMC 15440).
63 Byron is subjected to the linear exaggeration of caricature portraiture in Robert Cruikshank's *Management, or Butts & Hogsheads* (1812, BMC 11940), as well as being placed alongside Scott, Wordsworth, Coleridge, Southey and Matthew Lewis in Charles Williams's prints about the Poet Laureateship, *The Genius of the Times* (1812, BMC 11940) and *Rival Candidates for the Vacant Bays* (1813, BMC 12982). The Cruikshank brothers exploited Byron's separation from his wife and his departure from England in 1816 with *Fare Thee Well* (BMC 12827), *The Separation, A Sketch from the Private Life of Lord Iron* (BMC 12828), *Lobby Loungers* (BMC 12826) and *Fashionables of 1816 Taking the Air in Hyde Park!* (BMC 12825). On the image of Byron in satirical prints, see Tom Mole, *Byron's Romantic Celebrity* (Palgrave Macmillan, 2007), pp. 89–93.
64 Percy Shelley, 'Oedipus Tyrannus; or, Swellfoot the Tyrant', *The Collected Works of Percy Bysshe Shelley*, edited by Roger Ingen and Walter E. Peck, 10 vols. (London: Ernest Benn, 1927), vol. II, pp. 362–75.
65 See Iain Gordon Brown, 'Caricature: The Individual Contribution of John Kay', *The Edinburgh History of the Book in Scotland*, 2 vols., edited by Bill Bell (University of Edinburgh Press, 2012), vol. II, edited by Stephen W. Brown and Warren McDougall, pp. 107–10.
66 In 1818, Scott thanks his son in a letter for a present of some satirical prints: 'Mama and I like the caricatures very much. I think however scarce any shews the fancy and talent of old Gilray [sic]' (*Letters*, vol. V, p. 460).
67 See Olivia Ferguson, 'Gratifying Difficulty', *Essays in Criticism*, 70.3 (July 2020), pp. 376–77.
68 Robert L. Patten, *Cruikshank's Life, Times, and Art*, 2 vols. (New Brunswick, NJ: Rutgers University Press, 1992); Patten, *George Cruikshank: A Revaluation* (Princeton, NJ: Princeton University Press, 1974).
69 'Life and Genius of George Cruikshank', *Monthly Magazine*, 15.86 (February 1833), p. 135.
70 'Gillray's Caricatures', *Morning Chronicle* (25 October 1851), p. 7. This article is a review of Wright and Evans's *Historical and Descriptive Account of the Caricatures of James Gillray* (1851).
71 See 'James Gillray, and His Caricatures', *The Athenaeum*, 205 (1 October 1831), p. 633–34; 'Gillray's Caricatures', *Morning Chronicle* (25 October 1851), p. 7; and Scott, *Letters*, vol. V, p. 460.

72 John Barrell, 'A Smile at My Own Temerity', *London Review of Books*, 39.4 (February 2017), p. 8.
73 *The Monthly Magazine* 43.5 (1 June 1817), p. 453.
74 *The Complete Works of William Hazlitt*, 21 vols., edited by P. P. Howe (London: J. M. Dent, 1930–4), vol. X, p. 79.
75 'James Gillray, and His Caricatures', *Athenaeum*, p. 632.
76 Johann Kaspar Lavater, *Essays on Physiognomy*, 4 vols., translated by Thomas Holcroft (London: G. G. J. and J. Robinson, 1789–98, vol. I, p. 107, Holcroft's note.
77 *Physiognomische Fragmente zur Beförderung der Menschenkenntniß und Menschenliebe*, 3 vols. (Winterhur: Johann Michael Armbruster; Heinrich Steiners und Compagnie, 1783–7), vol. I, p. 192.
78 *Essays on Physiognomy*, pp. 198–99.
79 See Deidre Lynch, *The Economy of Character: Novels, Market Culture, and the Business of Inner Meaning* (University of Chicago Press, 1998), pp. 61–70.
80 'To the Authors of the Monthly Review', *The Monthly Review*, vol. XIX (September 1758), pp. 318–20.
81 Italics indicate the letter's quotation from Hogarth's caption for *The Bench*. 'To the Authors of the Monthly Review', *The Monthly Review*, vol. XIX (December 1758), pp. 605–7.
82 Hazlitt, 'On the Elgin Marbles', *The Examiner* (30 June 1816), p. 206; 'On the Imitation of Nature', *Complete Works*, vol. XVIII, pp. 114–15.
83 *Composers on Music*, ed. Josiah Fisk (Boston: Northeastern University Press, 1997), p. 85.
84 Unsigned review of *Tales of My Landlord*, *Edinburgh Review* (March 1817), p. 199.
85 Art. VIII.—*Manfred; a Dramatic Poem*', *Critical Review*, 5.6 (June 1817), p. 629.
86 Review of Joanna Bailie's *The Family Legend* and *A Series of Plays*, *The Monthly Review* (1 December 1812), pp. 382–93. The writer refers to Le Brun's *Méthode pour apprendre à dessiner les passions* (1698).
87 John Walker, *A Critical Pronouncing Dictionary & Expositor of the English Language* (London: Thomas Tegg, T. Kelly, G. Virtue; Manchester: J. Gleaves; Leicester: E. Allen, 1823).
88 Wollstonecraft, *A Vindication of the Rights of Woman*, p. 74; and see note on p. 383.
89 *Ibid.*, pp. 282–83.

Chapter 2

1 'On Fable and Romance', *Dissertations Moral and Critical*, 2 vols. (Dublin, 1783), vol. II, p. 306.
2 George Levine, *The Realistic Imagination* (Chicago: University of Chicago Press, 1983), pp. 19–20.

3 'Art. XI. 1. *Childe Harold's Pilgrimage* [...] 2. *The Prisoners of Chillon, and Other Poems*', *Eclectic Review*, 7.25 (March 1817), p. 301.
4 'Art. XII. *Frankenstein; or the Modern Prometheus*', *The British Critic* (October 1818), pp. 437–38.
5 *Introductions and Notes from the Magnum Opus: Waverley to A Legend of the Wars of Montrose*, edited by J. H. Alexander with P. D. Garside and Claire Lamont, p. 163. I discuss Scott's grotesquing of dwarf characters in Chapters 5 and 6.
6 '*Rob Roy*. By the Author of Waverley, &c.', *Scots Magazine*, 2.2 (February 1818), pp. 148, 151, 150.
7 John Frow, 'Spectacle Binding: On Character', *Poetics Today* 7 (1986): 227.
8 Lynch, *The Economy of Character*, pp. 1, 4.
9 *Ibid.*, p. 18.
10 Moi, 'Rethinking Character', in *Character: Three Inquiries in Literary Studies* (Chicago: University of Chicago Press, 2019), p. 28.
11 Anna Murphy Jameson, *Shakespeare's Heroines*, edited by Cheri L. Larsen Hoeckley (Peterborough: Broadview Press, 2005), p. 58.
12 Lynch, *The Economy of Character*, p. 133.
13 *Ibid.*, 135.
14 Frow, *Character and Person* (Oxford: Oxford University Press, 2014), p. 15.
15 *Ibid.*, p. 16
16 'Letter I. On Hogg's Memoirs', *Blackwood's Edinburgh Magazine*, 10.54 (August 1821), p. 52.
17 Karen Fang, 'A Printing Devil, a Scottish Mummy, and an Edinburgh Book of the Dead: James Hogg's Napoleonic Complex', *Studies in Romanticism*, 43.2 (2004), p. 81.
18 *Hypocrisy Unveiled and Calumny Detected in a Review of Blackwood's Magazine* (Edinburgh: Francis Pillans, 1818), pp. 53–4.
19 Nicholas Mason, General Introduction to *Blackwood's Magazine, 1817–25*, edited by Nicholas Mason, 6 vols. (London: Pickering & Chatto, 2006), vol. I, p. xi.
20 Tom Mole, '*Blackwood's* "Personalities"', in *Romanticism and Blackwood's Magazine: An Unprecedented Phenomenon*, edited by Robert Morrison and Daniel S. Roberts (Basingstoke: Palgrave, 2013), pp. 91–2.
21 'On the Cockney School of Poetry', *Blackwood's Edinburgh Magazine*, 16 (July 1818), p. 454.
22 *Ibid.*, p. 453.
23 Letter to Benjamin Bailey, 3 November 1817, in *The Letters of John Keats, 1814–1821*, edited by Hyder Edward Rollins, 2 vols. (Cambridge, MA: Harvard University Press, 2002), vol. I, pp. 179–80.
24 See James Mulvihill, *Notorious Facts* (Newark, NJ: University of Delaware Press, 2011), pp. 34–8.
25 See Michael Eberle-Sinatra's account in *Leigh Hunt and the London Literary Scene: A Reception History of His Major Works* (Abingdon: Routledge, 2005), pp. 74–91.

26 Unsigned review of *Hours of Idleness*, 'By George Gordon, Lord Byron, a Minor', *The Edinburgh Review* (January 1808), p. 285.
27 *Letters of Anna Seward: Written between the years 1784 and 1807*, edited by Walter Scott, 6 vols. (Edinburgh: Constable; London: Longman, Hurst, Rees, Orme, and Brown, William Miller, and John Murray, 1811), vol. VI, pp. 366–67.
28 Thomas De Quincey, *Confessions of an English Opium-Eater*, edited by Robert Morrison (Oxford: Oxford University Press, 2013), p. 3.
29 Samuel Taylor Coleridge, *The Friend*, 1 (London: Gale and Curtis, 1812), p. 6.
30 'Some Observations on the "Biographia Literaria" of S. T. Coleridge, Esq.— 1817', *Blackwood's Edinburgh Magazine*, 2.7 (October 1817), p. 6.
31 *The Mountain Bard; consisting of Legendary Ballads and Tales. By James Hogg, the Ettrick Shepherd. The Third Edition, Greatly Enlarged. To which is prefixed a Memoir of the Author's Life, written by himself* (Edinburgh: Oliver & Boyd, 1821), p. xxxi.
32 See MS 30,000 folios 14–17, National Library of Scotland, Edinburgh.
33 'Letter I. On Hogg's Memoirs', *Blackwood's Edinburgh Magazine*, p. 44. On the foregrounding and description of Hogg's body in Wilson's reviews, see Ian Duncan, 'Hogg's Body', *Scott's Shadow: The Novel in Romantic Edinburgh* (Princeton, NJ: Princeton University Press, 2007), pp. 173–82; Mark L. Shoenfield, 'Butchering James Hogg', in *At the Limits of Romanticism: Essays in Cultural, Feminist, and Materialist Criticism*, edited by Mary Favret and Nicola Watson (Bloomington: Indiana University Press, 1994), pp. 207–24; and Kelly E. Battles, 'Bad Taste, Gothic Bodies, and Subversive Aesthetics in Hogg's *Private Memoirs and Confessions of a Justified Sinner*', *Essays in Romanticism*, 19.5 (2012), pp. 49–64.
34 'Letter I. On Hogg's Memoirs', *Blackwood's Edinburgh Magazine* (1821), p. 43.
35 *Ibid.*, p. 52.
36 Walter Scott, *Letters*, vol. II, p. 109.
37 *Ibid.*, p. 116.
38 *Ibid.*, vol. XII, p. 446.
39 *Ibid.*, vol. V, pp. 154–56. On duelling and class, see Richard Cronin, *Paper Pellets: British Literary Culture after Waterloo* (Oxford: Oxford University Press, 2010), pp. 12–53.
40 'On the Cockney School of Poetry. No. I.', *Blackwood's Edinburgh Magazine*, 2.7 (October 1817), p. 39.
41 Marilyn Butler, *Maria Edgeworth: A Literary Biography* (Oxford: Oxford University Press, 1972), pp. 240, 241.
42 Butler and Tim McLoughlin, *The Works of Maria Edgeworth* (London: Routledge), vol. I, pp. vii–iii.
43 Butler, *Maria Edgeworth*, p. 241
44 *Ibid.*, p. 306
45 Quoted in Butler, *Maria Edgeworth*, p. 252.

46 *Ibid.*, pp. 248–49.
47 'Nightmare Abbey. By the Author of "Headlong Hall"', *The London Literary Gazette*, 99 (12 December 1818), p. 787.
48 Marilyn Butler, *Peacock Displayed: A Satirist in His Context* (Abingdon: Routledge, 1979), pp. 16–17, 19; Dyer, *British Satire and the Politics of Style*, p. 101.
49 Mulvihill, 'Peacock's Nightmare Abbey and the "Shapes" of Imposture', *Studies in Romanticism*, 34.4 (1995), p. 568.
50 *Headlong Hall. Nightmare Abbey. Maid Marian. Crotchet Castle. With corrections, and a preface, by the author* (London: Richard Bentley; Edinburgh: Bell and Bradfute; Dublin: J. Cumming, 1837), pp. v–vi; *Melincourt or Sir Oran Haut-ton* (London: Chapman and Hall, 1856), pp. iv.
51 Peacock claims to have written his own *Memoirs of Percy Bysshe Shelley* (1858–60) reluctantly, to correct the errors of previous biographers and to condemn the liberties they had taken. Indeed, the first part of the memoir is effectively a review of three recent biographies, Charles S. Middleton's *Shelley and His Writings* (1856), Edward Trelawny's *Recollections of the Last Days of Shelley and Byron* (1858) and Hogg's *The Life of Percy Bysshe Shelley* (1858).
52 On the reception of Hunt's memoir in the literary periodicals, see Eberle-Sinatra, *Leigh Hunt*, pp. 120–24.
53 *Lord Byron and Some of His Contemporaries* (London: Henry Colburn, 1828), pp. 87–8.
54 Peacock, *Crotchet Castle*, edited by Freya Johnston and Matthew Bevis (Cambridge: Cambridge University Press, 2016), p. 58.
55 *Ibid.*, pp. 43, 132.
56 *Ibid.* p. 153.
57 Felix Felton, *Thomas Love Peacock* (London: Allen & Unwin, 1973), p. 150.
58 Butler, *Peacock Displayed: A Satirist in His Context* (London: Routledge, 1979), p. 17.
59 Several of Dickens's letters to Hunt allude to the Skimpole caricature; there is no record of what Hunt said to Dickens on the subject, as Dickens appears to have burned all the letters his friend wrote to him. After Hunt's death, Dickens published a lengthy article in *All the Year Round* titled 'Leigh Hunt. A Remonstrance': a review of the new edition of Hunt's autobiography but also an apology and explanation for Harold Skimpole. See Luther A. Brewer, *Leigh Hunt and Charles Dickens: The Skimpole Caricature* (Cedar Rapids, IA: privately printed), 1930.
60 William Hazlitt, 'The Dandy School', *The Examiner* (18 November, 1827): see *Complete Works*, vol. XX, pp. 143–49.
61 Mary Brunton, *Discipline: a Novel* (Edinburgh: Manners and Miller; London: Longman, Hurst, Rees, Orme, and Brown, 1814), vol. II, p. 51.
62 Peacock, *Crotchet Castle*, p. 50.
63 See Cheryl A. Wilson, *Fashioning the Silver Fork Novel: Literary Texts and the Popular Marketplace* (London: Routledge, 2012), p. 27.
64 Butler, *Peacock Displayed*, p. 258.

65 Sydney, Lady Morgan, *Florence Macarthy: An Irish Tale*, 4 vols. (London: Colburn, 1818), vol. IV, p. 144–45.
66 Butler, *Peacock Displayed*, p. 257
67 *Introductions and Notes from the Magnum Opus: Waverley to a Legend of the Wars of Montrose*, p. 162.
68 Ibid., p. 159.
69 Ibid.
70 Ibid., p. 158, 162.
71 Ibid., p. 162.
72 Ibid., p. 158.
73 Anne Toner has argued that the lapse of the Licensing Act in 1695 partly accounts for texts' increased use of dashes, asterisks and blank spaces – 'blanks' – due to 'the loophole in libel laws that innuendo however blatant would not be permitted to constitute a libel'. See Anne Toner, *Ellipsis in English Literature: Signs of Omission* (Cambridge: Cambridge University Press, 2015), p. 58. In *Satire made Easy; or Instructions in the Art of Polite Censure* (1815), John Corry jokes that lawyers 'could measure a dash with mathematical precision, and expound an enigmatical libel with the aids of asterisks, or stars, with [...] astrological exactness'. *Satire made Easy; or Instructions in the Art of Polite Censure* (Manchester: Leigh, 1815), pp. 14–15.
74 Jane Austen, *Pride and Prejudice*, edited by Pat Rogers (Cambridge: Cambridge University Press, 2006). 82.
75 Anthony Trollope, *The Warden* (London: Longman, Brown, Green, and Longmans, 1855), p. 1.

Chapter 3

1 See William St. Clair, *The Reading Nation in the Romantic Period* (Cambridge: Cambridge University Press, 2004), p. 475.
2 Ibid., pp. 130–31, 274.
3 Jane Austen, *Northanger Abbey*, edited by Barbara M. Benedict and Deirdre Le Faye (Cambridge: Cambridge University Press, 2006), p. 31.
4 Theresa Shön, *A Cosmography of Man: Character Sketches in 'The Tatler' and 'The Spectator'* (De Gruyter, 2020), ch. 1, n. pag.
5 *Theophrastus His Morall Characters or Description of Maners*, translated by Joseph Healey (1628): www.eudaemonist.com/biblion/characters/healey.
6 Jean de la Bruyère, *The Characters, or the Manners of the Age. Made English with Several Hands. With the Characters of Theophrastus. With the Key Inserted in the Margent.* 4th ed. (London: Fr. Leach, 1705), p. 1.
7 'To the Right Honourable John Lord Sommers', *The Spectator*, 9th ed. (London: T. Jonson, 1729), vol. I, p. 4.
8 Brian Cowan, 'Mr. Spectator and the Coffeehouse Public Sphere', *Eighteenth-Century Studies* 37.3 (Spring 2004), p. 346.
9 Ibid., p. 347.

10 James Edward Austen-Leigh, *A Memoir of Jane Austen and Other Family Recollections*, edited by Kathryn Sutherland (Oxford: Oxford University Press, 2002), p. 118.
11 Thomas Randolph, *The Muses Looking-glass; (or, the Stage Re-view'd.) A Comedy* (London, 1706), p. 9.
12 See for example *The Law Corrupted* (1706), *The Characters and Conduct of Sir John Edgar* (1720), and *Tracts Consisting of Sermons, Discourses, and Letters* (1745), all cited in Ashley Marshall, *The Practice of Satire in England, 1658–1770* (Baltimore: Johns Hopkins University Press, 2016), p. 42.
13 Henry Fielding, *The History of the Adventures of Joseph Andrews and of His Friend Mr. Abraham Adams* (London: A. Millar, 1742), p. 162.
14 Jonathan Swift, *Verses on the Death of Dr. Swift* (London: Bathurst, 1739), p. 38.
15 Walter Scott, unsigned review of *Emma*, *Quarterly Review*, 14 (October 1815), p. 194.
16 Francis Jeffrey, unsigned review of *Waverley*, *Edinburgh Review* (November 1814), p. 209.
17 Unsigned review of *Waverley*, *Edinburgh Review* (November 1814), p. 210.
18 Shön, *A Cosmography of Man*, ch. 1, n. pag.
19 Richard Steele, *The Spectator*, 194 (London: G. Robertson), vol. III, pp. 337–40; Joseph Addison, *The Spectator*, 205 (London: G. Robertson), vol. III, pp. 390–95.
20 See Chester Noyes Greenough, *Bibliography of the English Theophrastan Character* (Cambridge, MA: Harvard University Press, 1947).
21 Ian Watt, *The Rise of the Novel: Studies in Defoe, Richardson and Fielding* (London: Chatto & Windus, 1957), p. 16.
22 Henry Home Kames, *Elements of Criticism*, 2nd ed. (Edinburgh: A. Kincaid & J. Bell; London: A. Millar), vol. I, pp. 4–5.
23 *Ibid.*, vol. III, pp. 198–99.
24 *Ibid.*, vol. I, pp. 5–6.
25 Quoted in Watt, *The Rise of the Novel*, p. 279.
26 Shön, *Cosmography*, n. pag.; J. W. Smeed, *The Theophrastan 'Character': The History of a Literary Genre* (Oxford: Clarendon Press, 1985), p. 2.
27 *London Magazine*, 33 (July 1764), p. 2.
28 Smeed, *Theophrastan 'Character'*, p. 2
29 E. Berens, ed., *A Second Selection from the Papers of Addison* (London: C. & J. Rivington, 1828), p. vii–viii.
30 Letter XLII, to P. Hill, *The Letters of Robert Burns* (London: T. Davison 1819), vol I, p. 91.
31 Further examples can be found in the critical apparatus of numerous eighteenth-century and nineteenth-century editions of the *Spectator*, for example in Robert Bisset's *The Spectator: A New Edition in Eight Volumes; with Illustrative Notes* (London: George Robertson; Edinburgh: Bell and Bradefute, 1793), and in reviews of new editions.

32 Samuel Johnson, *The Lives of the Most Eminent English Poets*, 2 vols. (London: C. Bathurst, etc., 1781), vol. II, pp. 442–43.
33 *The Spectator*, 8 vols. (London: Payne, Rivington, Davis, Longman, Dodsley, 1788), vol. VII, p. 174.
34 Alexander Chalmers, *The British Essayists; with Prefaces, Historical and Biographical*, x vols. (London: J. Johnson etc., 1808), vol. VI, p. xviii.
35 Lionel Thomas Berguer, *British Essayists; with Prefaces Biographical, Historical and Critical* (1823), vol. V, p. xxxvii.
36 Nathan Drake, *Essays, Biographical, Critical, and Historical; illustrative of the Tatler, Spectator, and Guardian*, 3 vols. (London: John Sharpe, 1805), vol. III, p. 19.
37 *Ibid.*, vol. I, pp. 235–36.
38 *Ibid.*, vol. I, p. 263–64.
39 Johnson, *Lives of the Poets*, vol. II, p. 442.
40 Berguer, *British Essayists*, vol. V, p. xxxvi.
41 Beattie, *The Papers of Joseph Addison*, vol. I, pp. xlii, xl–xli. The latter passage is reproduced with some alterations in punctuation and 'caricatura' changed to 'caricatures' in Chalmers, *British Essayists*, vol. VI, p. xxiii.
42 Beattie, *The Papers of Joseph Addison*, vol. I, p. xlii.
43 Lynch, *The Economy of Character*, p. 134.
44 Johnson, *Lives of the Poets*, vol. II, p. 442; Beattie, *The Papers of Joseph Addison*, vol. I, p. xlii.
45 Beattie, *The Papers of Joseph Addison*, vol. I, p. xlii.
46 Johnson, *Lives of the Poets*, vol. II, p. 367.
47 Beattie, *The Papers of Joseph* Addison, vol. I, p. xlii; reproduced in Chalmers, *British Essayists*, vol. VI, p. xviii.
48 Maurice Morgann, *Essay on the Dramatic Character of Sir John Falstaff* (London: P. T. Davies, 1777), p. 62; Thomas Robertson, 'An Essay on the Character of Hamlet', in *Transactions of the Royal Society of Edinburgh*, 2 (1788), quoted in Brian Vickers, *William Shakespeare: The Critical Heritage*, 6 vols. (London: Routledge, 1974), vol. VI, p. 482.
49 Berguer, *British Essayists*, vol. V, pp. xxxvi–ii.
50 George Saintsbury, ed., *Pride and Prejudice* (London: George Allen, 1894), pp. xii–xiii.
51 *Ibid.*, p. xvi.
52 *Ibid.*, pp. xvi, xvii.
53 Beattie, *Works of Addison*, vol. I, xlii.
54 Chalmers, *British Essayists*, vol. VI, p. xviii.
55 Johnson, *Lives of the Poets*, vol. II, p. 366. Quoted in Chalmers, vol. VI, pp. xiii–xiv.
56 Chalmers, *British Essayists*, vol. VI, p. xviii.
57 *The Spectator*, 8 vols. (London: Payne, Rivington, Davis, Longman, Dodsley, 1788), vol. VII, p. 174.
58 Joseph Meek, ed., *The De Coverley Papers from 'The Spectator'* (London: J. M. Dent, 1920), pp. 5–6.

59 *Ibid.*, p. 10.
60 For example, the contents page of *A Second Selection from the Papers of Addison*, edited by E. Berens (London: C. & J. Rivington, 1828).
61 Caleb Thomas Winchester, *The Sir Roger De Coverley Papers* (New York: American Book Company, 1904), pp. 30–1.
62 Watt, *The Rise of the Novel*, pp. 279–80.
63 Samuel Taylor Coleridge, *Seven Lectures on Shakespeare and Milton*, edited by J. Payne Collier (London: Chapman and Hall, 1856), pp. 57–8.
64 Chalmers, *British Essayists*, vol. VI, p. xx.
65 See also Lynch on the 'eerie thing-hood' of strong characters and their afterlives as collectibles in *The Economy of Character*, pp. 18–19.
66 T. E. Kebbel, 'Jane Austen at Home', *Fortnightly Review*, 37 (February 1885), pp. 262–70.
67 Unsigned review of *The Letters of Jane Austen*, *The Standard* (9 June 1884), p. 5.

Chapter 4

1 E. M. Forster, *Aspects of the Novel* (New York: Harcourt, Brace, and Co., 1927), p. 114.
2 Jane Stabler, 'Jane Austen and Caricature', *Nineteenth Century Studies*, 21 (2007), pp. 1–18.
3 Donald Greene, 'Jane Austen's Monsters', in John Halperin (ed.), *Jane Austen: Bicentenary Essays* (Cambridge: Cambridge University Press, 1975), pp. 262–78.
4 Rachel M. Brownstein, 'Character and Caricature: Jane Austen and James Gillray', *Persuasions*, 37 (2015), pp. 81–93.
5 *Ibid.*, p. 82.
6 Unsigned review of *Emma*, *The Gentleman's Magazine*, 86 (September 1816), pp. 248–49.
7 Unsigned review of Life and Adventures of Peter Wilkins, *The Retrospective Review*, 7 (1823), p. 131.
8 Richard Whately, unsigned review of *Northanger Abbey* and *Persuasion*, *Quarterly Review*, 24 (January 1821), pp. 353, 360, 368. On Austen's delicacy in the context of women's art more generally, see Francis Jeffrey's unsigned review of second editions of poems by Felicia Hemans, *Edinburgh Review*, 50 (October 1829), p. 473.
9 George Henry Lewes, 'The Novels of Jane Austen', *Blackwood's Edinburgh Magazine*, 86 (July 1859), p. 102.
10 Julia Kavanagh, *English Women of Letters*, 2 vols. (1862), vol. II, p. 252; Margaret Oliphant, review of *A Memoir of Jane Austen*; Margaret Oliphant, 'Miss Austen and Miss Mitford', *Blackwood's Magazine*, 107 (March 1870), p. 302.
11 Anna Laetitia Barbauld, 'Miss Burney', *British Novelists*, vol. XXXVIII (1810), pp. iii-iv; unsigned review of *Peter Wilkins*, *The Retrospective Review*, 7 (1823), p. 132; Toynbee, Paget, (ed.), *The Letters of Horace Walpole*, (Oxford: Clarendon, 1903–25), vol. XII, p. 339; 1 October 1782.

12 Thomas Babington Macaulay, unsigned review of *Diary and Letters of Madame D'Arblay*, *The Edinburgh Review*, 76 (January 1843), p. 562.
13 Kavanagh, *English Women of Letters*, pp. 94, 103.
14 Unsigned review of *The Letters of Jane Austen*, *The Standard* (9 June 1884), p. 5.
15 Unsigned review of *The Wanderer*, *The Edinburgh Review* (February 1815), p. 336.
16 *The Memoirs and Letters of Sara Coleridge*, ed. Edith Coleridge (Henry S. King & Co., 1873), vol I, p. 75; August 1834.
17 Mary Augusta Ward, 'Style and Miss Austen', *Macmillan's Magazine*, 51 (December 1884), p. 90. There are a great many more examples of women writing about Austen's femininity, each of which adds something new to the conversation. See Joanne Wilkes, *Women Reviewing Women in Nineteenth Century Britain: The Critical Reception of Jane Austen, Charlotte Brontë and George Eliot* (Farnham: Ashgate, 2010).
18 16–17 December 1816 in *Jane Austen's Letters*, edited by Deirdre Le Faye, 4th ed. (Oxford: Oxford University Press, 2011), p. 337.
19 See 'Tablet, memorandum', National Museums Scotland, A.1943.170 B (www.nms.ac.uk/explore-our-collections/collection-search-results/tablet-memorandum/357927). More luxurious polyptychs had ivory leaves inscribed with the days of the week, such as this one covered with a design of a nesting bird: 'Memorandum Tablet', Victoria and Albert Museum, T.170-1961: https://collections.vam.ac.uk/item/O316013/memorandum-tablet-unknown.
20 R. H. Hutton, unsigned review of *The Letters of Jane Austen*, 'The Charm of Miss Austen', *Spectator*, 64 (1890), pp. 403–4.
21 James Edward Austen-Leigh, *A Memoir of Jane Austen and Other Family Recollections*, edited by Kathryn Sutherland (Oxford University Press, 2002), p. 51. Anne Thackeray, 'Jane Austen', *Cornhill Magazine* 34 (1871), pp. 158–78. See Toner, *Jane Austen's Style: Narrative Economy and the Novel's Growth* (Cambridge: Cambridge University Press, 2020), pp. 23–4. See Barbara K. Seeber, *Jane Austen and Animals* (Farnham: Ashgate, 2013), pp. 2–4.
22 Richard Simpson, review of *Memoir of Jane Austen*, *North British Review*, 52 (April 1870), p. 130.
23 'Notice of Northanger Abbey and Persuasion', *The Edinburgh Magazine and Literary Miscellany; A New Series of the Scots Magazine*, vol. II (May 1818), pp. 453–55.
24 Excepting the weather-beaten faces of the ex-navy characters Admiral and Mrs Croft in *Persuasion*. *Sense and Sensibility*, edited by Edward Copeland (Cambridge: Cambridge University Press, 2006), pp. 40, 61; *Saint Ronan's Well*, edited by Mark A. Weinstein (Edinburgh: Edinburgh University Press, 1995), p. 134.
25 *Sense and Sensibility*, p. 8.
26 *Northanger Abbey*, edited by Barbara M. Benedict and Deirdre Le Faye (Cambridge: Cambridge University Press, 2006), p. 249.

27 *Sense and Sensibility*, p. 112.
28 *Northanger Abbey*, pp. 205–6.
29 Matthew G. Lewis, *The Monk*, eds. Howard Anderson and Emma McEvoy (Oxford: Oxford University Press, 2008), p. 441.
30 *Ibid.*, p. 442.
31 Walter Scott, unsigned review of *Emma*, *The Quarterly Review*, 14 (October 1815), p. 200.
32 *Sanditon* in *Jane Austen's Fiction Manuscripts*, edited by Kathryn Sutherland, b2, pp. 1–4: https://janeausten.ac.uk/manuscripts/sanditon/b1-2.html.
33 12 January 1848 in *The Letters of Charlotte Brontë: 1848–1851*, edited by Margaret Smith, 3 vols. (Oxford: Clarendon, 1995), vol. II, p. 10.
34 On disproportionately long speeches as a convention of exaggeration in *Mansfield Park* and *Emma*, see D. W. Harding, 'Character and Caricature in Jane Austen', in *Regulated Hatred and Other Essays on Jane Austen* (London: Athlone, 2000), pp. 83–86.
35 Mary Lascelles, *Jane Austen and Her Art* (Oxford: Oxford University Press, 1939), pp. 94–96. On the 'proper English' of Austen's novels, see Janet Sorenson, *The Grammar of Empire in Eighteenth-Century British Writing* (Cambridge: Cambridge University Press, 2000): pp. 198–200, 208, 210–13.
36 Marilyn Butler, 'Jane Austen's Word Process', review of *Computation into Criticism* by J. F. Burrows, *London Review of Books*, 9.12 (June 1987), p. 13.
37 Frances Ferguson, 'Austen, *Emma*, and the Impact of Form', *Modern Language Quarterly*, 61.1 (March 2000), pp. 157–80.
38 Macaulay, 'Madame D'Arblay', p. 43.
39 Richard Simpson, review of *Memoir of Jane Austen*, *North British Review*, 52 (April 1870), pp. 148–49.
40 Donald Greene, 'Jane Austen's Monsters', in *Jane Austen: Bicentenary Essays*, edited by John Halperin (Cambridge: Cambridge University Press, 1875), p. 272–73.
41 Barbara Z. Thaden, 'Figure and Ground: The Receding Heroine in Jane Austen's *Emma*', *South Atlantic Review*, 55.1 (January 1990), pp. 56–8.
42 Anne Toner, *Jane Austen's Style*, p. 14; see *Juvenilia*, ed. Peter Sabor (Cambridge: Cambridge University Press, 2006), p. xxiv.
43 R. W. Chapman, *Jane Austen: Facts and Problems* (Oxford: Clarendon, 1949), p. 208.
44 Michelle Levy, 'Jane Austen's Manuscripts and the Publicity of Print', *ELH*, 77.4 (2010), p. 1026.
45 B. C. Southam, *Jane Austen's Literary Manuscripts: A Study of the Novelist's Development through the Surviving Papers* (Oxford: Oxford University Press, 1964), pp. 135, 130.
46 Kathryn Sutherland, *Jane Austen's Textual Lives: From Aeschylus to Bollywood* (Oxford: Oxford University Press, 2005), p. 197.
47 D. W. Harding, 'Regulated Hatred', in *Regulated Hatred and Other Essays on Jane Austen*, edited by Monica Lawlor (London: Athlone, 1998), pp. 169–71.
48 Stabler, 'Jane Austen and Caricature', pp. 11–12.

49 *Northanger Abbey*, p. 249.
50 *Sense and Sensibility*, p. 6.
51 Giuseppe Baretti, *A Dictionary of the English and Italian Languages*, 1760.
52 *Sanditon* in *Jane Austen's Fiction Manuscripts*, edited by Kathryn Sutherland, b3, p. 12: https://janeausten.ac.uk/manuscripts/sanditon/b3-12.html.
53 See Jon Sleigh, 'The power paunch: body politics and eighteenth-century men's waistlines', *Art UK* (12 April 2021): https://artuk.org/discover/stories/the-power-paunch-body-politics-and-eighteenth-century-mens-waistlines.
54 See Freya Gowrley, 'Super-sized Georgians: why satirists were fixated with fatness', *History Extra* (3 November 2021): www.historyextra.com/period/georgian/super-sized-georgians-why-satirists-fixated-fatness. See also Gowrley's project 'Fatness and Its Images': https://flgowrley.wixsite.com/home/fatness-and-its-images.
55 Henry Fielding, *Amelia* (London: A. Millar, 1752), vol. II, p. 72.
56 Lewes, 'The Novels of Jane Austen', p. 99.
57 *Pride and Prejudice*, p. 72.
58 *Sanditon* in *Jane Austen's Fiction Manuscripts*, edited by Kathryn Sutherland, b3, p.16: https://janeausten.ac.uk/manuscripts/sanditon/b3-16.html.
59 Brownstein, 'Character and Caricature: Jane Austen and James Gillray', p. 92.
60 Michael Parrish Lee, 'The Nothing in the Novel: Jane Austen and the Food Plot', *NOVEL: A Forum on Fiction*, 45.3 (2012), p. 369.
61 *Mansfield Park*, edited by June Sturrock (Peterborough: Broadview Press, 2001), pp. 54 ('pop off'), 425 ('gouty symptoms'), 464 ('apoplexy and death'), 133 ('bon vivant', etc.), '132 ('eat, drink, and grow fat', etc.).
62 *Sanditon*, b3, pp. 15–22: https://janeausten.ac.uk/manuscripts/sanditon/b3-15.html.
63 *Ibid.*, b3, p. 21
64 *Ibid.*, b3, pp.17–18
65 *Ibid.*, b3, pp. 18–19.
66 *Ibid.*, b3, p. 13.
67 *Persuasion*, edited by Janet Todd and Antje Blank (Cambridge: Cambridge University Press, 2006), p. 42.
68 *Persuasion*, p. 73.
69 *Persuasion*, pp. 54–5.
70 May 1799, *Jane Austen's Letters* (2011) edited by Deirdre Le Faye, pp. 41, 42, 17.
71 *Sense and Sensibility*, p. 8.
72 *Teenage Writings*, edited by Freya Johnston and Kathryn Sutherland (Oxford: Oxford University Press, 2017), p. 26.
73 *Sanditon*, b3, pp. 16–21: https://janeausten.ac.uk/manuscripts/sanditon/b3-16.html.
74 *Ibid.*, b3, p. 21.
75 *Ibid.*, b3, p. 18.
76 Julienne Gehrer and Deirdre Le Faye, eds., *Martha Lloyd's Household Book: The Original Manuscript from Jane Austen's Kitchen* (Chicago: University of Chicago Press, 2021); Hannah Glasse, *The Art of Cookery Made Plain and Easy* (London: A. Millar and T. Trye, 1758), p. 190.

77 *Sanditon*, b3, p. 20: https://janeausten.ac.uk/manuscripts/sanditon/b3-20.html.
78 *Persuasion*, p. 73.
79 Ibid., pp. 73–4.
80 See Claudia Johnson, *Jane Austen: Women, Politics, and the Novel* (Chicago: University of Chicago Press, 1988), p. 150.
81 Marvin Mudrick, *Irony as Defense and Discovery* (Berkeley: University of California Press, 1968), p. 212.
82 Brownstein, 'Character and Caricature: Jane Austen and James Gillray', p. 89.
83 Alex Woloch, *The One vs. the Many: Minor Characters and the Space of the Protagonist in the Novel* (Princeton: Princeton University Press, 2003), p. 43.
84 Ibid., p. 84.
85 Michael McKeon, *The Secret History of Domesticity: Public, Private, and the Division of Knowledge* (Baltimore: Johns Hopkins University Press, 2005), p. 451.
86 Quoted in Woloch, *The One vs. the Many*, p. 29.

Chapter 5

1 See Victoria Henshaw, *Scotland and the British Army, 1700–1750: Defending the Union* (London: Bloomsbury, 2014), pp. 138–39.
2 The 'Old Tolbooth', which served as the city's jail, was established in the fourteenth century. Hugo Arnot's 1779 *History of Edinburgh* describes the 'slovenly condition' of the Tolbooth and the neglect suffered by the prisoners there (pp. 297–302). For an account of the Tolbooth's demolition as a metaphor for the progress of modernity, see Richard J. Hill, 'Reconstructing the Tolbooth: Alexander Nasmyth and *The Heart of Midlothian*', *Picturing Scotland through the Waverley Novels* (Farnham: Ashgate, 2010), pp. 135–40.
3 *The Heart of Mid-Lothian*, edited by David Hewitt and Alison Lumsden (Edinburgh: Edinburgh University Press, 2004), pp. 26–7.
4 Ibid., pp. 27–8.
5 See Nancy Armstrong, *Fiction in the Age of Photography: The Legacy of British Realism* (Cambridge, MA: Harvard University Press, 1999).
6 Hugh Paton, ed., *A Series of Original Portraits and Caricature Etchings by the Late John Kay, with Biographical Sketches and Anecdotes*, 2 vols. (Edinburgh: Paton), vol. I, p. iii.
7 The poem may be the work of George Galloway (b. 1755), whose name is written in pencil on the first page of Scott's copy of the pamphlet.
8 *Redgauntlet*, edited by G. A. M. Wood and David Hewitt (Edinburgh: Edinburgh University Press, 1997), p. 3. See Jonathan Henry Christie, 'Life of Lockhart', *The Quarterly Review*, 116 (1864), p. 447.
9 'Personal Sketch of the Duke of Wellington', *Dublin Literary Gazette*, reprinted in *The Kaleidoscope; or Literary and Scientific Mirror* (26 January 1830), p. 238.

10 Walker was depicted by Kay in two pen-and-ink drawings that are in Charles Kirkpatrick Sharpe's collection. Sharpe labelled them as 'George Walker, drawing master – in the uniform of the Defensive Band' and 'Walker – drawing master' (see 1994.189, Royal Scottish Academy).
11 *The Journal of Sir Walter Scott*, edited by W. E. K. Anderson (Oxford: Clarendon, 1972), p. 118; 1 March 1826.
12 *Rob Roy*, pp. 168, 95.
13 Isaac Cruikshank also made an etching of John Dhu, rhinophymic, sitting at a bar with a glass of whisky and cradling his Lochaber axe. The print is titled *John Dow Soldier of the City-Guard Edinburgh* (1784) and has a caption in Scots: 'And faithfully he toomed his Glass & Whisky was his kirn ay.' This choice of subject perhaps substantiates Robert Patten's suggestion that Isaac, who like Kay had no formal artistic training, studied with Kay in Edinburgh before leaving for London. See Patten, ODNB entry for 'Isaac Cruikshank'.
14 *Letters from Flushing. Containing an Account of the Expedition to Walcheren, Beveland [...] To which is added, A Topographical and Statistical Account of the Islands* (London: Richard Philips, 1809), p. 39.
15 On picturesque convention in Scott's novels, see Alexander M. Ross, *The Imprint of the Picturesque on Nineteenth-Century British Fiction* (Waterloo: Wilfrid Laurier University Press, 1986), pp. 46–72, and James Reed, *Sir Walter Scott: Landscape and Locality* (London: Bloomsbury, 1980). On Scott and the historical picturesque, see Rosemary Mitchell, *Picturing the Past: English History in Text and Image, 1830–1870* (Oxford: Clarendon, 2000), pp. 87–9. On picturesque human figures in the Waverley Novels, see P. D. Garside, 'Picturesque figure and landscape: Meg Merrilies and the gypsies', in *The Politics of the Picturesque: Literature, Landscape and Aesthetics Since 1770*, edited by Stephen Copley and P. D. Garside (Cambridge: Cambridge University Press, 1994), pp. 145–74.
16 *Guy Mannering*, edited by P. D. Garside (Edinburgh: Edinburgh University Press, 1999), pp. 114–15.
17 *Saint Ronan's Well*, edited by Mark Weinstein (Edinburgh: Edinburgh University Press, 1995), p. 33.
18 *London Magazine* (May 1822), p. 418.
19 On caricature as a critique of the picturesque, see Jonathan Bate, *The Song of the Earth* (London: Picador, 2000), pp. 133–36.
20 See for example *Sadak in Search of the Waters of Oblivion* (1812), Martin's first painting hung at the Royal Academy, now in the Saint Louis Art Museum (1566: 1983).
21 'On the Elgin Marbles', in *Criticisms on Art and Sketches of the Picture Galleries of England*, pp. 260–61.
22 *Ibid.*, p. 259.
23 'Rob Roy, Tales of my Landlord, 2d Series (Heart of Mid Lothian), Tales of My Landlord, 3d Series (Bride of Lammermoor, Montrose), Ivanhoe, Monastery, Abbot, Kenilworth', *Quarterly Review*, 26 (October 1822), p. 116.
24 *Ibid.*, p. 124.

25 *Ibid.*, pp. 123–24.
26 *Ibid.*, p. 123.
27 J. G. Lockhart, *Memoirs of the Life of Sir Walter Scott*, 10 vols. (London: Cadell, 1837), vol. VI, p. 88.
28 *Ibid.*, p. 51.
29 *Rob Roy*, p. 168.
30 *Ibid.*, p. 145, 168.
31 *Ibid.*, p. 121.
32 Entry for 12 June 1666: www.pepysdiary.com/diary/1666/06.
33 *Rob Roy*, p. 37.
34 *Saint Ronan's Well*, edited by Mark Weinstein (Edinburgh: Edinburgh University Press, 1995), p. 11.
35 Walter Scott, unsigned review, 'Frankenstein; or the Modern Prometheus. 3 vols. 8vo. London. Lackington, &c. 1818', *The Scots Magazine* 81 (March 1818), p. 249.
36 John Dunlop, *The History of Fiction* (London: Longman, Hurst, Rees, Orme, and Brown, 1814), vol. III, p. 379.
37 *Ibid.*, p. 380.
38 'De Foe's Memoirs of a Cavalier', *The Retrospective Review* 3 (1821), pp. 360–61.
39 Noctes Ambrosianae No. XXX, *Blackwood's Magazine* 21 (1827), pp. 107–8.
40 Glascock, 'Naval Novels', in *Metropolitan Magazine* 1 (1831), p. 370. Published in the *Naval Sketch Book* (1834) as 'Strictures on Smollett'.
41 'Waverley Novels; Revised and Corrected, with General Prefaces, and Notes, Historical and Illustrative, by the Author', *The North American Review* 32 (April 1831), pp. 404–5.
42 Anna Letitia Barbauld, *The British Novelists* (London: F. C. and J. Rivington, 1810), volume XXX, p. vii.
43 Claudia L. Johnson, '"Let Me Make the Novels of a Country": Barbauld's "The British Novelists" (1810/1820)', *NOVEL: A Forum on Fiction* 34, no. 2 (Spring 2001), pp. 163–79. On differences between Barbauld's and Scott's canonising novel series, see also Michael Gamer, 'The Select Collection and the Rise of the (Reprinted) Novel', in *Recognizing the Romantic Novel: New Approaches to British Fiction, 1780–1832*, edited by Jill Heydt-Stevenson and Charlotte Sussman (University of Liverpool Press, 2008), pp. 119–55.
44 Unsigned review of *Waverley*, *Edinburgh Review* (November 1814), p. 210.
45 Referring to long-serving admirals John Benbow (1653–1702), nicknamed 'Brave Benbow' and 'a Brother Tar', and Edward Boscawen (1711–61), nicknamed 'Old Dreadnought' and 'Wry-Necked Dick'. Scott, 'Prefatory Memoir to Smollett', in *The Novels of Tobias Smollett, M. D.* (London: Hurst, Robinson and Co.; Edinburgh: James Ballantyne and Co., 1821), pp. xl–li.
46 Scott, 'Prefatory Memoir', p. xlii. Cf. Hazlitt's suggestions that Rubens's paintings possessed 'a certain grossness of expression bordering on caricature' (*Complete Works*, vol. X, p.72), whereas Michelangelo 'enforced and expanded … a preconceived idea [of the human form], till he seems sometimes to tread on the verge of caricature' (vol. XVIII, p. 114).

47 Hunt, 'Smollett', *Table-Talk* (London: Smith, Elder and Co., 1870), p. 41.
48 Smollett, *The Expedition of Humphry Clinker*, edited by Lewis M. Knapp and Paul-Gabriel Boucé (Oxford: Oxford University Press, 2009), p. 188.
49 *Ibid.*, p. 191.
50 *Ibid.*, p. 300.
51 *Ibid.*, p. 201.
52 Lismahago's history, at least, was based on a real individual, Captain Robert Stobo. See George M. Kahrl, 'Captain Robert Stobo', in *Virginia Magazine of History and Biography*, 49 (1941), pp. 254–68; Louis L. Martz, *The Later Career of Tobias Smollett* (New Haven, CT: Yale University Press, 1942); and Lewis M. Knapp, *Tobias Smollett: Doctor of Men and Manners* (Princeton, NJ: Princeton University Press, 1949), pp. 274–75. Scott, 'Prefatory Memoir to Smollett', p. xx.
53 Scott, *The Miscellaneous Prose Works of Sir Walter Scott*, edited by J. G. Lockhart (Edinburgh: Cadell, 1827), vol. III, p. 201.
54 Ann Rigney, *The Afterlives of Walter Scott: Memory on the Move* (Oxford University Press, 2015), p. 107.
55 *The Journal of Sir Walter Scott*, pp. 129, 333.
56 Angela Esterhammer, '1824: Improvisation, Speculation, and Identity-Construction', in *BRANCH: Britain, Representation and Nineteenth-Century History* (July 2012), n. pag.
57 *The Journal of Walter Scott*, p. 491.
58 *The Monastery*, edited by Penny Fielding (Edinburgh: Edinburgh University Press, 2008), p. 52.
59 *Letters*, vol. VII, p. 354.
60 *Ibid.*,. 364
61 J. H. Alexander, P. D. Garside, and Claire Lamont, eds., *Introductions and Notes from the Magnum Opus*, 2 vols. (Edinburgh: Edinburgh University Press, 2012), vol. I, pp. lii–iii.
62 George L. Craik and Charles Mac Farlane, *The Pictorial History of England during the Reign of George the Third: Being a History of the People, as Well as a History of the Kingdom, Illustrated with Several Hundred Woodcuts*, 3 vols. (London: Charles Knight and Co., 1841), vol. III, p. 385.
63 Anthony Trollope, 'On English Prose Fiction as a Rational Amusement', in *An Autobiography and Other Writings*, edited by Nicholas Shrimpton (Oxford University Press, 2014), p. 236.
64 The OED's methods of gathering citations have resulted in Scott's works being its third most-cited source, after Shakespeare and the Bible. Of 17,134 quotations from Scott, 444 are taken as first evidence of a word, and 2,104 provide evidence of a particular meaning. See Charlotte Brewer, 'The Use of Literary Quotations in the *Oxford English Dictionary*', *The Review of English Studies* 61.248 (2010), pp. 93–125.
65 Wilson, *John Lyly* (New York: Haskell, 1970), p. 11.
66 *Introductions and Notes from the Magnum Opus*, vol. I, p. 49.
67 *Ibid.*, pp. 49–52.

68 Ibid., p. 52.
69 Unsigned review of *Tales of My Landlord, Edinburgh Review* (March 1817): p. 197.
70 See John Walker, *Essay on the Revival of the Drama in Italy* (Edinburgh: Mundell and Son; London: Longman, Hurst, Rees, and Orme, 1805), p. 249.
71 Richard Andrews, *The Commedia Dell'Arte of Flaminio Scala: A Translation and Analysis of 30 Scenarios* (Plymouth: Scarecrow, 2008), p. xxiii.
72 Smollett, *The Reprisal; or, the Tars of Old England* (London: R. Baldwin, 1757), p. 8.
73 Coleridge, *Shorter Works and Fragments*, edited by H. J. Jackson and J. R. de J. Jackson (Princeton, NJ: Princeton University Press, 1995), vol. I, p. 336.
74 *Introductions and Notes from the Magnum Opus*, vol. II, pp. 51–2.
75 *Introductions and Notes from the Magnum Opus*, vol. I, p. 344.
76 Ibid., vol. II, p. 52.
77 Homer, *Ars Poetica*, "Quodcumque ostendis mihi sic, incredulus odi." Alexander, Garside, and Lamont, eds., *Introduction and Notes from the Magnum Opus*, vol. II, p. 52. On *incredulus odi* in criticism of Gothic literature, see E. J. Clery and Robert Miles, *Gothic Documents: A Sourcebook, 1700–1820* (Manchester: Manchester University Press, 2000), p. 173.
78 *Introductions and Notes from the Magnum Opus*, vol. II, p. 11.
79 *Ivanhoe*, edited by Graham Tulloch (Edinburgh: Edinburgh University Press, 1998), p. 7.
80 Ibid., p. 6.
81 *The Monastery*, p. 201.
82 Ibid., p. 134.
83 *Ivanhoe*, p. 52; *Introductions and Notes from the Magnum Opus*, vol. II, p. 394.
84 *The Monastery*, p. 134.
85 The work's full title is specific about its historical referents and provenance: *Memoirs of a Cavalier; or A Military Journal of the Wars in Germany, and the Wars in England. From the Years 1632 to 1648. Written threescore years ago, by an English gentleman, who served first in the army of Gustavus Adolphus, the Glorious King of Sweden, till his death, and after that in the Royal Army of King Charles the First, from the beginning of the Rebellion to the end of the War.*
86 *Retrospective Review*, p. 363.
87 Quoted in Watt, *Rise of the Novel*, p. 16.
88 Francis Jeffrey, unsigned review of *Waverley*, *Edinburgh Review* (November 1814), p. 210.
89 *Retrospective Review*, p. 367.
90 Georg Lukács, *The Historical Novel*, translated by Hannah Mitchell and Stanley Mitchell (London: Merlin, 1962), p. 60.
91 Ibid., pp. 50, 43.
92 Thomas Carlyle, 'Memoirs of the Life of Sir Walter Scott, Baronet. Vol. i–vi. Cadell. Edinburgh, 1837', *The London and Westminster Review* (January 1838), pp. 336–37.
93 Timothy Campbell, *Historical Style: Fashion and the New Mode of History, 1740–1830* (Philadelphia: University of Pennsylvania Press, 2016), p. 2.

94 *Ibid.*, p. 208–22.
95 *The Black Dwarf*, edited by P. D. Garside (Edinburgh: Edinburgh University Press, 1993) pp. 13, 12; see notes 12.13–15 and 12.19.
96 *Ibid.*, pp. 29, 31.
97 *Kenilworth*, edited by J. H. Alexander (Edinburgh: Edinburgh University Press, 1993), pp. 259–60.
98 Scott, *The Pirate*, edited by Mark Weinstein and Alison Lumsden (Edinburgh: Edinburgh University Press, 2001), pp. 256, 280, 283, 358.
99 Scott, *Peveril of the Peak*, edited by Alison Lumsden (Edinburgh: Edinburgh University Press , 2007), pp. 359, 363.
100 *Talisman*, p. 51.
101 *Ibid.*, p. 53.
102 *Peveril*, p. 352.
103 *Ibid.*, p. 363.
104 *Ibid.*, p. 352.
105 *Rob Roy*, p. 187.
106 *Black Dwarf*, p. 124.
107 *Introductions and Notes from the Magnum Opus*, vol. I, p. 161.
108 *Ibid.*, p. 230.
109 *Introductions and Notes from the Magnum Opus*, vol. II, p. 271.
110 *Peveril*, p. 352.
111 *Introductions and Notes from the Magnum Opus*, vol. II, p. 272.
112 *Peveril*, p. 367; see pp. 366–67.
113 *Ibid.*, p. 353.
114 Francis Bacon, 'Of Deformity' (1597), in *Lord Bacon's Essays, or Counsels Moral and Civil*, translated by William Willimot, 2 vols. (London: H. Parson, J. Brotherton and W. Meadows, A. Bettesworth, S. Ballard, R. Gosling, and C. King, 1720).
115 *Peveril*, p. 353.
116 *Peveril*, p. 350; *Talisman*, p. 51.
117 *Talisman*, p. 51; *Black Dwarf*, p. 29.
118 *Introductions and Notes from the Magnum Opus*, vol. I, p. 159.
119 *Rob Roy*, p. 87.
120 *Rob Roy*, p. 88
121 'On the Scotch Character. (A Fragment.)', *The Liberal: Verse and Prose from the South* (London: John Hunt, 1822) pp. 367–68.
122 See Gordon Pentland, '"We Speak for the Ready": Images of Scots in Political Prints, 1707–1832', *The Scottish Historical Review*, 90.1 (2011), p. 78.
123 In Exodus, the Israelites plunder gold, silver and clothing after the Egyptians have suffered ten plagues: '"It's a mere spoiling o' the Egyptians', says Andrew, '[P]uir old Scotland suffers aneugh by thae blackguard lowns o' excisemen and gaugers, that hae come down on her like locusts since the sad and sorrowfu' Union"' (p. 151).

124 Hazlitt accuses 'the Great Unknown' of 'talk[ing] of the Scotch novels in all companies; and by waving the title of the author, is at liberty to repeat the subject *ad infinitum*' (p. 368).
125 Written during the Seven Years' War, a period when the British navy grew from approximately 17,000 to 75,000 personnel, *The Reprisal* makes sailors symbolic of a pan-British nationalism.
126 Scott, 'Prefatory Memoir', p. xx.
127 *Reprisal*, p. 19.
128 11 June 1821, *Letters*, p. 462; see also pp. 458, 464–65, 479.
129 *The Heart of Mid-Lothian*, p. 356.
130 *Tales of My Landlord, Second Series*, 4 vols. (Edinburgh: Archibald Constable and Company, 1818), vol. I, pp. 288–89.
131 Ibid., vol. IV, pp. 13–14.
132 Ibid., vol. III, pp. 71–2.
133 Ibid., p. 61.
134 Ibid., p. 62.
135 *Ivanhoe*, p. 48.
136 *A Vindication of the Rights of Woman*, pp. 282–83.
137 *Ivanhoe*, p. 47.
138 Ibid., p. 61
139 Ibid., p. 63
140 Ibid., p. 65.
141 See Judith W. Page, *Imperfect Sympathies: Jews and Judaism in British Romantic Literature and Culture* (New York: Palgrave Macmillan, 2004), pp. 11–14.
142 Maria Edgeworth, *Harrington, A Tale; and Ormond, A Tale*, 3 vols. (London: R. Hunter, and Baldwin, Cradock, and Joy, 1817), vol. I, p. 271.
143 Ibid., p. 254.
144 Ibid., p. 263.
145 Ibid., pp. 30–1.
146 *Ivanhoe*, p. 62.

Chapter 6

1 Denise Gigante, 'Facing the Ugly: The Case of 'Frankenstein', *ELH* 67.2 (2000), pp. 565–97.
2 Edmund Burke, *A Philosophical Enquiry into the Origin of Our Ideas of the Sublime and Beautiful*, edited by Paul Guyer (Oxford: Oxford University Press, 2015), p. 96.
3 Gigante, 'Facing the Ugly', p. 574
4 *Frankenstein or, the Modern Prometheus: 1818 Text*, edited by Marilyn Butler (Oxford: Oxford University Press, 2008), p. 39.
5 Essaka Joshua, *Physical Disability in British Romantic Literature* (Cambridge: Cambridge University Press, 2020), p. 158.

6. MS Abinger c. 56, 38v–r.
7. MS Abinger c. 57, 80r.
8. Anne K. Mellor, *Romanticism and Gender* (New York: Routledge, 1993), p. 63.
9. Jonathan Swift, *Gulliver's Travels*, edited by Ian Higgins (Oxford: Oxford University Press, 2008) pp. 82–3.
10. Mellor, *Romanticism and Gender*, p. 63.
11. MS Abinger c. 57, 83r.
12. MS Abinger c. 57, 91r.
13. MS Abinger c. 58, 25r.
14. Burke, *Enquiry*, p. 82.
15. Anne Mathews, *Memoirs of Charles Mathews, Comedian* (London: Bentley, 1839), p. 231.
16. Scott, *Peveril of the Peak*, edited by Alison Lumsden (Edinburgh: Edinburgh University Press and Columbia University Press, 2007), p. 352.
17. Charles Dickens, *The Old Curiosity Shop* (London: Chapman & Hall, 1840), p. 17.
18. *Rob Roy*, p. 187.
19. Scott, *The Pirate*, edited by Mark Weinstein and Alison Lumsden (Edinburgh: Edinburgh University Press and Columbia University Press, 2001), pp. 183, 256.
20. MS Abinger, c. 57, 21r.
21. Ann Radcliffe, 'On the Supernatural in Poetry', *Gothic Documents: A Sourcebook, 1700–1820*, edited by E. J. Clery and Robert Miles (Manchester: Manchester University Press, 2000), pp. 145–52.
22. George Levine, *The Realistic Imagination*, pp. 27–8.
23. Essaka Joshua, *Physical Disability in British Romantic Literature*, p. 163
24. Scott, *Peveril of the Peak*, p. 360.
25. Scott, *The Talisman*, p. 120.
26. Scott, *The Pirate*, p. 256.
27. These phrases distinguishing terror from horror are taken from Radcliffe's 'Essay on the Supernatural', *Gothic Documents*, pp. 169, 168.
28. Scott, *The Talisman*, p. 51.
29. *Ibid.*, pp. 50–1.
30. *Ibid.*, pp. 51–2.
31. Watt, *The Rise of the Novel*, pp. 16–17.
32. Anthony Ashley Cooper, Earl of Shaftesbury, *Sensus Communis: An Essay on the Freedom of Wit and Humour. In a letter to a Friend* (London: for Egbert Sanger, 1709), p. 113.
33. Kames, *Elements of Criticism*, vol. III, pp. 198–99.
34. Scott, *The Pirate*, p. 257.
35. MS Abinger c. 58, 83r.
36. On facial physiognomy and the emotions, see Jean-Jacques Courtine and Claudine Haroche, *Histoire du visage: exprimer et taire ses émotions, XVIe-début XIXe siècle* (Paris: Rivages, 1988).
37. *Lodore*, 3 vols. (London: Bentley, 1835), vol. II, pp. 186, 193.
38. *Falkner*, 3 vols. (London: Saunders and Otley, 1837), vol. I, p. 37.

39 Francis Bacon, 'Of Deformity' (1625): www.ourcivilisation.com/smartboard/shop/baconf/deform.htm.
40 *Frankenstein; or, the Modern Prometheus* (London: Colburn and Bentley, 1831), p. 21.
41 David T. Mitchell and Sharon L. Snyder, *Narrative Prosthesis: Disability and the Dependencies of Discourse* (Ann Arbor: University of Michigan Press, 2000), p. 132; Paul Youngquist, *Monstrosities: Bodies and British Romanticism* (Minneapolis: University of Minnesota Press, 2003), p. 55.
42 Lee Sterrenburg, 'Mary Shelley's Monster: Politics and Psyche in *Frankenstein*', in *The Endurance of 'Frankenstein': Essays on Mary Shelley's Novel*, edited by George Levine and U. C. Knoepflmacher (Berkeley: University of California Press, 1979), p. 145.
43 See Burke (quoting Jean-Frédéric de la Tour du Pin's address to the National Assembly), *Reflections on the Revolution in France*, ed. L. G. Mitchell (Oxford University Press, 2009), p. 213; Thomas Paine, *Rights of Man: Being an Answer to Mr. Burke's Attack on the French Revolution* (London: J. S. Jordan, 1791), pp. 35, 70; William Godwin, *An Enquiry concerning Political Justice, and Its Influence on General Virtue and Happiness*, 2 vols. (London: G. G. J. and J. Robinson, 1793), vol. II, p. 583.
44 See Taylor, *The Politics of Parody: A Literary History of Caricature* (Princeton, NJ: Princeton University Press, 2018).
45 John Locke, *Some Thoughts Concerning Education* (London: for A. and J. Churchill, 1693), pp. 11–12.
46 William Cadogan, *An Essay upon Nursing, and the Management of Children, from Their Birth to Three Years of Age* (London: J. Roberts), p. 10.
47 Jean-Jacques Rousseau, *Emilius; or, an Essay on Education*, 2 vols., trans. Thomas Nugent (London: Nourse and Vaillant, 1763), vol. I, p. 20.
48 *Ibid.*, vol. II, p. 19.
49 Cadogan, *Nursing*, p. 11.
50 On the meanings of women's foundation garments in sixteenth- and seventeenth-century England, women's lived experience of wearing 'bodies' and 'farthingales', and changing attitudes to foundation garments in the early eighteenth century, see Sarah Bendall, *Shaping Femininity: Foundation Garments, the Body and Women in Early Modern England* (Bloomsbury, 2021).
51 William Godwin, *An Enquiry concerning Political Justice, and Its Influence on General Virtue and Happiness*, 2 vols. (London: G. G. J. and J. Robinson, 1793), vol. II, p 217.
52 William Buchan, *Domestic Medicine*, 17th ed. (London: Strahan, Cadell and Davies; Edinburgh: Balfour and Creech, 1800), p. 11. Subsequent references in the text.
53 Buchan, *Advice to Mothers, on the Subject of Their Own Health*, 2nd ed. (London: Cadell and Davies, 1811), pp. 249–50.
54 J. P. Malcolm, *An Historical Sketch of the Art of Caricaturing* (London: Hurst, Rees, Orme and Brown, 1813), p. 1.
55 Buchan, *Advice to Mothers*, pp. 249–50.

56 Walter Harris, *A Full View of All the Diseases Incident to Children* (London: A. Millar, 1742), p. 197.
57 David M. Turner, 'Impaired Children in Eighteenth-Century England', *Social History of Medicine* 30.4 (1 November 2017), p. 794.
58 Ellen Moers, *Literary Women: The Great Writers* (New York: Doubleday, 1976), p. 93. Moers' essay was first published on 21 March 1974 in *The New York Review of Books* as 'Female Gothic: The Monster's Mother'.
59 Anne K. Mellor, *Mary Shelley: Her Life, Her Fiction, Her Monsters* (New York: Methuen, 1988), p. 38.
60 Malcolm, *Historical Sketch*, pp. 2–3.
61 *The Prognostics and Prorrhetics of Hippocrates*, translated and edited by John Moffat (London: Elliot, Kay & Co., 1788), p. 3.
62 Browne, *Letter to a Friend, Upon Occasion of the Death of his Intimate Friend* (London: Brome, 1690), pp. 3–5.
63 Bartholomew Parr, *The London Medical Dictionary* (London: J. Johnson, F. and C. Rivington, etc., 1809), 2 vols, vol. I, p. 638.
64 John Moffat, trans., *The Prognostics and Prorrhetics of Hippocrates* (London: T. Bensley, 1788), p. 5.
65 H. G. Wells, *The Island of Doctor Moreau: A Possibility* (London: William Heinemann, 1896), p. 129 ('disproportion'), pp. 53, 94, 143, 184 ('misshapen'), pp. 38, 49, 91, 130, 143 ('distorted').
66 Victor Hugo, *L'Homme Qui Rit*, 4 vols. (Paris: A. Lacroix, 1869), p. 66. Hugo's fanciful notion of a Chinese dwarfing vase may also have been partly suggested by the well-attested practice, in royal courts across Europe and Russia in the sixteenth and seventeenth centuries, of containing dwarfs in cages or other confined spaces for amusement, such as the conventional party piece of a court dwarf emerging from a pie. See Scott, *Peveril of the Peak*, pp. 355–57.
67 Wells, *The Island of Dr Moreau*, pp. 110–11.

Afterword

1 David Taylor, 'The practice of caricature in 18th-century Britain', *Literature Compass* (2017): https://doi.org/10.1111.lic3.12383.
2 James Chandler, 'The Age of the Spirit of the Age', in *England in 1819: The Politics of Literary Culture and the Case of Romantic Historicism* (Chicago: University of Chicago Press, 1998), pp. 105–13.
3 'The Mirror of Fashion', *Morning Chronicle* (August 1796), p. 7.
4 E. J. Clery, *The Rise of Supernatural Fiction 1762–1800* (Cambridge: Cambridge University Press, 1995), p. 172.
5 '*Frankenstein; or the Modern Prometheus.*', *Scots Magazine*, 2.3 (March 1818), pp. 249, 253.
6 *Ibid.*, p. 253.
7 'Notice of Northanger Abbey and Persuasion', *Edinburgh Magazine and Literary Miscellany* (May 1818), pp. 453–55.

Bibliography

Primary Sources

Works of literary criticism are included here when used as primary sources, for example in Chapter 4's discussion of the critical tradition on Austen and caricature.

Book reviews used as primary sources are listed separately.

Addison, Joseph and Richard Steele, *The Spectator*, 9th ed. (London: T. Jonson, 1729).
  The Spectator, 8 vols. (London: Payne, Rivington, Davis, Longman, Dodsley, 1788).
Anderson, W. E. K., ed., *The Journal of Walter Scott* (Oxford: Clarendon Press, 1972).
Arnot, Hugo, *The History of Edinburgh* (Edinburgh: William Creech, 1779).
Ashley-Cooper, Anthony, *The Moralists, a Philosophical Rhapsody: Being a Recital of Certain Conversations upon Natural and Moral Subjects* (London: Wyat, 1709).
Austen, Jane, Add MS 41253 ['Opinions by various people of Jane Austen's work'], British Library, London.
  Emma, eds. Richard Cronin and Dorothy Macmillan (Cambridge: Cambridge University Press, 2005).
  Juvenilia, ed. Peter Sabor (Cambridge: Cambridge University Press, 2006).
  Later Manuscripts, eds. Janet Todd and Linda Bree (Cambridge: Cambridge University Press, 2008).
  Mansfield Park, ed. John Wiltshire (Cambridge: Cambridge University Press, 2006).
  Northanger Abbey, eds. Barbara M. Benedict and Deirdre Le Faye (Cambridge: Cambridge University Press, 2006).
  Persuasion, eds. Antje Blank and Janet Todd (Cambridge: Cambridge University Press, 2006).
  Pride and Prejudice, ed. Pat Rogers (Cambridge: Cambridge University Press, 2006).
  Sanditon, ed. Kathryn Sutherland: https://janeausten.ac.uk/manuscripts/sanditon.
  Sense and Sensibility, ed. Edward Copeland (Cambridge: Cambridge University Press, 2006).

Teenage Writings, eds. Freya Johnston and Kathryn Sutherland (Oxford: Oxford University Press, 2017).

Austen, Henry, 'Biographical Notice of the Author', prefacing *Northanger Abbey and Persuasion*, 4 vols. (London: John Murray, 1818), vol. I, pp. v–xix.

Austen-Leigh, James Edward, *A Memoir of Jane Austen and Other Family Recollections*, ed. Kathryn Sutherland (Oxford: Oxford University Press, 2002).

Bacon, Francis, 'Of Deformity', in *Lord Bacon's Essays, or Counsels Moral and Civil*, trans. William Willimot, 2 vols. (London: H. Parson, J. Brotherton and W. Meadows, A. Bettesworth, S. Ballard, R. Gosling and C. King, 1720).

Barbauld, Anna Laetitia, 'Miss Burney', in *British Novelists*, 50 vols., ed. Anna Laetitia Barbauld (London: F. C. and J. Rivington, 1810), vol. XXXVIII, pp. i–xi.

'Smollett', in *The British Novelists*, 50 vols., ed. Anna Laetitia Barbauld (London: F. C. and J. Rivington, 1810), vol. XXX, pp. i–xviii.

Baretti, Giuseppe, *A Dictionary of the English and Italian Languages, by Joseph Baretti*, 2nd ed. (London: C. Hitch and L. Lawes, R. Baldwin, W. Johnston, W. Owen. J. Richardson, G. Keith, T. Longman, S. Crowder and Co., P. Davey and B. Law, and H. Woodgate and S. Brookes, 1760).

Barruel, Augustin, *Memoirs Illustrating the History of Jacobinism*, 3rd ed., 3 vols., trans. Robert Clifford (London: Burton, 1798).

Beattie, James, 'On Fable and Romance', in *Dissertations Moral and Critical*, 2 vols. (London: W. Strahan, T. Cadell; Edinburgh: William Creech, 1783).

The Papers of Joseph Addison, Esq. in the Tatler, Spectator, Guardian, and Freeholder, 4 vols. (Edinburgh: William Creech, 1790).

Berens, E., ed., *A Second Selection from the Papers of Addison* (London: C. & J. Rivington, 1828).

Berguer, Lionel Thomas, *British Essayists; with Prefaces Biographical, Historical and Critical*, 45 vols. (London: T. and J. Allman, 1823).

Bisset, Robert, *The Spectator: A New Edition in Eight Volumes; with Illustrative Notes* (London: George Robertson; Edinburgh: Bell and Bradefute, 1793).

Blackie, John (ed.), 'Portrait of Burns, from an Original Drawing by Skirving', in *The Works of Robert Burns*, 2 vols. (Glasgow: Blackie and Son, 1844), vol. I, n. pag.

Blackstone, William, *Commentaries on the Laws of England*, 4 vols. (Oxford: Clarendon, 1765–69).

Blind, Mathilde, *George Eliot* (London: W. H. Allen and Co., 1883).

Browne, Thomas, *Letter to a Friend, Upon Occasion of the Death of His Intimate Friend* (London: Brome, 1690).

Brunton, Mary, *Discipline*, 3 vols. (Edinburgh: Manners and Miller; London: Longman, Hurst, Rees, Orme, and Brown, 1814).

Self-control, 2 vols. (Edinburgh: Manners and Miller; London: Longman, Hurst, Rees, Orme, and Brown, 1811).

Self-control, ed. Anthony Mandal (Abingdon: Routledge, 2015).

Buchan, William, *Advice to Mothers, on the Subject of Their Own Health; and on the Means of Promoting the Health, Strength, and Beauty of Their Offspring*, 2nd ed. (London: Cadell and Davies, 1811).
   Domestic Medicine: or, a Treatise on the Prevention and Cure of Diseases by Regimen and Simple Medicines, 17th ed. (London: Strahan, Cadell, and Davies; Edinburgh: Balfour and Creech, 1800).
Burke, Edmund, *A Philosophical Enquiry into the Origin of Our Ideas of the Sublime and Beautiful*, ed. Paul Guyer (Oxford: Oxford University Press, 2015).
   Reflections on the Revolution in France, ed. L. G. Mitchell (Oxford: Oxford University Press, 2009).
Cadogan, William, *An Essay Upon Nursing, and the Management of Children, from their Birth to Three Years of Age* (London: J. Roberts, 1748).
Chalmers, Alexander, *The British Essayists; with Prefaces, Historical and Biographical*, 45 vols. (London: J. Johnson etc., 1808).
Chapman, R. W., *Jane Austen: Facts and Problems* (Oxford: Clarendon, 1949).
Cohen, Jeffrey Jerome, *Of Giants: Sex, Monsters, and the Middle Ages* (Minneapolis: University of Minnesota Press, 1999).
Coleridge, Samuel Taylor, *The Friend, 1* (London: Gale and Curtis, 1812).
   Seven Lectures on Shakespeare and Milton, ed. J. Payne Collier (London: Chapman and Hall, 1856).
   Shorter Works and Fragments, 2 vols., eds. H. J. Jackson and J. R. de J. Jackson (Princeton, NJ: Princeton University Press, 1995).
Coleridge, Sara, *The Memoirs and Letters of Sara Coleridge*, 2 vols., ed. Edith Coleridge (Henry S. King & Co., 1873).
Cooper, Anthony Ashley, 'Earl of Shaftesbury', in *Sensus Communis: An Essay on the Freedom of Wit and Humour. In a letter to a Friend* (London: for Egbert Sanger, 1709).
   The Moralists: A Philosophical Rhapsody (London: John Wyat, 1709).
Corry, John, *Satire Made Easy; or Instructions in the Art of Polite Censure* (Manchester: Leigh, 1815).
Craik, George L. and Charles MacFarlane, *The Pictorial History of England during the Reign of George the Third: Being a History of the People, as Well as a History of the Kingdom, Illustrated with Several Hundred Woodcuts*, 3 vols. (London: Charles Knight, 1841–44).
Cumberland, Richard, *Henry*, 4 vols. (London: Charles Dilly, 1795).
Darly, Mary, *A Book of Carricaturas* (London: Darly, 1762).
De la Bruyère, Jean, *The Characters, or the Manners of the Age. Made English with Several Hands. With the Characters of Theophrastus. With the Key Inserted in the Margent*, 4th ed. (London: Fr. Leach, 1705).
De Quincey, Thomas, 'Autobiography of an English Opium Eater. Literary Connexions or Acquaintances', *Tait's Magazine*, 4 (March 1837), 169–76.
   Confessions of an English Opium-Eater, ed. Robert Morrison (Oxford: Oxford University Press, 2013).
Dickens, Charles, *The Old Curiosity Shop* (London: Chapman & Hall, 1840).

Drake, Nathan, *Essays Biographical, Critical and Historical; Illustrative of the Tatler, Spectator and Guardian*, 3 vols. (London: John Sharpe, 1805).
Dunlop, John, *The History of Fiction*, 3 vols. (London: Longman, Hurst, Rees, Orme, and Brown, 1814).
Edgeworth, Maria, *Belinda*, ed. Kathryn J. Kirkpatrick (Oxford: Oxford University Press, 2008).
  Castle Rackrent and Ennui, ed. Marilyn Butler (London: Penguin, 1992).
  Harrington, A Tale; and Ormond, A Tale, 3 vols. (London: R. Hunter, and Baldwin, Cradock, and Joy, 1817).
  Helen (London: Pandora, 1987).
Fielding, Henry, *Amelia* (London: A. Millar, 1752).
  The History of the Adventures of Joseph Andrews and of His Friend Mr. Abraham Adams (London: A. Millar, 1742).
Fisk, Josiah (ed.), *Composers on Music* (Boston: Northeastern University Press, 1997).
Forster, E. M., *Aspects of the Novel* (New York: Harcourt, Brace, and Co., 1927).
Gardiner, Marguerite, *The Works of Lady Blessington* (Philadelphia: Carey and Hart, 1838).
Gehrer, Julienne and Deirdre Le Faye (eds.), *Martha Lloyd's Household Book: The Original Manuscript from Jane Austen's Kitchen* (Chicago: University of Chicago Press, 2021).
Gillray, James, 'Correspondence with James Gillray', 1798–1802, Add MS 27337 ff31–44, British Library, London.
Glasse, Hannah, *The Art of Cookery Made Plain and Easy* (London: A. Millar and T. Trye, 1758).
Godwin, William, *An Enquiry Concerning Political Justice, and Its Influence on General Virtue and Happiness*, 2 vols. (London: G. G. J. and J. Robinson, 1793).
  Fleetwood: Or, the New Man of Feeling (London: Colburn and Bentley, 1831).
Gordon, Mary Wilson, *'Christopher North': A Memoir of John Wilson*, 2 vols. (Edinburgh: Edmonston and Douglas, 1862).
Grierson, Herbert (ed.), *The Letters of Walter Scott*, 12 vols. (London: Constable, 1932–37).
Grose, Francis, *Rules for Drawing Caricaturas* (London: Bagster, 1788).
Grosley, Pierre Jean, *A Tour to London; or, New Observations on England, and Its Inhabitants*, 2 vols., trans. Thomas Nugent (London: Lockyer Davis, 1772).
Guiccoli, Teresa, *My Recollections of Lord Byron*, trans. Hubert E. H. Jerningham (Cambridge: Cambridge University Press, 2014).
Harding, D. W., 'Character and Caricature in Jane Austen', in *Regulated Hatred and Other Essays on Jane Austen*, ed. Monica Lawlor (London: Athlone, 1998), pp. 80–105.
  'Regulated Hatred', in *Regulated Hatred and Other Essays on Jane Austen*, ed. Monica Lawlor (London: Athlone, 1998), pp. 5–26.
Hardy, Barbara, *A Reading of Jane Austen* (London: Athlone, 1979).
Harris, Walter, *A Full Account of Diseases Incident to Children* (London: Millar, 1742).

Hazlitt, William, 'On the Elgin Marbles', in *Criticisms on Art and Sketches of the Picture Galleries of England*, ed. William Hazlitt Jr. (London: John Templeman, 1843), pp. 240–83.
  'On the Scotch Character. (A Fragment.)', in *The Liberal: Verse and Prose from the South*, 1 (London: John Hunt, 1822), pp. 367–76.
Healey, Joseph, transl. *Theophrastus His Morall Characters or Description of Maners* (1628): www.eudaemonist.com/biblion/characters/healey.
Hill, P., ed., *The Letters of Robert Burns* (London: T. Davison, 1819).
Hippocrates, *The Prognostics and Prorrhetics of Hippocrates*, trans. and ed. John Moffat (London: Elliot, Kay & Co., 1788).
Hogg, James, *The Mountain Bard; Consisting of Legendary Ballads and Tales. By James Hogg, the Ettrick Shepherd. The Third Edition, Greatly Enlarged. To which is prefixed A Memoir of the Author's Life, written by himself* (Edinburgh: Oliver & Boyd, 1821).
Howe, P. P., ed., *The Complete Works of William Hazlitt*, 21 vols. (London: J. M. Dent, 1930–4).
Hughes, John, 'To the Spectator', *The Spectator*, 537 (15 November 1712), p. 1.
Hugo, Victor, *L'Homme Qui Rit*, 4 vols. (Paris: A. Lacroix, 1869).
Hunt, Leigh, *Lord Byron and Some of His Contemporaries* (London: Henry Colburn, 1828).
  'Smollett', in *Table-Talk* (London: Smith, Elder and Co., 1870), pp. 40–2.
Ingen, Roger and Walter E. Peck, *The Collected Works of Percy Bysshe Shelley*, 10 vols. (London: Ernest Benn, 1927).
Jameson, Anna Murphy, *Shakespeare's Heroines*, ed. Cheri L. Larsen Hoeckley (Peterborough, ON: Broadview Press, 2005).
Jewsbury, Maria Jane, 'Literary Women. No. II. Jane Austen', *Athenaeum*, 27 (August 1831), pp. 553–54.
Johnson, Samuel, *Johnson's Dictionary of the English Language, in Miniature* (Edinburgh: W. Creech, Peter Hill, Ogle & Aikman and J. Thomson, Jun. & Co.; Glasgow: Brash & Reid, 1808).
  The Lives of the Most Eminent English Poets, 2 vols. (London: C. Bathurst, 1781).
Johnson, Samuel and John Walker, *Johnson's Dictionary of the English Language with Walker's Pronunciation of All the Difficult or Doubtful Words* (London: C. Corall and Thomas Hurst, Edward Chance & Co., 1827).
Kames, Henry Home, *Elements of Criticism*, 2nd ed., 3 vols. (Edinburgh: A. Kincaid & J. Bell; London: A. Millar).
Kavanagh, Julia, *English Women of Letters*, 2 vols. (London: Hurst and Blackett, 1863).
Landseer, John, 'Mr. Landseer's Apology for James Gillray', *The Athenaeum*, 207 (15 October 1831), pp. 667–68.
Lascelles, Mary, *Jane Austen and Her Art* (Oxford: Oxford University Press, 1939).
Lavater, Johann Kaspar, *Essays on Physiognomy*, 4 vols., trans. Thomas Holcroft (London: G. G. J. and J. Robinson, 1789–98).

Physiognomische Fragmente zur Beförderung der Menschenkenntniß und Menschenliebe, 3 vols. (Winterhur: Johann Michael Armbruster, Heinrich Steiners und Compagnie, 1783–87).

Le Faye, Deirdre (ed.), *Jane Austen's Letters*, 4th ed. (Oxford: Oxford University Press, 2011).

Lewis, Matthew G., *The Monk*, eds. Howard Anderson and Emma McEvoy (Oxford: Oxford University Press, 2008).

Litz, A. Walton, *Jane Austen: A Study of Her Artistic Development* (Oxford: Oxford University Press, 1965).

Locke, John, *Some Thoughts Concerning Education* (London: for A. and J. Churchill, 1693).

Lockhart, J. G., *Memoirs of the Life of Sir Walter Scott*, 10 vols. (London: Cadell, 1837).

The Miscellaneous Prose Works of Sir Walter Scott, 6 vols., ed. J. G. Lockhart (Edinburgh: Cadell, 1827).

'On the Cockney School of Poetry. No. I', *Blackwood's Edinburgh Magazine* (October 1817), p. 36–41.

'On the Cockney School of Poetry. No. II', *Blackwood's Edinburgh Magazine* (November 1817), pp. 194–201.

'On the Cockney School of Poetry. III', *Blackwood's Edinburgh Magazine* (July 1818), pp. 453–56.

Lukács, *The Historical Novel*, trans. Hannah Mitchell and Stanley Mitchell (London: Merlin, 1962).

Macaulay, Thomas Babington, *Critical and Historical Essays Contributed to the Edinburgh Review*, 4 vols. (London: Longmans, Green, and Co., 1874).

Malcolm, James Peller, *An Historical Sketch of the Art of Caricaturing* (London: Hurst, Rees, Orme, and Brown, 1813).

Marrs, Edwin W. Jr. (ed.), *The Letters of Charles and Mary Anne Lamb*, 3 vols. (London: Cornell University Press, 1975–78).

Martin, John, *Sadak in Search of the Waters of Oblivion*, painting, 1812 (Saint Louis Art Museum, 1566: 1983).

Mathews, Anne, *Memoirs of Charles Mathews, Comedian* (London: Bentley, 1839).

Meek, Joseph, ed., *The De Coverley Papers from 'The Spectator'* (London: J. M. Dent, 1920).

Moffat, John, trans. and ed., *The Prognostics and Prorrhetics of Hippocrates* (London: Elliot, Kay & Co., 1788).

Morgann, Maurice, *Essay on the Dramatic Character of Sir John Falstaff* (London: P. T. Davies, 1777).

Morley, Edith (ed.), *Henry Crabb Robinson on Books and Their Writers*, 3 vols. (London: Dent, 1938).

Mudrick, Marvin, *Irony as Defense and Discovery* (Berkeley: University of California Press, 1968).

Napier, Macvey, *Hypocrisy Unveiled and Calumny Detected in a Review of Blackwood's Magazine* (Edinburgh: Francis Pillans, 1818).

Paine, Thomas, *Rights of Man* (London: J. S. Jordan, 1791).
Parr, Bartholomew, *The London Medical Dictionary*, 2 vols. (London: J. Johnson, F. and C. Rivington, etc., 1809).
Paton, Hugh (ed.), *A Series of Original Portraits and Caricature Etchings by the Late John Kay, with Biographical Sketches and Anecdotes*, 2 vols. (Edinburgh: Paton, 1842).
Peacock, Thomas Love, *Crotchet Castle*, eds. Freya Johnston and Matthew Bevis (Cambridge: Cambridge University Press, 2016).
  Crotchet Castle (London: T. Hookham, 1831).
  Headlong Hall. Nightmare Abbey. Maid Marian. Crotchet Castle, with corrections, and a preface, by the author (London: Richard Bentley; Edinburgh: Bell and Bradfute; Dublin: J. Cumming, 1837).
  Melincourt or Sir Oran Haut-ton (London: Chapman and Hall, 1856).
  'Memoirs of Percy Bysshe Shelley', *Fraser's Magazine* (June 1858), pp. 643–59.
  Nightmare Abbey (London: T. Hookham, and Baldwin, Cradock and Joy, 1818).
  The Works of Thomas Love Peacock, 3 vols., ed. Henry Cole (London: Richard Bentley and Son, 1875).
Perlemuter, Vlado, *Ravel According to Ravel*, trans. Frances Tanner, ed. Harold Taylor (London: Kahn & Averill, 1990).
Pittock, Malcolm, 'Jane Austen and Her Critics', *The Cambridge Quarterly*, 32.3 (2003), pp. 251–75.
Pratt, Lynda, Tim Fulford and Ian Packer, eds., *The Collected Letters of Robert Southey: Part Two, 1798–1803* (Romantic Circles, 2011): https://romantic-circles.org/editions/southey_letters/Part_Two/index.html.
Randolph, Thomas, *The Muses Looking-Glass; (Or, the Stage Re-view'd). A Comedy* (London, 1706).
Robertson, Thomas, 'An Essay on the Character of Hamlet' *Transactions of the Royal Society of Edinburgh*, 2 (1788).
Rollins, Hyder Edward (ed.), *The Letters of John Keats, 1814–1821*, 2 vols. (Cambridge, MA: Harvard University Press, 2002).
Rousseau, Jean-Jacques, *Emilius; Or, an Essay on Education*, 2 vols., trans. Thomas Nugent (London: Nourse and Vaillant, 1763).
Saintsbury, George, ed., *Pride and Prejudice* (London: George Allen, 1894).
Sato, Takero, and the Centre for Research Collections, Edinburgh University Library, *The Letters of Sir Walter Scott: E-text*: www.walterscottlib.ed.ac.uk/etexts/etexts/letters.html.
Scott, Walter, *The Black Dwarf*, ed. P. D. Garside (Edinburgh: Edinburgh University Press and Columbia University Press, 1993).
  'Essay on the Drama', in *The Miscellaneous Prose Works of Sir Walter Scott*, 6 vols., ed. J. G. Lockhart (Edinburgh: Cadell, 1827), vol. VI, pp. 658–700.
  Guy Mannering, ed. P. D. Garside (Edinburgh: Edinburgh University Press and Columbia University Press, 1999).
  The Heart of Mid-Lothian, eds. David Hewitt and Alison Lumsden (Edinburgh: Edinburgh University Press and Columbia University Press, 2004).

Introductions and Notes from the Magnum Opus, 2 vols., eds. J. H. Alexander, P. D. Garside and Claire Lamont (Edinburgh: Edinburgh University Press and Columbia University Press, 2012).

Ivanhoe, ed. and with introduction by Graham Tulloch (London: Penguin, 2000).

Kenilworth, ed. J. H. Alexander (Edinburgh: Edinburgh University Press and Columbia University Press, 1993).

A Legend of the Wars of Montrose, ed. J. H. Alexander (Edinburgh: Edinburgh University Press and Columbia University Press, 1995).

(ed.), *Letters of Anna Seward: Written between the Years 1784 and 1807*, 6 vols. (Edinburgh: Constable; London: Longman, Hurst, Rees, Orme and Brown, William Miller and John Murray, 1811).

The Monastery, ed. Penny Fielding (Edinburgh: Edinburgh University Press and Columbia University Press, 2008).

The Monastery. A Romance, 3 vols. (Edinburgh: Archibald Constable and Co., and John Ballantyne; London: Longman, Hurst, Rees, Orme, and Brown, 1820).

Peveril of the Peak, eds. Mark Weinstein and Alison Lumsden (Edinburgh: Edinburgh University Press and Columbia University Press, 2007).

The Pirate, ed. Alison Lumsden (Edinburgh: Edinburgh University Press and Columbia University Press, 2001).

'Prefatory Memoir to Smollett', in *The Novels of Tobias Smollett, M. D.* (London: Hurst, Robinson and Co.; Edinburgh: James Ballantyne and Co., 1821), pp. i–xlii.

Redgauntlet, eds. G. A. M. Wood and David Hewitt (Edinburgh: Edinburgh University Press and Columbia University Press, 1997).

Rob Roy, ed. David Hewitt (Edinburgh: Edinburgh University Press and Columbia University Press, 2008).

Saint Ronan's Well, ed. Mark A. Weinstein (Edinburgh: Edinburgh University Press and Columbia University Press, 1995).

Tales of My Landlord, Second Series, 4 vols. (Edinburgh: Archibald Constable and Co., 1818).

Tales of the Crusaders, 4 vols. (Edinburgh: Archibald Constable and Co.; London: Hurst, Robinson, and Co., 1825).

The Talisman, ed. J. B. Ellis with J. H. Alexander, P. D. Garside and David Hewitt (Edinburgh: Edinburgh University Press and Columbia University Press, 2009).

Waverley; or, 'Tis Sixty Years Since, ed. Claire Lamont (Oxford: Oxford University Press, 2008).

Shelley, Mary, *Falkner*, 3 vols. (London: Saunders and Otley, 1837).

Frankenstein or, the Modern Prometheus: 1818 Text, ed. Marilyn Butler (Oxford: Oxford University Press, 2008).

Frankenstein, or, The Modern Prometheus, 3 vols. (London: Lackington, Hughes, Harding, Mavor, & Jones, 1818).

Frankenstein; or, the Modern Prometheus (London: Colburn and Bentley, 1831).

The Last Man, ed. Morton D. Paley (Oxford: Oxford University Press, 2008).

Lodore, 3 vols. (London: Bentley, 1835).
  with Percy Shelley, MS Abinger c. 56–8.
  Rambles in Germany and Italy in 1840, 1842, and 1843, 3 vols. (London: Moxon, 1844).
  'Transformation: A Tale', in *The Keepsake for MDCCCXXXI*, ed. Frederic Mansel Reyolds (London: Hurst and Co., Jennings and Co., 1830), pp. 18–39.
Sheridan, Thomas, *A Complete Dictionary of the English Language, Both with Regard to Sound and Meaning*, 4th ed. (Dublin: Pat. Wogan, Pat. Burne, 1790).
Skirving, Archibald, Chalk drawing of Robert Burns (c. 1796–98), Scottish National Portrait Gallery, PG 745.
Smith, Margaret (ed.), *The Letters of Charlotte Brontë: 1848–1851*, 3 vols. (Oxford: Clarendon, 1995).
Smollett, Tobias, *The Expedition of Humphry Clinker*, eds. Lewis M. Knapp and Paul-Gabriel Boucé (Oxford: Oxford University Press, 2009).
  The Reprisal; or, the Tars of Old England (London: R. Baldwin, 1757).
Southam, B. C., *Jane Austen's Literary Manuscripts: A Study of the Novelist's Development through the Surviving Papers* (Oxford: Oxford University Press, 1964).
Steele, Richard, 'The Satyrist and the Libeller Differ...', *The Tatler*, 92 (10 November 1709).
Summerscale, Ann (ed. and trans.), *Malvasia's Life of the Carracci* (University Park, PA: Penn State University Press, 2000).
Sutherland, Kathryn (ed.) *Jane Austen's Fiction Manuscripts*: www.janeausten.ac.uk.
Swift, Jonathan, *Gulliver's Travels*, ed. Ian Higgins (Oxford: Oxford University Press, 2008).
  A Tale of a Tub [...] To which Is Added, an Account of a Battel between the Antient and Modern Books in St. James's Library (London: John Nutt, 1704).
  Verses on the Death of Dr. Swift (London: Bathurst, 1739).
Sydney, Lady Morgan, *Florence Macarthy: An Irish Tale*, 4 vols. (London: Colburn 1818).
Thackeray, William Makepeace, unsigned essay, 'Life and Genius of George Cruikshank', *The Monthly Magazine*, 15.86 (February 1833), pp. 131–47.
  Vanity Fair: A Novel without a Hero, ed. Helen Small (Oxford: Oxford University Press, 2015).
Thaden, Barbara Z., 'Figure and Ground: The Receding Heroine in Jane Austen's *Emma*', *South Atlantic Review*, 55.1 (January 1990), pp. 47–62.
Tissot, Auguste, *Advice to the People in General, with Regard to Their Health*, trans. J. Kirkpatrick (Dublin: J. Hoey sr., P. Wilson, S. Cotter, W. Sleater, J. Potts, S. Watson, J. Hoey Jr., J. Williams, and J. Sheppherd, 1766), pp. 271–72.
Todd, H. J. (ed.), *A Dictionary of the English Language by Samuel Johnson, LL.D, with numerous corrections, and with the addition of several thousand words*, 4 vols. (London: Longman, Hurst, Rees, Orme, and Brown, 1818).

Toynbee, Paget (ed.), *The Letters of Horace Walpole*, 16 vols. (Oxford: Clarendon, 1903–25).

Trollope, Anthony, 'On English Prose Fiction as a Rational Amusement', in *An Autobiography and Other Writings*, ed. Nicholas Shrimpton (Oxford: Oxford University Press, 2014).

The Warden (London: Longman, Brown, Greene, and Longmans, 1855).

Unsigned, 'Account of George Steevens, Esq. the Celebrated Commentator on Shakespeare', *The Edinburgh Magazine and Literary Miscellany* (April 1800), pp. 289–94.

Unsigned advertisement for a performance of *The Ugly Club*, *Morning Post and Gazetteer*, 13619 (14 September 1814), p. 3.

Unsigned advertisement for George Cruikshank's print *The Modern Prometheus, or Downfall of Tyranny*, *The Morning Post* (28 April 1814).

Unsigned, 'Art. XVI. *A Treatise on the Lues Bovilla, or Cow-Pox*', *The Monthly Review* (August 1805), pp. 427–31.

Unsigned, 'Celebrated Deformed Men', *The Scots Magazine* (1 November 1797), p. 796.

Unsigned, 'Characters of Eminent Members of the National Assembly of France', Oracle Bell's *New World*, 130 (29 October 1789), p. 3.

Unsigned letter, *Morning Herald* (26 January 1781), p. 2.

Unsigned letter attributed to 'Patrick', 'The Peace', *Morning Post* (12 December 1815), p. 2.

Unsigned letter, 'Poor Laws', *Cobbett's Weekly Political Register* (12 December 1807), p. 18.

Unsigned 'Letter to the Editor, March 20', *Morning Post and Daily Advertiser*, 774 (20 April 1775).

Unsigned, *Letters from Flushing. Containing an Account of the Expedition to Walcheren, Beveland ... To which is added, A Topographical and Statistical Account of the Islands* (London: Richard Philips, 1809).

Unsigned letter, 'To the Authors of the Monthly Review', *The Monthly Review*, vol. 19 (September 1758), pp. 318–20.

Unsigned letter, 'To the Authors of the Monthly Review', *The Monthly Review*, vol. 19 (December 1758), pp. 605–7.

Unsigned, 'Lord Holdernesse', *Morning Post and Advertiser*, 1129 (7 June 1776), p. 4.

Unsigned notice of a caricature print, *Morning Herald*, 5668 (17 November 1798), p. 2.

Unsigned, 'Ode, on the Success of His Majesty's Arms', *London Evening Post* (9–11 December 1777), p. 14.

Unsigned, 'Personal Sketch of the Duke of Wellington', originally published in the *Dublin Literary Gazette*, reprinted in *The Kaleidoscope; or Literary and Scientific Mirror* (26 January 1830), pp. 238–39.

Unsigned report on Benjamin Franklin's departure to Prussia, *General Evening Post* (20 September 1777), p. 2.

Unsigned, *Satire Made Easy; or Instructions in the Art of Polite Censure* (Manchester: Leigh, 1815).

Unsigned, 'The Brain-Sucker. Or, the Distress of Authorship. A Serio-Comic Caricature. In a Letter from Farmer Homely, to an Absent Friend', *The Morning Star*, 191 (23 September 1798), p. 4.

Unsigned, 'The Mirror of Fashion', *Morning Chronicle* (August 1796), p. 7.

Unsigned, 'The Mirror of French Manners. On Caricatures', *La Belle Assemblée; Or, Bell's Court and Fashionable Magazine*, 76 (1 October 1815), p. 189.

Walker, John, *A Critical Pronouncing Dictionary & Expositor of the English Language* (London: Thomas Tegg, T. Kelly, G. Virtue; Manchester: J. Gleaves; Leicester: E. Allen, 1823).

Johnson's Dictionary of the English Language with Walker's Pronunciation of All the Difficult or Doubtful Words (London: C. Corall; Thomas Hurst, Edward Chance, & Co., 1827).

Walker, Joseph John, *Essay on the Revival of the Drama in Italy* (Edinburgh: Mundell and Son; London: Longman, Hurst, Rees, and Orme, 1805).

Ward, Mary Augusta, 'Style and Miss Austen', *Macmillan's Magazine*, 51 (December 1884), pp. 84–91.

Wells, H. G., *The Island of Doctor Moreau: A Possibility* (London: William Heinemann, 1896).

Wilson, John, 'Noctes Ambrosianae No. XXX', *Blackwood's Magazine* (January 1827), pp. 100–17.

'On the Personalities of the Augustan Age of English Literature', *Blackwood's Edinburgh Magazine*, 10.56 (October 1821), pp. 312–15.

Wilson, John Dover, *John Lyly* (New York: Haskell, 1970).

Wilson, Thomas, *A Catalogue Raisonné of the Select Collection of Engravers of an Amateur* (London, 1828).

Winchester, Caleb Thomas, *The Sir Roger De Coverley Papers* (New York: American Book Company, 1904).

Wollstonecraft, Mary, *A Vindication of the Rights of Woman and A Vindication of the Rights of Men*, ed. Janet Todd (Oxford: Oxford University Press, 2008).

Vickers, Brian, ed., *William Shakespeare: The Critical Heritage*, 6 vols. (London: Routledge, 1974).

Primary Sources: Book Reviews

Anonymous reviews are listed under the names of their authors, where known.

Reviews by unidentified writers are labelled 'unsigned' and listed chronologically within that category.

Brougham, Henry, unsigned review of *Hours of Idleness*, 'By George Gordon, Lord Byron, a Minor', *The Edinburgh Review* (January 1808), pp. 285–89.

Burney, Charles, unsigned review of *Lyrical Ballads*, *The Monthly Review* (June 1799), pp. 202–10.

Carlyle, Thomas, review of Lockhart's *Memoirs of the Life of Sir Walter Scott*, *The London and Westminster Review* (January 1838), pp. 293–345.

Christie, Jonathan Henry, 'Life of Lockhart', *The Quarterly Review*, 116 (1864), p. 439–82.

Glascock, William Nugent, 'Naval Novels', *The Metropolitan*, 1 (May–August 1831), pp. 370–76.
Hutton, R. H., unsigned review of *The Letters of Jane Austen*, 'The Charm of Miss Austen', *Spectator*, 64 (1890), pp. 403–4.
Jeffrey, Francis, unsigned review of *Waverley*, *Edinburgh Review* (November 1814), pp. 208–43.
  unsigned review of *Tales of My Landlord*, *Edinburgh Review* (March 1817), pp. 193–259.
  unsigned review of *The Fortunes of Nigel*, *Edinburgh Review* (June 1822), pp. 204–25.
  unsigned review of second editions of poems by Felicia Hemans, *Edinburgh Review*, 50 (October 1829), pp. 473–78.
Kebbel, T. E., 'Jane Austen at Home', *Fortnightly Review*, 37 (February 1885), pp. 262–70.
Lewes, George Henry, 'The Novels of Jane Austen', *Blackwood's Edinburgh Magazine*, 86 (July 1859), pp. 99–113.
Macaulay, Thomas Babington, unsigned review of *Diary and Letters of Madame D'Arblay*, *The Edinburgh Review*, 76 (January 1843), pp. 523–70.
Malcolm, James Peller, letter labelled 'Critical remarks on *Pizarro*/Modern novels censured', *Gentleman's Magazine*, 68 (September 1798), pp. 919–20.
Oliphant, Margaret, review of *A Memoir of Jane Austen*, 'Miss Austen and Miss Mitford', *Blackwood's Magazine*, 107 (March 1870), pp. 290–313.
Pollock, W. F., 'British Novelists – Richardson, Miss Austen, Scott', *Fraser's Magazine*, 61 (January 1860), pp. 20–38.
Senior, Nassau William, unsigned review of Scott's novels to 1822, *Quarterly Review*, 26 (October 1822), pp. 109–48.
Scott, Walter, unsigned review of *Emma*, *Quarterly Review*, 14 (October 1815), pp. 188–201.
  unsigned review of *Frankenstein*, *The Scots Magazine*, 81 (March 1818), p. 249.
Simpson, Richard, review of *Memoir of Jane Austen*, *North British Review*, 52 (April 1870), pp. 129–52.
Southey, Robert, unsigned review of *Lyrical Ballads*, *Critical Review* (October 1798), pp. 197–204.
Thackeray, Anne, 'Jane Austen', *Cornhill Magazine*, 34 (1871), pp. 158–78.
Unsigned review of *Santa Maria; or, The Mysterious Pregnancy*, *The Gentleman's Magazine* (September 1798), pp. 786–87.
Unsigned review of *Lyrical Ballads*, *The British Critic* (October 1799), pp. 364–69.
Unsigned review of Joanna Bailie's *The Family Legend* and *A Series of Plays*, *The Monthly Review* (1 December 1812), pp. 382–93.
Unsigned review of *Pride and Prejudice*, *Critical Review*, 4.3 (March 1813), pp. 318–24.
Unsigned review of *The Wanderer*, *The Edinburgh Review* (February 1815), pp. 320–38.

Unsigned review of *Hebrew Melodies*, *Critical Review*, 2.1 (July 1815), pp. 166–71.
Unsigned review of *Emma*, *The Gentleman's Magazine*, 86 (September 1816), pp. 248–49.
Unsigned review of *Childe Harold's Pilgrimage* and *The Prisoners of Chillon*, *Eclectic Review*, 7.25 (March 1817), pp. 292–304.
Unsigned review of *Tales of My Landlord*, *Edinburgh Review* (March 1817), pp. 193–259.
Unsigned review of *Manfred*, *Critical Review*, 5.6 (June 1817), pp. 622–29.
Unsigned review of *Manfred*, *The European Magazine and London Review*, 72 (August 1817), pp. 150–52.
Unsigned review of *Six Week's at Long's*, *The Monthly Magazine*, 43.5 (1 June 1817), p. 453.
Unsigned review of *Rob Roy*, *Scots Magazine*, 2.2 (February 1818), pp. 148–52.
Unsigned review of *Frankenstein*, *Scots Magazine*, 2.3 (March 1818), pp. 249–53.
Unsigned review of *Frankenstein*, *Blackwood's Edinburgh Magazine*, 2.12 (March 1818), pp. 613–20.
Unsigned 'Notice of Northanger Abbey and Persuasion', *Edinburgh Magazine and Literary Miscellany*, 81 (May 1818), pp. 453–55.
Unsigned review of *Frankenstein*, *British Critic* (October 1818), pp. 432–38.
Unsigned review of *Nightmare Abbey*, *The London Literary Gazette*, 99 (12 December 1818), pp. 787–88.
Unsigned review of *Memoirs of a Cavalier*, *The Retrospective Review*, 3 (1821), pp. 354–79.
Unsigned review of *Life and Adventures of Peter Wilkins*, *The Retrospective Review*, 7 (1823), pp. 131–35.
Unsigned review of the Waverley Novels, *The North American Review*, 32 (April 1831), pp. 404–45.
Unsigned, 'James Gillray, and His Caricatures', *The Athenaeum*, 205 (1 October 1831), pp. 632–34.
Unsigned review of *Historical and Descriptive Account of the Caricatures of James Gillray*, 'Gillray's Caricatures', *Morning Chronicle* (25 October 1851), p. 7.
Unsigned review of *The Mill on the Floss*, *Saturday Review*, 9 (April 1860), pp. 470–71.
Unsigned review of *The Letters of Jane Austen*, *The Standard* (9 June 1884), p. 5.
Unsigned review of *English Caricaturists and Graphic Humourists of the Nineteenth Century, and How They Illustrated and Interpreted Their Times*, *The Athenaeum*, 3064 (17 July 1886), pp. 85–7.
Ward, Mary, 'Style and Miss Austen', *Macmillan's Magazine*, 51 (December 1884), pp. 84–91.
Whately, Richard, 'Modern Novels', unsigned review of *Northanger Abbey* and *Persuasion*, *Quarterly Review*, 24 (January 1821), pp. 352–76.
Wilson, John, 'Letter I. On Hogg's Memoirs', *Blackwood's Edinburgh Magazine*, 10.54 (August 1821), pp. 43–52.
— 'Some Observations on the "Biographia Literaria" of S. T. Coleridge, Esq. — 1817', *Blackwood's Edinburgh Magazine*, 2.7 (October 1817), pp. 3–18.

Primary Sources: Prints, Drawings, Paintings

British Museum, London

Aiken, Henry Thomas, *Calves' Heads and Brains or a Phrenological Lecture*, 1826, BM Satires 15158.
Beauclerk, Diana, portraits of Edward Gibbon, BMC Binyon 1898–1907 1.
Cruikshank, George, *The Modern Prometheus, or Downfall of Tyranny*, 1814, BM Satires 12299.
  The Night Mare, 1816, BMC 12817.
Cruikshank, George and Robert Isaac, *Fare Thee Well*, 1816, BM Satires 12927.
  Fashionables of 1816 Taking the Air in Hyde Park!, 1816, BM Satires 12825.
  Lobby Loungers, 1816, BM Satires 12826.
  The Separation, A Sketch from the Private Life of Lord Iron, 1816, BM Satires 12828.
Cruikshank, Isaac, *John Dow Soldier of the City-Guard Edinburgh*, 1784, BM Satires 6689.
Cruikshank, Robert Isaac, *The Great Unknown Cutting Up Napoleon the Great*, 1827, BM Satires 14825.
  The Great Unknown Lately Discovered in Ireland, 1825, BM Satires 14825.
  Management, or Butts & Hogsheads, 1812, BM Satires 11940.
Doyle, John, *The Balance of Public Favor*, 1827, BM Satires 15440.
Gillray, James, *The Apotheosis of Hoche*, 1798, BM Satires 9156.
Hogarth, William, *The Bench*, 1758, BM Satires 3662.
Hood, Thomas, *The Progress of Cant*, 1815, BM Satires 14815.
Rowlandson, Thomas, *The Covent Garden Night Mare*, 1784, BM Satires 6543.
  Dutch Night-Mare or the Fraternal Hug Returned with a Dutch Squeeze, 1813, BM Satires 12105.
Williams, Charles, *The Genius of the Times*, 1812, BM Satires 11940.
  Rival Candidates for the Vacant Bays, 1813, BM Satires 12982.
Spencer, Lavinia, portraits of Edward Gibbon, BMC Binyon 1898–1904 4.

National Galleries of Scotland, Edinburgh

Clerk, George, *Caricature of a Hedgehog Dressed as a Woman*, NGS D 5057.79 A.
  Caricature of a Man in a Wig, NGS D 5057.73 A.
  Heads of Two Men, NGS D 5057.92 B.
  ink drawing, *Woman Wearing a Fancy Bonnet*, NGS D 5057.94 A.
Ghezzi, Pier Leone, portrait of Lord Southesk in Rome, NGS PG 2452.
Grose, Francis, *Caricature of Gluttons at Table*, NGS D 5057.69 A.
Sharpe, Charles Kirkpatrick, *Caricature of Fanny Persiani, Italian Soprano*, NGS D 2381.
  The Music Room, Oxford, 1802, NGS D 4800 H.
Wood, John Muir, *The Professor*, NGS PGP.W.113.

Royal Collection Trust

Taylor, Ella, *A celebrated noble Lord in sporting dress*, 1859, DM 5288.
 Drawing of Count B. Chotek, DM 4262.
 Drawing of Count Kielmansegge, DM 5266.
 Drawing of Isidore Brasseur, DM 5263.
 Drawing of presentation to Queen Victoria, 1869, RCIN 918861.
 Four Caricatures of Dr Quin's adventures on his way to Cambridge Cottage, 1860, RCIN 918820.
 Sketches made at the Opening of Parliament, 1861, RCIN 918824.

Other Collections

English Fire-side, 'Portfolio of Caricatures, Coloured', Abbotsford Collection, Advocates Library, National Library of Scotland, Edinburgh.
Kay, John, *George Walker, Drawing Master – in the Uniform of the Defensive Band*, 1994.189, Royal Scottish Academy, Edinburgh.
Martin, David, *Sadak in Search of the Waters of Oblivion*, 1812, 1566: 1983, Saint Louis Art Museum, Missouri.
Spencer, Lavinia, *Gallant and Gay Lothario*, T10114, Tate Britain, London.

Secondary Sources

Ailwood, Sarah, *Jane Austen's Men: Rewriting Masculinity in the Romantic Era* (Abingdon: Routledge, 2019).
Andrews, Richard, *The Commedia Dell'Arte of Flaminio Scala: A Translation and Analysis of 30 Scenarios* (Plymouth: Scarecrow, 2008).
Armstrong, Nancy, *Fiction in the Age of Photography: The Legacy of British Realism* (Cambridge, MA: Harvard University Press, 1999).
Baker, James, *The Business of Satirical Prints in Late-Georgian England* (New York: Palgrave Macmillan, 2017).
Baldick, Chris, 'The Politics of Monstrosity', in *Frankenstein's Shadow: Myth, Monstrosity, and Nineteenth-Century Writing* (Oxford: Clarendon, 1987), pp. 11–29.
Banerji, Christine and Diana Donald, *Gillray Observed: The Earliest Account of His Caricatures in London und Paris* (Cambridge: Cambridge University Press, 1999).
Barrell, John, 'London in the 1790s', in *The Cambridge History of English Literature: The Romantic Period*, ed. James Chandler (Cambridge: Cambridge University Press, 2009), pp. 127–58.
 'A Smile at My Own Temerity', *London Review of Books*, 39.4 (February 2017), pp. 8–10.
Bate, Jonathan, *The Song of the Earth* (London: Picador, 2000).

Battles, Kelly E., 'Bad Taste, Gothic Bodies, and Subversive Aesthetics in Hogg's *Private Memoirs and Confessions of a Justified Sinner*', *Essays in Romanticism*, 19.5 (2012), pp. 49–64.

Bendall, Sarah, *Shaping Femininity: Foundation Garments, the Body and Women in Early Modern England* (London: Bloomsbury, 2021).

Bove, Alexander, 'The "Unbearable Realism of a Dream": On the Subject of Portraits in Austen and Dickens', *ELH*, 74.3 (2007), pp. 655–79.

Bray, Joe, *The Portrait in Fiction of the Romantic Period* (Abingdon: Routledge, 2016).

Brewer, Charlotte, 'The Use of Literary Quotations in the Oxford English Dictionary', *The Review of English Studies*, 61.248 (2010), pp. 93–125.

Brewer, Luther A., *Leigh Hunt and Charles Dickens: The Skimpole Caricature* (Cedar Rapids, IA: privately printed, 1930).

Brown, Iain Gordon, 'Caricature: The Individual Contribution of John Kay', in *The Edinburgh History of the Book in Scotland*, 2 vols., ed. Bill Bell (University of Edinburgh Press, 2012), vol. II, *Enlightenment and Expansion 1707–1800*, eds. Stephen W. Brown and Warren McDougall, pp. 107–11.

Brownstein, Rachel, 'Character and Caricature: Jane Austen and James Gillray', *Persuasions*, 37 (2015), pp. 81–93.

Butler, Marilyn, 'Jane Austen's Word Process', review of *Computation into Criticism* by J. F. Burrows, *London Review of Books*, 9.12 (June 1987), pp. 11–13.

  Maria Edgeworth: A Literary Biography (Oxford: Oxford University Press, 1972).

  Peacock Displayed: A Satirist in His Context (Abingdon: Routledge, 1979).

Butler, Marilyn and Tim McLoughlin, *The Works of Maria Edgeworth* (London: Routledge), vol. I.

Campbell, Timothy, *Historical Style: Fashion and the New Mode of History, 1740–1830* (Philadelphia: University of Pennsylvania Press, 2016).

Chandler, James, *England in 1819: The Politics of Literary Culture and the Case of Romantic Historicism* (Chicago: Chicago University Press, 1998).

Clery, E. J., *The Rise of Supernatural Fiction 1761–1800* (Cambridge: Cambridge University Press, 1995).

Clery, E. J. and Robert Miles, *Gothic Documents: A Sourcebook, 1700–1820* (Manchester: Manchester University Press, 2000).

Connelly, Frances S., *The Grotesque in Western Art and Culture: The Image at Play* (Cambridge: Cambridge University Press, 2012).

Cowan, Brian, 'Mr. Spectator and the Coffeehouse Public Sphere', *Eighteenth-Century Studies* 37.3 (Spring 2004): 345–66.

Cronin, Richard, *Paper Pellets: British Literary Culture after Waterloo* (Oxford: Oxford University Press, 2010).

Daiches, David, 'Walter Scott and History', *Études Anglais*, 24 (1971), pp. 458–77.

Dickerson, Claude Douglas, *Raw Painting: The Butcher's Shop by Annibale Carracci* (New Haven, CT: Yale University Press, 2010).
Dickinson, H. T., *Caricatures and the Constitution 1760–1832* (Cambridge: Chadwyck-Healey, 1986).
Donald, Diana, *The Age of Caricature: Satirical Prints in the Reign of George III* (New Haven, CT: Yale University Press, 1996).
Duncan, Ian, *Scott's Shadow: The Novel in Romantic Edinburgh* (Princeton, NJ: Princeton University Press, 2007).
Dyer, Gary, *British Satire and the Politics of Style, 1789–1832* (Cambridge: Cambridge University Press, 1997).
Eberle-Sinatra, Michael, *Leigh Hunt and the London Literary Scene: A Reception History of His Major Works* (Abingdon: Routledge, 2005).
Esterhammer, Angela, '1824: Improvisation, Speculation, and Identity-Construction', *BRANCH: Britain, Representation and Nineteenth-Century History*, ed. Dino Franco Felluga, *Romanticism and Victorianism on the Net* (July 2012).
Fang, Karen, 'A Printing Devil, a Scottish Mummy, and an Edinburgh Book of the Dead: James Hogg's Napoleonic Complex', *Studies in Romanticism*, 43.2 (2004), pp. 161–85.
Felton, Felix, *Thomas Love Peacock* (London: Allen & Unwin, 1973).
Ferguson, Frances, 'Austen, *Emma*, and the Impact of Form', *Modern Language Quarterly*, 61.1 (March 2000), pp. 157–80.
Ferguson, Olivia, 'Gratifying Difficulty', review of David Taylor's *Politics of Parody* (2018), *Essays in Criticism*, 70.3 (July 2020), pp. 376–82.
  'Jane Austen Caricature, and the Fat Self', in *The Edinburgh Companion to Jane Austen and the Arts*, eds. Joe Bray and Hannah Moss (Edinburgh: Edinburgh University Press, 2023), forthcoming.
  'Walter Scott and the Future of Caricature in the Novel', *Studies in Romanticism*, 60.2 (2021), pp. 205–27.
  'Wellington's Rats in the Illustrated *Devil's Walk*', *Notes and Queries*, 61.1 (2014), pp. 54–6.
  '*The Unwelcome Guest*: A Poem on John Kay, Caricaturist', *Notes and Queries*, 65.2 (2018), pp. 316–19.
Frow, John, *Character and Person* (Oxford: Oxford University Press, 2014).
  'Spectacle Binding: On Character', *Poetics Today*, 7 (1986), pp. 227–50.
Frye, Northrop, 'The Four Forms of Prose Fiction', in *Modern Literary Criticism: 1900–1970*, eds. Lawrence I. Lipking and A. Walton Litz (New York: Athenaeum, 1972), pp. 208–14.
Gamer, Michael, 'The Select Collection and the Rise of the (Reprinted) Novel', in *Recognizing the Romantic Novel: New Approaches to British Fiction, 1780–1832*, eds. Jill Heydt-Stevenson and Charlotte Sussman (Liverpool: University of Liverpool Press, 2008), pp. 119–55.
Garside, P. D., 'Picturesque Figure and Landscape: Meg Merrilies and the Gypsies', in *The Politics of the Picturesque: Literature, Landscape and*

Aesthetics Since 1770, eds. Stephen Copley and P. D. Garside (Cambridge: Cambridge University Press, 1994), pp. 145–74.
  'Scott and the "Philosophical Historians"', *Journal of the History of Ideas*, 36 (1975), pp. 497–512.
Gigante, Denise, 'Facing the Ugly: The Case of "Frankenstein"', *ELH*, 67.2 (2000), pp. 565–97.
Gombrich, E. H., 'Imagery and Art in the Romantic Period', in *The Essential Gombrich: Selected Writings on Art and Culture*, ed. Richard Woodfield (New York: Phaidon, 1996), pp. 529–38.
Gombrich, E. H., and Ernst Kris, *Caricature* (London: Penguin, 1940).
Gottlieb, Evan, *Feeling British: Sympathy and National Identity in Scottish and English Writing, 1707–1832* (Cranbury, NJ: Rosemont, Associated University Presses, 2007).
  'Fools of Prejudice: Sympathy and National Identity in the Scottish Enlightenment and *Humphry Clinker*', *Eighteenth-Century Fiction*, 18 (2005), pp. 81–106.
Gowrley, Freya, 'Super-Sized Georgians: Why Satirists Were Fixated with Fatness', *History Extra* (3 November 2021): www.historyextra.com/period/georgian/super-sized-georgians-why-satirists-fixated-fatness.
Greene, Donald, 'Jane Austen's Monsters', in *Jane Austen: Bicentenary Essays*, ed. John Halperin (Cambridge: Cambridge University Press, 1975), pp. 262–78.
Greenough, Chester Noyes, *Bibliography of the English Theophrastan Character* (Cambridge, MA: Harvard University Press, 1947, reprinted 2014).
Grigsby, Darcy Grimaldo, 'Nudity à la grecque in 1799', *The Art Bulletin*, 80.2 (June 1998), pp. 311–35.
Habermas, Jürgen, *The Structural Transformation of the Public Sphere*, trans. Thomas Burger (Cambridge, MA: MIT Press, 1989).
Hagstrum, Jean H., 'Verbal and Visual Caricature in the Age of Dryden, Swift, and Pope', in *England in the Restoration and Early Eighteenth Century: Essays on Culture and Society*, ed. H. T. Swedenberg, Jr. (Berkeley: University of California Press, 1972), pp. 173–86.
Halsey, Katie, *Jane Austen and Her Readers, 1786–1845* (London: Anthem, 2012).
Haywood, Ian, *Romanticism and Caricature* (Cambridge: Cambridge University Press, 2014).
Henshaw, Victoria, *Scotland and the British Army, 1700–1750: Defending the Union* (London: Bloomsbury, 2014).
Higgins, David, *Romantic Genius and the Literary Magazine: Biography, Celebrity, Politics* (New York: Routledge, 2005).
Hill, Draper, *Mr. Gillray: The Caricaturist* (New York: Phaidon, 1965).
Hill, Richard J., 'Reconstructing the Tolbooth: Alexander Nasmyth and *The Heart of Midlothian*', in *Picturing Scotland through the Waverley Novels* (Farnham: Ashgate, 2010).
Hinde, Wendy, *George Canning* (London: Purnell, 1973).

Ingram, Allan with Michelle Faubert, *Cultural Constructions of Madness in Eighteenth-Century Writing: Representing the Insane* (Basingstoke: Palgrave Macmillan, 2005).
Johnson, Claudia, '"Let Me Make the Novels of a Country": Barbauld's "The British Novelists" (1810/1820)', *NOVEL: A Forum on Fiction*, 34.2 (Spring 2001), pp. 163–79.
   Jane Austen: Women, Politics, and the Novel (Chicago: University of Chicago Press, 1988).
Joshua, Essaka, *Physical Disability in British Romantic Literature* (Cambridge: Cambridge University Press, 2020).
Kahrl, George M., 'Captain Robert Stobo', *Virginia Magazine of History and Biography*, 49 (1941), pp. 254–68.
Kerr, David, *Caricature and French Political Culture, 1830–1848* (Oxford: Oxford University Press, 2000).
Knapp, Lewis M., *Tobias Smollett: Doctor of Men and Manners* (Princeton, NJ: Princeton University Press, 1949).
Kris, Ernst, *Psychoanalytic Exploration in Art* (New York: Schoken, 1952).
Lascelles, Mary, *Jane Austen and her Art* (Oxford: Oxford University Press, 1939).
Lee, Michael Parrish, 'The Nothing in the Novel: Jane Austen and the Food Plot', *NOVEL: A Forum on Fiction*, 45.3 (2012), pp. 368–88.
Levine, George, *The Realistic Imagination* (Chicago: University of Chicago Press, 1983).
Levy, Michelle, 'Jane Austen's Manuscripts and the Publicity of Print', *ELH*, 77.4 (2010), pp. 1015–40.
Lynch, Deidre, *The Economy of Character: Novels, Market Culture, and the Business of Inner Meaning* (Chicago: Chicago University Press, 1998).
   (ed.), *Janeites: Austen's Disciples and Devotees* (Princeton, NJ: Princeton University Press, 2000).
Maidment, Brian, *Comedy, Caricature, and the Social Order, 1820–50* (Manchester: Manchester University Press, 2013).
Marshall, Ashley, *The Practice of Satire in England, 1658–1770* (Baltimore: Johns Hopkins University Press, 2016).
Martz, Louis L. *The Later Career of Tobias Smollett* (New Haven, CT: Yale University Press, 1942).
Mason, Nicholas (ed.), *Blackwood's Magazine, 1817–25*, 6 vols. (London: Pickering & Chatto, 2006).
McCreery, Cindy, *The Satirical Gaze: Prints of Women in Late Eighteenth-Century England* (Oxford: Oxford University Press, 2004).
McKeon, Michael, *The Secret History of Domesticity: Public, Private, and the Division of Knowledge* (Baltimore: Johns Hopkins University Press, 2005).
Mellor, Anne K., *Mary Shelley: Her Life, Her Fiction, Her Monsters* (New York: Methuen, 1988).
   Romanticism and Gender (New York: Routledge, 1993).
Mitchell, David and Sharon L. Snyder, *Narrative Prosthesis: Disability and the Dependencies of Discourse* (Ann Arbor: University of Michigan Press, 2000).

Mitchell, Rosemary, *Picturing the Past: English History in Text and Image, 1830–1870* (Oxford: Clarendon, 2000).
Moers, Ellen, *Literary Women: The Great Writers* (New York: Doubleday, 1976).
Moi, Toril, 'Rethinking Character', in *Character: Three Inquiries in Literary Studies* (Chicago: University of Chicago Press, 2019).
Mole, Tom, (ed.), *Blackwood's Magazine: Selected Criticism, 1817–19* (London: Pickering & Chatto, 2006).
   '*Blackwood's* "Personalities"', in *Romanticism and Blackwood's Magazine: An Unprecedented Phenomenon*, eds. Robert Morrison and Daniel S. Roberts (Basingstoke: Palgrave Macmillan, 2013), pp. 89–99.
   Byron's Romantic Celebrity: Industrial Culture and the Hermeneutic of Intimacy (New York: Palgrave Macmillan, 2007).
Mulvihill, James, *Notorious Facts* (Newark, NJ: University of Delaware Press, 2011).
   'Peacock's Nightmare Abbey and the "Shapes" of Imposture', *Studies in Romanticism*, 34.4 (1995), pp. 553–68.
   Thomas Love Peacock (Boston: G. K. Hall & Co., 1987).
Mudrick, Marvin, *Irony as Defense and Discovery* (Berkeley: University of California Press, 1968).
Nicholson, Eirwen E. C., 'Consumers and Spectators: The Public of the Political Print in Eighteenth-Century England', *History*, 81.261 (1996), pp. 5–21.
Odumosu, Temi, *Africans in English Caricature, 1769–1819: Black Jokes, White Humour* (London: Harvey Miller, 2017).
O'Neill, Michael, 'Mournful Ditties and Merry Measures: Feeling and Form in the Romantic Short Lyric and Song', in *A Companion to Romantic Poetry*, ed. Charles Mahoney (Hoboken, NJ: Wiley-Blackwell, 2010), pp. 7–24.
Page, Judith W., *Imperfect Sympathies: Jews and Judaism in British Romantic Literature and Culture* (New York: Palgrave Macmillan, 2004).
Patten, Robert L., 'Conventions of Georgian Caricature', *Art Journal*, 43.4 (1983), pp. 331–38.
   Cruikshank's Life, Times, and Art, 2 vols. (New Brunswick, NJ: Rutgers University Press, 1992).
   George Cruikshank: A Revaluation (Princeton, NJ: Princeton University Press, 1974).
Pentland, Gordon, '"We Speak for the Ready": Images of Scots in Political Prints, 1707–1832', *The Scottish Historical Review*, 90.1 (2011), pp. 64–95.
Porterfield, Todd (ed.), *The Efflorescence of Caricature, 1759–1838* (Abingdon: Routledge, 2011).
Posner, Donald, *Annibale Carracci: A Study in the Reform of Italian Painting around 1590* (London: Phaidon, 1971).
Rauser, Amelia, *Caricature Unmasked: Irony, Authenticity, and Individualism in Eighteenth-Century English Prints* (Newark, NJ: University of Delaware Press, 2008).
   'Hair, Authenticity, and the Self-Made Macaroni', *Eighteenth-Century Studies*, 38.1 (2004), pp. 101–17.

Reed, James, *Sir Walter Scott: Landscape and Locality* (London: Bloomsbury, 1980).
Rigney, Ann, *The Afterlives of Walter Scott: Memory on the Move* (Oxford: Oxford University Press, 2015).
Robertson, Clare, *The Invention of Annibale Carracci* (Milan: Silvana Editoriale, 2008).
Ross, Alexander M., *The Imprint of the Picturesque on Nineteenth-Century British Fiction* (Waterloo: Wilfrid Laurier University Press, 1986.
Schoenfield, Mark L., 'Butchering James Hogg', in *At the Limits of Romanticism: Essays in Cultural, Feminist, and Materialist Criticism*, eds. Mary Favret and Nicola Watson (Bloomington: Indiana University Press, 1994).
Schön, Theresa, *A Cosmography of Man: Character Sketches in 'The Tatler' and 'The Spectator'* (Berlin: De Gruyter, 2020).
Seeber, Barbara K., *Jane Austen and Animals* (Farnham: Ashgate, 2013).
Sleigh, Jon, 'The Power Paunch: Body Politics and Eighteenth-Century Men's Waistlines', *Art UK* (12 April 2021): https://artuk.org/discover/stories/the-power-paunch-body-politics-and-eighteenth-century-mens-waistlines#.
Smeed, J. W., *The Theophrastan 'Character': The History of a Literary Genre* (Oxford: Clarendon Press, 1985).
Sorenson, Janet, *The Grammar of Empire in Eighteenth-Century British Writing* (Cambridge: Cambridge University Press, 2000).
Stabler, Jane, 'Jane Austen and Caricature', *Nineteenth Century Studies*, 21 (2007), pp. 1–18.
St. Clair, William, *The Reading Nation in the Romantic Period* (Cambridge: Cambridge University Press, 2004).
Sterrenburg, Lee, 'Mary Shelley's Monster: Politics and Psyche in *Frankenstein*', in *The Endurance of 'Frankenstein': Essays on Mary Shelley's Novel*, eds. George Levine and U. C. Knoepflmacher (Berkeley: University of California Press, 1979).
Summerscale, Ann, (ed. and trans.), *Malvasia's Life of the Carracci* (University Park, PA: Penn State University Press, 2000).
Sutherland, Kathryn, *Jane Austen's Textual Lives: From Aeschylus to Bollywood* (Oxford: Oxford University Press, 2005).
Taylor, David F., 'Edgeworth's *Belinda* and the Gendering of Caricature', *Eighteenth-Century Fiction*, 26.4 (2014), pp. 493–624.
 The Politics of Parody: A Literary History of Caricature, 1760–1830 (New Haven, CT: Yale University Press, 2018).
 'The Practice of Caricature in 18th-century Britain', *Literature Compass* (2017): https://doi.org/10.1111/lic3.12383.
Thaden, Barbara Z., 'Figure and Ground: The Receding Heroine in Jane Austen's *Emma*', *South Atlantic Review*, 55.1 (January 1990), pp. 47–62.
Toner, Anne, *Ellipsis in English Literature: Signs of Omission* (Cambridge: Cambridge University Press, 2015).
 Jane Austen's Style: Narrative Economy and the Novel's Growth (Cambridge: Cambridge University Press, 2020).

Tracy, Ann B., *The Gothic Novel 1790–1830: Plot Summaries and Index to Motifs* (Lexington: The University Press of Kentucky, 1981).
Vogler, Richard A. (ed.), *Graphic Works of George Cruikshank* (New York: Dover, 1979).
Wardroper, John, *Kings, Lords and Wicked Libellers: Satire and Protest 1760–1837* (London: Murray, 1973).
Warner, Michael, *Publics and Counterpublics* (Princeton, NJ: Zone Books, 2002).
Watt, Ian, *The Rise of the Novel: Studies in Defoe, Richardson and Fielding* (London: Chatto & Windus, 1957).
Wilkes, Joanne, *Women Reviewing Women in Nineteenth-Century Britain: The Critical Reception of Jane Austen, Charlotte Brontë, and George Eliot* (Abingdon: Routledge, 2010).
Wilson, Cheryl A., *Fashioning the Silver Fork Novel: Literary Texts and the Popular Marketplace* (London: Routledge, 2012).
Woloch, Alex, *The One vs. the Many: Minor Characters and the Space of the Protagonist in the Novel* (Princeton, NJ: Princeton University Press, 2003).
Youngquist, Paul, *Monstrosities: Bodies and British Romanticism* (Minneapolis: University of Minnesota Press, 2003).

Index

Addison, Joseph, 53, 72, 74–78
Aiken, Henry Thomas, 18
Alexander, J. H., 141
Allan, David, 130
amateur caricature drawing, 12–14, 16–17, 35, 95, 114–15
   and the elite, 12–15, 21, 35
   and professional graphic satirists, 14–15
Andrews, Richard, 145
anti-caricature, 27–32, 34, 49, 73–77, 81, 93, 97–98, 103, 106–8, 125, 131, 204, 206
   and Englishness, 93, 101, 107
   and femininity, 93, 98–100
   and *troppo caricato*, 23–25, 27–28, 169
Anti-Jacobin Magazine, 17–18
anti-Semitism, 127, 162–67
Armstrong, Nancy, 129
Arthur Parker (character in *Sanditon*), 117–19, 121–22
Austen, Cassandra, 95
Austen, Jane, 61, 86, 93–101, 155
   Emma, 8, 97, 105, 108, 117
   free indirect style, 107
   History of England, 95
   juvenilia, 108, 120
   Mansfield Park, 97, 105, 117–18, 120
   Northanger Abbey, 52, 86, 102–3
   'Opinions of Mansfield Park and Opinions of Emma' (BL Add. MSS. 41253A), 96–98
   Persuasion, 108, 112, 115–16, 119–20, 122–23
   Pride and Prejudice, 48, 61, 76–77, 97, 105, 110
   Sanditon, 105, 107–9, 112–13, 115, 120–22
   Sense and Sensibility, 16, 101–4, 117–18, 157
   and satirical prints, 94–95
Austen-Leigh, James Edward, 57, 100
autobiography, 39–41

Bacon, Francis, 155, 193
Baker, James, 9, 15
Barbauld, Anna Letitia, 99, 137

Barett, Eaton Stannard, 46
Baretti, Giuseppe
   Dictionary of the English and Italian Languages, 3–7, 23, 25, 111–12
Barrell, John, 20
Beattie, James, 28, 71, 74–75, 77
Beauclerk, Diana, 114
beauty, 186–88, 171–73, 176–79
Bell, Vanessa, 14
Berguer, Lionel Thomas, 72, 74, 76
Berlioz, Hector, 25
Blackburn, Jemima, 14
Blackwood, William, 37
Blackwood's Magazine, 36–42
Bonaparte, Napoleon, 10–11, 195, 205–6
Brontë, Charlotte, 105
Brougham, Henry, 39
Browne, Thomas, 4, 201
Brownstein, Rachel, 95–96, 117, 123
Brunton, Mary, 16–17, 45
Buchan, William, 198–99
Budgell, Eustace, 77, 78
Burke, Edmund, 171, 175–76, 178, 185, 190
Burney, Fanny, 8, 99, 107
Burns, Robert, 71
Burrows, J. F., 106
Butler, Marilyn, 42–43, 45, 106
Butler, Samuel, 27
Byron, 18, 25, 30, 39, 44, 198, 206

Cadogan, William, 197
Campbell, Timothy, 150
Canning, George, 15, 17
caricature
   the 'Age of', 8–9, 20, 94–96, 114, 204–6
   and animals, 180, 184
   and contrast, 7, 16, 21, 50, 126, 131–34, 173, 186–88
   and cooking, 101, 138, 147
   and intimacy, 14, 35, 114
   belaboured, 133–35

255

caricature (cont.)
  editorial, 5
  ephemerality, topicality of, 20–21, 52, 107, 144–45, 167–68
  and the literary canon, vii, 107, 139
  of lower-class people, 42–43, 99–101, 105, 136
  and novelty, 30, 133, 147
  not pictorial, 5–7, 8, 25–26, 111
  not satirical prints, 8, 10–11, 19, 204
  of oneself, 39, 109–12, 115, 117, 156, 162–64
  oral, 6–7, 42
  and realism, 29, 34–35, 125, 130, 133, 146
  and size, 7, 25, 77, 111–13
  and superaddition, 30, 39, 133
  and violation, 7, 15, 35, 47–48, 56, 58
  and weight, 4, 111–13
  taste for, 101, 136, 204–6
  textual styling of, 121–23
  verisimilitude of, 34, 129–30, 139, 143
caricature studies, 9–10, 94–96
caricature talk, 32–34, 49, 60–62, 65, 69, 71–77, 91, 96, 105, 112, 125, 169, 202, 206
  in cooperation with characterisation technique, 50–87, 109, 124–25, 169–83
caricature, term
  coincidental resemblance to *character*, 24
  and *caricatúra*, 3–8, 11–12, 111
  earliest usage in English, 4
  and *overcharged*, 7–8, 26, 28, 97, 99, 107, 136–37
Carlyle, Thomas, 149
Carr, John, 43
Carracci family, 11–12, 24
celebrity, 15, 17–18, 35, 114
Chalmers, Alexander, 71, 77, 84
Chambers, Robert, 141–42, 155
Chambers, William, 141
Chandler, James, 204
Chapman, R. W., 108
character sketch, 53, 63, 66, 69
characters, fictive, 30–32, 34, 135
  identifiable as portraits of real 'originals', 42–48, 69, 73, 139
  non-protagonist ('minor'), 32, 50–52, 63, 71, 74–77, 80–82, 105–8, 124, 131, 133–36, 141–42
  originality of, 58, 62, 69, 72–73, 85–86
  and parasociality, 74, 80–81
  as the property of authors and readers, 58, 72, 77, 84
  as real people, 32–34, 49
Clarke, Mary Cowden, 33
Clery, E. J., 205
clothing, 148–50, 155, 186–87

Coleridge, Samuel Taylor, 17, 43, 65, 80, 82
commedia dell'arte, 145
Conder, Josiah, 30
Constable, Archibald, 37, 141
Cooke, Thomas, 201
Cooper, James Fenimore, 137
Cowan, Brian, 55
critical character studies, 32–35, 52–53
  and character appreciation, 51, 71–72, 74–76, 82, 93, 110
  and character talk, 32, 91, 124–25
  and formal realism, 169
Croker, John Wilson, 47
Cruikshank, George, 10, 15, 20
Cruikshank, Isaac, 20
Cruikshank, Robert Isaac, 18, 20
Cunningham, Allan, 137

Darly, Mary, 12–14
De Cervantes, Miguel, 18, 51, 78, 140
De la Bruyère, Jean, 67
De Quincey, Thomas, 40
Defoe, Daniel, 136, 148
deformity, concept of, 155, 169–71, 173–76, 184, 193–94, 199
Dickens, Charles, 117
Dickinson, H. T., 15
disproportion, 31, 115, 122, 152–53, 169–76, 180, 182, 184, 199
Dissenters, 27
Donald, Diana, 9
Doyle, John, 18
Drake, Nathan, 71–72
Dunlop, John, 136
dwarfs and dwarfism, 24, 31, 47–48, 127, 150–55, 169–70, 176–80, 183–86, 195, 199
Dyer, Gary, 43

eating, 112, 117–19, 122
Edgeworth, Maria, 17, 42–43, 46–47, 99, 164–66
Esterhammer, Angela, 140
Euphuism, 143–45, 148

fatness, 94–95, 112–16, 121–23
  fat-hating, 113–16, 123–24
femininity, 27
Fergusson, Adam, 47
Fergusson, Robert, 128
Ferrier, Susan, 99, 142
Fielding, Henry, 65, 107, 136, 138
  Amelia, 115
  Joseph Andrews, 60
  Tom Jones, 82

flesh-caricature, 22–23, 26–27, 164, 169, 195, 200, 202–3
Forster, E. M., 100
Franklin, Benjamin, 10
French Revolution, 205
Frow, John, 32–33
Fuseli, Henri, 16, 30

George III, 15
George IV, 15, 38, 113
George, Mary Dorothy, 9
Gibbon, Edward, 114
Gigante, Denise, 170–71
gigantism, 24–25, 28, 127, 152, 154, 172–73, 175–80, 184, 186
Gillray, James, 11, 18–19, 95–96, 123, 195
Godwin, William, 197
Goethe, Johann Wolfgang von, 125, 149
Gombrich, E. H., 11, 12
Gothic, 103
Graglia, Giuspano
 New Pocket Dictionary of the English and Italian Languages, 4
Greene, Donald, 95, 107
Grose, Francis, 7–8, 13
grotesque portraiture
 pre-*caricatúra*, 11

Harding, D. W., 109
Harris, Walter, 200
Haywood, Ian, 10–11
Hazlitt, William, 20, 25, 45, 132–33, 160, 162
Hippocratic face, 201–2
historical character, 127, 129, 167
Hogarth, William, 95, 177
Hogg, James, 37, 40–42, 45
Holcroft, Thomas, 22
Home, Henry (Lord Kames), 63–64, 188
Hood, Thomas, 18
horror, 8, 30, 169–70, 177, 181–84, 186, 190, 196, 198, 202–3
Hudson, Jeffrey (inspiration for character in *Peveril of the Peak*), 152–55, 178
Hugo, Victor, 182, 202–3
humours, 146
Hunt, Leigh, 37–38
Hutton, R. H., 100

imagination, 30, 56–57, 72–73, 108, 133, 178, 181–82, 188, 190

Jameson, Anna Murphy, 32
Jameson, Fredric, 33
Jeffrey, Francis, 25, 61, 145, 149
Johnson, Samuel, 74–75, 77

Jonson, Ben, 144, 146
Joshua, Essaka, 171, 183

Kavanagh, Julia, 98–99
Kay, John, 114, 127–31, 138
Keats, John, 38
Knights, L. C., 33

Lamb, Caroline, 45
Lamb, Charles, 17
landscape, 132–33, 134, 135
Langan, John (inspiration for *Castle Rackrent*), 42–43
Lascelles, Mary, 106
Lavater, Johann Caspar, 22–23
Le Brun, Charles, 25
Lear, Edward, 14
Lee, Michael Parrish, 117
Levine, George, 29, 183
Levy, Michelle, 108
Lewes, George Henry, 98, 116–17
Lewis, Matthew G.
 The Monk, 103, 181
libel, 38, 56, 58–60
Locke, John, 196–98
Lockhart, John Gibson, 37–38, 134
Lukács, Georg, 125
Lynch, Deidre, 23, 32–33, 74–75

Macaulay, Thomas Babington, 8, 99, 107
Mackenzie, Henry, 33
Malcolm, James Peller, 199–201
Martin, John, 133
masculinity, 135
McKeon, Michael, 125
Medwin, Thomas, 44
Meek, Joseph, 79–80
Mendelssohn, Felix, 25
Mercutio (character in *Romeo and Juliet*), 83, 144
Michelangelo, 25
mimicry, 42
Miss Bates (character in *Emma*), 8, 74, 85, 97
Mitchell, David, 194
Moers, Ellen, 200
Moi, Toril, 32, 61
Moore, Thomas, 44
Morgann, Maurice, 33, 75
Mr Collins (character in *Pride and Prejudice*), 34, 74, 76, 85, 97, 107, 110, 117, 124–25
Mudrick, Marvin, 120, 123
Mulvihill, James, 44

Napier, Macvey, 37
national character, 136, 139, 141, 155–67
Nicholson, Eirwen E. C., 9, 15

O'Neill, Michael, 9
Odumosu, Temi, 10
Oliphant, Margaret, 98
Ovid, 66–67
Owenson, Sydney, 46

Paton, Hugh, 129
Patten, Robert, 11, 20
Peacock, Thomas Love, 20, 43–46, 145–46
Pepys, Samuel, 135
personality (OED n. 6b), 36
physiognomy, 44, 115, 163–64, 170, 192–94
  moral, 163, 192–94, 201
  prognostic, 4, 200–2
picturesque, 101–2, 131, 133, 134, 149
Pollock, W. F., 106
Pope, Alexander, 3
Porterfield, Todd, 10
Posner, Donald, 12

Quakers, 199–200

Radcliffe, Ann, 103, 181
Randolph, Thomas, 59–60
Rauser, Amelia, 10
reading public, 44
  of women, 52
realism, 12, 28–29, 32, 34–35, 49, 51, 61–63, 65, 69, 74, 77, 80–82, 86, 91, 93–94, 98, 104, 106–7, 124–25, 127, 134, 148–49, 167–69, 177, 182, 188, 203–4, 206
  compendious, 126–27, 131, 135, 150, 167
  and elision, redaction, 146
  horrid, 86, 169–77, 182–92, 194–95, 200–3
  at odds with pictorial caricature, 21
  pseudo-sensory enjoyment of, 63–64, 66, 203
Richardson, Samuel, 107
Richardson, William, 33
Ritchie, David (inspiration for *The Black Dwarf*), 47–48, 141, 153, 155, 179, 202
ritratti carichi, 11–14, 35–36, 114, 129
Robertson, Thomas, 75
roman à clef, 46
Romanticism, 8–9, 11, 33, 39, 57, 131
Rousseau, Jean Jacques, 197–98

Saintsbury, George, 76, 85
satire, 48, 53, 55–56, 59, 60, 91, 93, 113–14, 144
satirical prints, 8–11, 95, 113–14, 129, 195
  and the elite, 11–18
  literary figures represented in, 17–18
  referenced in literature of the Romantic period, 18–19
  Scottishness, 19–20

Scott, Walter, 41–42, 61, 65, 76, 86, 104, 130, 176, 202, 205–6
  The Black Dwarf, 31, 42, 47–48, 151, 153, 155, 179–80, 184–85, 187
  The Bride of Lammermoor, 134, 146
  Guy Mannering, 25, 132–33, 135, 141
  The Heart of Mid-Lothian, 127–29, 159–62, 167
  Ivanhoe, 142, 147–48, 162–64, 166–67
  Kenilworth, 150–51, 154
  A Legend of Montrose, 148
  Magnum Opus, 30, 47–48, 140–48, 153–55, 167, 184
  The Monastery, 140–45, 148, 150
  Peveril of the Peak, 151–55, 178, 184
  The Pirate, 151, 179, 184, 188
  Redgauntlet, 129
  Rob Roy, 4–5, 31, 130, 135, 153, 156–60, 162, 179–80
  Saint Ronan's Well, 132, 136
  The Talisman, 148, 151–52, 155, 180, 185, 187
  Waverley, 61, 141
Senior, Nassau, 134, 139, 141
Seward, Anna, 39
Shaftesbury, 10, 148, 188
Shakespeare, William, 76, 205
  and character criticism, 33
  in character criticism, 75, 82–83
  Henry V, 201
  Romeo and Juliet, 82–83, 144
Sharpe, Charles Kirkpatrick, 14
Shelley, Mary, 45, 86
  Falkner, 193
  Frankenstein, 10, 30, 170–76, 180–96, 200–3, 205
  Lodore, 193
  'Transformation', 176, 179–82, 190–92
Shelley, Percy, 43, 45, 173–76
Shön, Theresa, 53
silver-fork novels, 45–46
Simpson, Richard, 100, 107
Sir Piercie Shafton (character in *The Monastery*), 134, 145, 151
Sir Roger de Coverley (character in the *Spectator*), 34, 50–51, 71, 76–81, 83–85, 87
Skirving, Archibald, 130
Smollett, Tobias, 136–39, 146
Snyder, Sharon, 194
Southam, B. C., 108
Southey, Robert, 17–18, 43
speech, 143, 148
  and dialect, 145–46, 166

Spencer, Lavinia, 114
Stabler, Jane, 95, 109
Steele, Richard, 72–73, 77
Stephens, Frederic George, 9
Sterrenburg, Lee, 194
sublime, 30, 102–5, 133, 177–78, 181, 185, 187
Sutherland, Kathryn, 108
Swift, Jonathan, 60, 174

Taylor, David, 10, 15, 204
Taylor, Ella, 14
Thackeray, William Makepeace, 14
Thaden, Barbara, 107
The Spectator, 50–57, 62–63, 71–73, 77–81, 83–86
Theophrastus, 53, 62, 67–68, 70
Toner, Anne, 108
Trollope, Anthony, 49, 143
Turner, David, 200

uncanny, 22, 110, 153, 180

Walker, George, 130
Walker, Joseph, 145
Ward, Mary, 99
Watt, Ian, 65, 104, 188
Wellington, 17, 129
Wells, H. G., 202–3
Whately, Richard, 98
Williams, Charles, 18
Wilson, John, 36, 40, 44
Winchester, C. T., 81
Wollstonecraft, Mary
  Vindication of the Rights of Woman, 5, 8, 26–27, 164, 198
Woloch, Alex, 124
Woolf, Virginia, 14
Wordsworth, William, 39

Youngquist, Paul, 194

CAMBRIDGE STUDIES IN ROMANTICISM

General Editor
James Chandler, University of Chicago

1. Romantic Correspondence: Women, Politics and the Fiction of Letters
   MARY A. FAVRET
2. British Romantic Writers and the East: Anxieties of Empire
   NIGEL LEASK
3. Poetry as an Occupation and an Art in Britain, 1760–1830
   PETER MURPHY
4. Edmund Burke's Aesthetic Ideology: Language, Gender and Political Economy in Revolution
   TOM FURNISS
5. In the Theatre of Romanticism: Coleridge, Nationalism, Women
   JULIE A. CARLSON
6. Keats, Narrative and Audience
   ANDREW BENNETT
7. Romance and Revolution: Shelley and the Politics of a Genre
   DAVID DUFF
8. Literature, Education, and Romanticism: Reading as Social Practice, 1780–1832
   ALAN RICHARDSON
9. Women Writing about Money: Women's Fiction in England, 1790–1820
   EDWARD COPELAND
10. Shelley and the Revolution in Taste: The Body and the Natural World
    TIMOTHY MORTON
11. William Cobbett: The Politics of Style
    LEONORA NATTRASS
12. The Rise of Supernatural Fiction, 1762–1800
    E. J. CLERY
13. Women Travel Writers and the Language of Aesthetics, 1716–1818
    ELIZABETH A. BOHLS
14. Napoleon and English Romanticism
    SIMON BAINBRIDGE
15. Romantic Vagrancy: Wordsworth and the Simulation of Freedom
    CELESTE LANGAN
16. Wordsworth and the Geologists
    JOHN WYATT
17. Wordsworth's Pope: A Study in Literary Historiography
    ROBERT J. GRIFFIN

18 The Politics of Sensibility: Race, Gender and Commerce in the Sentimental Novel
   MARKMAN ELLIS
19 Reading Daughters' Fictions, 1709–1834: Novels and Society from Manley to Edgeworth
   CAROLINE GONDA
20 Romantic Identities: Varieties of Subjectivity, 1774–1830
   ANDREA K. HENDERSON
21 Print Politics: The Press and Radical Opposition in Early Nineteenth-Century England
   KEVIN GILMARTIN
22 Reinventing Allegory
   THERESA M. KELLEY
23 British Satire and the Politics of Style, 1789–1832
   GARY DYER
24 The Romantic Reformation: Religious Politics in English Literature, 1789–1824
   ROBERT M. RYAN
25 De Quincey's Romanticism: Canonical Minority and the Forms of Transmission
   MARGARET RUSSETT
26 Coleridge on Dreaming: Romanticism, Dreams and the Medical Imagination
   JENNIFER FORD
27 Romantic Imperialism: Universal Empire and the Culture of Modernity
   SAREE MAKDISI
28 Ideology and Utopia in the Poetry of William Blake
   NICHOLAS M. WILLIAMS
29 Sexual Politics and the Romantic Author
   SONIA HOFKOSH
30 Lyric and Labour in the Romantic Tradition
   ANNE JANOWITZ
31 Poetry and Politics in the Cockney School: Keats, Shelley, Hunt and Their Circle
   JEFFREY N. COX
32 Rousseau, Robespierre and English Romanticism
   GREGORY DART
33 Contesting the Gothic: Fiction, Genre and Cultural Conflict, 1764–1832
   JAMES WATT
34 Romanticism, Aesthetics, and Nationalism
   DAVID ARAM KAISER
35 Romantic Poets and the Culture of Posterity
   ANDREW BENNETT
36 The Crisis of Literature in the 1790s: Print Culture and the Public Sphere
   PAUL KEEN

37 Romantic Atheism: Poetry and Freethought, 1780–1830
MARTIN PRIESTMAN
38 Romanticism and Slave Narratives: Transatlantic Testimonies
HELEN THOMAS
39 Imagination under Pressure, 1789–1832: Aesthetics, Politics, and Utility
JOHN WHALE
40 Romanticism and the Gothic: Genre, Reception, and Canon Formation, 1790–1820
MICHAEL GAMER
41 Romanticism and the Human Sciences: Poetry, Population, and the Discourse of the Species
MAUREEN N. MCLANE
42 The Poetics of Spice: Romantic Consumerism and the Exotic
TIMOTHY MORTON
43 British Fiction and the Production of Social Order, 1740–1830
MIRANDA J. BURGESS
44 Women Writers and the English Nation in the 1790s
ANGELA KEANE
45 Literary Magazines and British Romanticism
MARK PARKER
46 Women, Nationalism and the Romantic Stage: Theatre and Politics in Britain, 1780–1800
BETSY BOLTON
47 British Romanticism and the Science of the Mind
ALAN RICHARDSON
48 The Anti-Jacobin Novel: British Conservatism and the French Revolution
M. O. GRENBY
49 Romantic Austen: Sexual Politics and the Literary Canon
CLARA TUITE
50 Byron and Romanticism
JEROME MCGANN and JAMES SODERHOLM
51 The Romantic National Tale and the Question of Ireland
INA FERRIS
52 Byron, Poetics and History
JANE STABLER
53 Religion, Toleration, and British Writing, 1790–1830
MARK CANUEL
54 Fatal Women of Romanticism
ADRIANA CRACIUN
55 Knowledge and Indifference in English Romantic Prose
TIM MILNES
56 Mary Wollstonecraft and the Feminist Imagination
BARBARA TAYLOR
57 Romanticism, Maternity and the Body Politic
JULIE KIPP

58 Romanticism and Animal Rights
   DAVID PERKINS
59 Georgic Modernity and British Romanticism: Poetry and the Mediation of History
   KEVIS GOODMAN
60 Literature, Science and Exploration in the Romantic Era: Bodies of Knowledge
   TIMOTHY FULFORD, DEBBIE LEE, and PETER J. KITSON
61 Romantic Colonization and British Anti-Slavery
   DEIRDRE COLEMAN
62 Anger, Revolution, and Romanticism
   ANDREW M. STAUFFER
63 Shelley and the Revolutionary Sublime
   CIAN DUFFY
64 Fictions and Fakes: Forging Romantic Authenticity, 1760–1845
   MARGARET RUSSETT
65 Early Romanticism and Religious Dissent
   DANIEL E. WHITE
66 The Invention of Evening: Perception and Time in Romantic Poetry
   CHRISTOPHER R. MILLER
67 Wordsworth's Philosophic Song
   SIMON JARVIS
68 Romanticism and the Rise of the Mass Public
   ANDREW FRANTA
69 Writing against Revolution: Literary Conservatism in Britain, 1790–1832
   KEVIN GILMARTIN
70 Women, Sociability and Theatre in Georgian London
   GILLIAN RUSSELL
71 The Lake Poets and Professional Identity
   BRIAN GOLDBERG
72 Wordsworth Writing
   ANDREW BENNETT
73 Science and Sensation in Romantic Poetry
   NOEL JACKSON
74 Advertising and Satirical Culture in the Romantic Period
   JOHN STRACHAN
75 Romanticism and the Painful Pleasures of Modern Life
   ANDREA K. HENDERSON
76 Balladeering, Minstrelsy, and the Making of British Romantic Poetry
   MAUREEN N. MCLANE
77 Romanticism and Improvisation, 1750–1850
   ANGELA ESTERHAMMER
78 Scotland and the Fictions of Geography: North Britain, 1760–1830
   PENNY FIELDING

79 Wordsworth, Commodification and Social Concern: The Poetics of Modernity
   DAVID SIMPSON
80 Sentimental Masculinity and the Rise of History, 1790–1890
   MIKE GOODE
81 Fracture and Fragmentation in British Romanticism
   ALEXANDER REGIER
82 Romanticism and Music Culture in Britain, 1770–1840: Virtue and Virtuosity
   GILLEN D'ARCY WOOD
83 The Truth about Romanticism: Pragmatism and Idealism in Keats, Shelley, Coleridge
   TIM MILNES
84 Blake's Gifts: Poetry and the Politics of Exchange
   SARAH HAGGARTY
85 Real Money and Romanticism
   MATTHEW ROWLINSON
86 Sentimental Literature and Anglo-Scottish Identity, 1745–1820
   JULIET SHIELDS
87 Romantic Tragedies: The Dark Employments of Wordsworth, Coleridge, and Shelley
   REEVE PARKER
88 Blake, Sexuality and Bourgeois Politeness
   SUSAN MATTHEWS
89 Idleness, Contemplation and the Aesthetic
   RICHARD ADELMAN
90 Shelley's Visual Imagination
   NANCY MOORE GOSLEE
91 A Cultural History of the Irish Novel, 1790–1829
   CLAIRE CONNOLLY
92 Literature, Commerce, and the Spectacle of Modernity, 1750–1800
   PAUL KEEN
93 Romanticism and Childhood: The Infantilization of British Literary Culture
   ANN WEIRDA ROWLAND
94 Metropolitan Art and Literature, 1810–1840: Cockney Adventures
   GREGORY DART
95 Wordsworth and the Enlightenment Idea of Pleasure
   ROWAN BOYSON
96 John Clare and Community
   JOHN GOODRIDGE
97 The Romantic Crowd
   MARY FAIRCLOUGH
98 Romantic Women Writers, Revolution and Prophecy
   ORIANNE SMITH

99 Britain, France and the Gothic, 1764–1820
ANGELA WRIGHT
100 Transfiguring the Arts and Sciences
JON KLANCHER
101 Shelley and the Apprehension of Life
ROSS WILSON
102 Poetics of Character: Transatlantic Encounters 1700–1900
SUSAN MANNING
103 Romanticism and Caricature
IAN HAYWOOD
104 The Late Poetry of the Lake Poets: Romanticism Revised
TIM FULFORD
105 Forging Romantic China: Sino-British Cultural Exchange 1760–1840
PETER J. KITSON
106 Coleridge and the Philosophy of Poetic Form
EWAN JAMES JONES
107 Romanticism in the Shadow of War: Literary Culture in the Napoleonic War Years
JEFFREY N. COX
108 Slavery and the Politics of Place: Representing the Colonial Caribbean, 1770–1833
ELIZABETH A. BOHLS
109 The Orient and the Young Romantics
ANDREW WARREN
110 Lord Byron and Scandalous Celebrity
CLARA TUITE
111 Radical Orientalism: Rights, Reform, and Romanticism
GERARD COHEN-VRIGNAUD
112 Print, Publicity, and Popular Radicalism in the 1790s
JON MEE
113 Wordsworth and the Art of Philosophical Travel
MARK OFFORD
114 Romanticism, Self-Canonization, and the Business of Poetry
MICHAEL GAMER
115 Women Wanderers and the Writing of Mobility, 1784–1814
INGRID HORROCKS
116 Eighteen Hundred and Eleven: Poetry, Protest and Economic Crisis
E. J. CLERY
117 Urbanization and English Romantic Poetry
STEPHEN TEDESCHI
118 The Poetics of Decline in British Romanticism
JONATHAN SACHS
119 The Caribbean and the Medical Imagination, 1764–1834: Slavery, Disease and Colonial Modernity
EMILY SENIOR

120 Science, Form, and the Problem of Induction in British Romanticism
   DAHLIA PORTER
121 Wordsworth and the Poetics of Air
   THOMAS H. FORD
122 Romantic Art in Practice: Cultural Work and the Sister Arts, 1760–1820
   THORA BRYLOWE
123 European Literatures in Britain, 1815–1832: Romantic Translations
   DIEGO SIGALIA
124 Romanticism and Theatrical Experience: Kean, Hazlitt and Keats in the Age of Theatrical News
   JONATHAN MULROONEY
125 The Romantic Tavern: Literature and Conviviality in the Age of Revolution
   IAN NEWMAN
126 British Orientalisms, 1759–1835
   JAMES WATT
127 Print and Performance in the 1820s: Improvisation, Speculation, Identity
   ANGELA ESTERHAMMER
128 The Italian Idea: Anglo-Italian Radical Literary Culture, 1815–1823
   WILL BOWERS
129 The Ephemeral Eighteenth Century: Print, Sociability, and the Cultures of Collecting
   GILLIAN RUSSELL
130 Physical Disability in British Romantic Literature
   ESSAKA JOSHUA
131 William Wordsworth, Second-Generation Romantic: Contesting Poetry after Waterloo
   JEFFREY COX
132 Walter Scott and the Greening of Scotland: The Emergent Ecologies of a Nation
   SUSAN OLIVER
133 Art, Science and the Body in Early Romanticism
   STEPHANIE O'ROURKE
134 Honor, Romanticism, and the Hidden Value of Modernity
   JAMISON KANTOR
135 Romanticism and the Biopolitics of Modern War Writing
   NEIL RAMSEY
136 Jane Austen and Other Minds: Ordinary Language Philosophy in Literary Fiction
   ERIC REID LINDSTROM
137 Orientation in European Romanticism: The Art of Falling Upwards
   PAUL HAMILTON
138 Romanticism, Republicanism, and the Swiss Myth
   PATRICK VINCENT
139 Coleridge and the Geometric Idiom: Walking with Euclid
   ANN C. COLLEY

140 Late Romanticism and the End of Politics: Byron, Mary Shelley, and the Last Men
    JOHN HAVARD
141 Experimentalism in Wordsworth's Later Poetry: Dialogues with the Dead
    TIM FULFORD
142 Romantic Fiction and Literary Excess in the Minerva Press Era
    HANNAH DOHERTY HUDSON
143 Byron's *Don Juan*: The Liberal Epic of the Nineteenth Century
    RICHARD CRONIN
144 Sound and Sense in British Romanticism
    JAMES GRANDE and CARMEL RAZ
145 Wordsworth After War: Recovering Peace in the Later Poetry
    PHILIP SHAW
146 Staël, Romanticism and Revolution: The Life and Times of the First European
    JOHN CLAIBORNE ISBELL
147 Romantic Epics and the Mission of Empire
    MATTHEW LEPORATI
148 Caricature and Realism in the Romantic Novel
    OLIVIA FERGUSON

For EU product safety concerns, contact us at Calle de José Abascal, 56–1°,
28003 Madrid, Spain or eugpsr@cambridge.org.

www.ingramcontent.com/pod-product-compliance
Ingram Content Group UK Ltd.
Pitfield, Milton Keynes, MK11 3LW, UK
UKHW020827291025
464422UK00020B/1014